The **Rough Guide** to

Yellowstone and Grand Teton

written and researched by

Stephen Timblin

NEW YORK • LONDON • DELHI

www.roughguides.com

Contents

The wolves of Yellowstone color section following p.64

Hydrothermal Yellowstone color section following p.160

◀◀ Grand Tetons in fall ◀ Grand Canyon of the Yellowstone

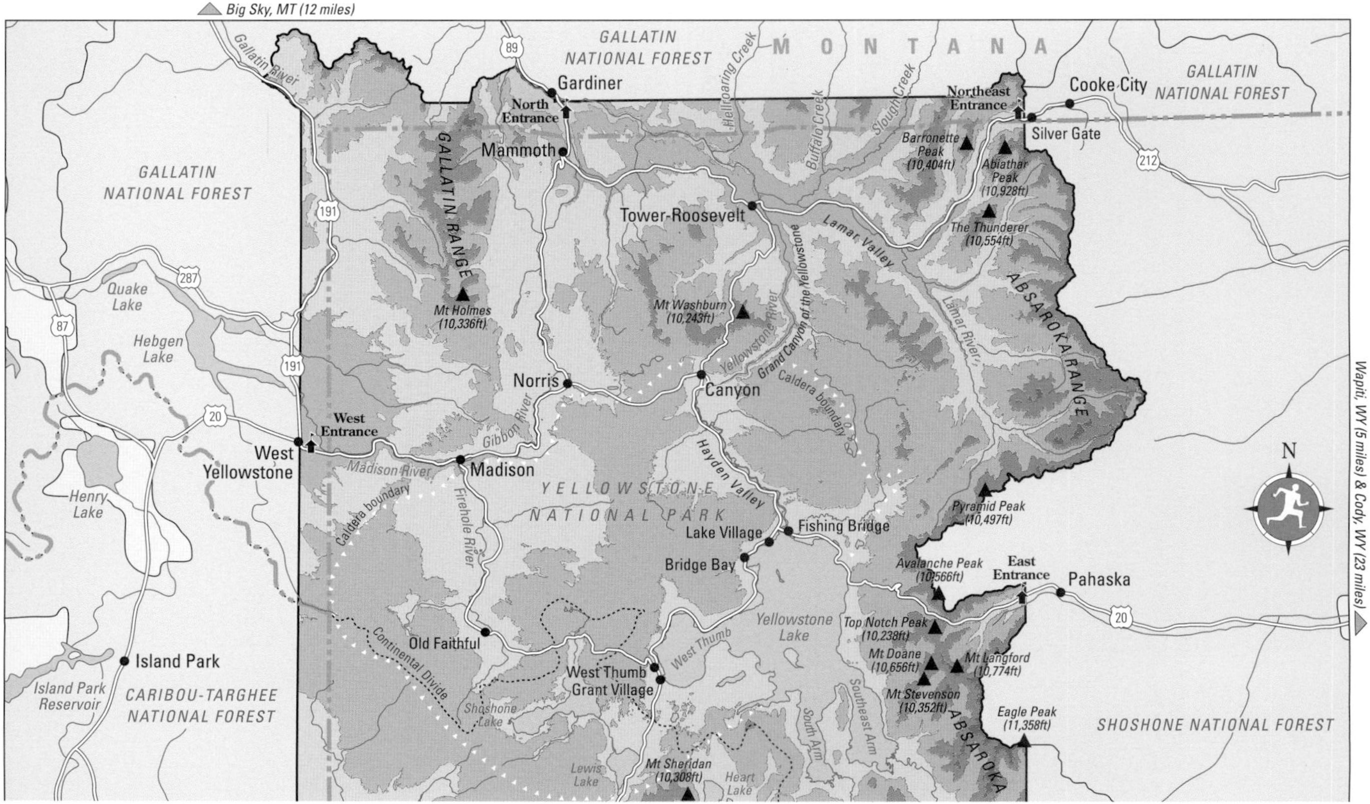

Big Sky, MT (12 miles)
Wapiti, WY (5 miles) & Cody, WY (23 miles)
MONTANA
GALLATIN NATIONAL FOREST
GALLATIN NATIONAL FOREST
GALLATIN NATIONAL FOREST
CARIBOU-TARGHEE NATIONAL FOREST
SHOSHONE NATIONAL FOREST
YELLOWSTONE NATIONAL PARK
N
Gardiner
North Entrance
Mammoth
Cooke City
Northeast Entrance
Silver Gate
Tower-Roosevelt
Norris
Canyon
Madison
West Entrance
West Yellowstone
Fishing Bridge
Lake Village
Bridge Bay
East Entrance
Pahaska
Old Faithful
West Thumb
Grant Village
Island Park
GALLATIN RANGE
ABSAROKA RANGE
ABSAROKA
Mt Holmes (10,336ft)
Mt Washburn (10,243ft)
Barronette Peak (10,404ft)
Abiathar Peak (10,928ft)
The Thunderer (10,554ft)
Pyramid Peak (10,497ft)
Avalanche Peak (10,566ft)
Top Notch Peak (10,238ft)
Mt Doane (10,656ft)
Mt Langford (10,774ft)
Mt Stevenson (10,352ft)
Eagle Peak (11,358ft)
Mt Sheridan (10,308ft)
Gallatin River
Hellroaring Creek
Buffalo Creek
Slough Creek
Lamar Valley
Lamar River
Yellowstone River
Grand Canyon of the Yellowstone
Caldera boundary
Caldera boundary
Hayden Valley
Gibbon River
Madison River
Firehole River
Continental Divide
Yellowstone Lake
West Thumb
South Arm
Southeast Arm
Shoshone Lake
Lewis Lake
Heart Lake
Quake Lake
Hebgen Lake
Henry Lake
Island Park Reservoir
89
191
191
287
87
20
20
212

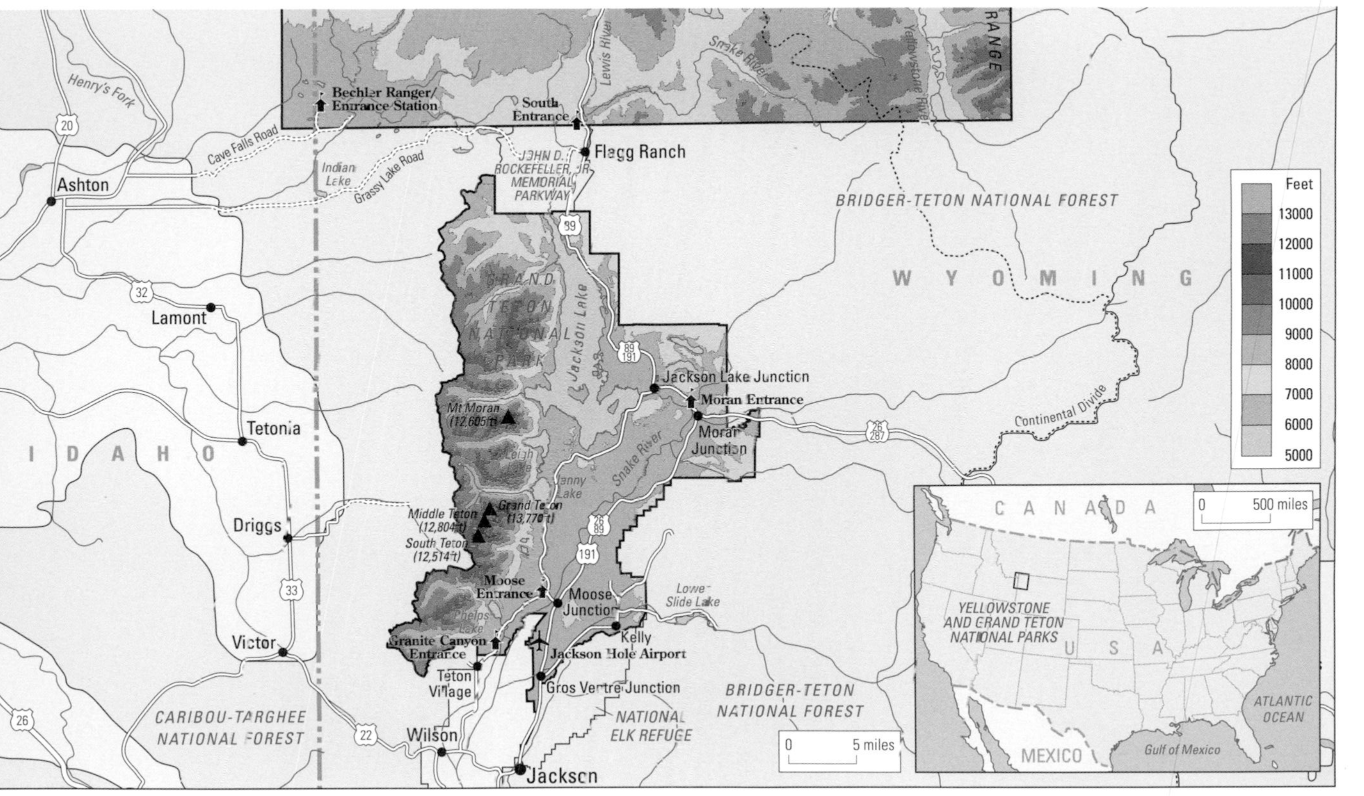
Henry's Fork
20
Ashton
Cave Falls Road
Grassy Lake Road
Indian Lake
Bechler Ranger/ Entrance Station
South Entrance
Lewis River
Snake River
Yellowstone River
RANGE
Flagg Ranch
JOHN D. ROCKEFELLER, JR. MEMORIAL PARKWAY
89
BRIDGER-TETON NATIONAL FOREST
Feet
13000
12000
11000
10000
9000
8000
7000
6000
5000
W Y O M I N G
32
Lamont
GRAND TETON NATIONAL PARK
Jackson Lake
89 191
Jackson Lake Junction
Moran Entrance
Moran Junction
26 287
Continental Divide
Mt Moran (12,605ft)
Tetonia
I D A H O
Leigh Lake
Jenny Lake
Snake River
Grand Teton (13,770ft)
Middle Teton (12,804ft)
South Teton (12,514ft)
Driggs
26 89
191
33
Moose Entrance
Moose Junction
Lower Slide Lake
Phelps Lake
Granite Canyon Entrance
Kelly
Jackson Hole Airport
Victor
Teton Village
Gros Ventre Junction
BRIDGER-TETON NATIONAL FOREST
NATIONAL ELK REFUGE
CARIBOU-TARGHEE NATIONAL FOREST
26
22
Wilson
Jackson
0 5 miles
C A N A D A
0 500 miles
YELLOWSTONE AND GRAND TETON NATIONAL PARKS
U S A
MEXICO
Gulf of Mexico
ATLANTIC OCEAN

Introduction to

Yellowstone and Grand Teton

Often called "America's greatest idea," Yellowstone became the world's first national park in 1872. From its inception, it took six decades for the storied park to celebrate its three millionth visitor. Nowadays, that many sightseers and outdoor enthusiasts arrive annually from across the globe. But even given the frequent crowds, the park's original nickname – Wonderland – remains an apt one. Yellowstone can be fairly described as Mother Nature's theme park, as within the boundaries of the lower 48's second largest national park (only Death Valley is larger) sit one unique sight after another, from magnificent mountain scenery and remarkable wildlife to hydrothermal phenomena on a mind-bending scale.

Carved out of a block of Edenic wilderness in northwest Wyoming, Montana, and Idaho, the 2.2 million acre park takes in the glorious colors of the **Grand Canyon of the Yellowstone**, stormy **Yellowstone Lake** and rainbow-hued hot springs, along with the sounds of roaring waterfalls, belching mudpots, and, of course, the rowdy spectacles of geysers like **Old Faithful**. All of this would be more than enough to justify its status as the country's premier national park, but Yellowstone is further blessed with an astonishing array of wildlife. More than sixty species of mammals call the park home, including huge populations of easily spotted **bison** and **elk** along with more reclusive scatterings of **wolves**, **bighorn sheep**, and **grizzlies**. More than three hundred species of birds swoop through the area, while a variety of trout

▲ Bald eagle

– including the celebrated **cutthroat** – swim within the seemingly countless streams and lakes.

Just down the road – and part and parcel of anything more than a quick visit to Yellowstone's highlights – are the scenic hiking trails and jagged mountains of Grand Teton. Pieced together in 1929 from federally owned forests and privately owned ranches, the sheer-faced cliffs of the national park's **Teton Range** make a magnificent spectacle, rising abruptly to tower 7000ft above the valley floor. A string of gem-like lakes brush the foot of the mountains, while beyond them lies the broad, sagebrush-covered **Jackson Hole** river basin, broken by the winding **Snake River**. Wildlife is also prevalent in Grand Teton, including healthy populations of gangly **moose** and speedy **pronghorns**.

The **popularity** of the parks is the area's Achilles heel, both from the point of view of the enjoyment of the visitor and the pressure put on the environment by so much human traffic. Rapidly expanding communities, including huge vacation "cabins" for the uber-rich, are gobbling up virgin landscapes at a frightening pace, and if you visit during the height of summer be prepared for hordes of tourists. But if you let yourself get frustrated by it all, you'll be missing something very special. Speeding through the parks, checking off sight after sight in quick succession is the wrong way to visit. Unless you have two weeks and look forward to covering long distances by car, forget about trying to see everything. Chance **encounters** – be it a rare geyser eruption, a wolf or grizzly sighting, or that perfect Teton sunset – are the most memorable moments, and these require an easy pace filled with patient lingering. Getting out of the car and *into* the parks is essential, so budget plenty of time for both

Chance encounters – be it a rare geyser eruption, a wolf or grizzly sighting, or that perfect Teton sunset – are the most memorable moments

▲ Backpacking through Yellowstone

hikes – including at least one overnight hike if possible – and lazy picnics, along with other **outdoor activities** ranging from fishing and boating to horseback riding and mountain climbing.

Where to go

Given Yellowstone's immense size – it's larger than the states of Rhode Island and Delaware combined – and the fact that it's accessible from all directions, there's no park center to speak of. Instead, there are nearly a dozen "village" hubs of various sizes located near the busiest junctions on the park's 150-mile long **Grand Loop Road**. Shaped like a giant figure eight, the Grand Loop was designed to pass most of the park's main attractions, and it does so admirably. While the entire road could conceivably be travelled in a very long day – frequent "bison-jams" and speed limits keep traffic moving slowly – it deserves at minimum three or four days, not including time for serious hikes or other outdoor activities.

To keep things manageable, we've grouped the Grand Loop's top half, along with the highways branching off to the North and Northeast entrances, into Northern Yellowstone (Chapter 1). The two main villages here are **Mammoth Hot Springs** and **Canyon Village**, the former is home to an old army fort and bizarre travertine terraces and the

▲ Mammoth Hot Springs

latter centered on the magnificent **Grand Canyon of the Yellowstone**. Other must-see sights in the park's northern half include the wildlife-rich **Lamar Valley** and the alien landscape of the superheated **Norris Geyser Basin.**

▲ Morning Glory Pool

Southern Yellowstone (Chapter 2) takes in the longer, lower half of the Grand Loop, as well as the highways to the West, South and East entrances. Here bison graze contentedly by the steaming geysers of the **Upper, Midway, and Lower Geyser Basins**, while patches of bright yellow monkey flowers and frequent rainbows add color to the already vivid palette of bright blues and emerald greens swirling in the numerous hot springs. The village at **Old Faithful** is the biggest in the park, with a mix of historic buildings and tacky trinket shops vying for your attention. To the east, the **West Thumb Geyser Basin** sits on the shores of **Yellowstone Lake**, the park's largest, most tempestuous attraction. Along its northern shores, **Bridge Bay**, **Lake Village** and **Fishing Bridge** host most of the lakeside activity, including a marina and historic hotel. To the south and east of Yellowstone Lake lies untrammeled wilderness laced with some of the park's best hiking trails, while north towards Canyon Village is the **Hayden Valley**, a paradise for bison and a great place to end the day watching the sunset glow on the **Yellowstone River**.

Due south, **Grand Teton National Park** (Chapter 3) can more easily be enjoyed in a couple of days, though even that gives scant time for sampling the long menu of outdoor activities. After gawking at the brash **Teton Range** from some of the fine roadside viewpoints – including the **Snake River Overlook**, **Oxbow Bend**, and towering **Signal Mountain Summit Road** – your best bet is to either start hiking or paddling. The trail to **Hidden Falls** and **Inspiration Point** reached via ferry across idyllic **Jenny Lake** is a superb first jaunt into the Tetons, while the relaxed float trips take you right through the heart of the park on the curvy **Snake River** rarely disappoint.

As for the outlying towns, choosing which to visit can be more a matter of location than of preference. Montana's **West Yellowstone** (Chapter 12), **Gardiner** (Chapter 13), and tiny **Cooke City** (Chapter 14) all border

Yellowstone, and make convenient stopovers for supplies and a friendly sit-down meal. West Yellowstone is the gateway to **Big Sky** country, home to an eponymous ski resort and top-class whitewater rafting, while smaller Gardiner hosts the new Yellowstone Heritage and Research Center. Wyoming's **Cody** (Chapter 15) is the eastern gateway to Yellowstone, and the pretty hour-long drive to visit the Buffalo Bill Historical Center is essential for anyone interested in Western history. Five miles south of Grand Teton, trendy **Jackson** (Chapter 11) is the region's most buzzing getaway. At one time a laidback ranching town, Jackson now boasts a cosmopolitan blend of galleries, restaurants and high-end hotels, along with one of the country's finest ski resorts.

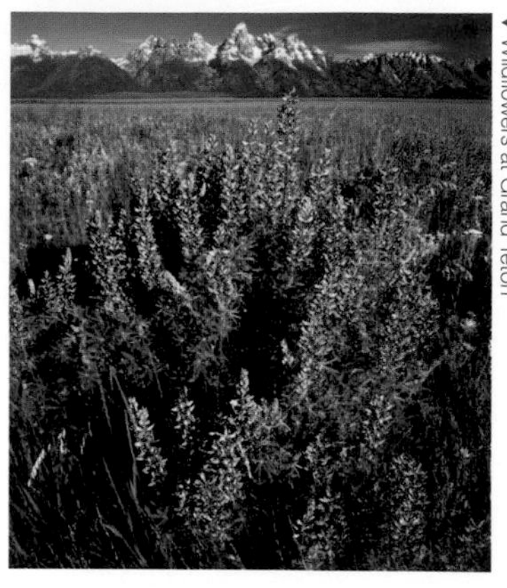
▲ Wildflowers at Grand Teton

When to go

Traditionally running between Memorial Day in late May and Labor Day in early September, the **summer** high season sees a steady stream of vacationing families lined up at the entrance gates of both Yellowstone and Grand Teton. Campgrounds quickly fill up, while visitor centers and boardwalks are clogged with a maddening mix of camera-crazed tour groups and cranky kids. Weather, however, is typically best through summer, as are trail conditions, with wildflowers blooming and winter snow and spring mud having largely dried up. It's worth keeping in mind that even during the busiest late-June to mid-August timeframe, hikers will find ample solitude and plenty of free backcountry sites, and those willing to be out at dawn will have a couple hours of peaceful wildlife spotting ahead of them.

If the thought of sharing Old Faithful with a thousand strangers is still too much to bear, consider visiting during one of the **shoulder seasons**. Weather is far more temperamental and area amenities are often shuttered, but the more relaxed pace can make up for the inconveniences. **Spring** is a transitional time, with snow gradually receding to leave behind muddy bogs and roaring waterfalls. Some roads and many trails remain closed through mid-May, with the weeks around late May and early June offering fine opportunities for relatively quiet early summer traveling. **Fall** is the best time to miss the crowds but still experience all, or most, that the parks have to offer.

With many schools starting back up in mid-August nowadays, the week before Labor Day is a golden time to visit, while the rest of September and early October sees great fishing and hiking conditions, along with active wildlife spotting as creatures enter a feeding frenzy in preparation for **winter**. This final season is a magical and secluded time, but road closures, perilously cold temperatures, and greatly limited conveniences complicate travel and must be considered before planning a trip.

▲ Hot springs at Yellowstone Lake

While the **climate** varies a good deal with both the **season** and the **altitude**, it can snow at any time throughout the year; a waterproof jacket, fleece, hat, and gloves are all essential wardrobe companions. Throughout the **summer**, expect warmish sunny days punctuated by short but possibly fierce mid-afternoon thunderstorms leaving brilliant rainbows in their wake. Evening temperatures flirt with freezing, keeping campers rolled up tight in their sleeping bags. Additional gear and caution is required through the late **spring** and **fall**, when periods of mild, near-perfect hiking conditions are balanced with freezing rain and sudden snowstorms. **Winter** temperatures are guaranteed to be frigid, and whether skiing at one of the superb regional resorts or tucked into the backseat of an unheated snowcoach, you'll want to be bundled up in multiple layers of warm clothing.

Average temperatures and rainfall

	Jan	Feb	Mar	Apr	May	Jun	Jul	Aug	Sep	Oct	Nov	Dec
Old Faithful, Yellowstone												
High (°F/°C)	23/-5	28/-2	35/2	42/6	51/11	61/16	70/21	70/21	60/16	48/9	33/1	25/-4
Low (°F/°C)	-3/-19	0/-18	4/-16	16/-9	25/-4	34/1	37/3	36/2	29/-2	21/-6	9/-13	1/-17
Rainfall (in)	2	1.5	1.8	1.5	2.1	2.1	1.7	1.7	1.6	1.3	1.7	1.7
Gardiner, MT												
High (°F/°C)	33/1	40/4	46/8	57/14	67/19	77/25	85/29	84/29	74/23	60/16	41/5	32/0
Low (°F/°C)	14/-10	18/-8	25/-4	31/-1	38/3	47/8	53/12	52/11	43/6	34/1	23/-5	14/-10
Rainfall (in)	.4	.3	.6	.6	1.6	1.4	1.2	.8	.9	.7	.7	.5
Jackson, WY												
High (°F/°C)	24/-4	31/1	40/4	49/9	59/15	70/21	80/27	79/26	71/22	55/13	37/3	26/-3
Low (°F/°C)	0/-18	3/-16	12/-11	20/-7	30/-1	37/3	41/5	39/4	33/1	24/-4	13/-11	1/-17
Rainfall (in)	2.5	2	1.7	1.4	1.9	1.9	1.3	1.3	1.4	1.2	2.2	2.4

22 things not to miss

It's not possible to see everything in and around Yellowstone and Grand Teton in one trip – and we don't suggest you try. What follows is a selective look at the highlights in and around the parks, including unforgettable hikes, fly-fishing, photogenic landscapes, and the best places to relax and relive the day's excitement. The highlights are arranged in five color-coded categories to help you find the very best things to see, do, eat, and experience. All highlights have a page reference to take you straight into the guide, where you can find out more.

01 The Lamar Valley Page **52** • Not only is the wide valley itself breathtaking, but it's also the pre-eminent setting within the Rockies for spotting bison, elk, pronghorn, and predators including wolves and grizzly bears.

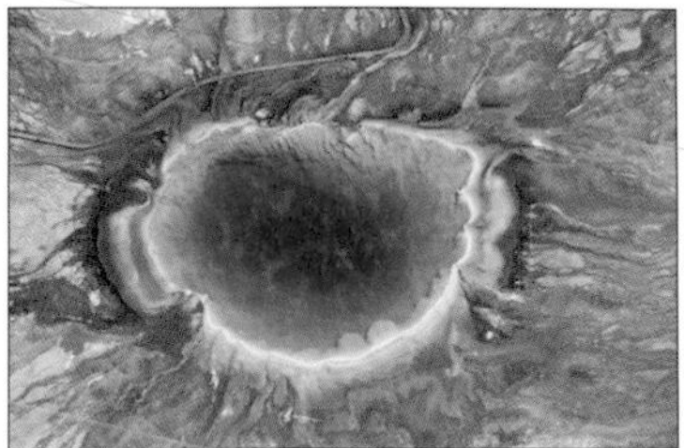

02 Grand Prismatic Spring Page **72** • The largest hot spring in Yellowstone is also the most brilliantly colored, ranging from deep ocean-blue to a fiery lava-like orange.

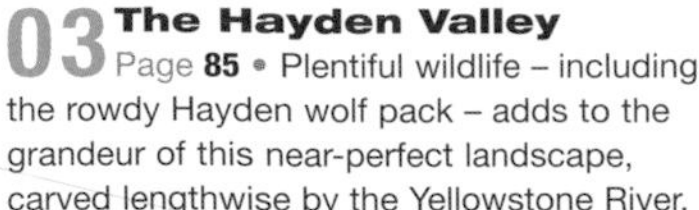

03 The Hayden Valley Page **85** • Plentiful wildlife – including the rowdy Hayden wolf pack – adds to the grandeur of this near-perfect landscape, carved lengthwise by the Yellowstone River.

04 Sunset on Lunch Tree Hill Page **111** • Overlooking moose-rich Willow Flats, this historic spot is a peaceful place to watch the sun dip behind the shark-toothed Tetons.

05 Wolf-watching with the Yellowstone Institute Page **203** & ***The wolves of Yellowstone* color section** • Increase your chances of spotting one of these captivating creatures and learn plenty in the process on a course run by this hardworking nonprofit dedicated to Yellowstone's preservation.

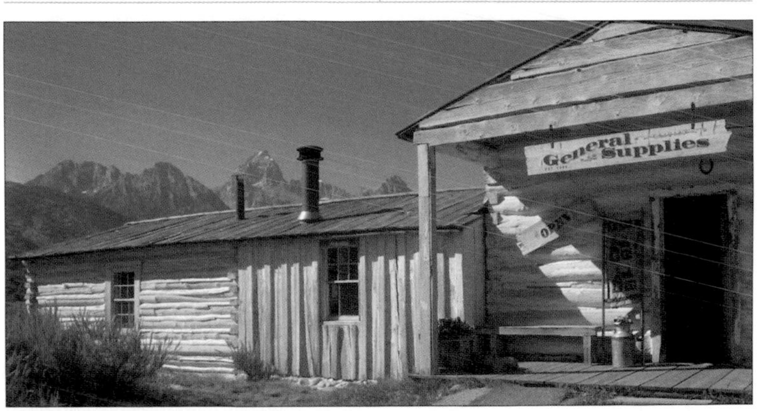

06 Menor's Ferry Historic District Page **95** • A restored homestead cabin and replica ferry in the heart of Grand Teton give great insight into the lives of Jackson's early settlers.

07 Old Faithful Page **70** • Yellowstone's essential must-see sight, as much to witness the dependable 105–185ft eruptions as to answer questions from curious friends back home.

08 West Thumb Geyser Basin Page **79** • A dramatically set geyser basin where bright-blue springs and mudpots bubble away only steps from immense Yellowstone Lake.

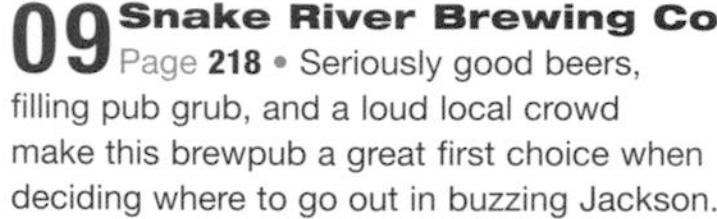

09 Snake River Brewing Co Page **218** • Seriously good beers, filling pub grub, and a loud local crowd make this brewpub a great first choice when deciding where to go out in buzzing Jackson.

10 Bechler Meadows Page **137** • A hike through this sea of waving grasses is a must for those venturing into Yellowstone's isolated Cascade Corner.

11 Fly-fishing in Yellowstone Page **160** • From the steaming Firehole River early in summer to Slough Creek in fall, Yellowstone's 200-plus trout-filled streams are fabled fishing grounds that draw anglers from around the world.

12 Artist Point Page **59** • Often thronged with visitors, this stunning viewpoint over the Grand Canyon of the Yellowstone and thundering Lower Falls never disappoints.

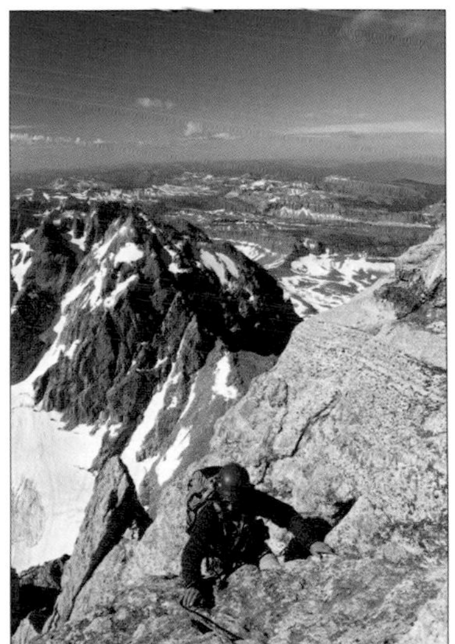

14 Climbing Grand Teton Page **170** • The view from afar is always spectacular, but for a truly unforgettable experience even reasonably fit rookies can crest this peak on a three-day climbing course.

13 Bike and hike to Osprey Falls Page **122** • Mountain bike the first three miles and then dismount to hike down Yellowstone's precipitous Sheepeater Canyon to the 150-foot wall of thundering foam that is Osprey Falls.

15 Winter in the parks Page **172** • Visiting in winter isn't always easy – many roads close completely and temperatures plummet – but the solitude and snowy scenery make it well worthwhile.

16 Old Faithful Inn Page **188** • A "log cabin" of epic proportions, soaring interior of the beloved *Old Faithful Inn* has wowed visitors for over a century, and a recent facelift had brought back to life numorous original flourishes.

17 Rafting the Gallatin Page **236** • Whooshing through a scenic and narrow valley within Big Sky country, the Gallatin River makes for a thrilling, if cold, whitewater rafting trip.

19 Helen's Corral Drive-Inn Page **242** • Gloriously greasy, the plate-sized burgers at this Gardiner institution are the perfect post-hike reward after days spent nibbling on trail mix.

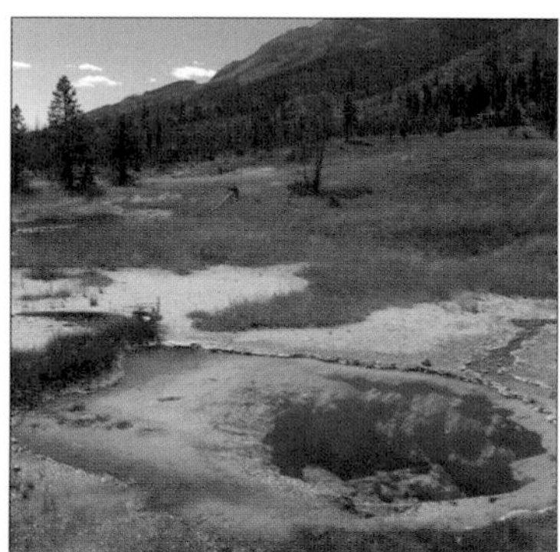

21 Hiking to Heart Lake and Mount Sheridan Page **155** • One of Yellowstone's finest overnight – or very long day – hikes takes in isolated hot springs, a gem of a backcountry lake, and a steep slog to incredible panoramic views in the region.

18 Buffalo Bill Historical Center Page **254** • Cody's marquee attraction and one of the most interesting museums in – and on – the West, with plenty beyond just Buffalo Bill ephemera.

20 Jackson Hole Mountain Resort Page **220** • The complete package for expert skiers, with hair-rising chutes, ultra steep bowls, formidable backcountry routes, and even the occasional foraging moose providing enough challenges for trips of any length.

22 Jenny Lake Page **107** • The prettiest of Grand Teton's many glacial lakes can be crossed throughout the day on a short, charming ferry ride.

Basics

Basics

Getting there

When flying into Yellowstone, the first order of business is picking which airport to land at – there are several air links to the region, but for the most part these are smaller airports, requiring a connection via a larger international airport, typically Denver and Salt Lake City, meaning cheap tickets are harder to find. Given the lack of nearby depots and the nearly non-existent public transportation in the area, trains and buses aren't much of an option. Considering the importance of having a car to get around most of the region, if you live within a day or two's drive from the parks, simply packing up the old station wagon and driving the entire distance may be the most efficient option.

Flights from the US and Canada

If you're willing to tack on a half day's drive, the airport at **Salt Lake City** (SLC; ⓦwww.slcairport.com) has excellent links to the rest of the USA and Canada, with direct flights arriving daily from many major towns and cities in the country. Barring a fare war, round-trip prices to Salt Lake City start at around $250 from New York, $150 respectively from Los Angeles, and around CAN$400 from Vancouver and Calgary (the only two Canadian cities with direct flights).

To land close by the parks – or in the case of Jackson Hole's airport, *within* one of them – you'll have to pay more, though prices tend to fluctuate wildly based on availability and the season. **Jackson Hole Airport** (JAC; ⓣ307/733-7682, ⓦwww.jacksonholeairport.com) has direct flights from Boise, Chicago, Dallas, Denver, Minneapolis/St. Paul, and Salt Lake City throughout most of the year, while Bozeman's **Gallatin Field Airport** (BZN; ⓣ406/388-8321, ⓦwww.gallatinfield.com) fields direct flights from Boise, Denver, Minneapolis/St. Paul, Salt Lake City, and Seattle/Tacoma. Cody's **Yellowstone Regional Airport** (YRA) (ⓣ307/587-5096, ⓦwww.flyyra.com) has direct flights from Denver and Salt Lake City throughout the summer, while West Yellowstone's tiny airport hosts SkyWest (a Delta airline) flights from Salt Lake City in summer only as well. For more information on these airports, see Chapters 11, 12, & 15.

Flights from the UK and Ireland

Whether you're flying from London or one of Britain's many regional airports, flying to within driving distance Yellowstone requires at least one stopover. One of the quickest routes is to Jackson Hole via Denver on British Airways (from London's Gatwick airport). The flight to Denver takes around ten hours, while the leg onwards to Jackson (via United) adds on another hour, not including layover. For **two-stop flights** travelers can choose between a wide array of options on American, British Airways, Delta, Northwest, United, and others, with connections through Atlanta, Chicago, Dallas, Denver, Minneapolis or Salt Lake City. You'll end up changing planes repeatedly, and waiting times between flights vary wildly. A basic round-trip economy-class ticket to Jackson or Bozeman from London will cost around £700 in high season and about £100–200 less during other times; flying into Salt Lake City and driving north instead should shave around £100 off the ticket price.

The best choices for those who don't live around London are similar. The quickest services will involve taking a flight to the US from a regional airport like Manchester or Glasgow (both offered by Continental), then a connecting flight from a US airport. The cheapest services are, however, usually offered by European carriers, who will fly you to a hub like Paris, Amsterdam, or Frankfurt for a connecting flight to the US, then another on to the Yellowstone region. These trips can become eighteen- to twenty-hour odysseys, but might be worth it if the fare is right.

Flights from Australia and New Zealand

There are no direct flights from **Australia** and **New Zealand** to anywhere near Yellowstone, be it Salt Lake City or the smaller airports closer to the parks. Whether you go via the Pacific or the more roundabout route through Asia, you'll have to touch down on the US West Coast – in Los Angeles or San Francisco – before taking a connection to Salt Lake City or two connections to the closer airports in Wyoming or Montana. Via the Pacific most flights are nonstop to the West Coast, with traveling time from Auckland/Sydney taking twelve to fourteen hours; some flights allow for stopovers in Honolulu or one of a number of the South Pacific Islands. If you go via Asia, you'll usually have to spend a night, or the best part of a day, in the airline's home city.

Traveling from Australia's east-coast cities, **fares** to Salt Lake City cost around A$1500–1700, while from Perth they may be A$300–400 more. There are daily flights from Sydney to Salt Lake City via Los Angeles or San Francisco on United and

Fly less – stay longer! Travel and climate change

Climate change is the single biggest issue facing our planet. It is caused by a build-up in the atmosphere of carbon dioxide and other greenhouse gases, which are emitted by many sources – including planes. Already, flights account for around 3–4% of human-induced global warming: that figure may sound small, but it is rising year on year and threatens to counteract the progress made by reducing greenhouse emissions in other areas.

Rough Guides regard travel, overall, as a global benefit, and feel strongly that the advantages to developing economies are important, as are the opportunities for greater contact and awareness among peoples. But we all have a responsibility to limit our personal "carbon footprint". That means giving thought to how often we fly and what we can do to redress the harm that our trips create.

Flying and climate change

Pretty much every form of motorized travel generates CO_2, but planes are particularly bad offenders, releasing large volumes of greenhouse gases at altitudes where their impact is far more harmful. Flying also allows us to travel much further than we would contemplate doing by road or rail, so the emissions attributable to each passenger become truly shocking. For example, one person taking a return flight between Europe and California produces the equivalent impact of 2.5 tonnes of CO_2 – similar to the yearly output of the average UK car.

Less harmful planes may evolve but it will be decades before they replace the current fleet – which could be too late for avoiding climate chaos. In the meantime, there are limited options for concerned travellers: to reduce the amount we travel by air (take fewer trips, stay longer!), to avoid night flights (when plane contrails trap heat from Earth but can't reflect sunlight back to space), and to make the trips we do take "climate neutral" via a carbon offset scheme.

Carbon offset schemes

Offset schemes run by **climatecare.org**, **carbonneutral.com** and others allow you to "neutralize" the greenhouse gases that you are responsible for releasing. Their websites have simple calculators that let you work out the impact of any flight. Once that's done, you can pay to fund projects that will reduce future carbon emissions by an equivalent amount (such the distribution of low-energy lightbulbs and cooking stoves in developing countries). Please take the time to visit our website and make your trip climate neutral.

www.roughguides.com/climatechange

Qantas/American. Adding another connection onwards to Jackson Hole or Bozeman's Gallatin Field airports adds another A$200–300. Via Asia, the lowest fares are likely with JAL, which flies out of Sydney, Brisbane, and Cairns with a transfer in Tokyo, or Korean Air, which makes a similar change in Seoul. Expect flights to start around A$1500 in low season; add an additional A$400–600 at peak times.

From **New Zealand**, most flights are out of **Auckland** (add NZ$200–250 for Christchurch and Wellington departures), with the best deals on Air New Zealand (either nonstop or via Honolulu, Fiji, or Tonga) and Qantas (direct or via Sydney) to Los Angeles, where you would link with American for the onward flight to Salt Lake (NZ$2200–2600). United Airlines have regular deals on fares all the way to Salt Lake that may undercut their competition. Via Asia, Singapore Airlines has convenient connecting services to LA and San Francisco from NZ$2300, while the best value for money (NZ$2000–2100) is on JAL via Tokyo.

Trains

For the first half of the twentieth century, traveling to Yellowstone by **train** on the Union Pacific was the most popular mode of arrival. By 1960, however, regular services to West Yellowstone's depot were suspended, and nowadays traveling by train is mainly an option for those who refuse to fly or drive a long distance. **Amtrak** does not have a single passenger train running through Wyoming or southern Montana, meaning the closest train passengers can get to the parks is around 300 miles, from where they'll need to rent a car and drive the remaining distance.

The most northerly Amtrak route, the **Empire Builder**, connects Seattle to Chicago (46 hours). This is a good option if you're planning on also visiting Montana's Glacier National Park, as the train makes several stops in the area. To the south, the **California Zephyr**, which runs from Chicago to San Francisco (53 hours), calls in at Salt Lake City, Utah.

Amtrak **fares** are more often than not more expensive than flying. For all **information** on fares and schedules, and to make **reservations**, use the toll-free number ⓣ1-800/USA-RAIL or website (ⓦwww.amtrak.com). Do not call individual stations.

Buses

Bus travel is the most tedious and time-consuming way to get to Yellowstone, and, for all the discomfort, it won't really save you much money. **Greyhound** (ⓣ1-800/231-2222, ⓦwww.greyhound.com), the sole long-distance operator, stops off only at Cody, Wyoming and Bozeman, Montana, in the area, meaning visitors still need to rent a car or book a local shuttle service to get into the parks (the latter are detailed on pp. 26 and 204 respectively).

The only reason to go Greyhound is if you're planning to visit a number of other places en route; the company's domestic **Discovery Pass** (ⓦwww.discoverypass.com) is good for unlimited travel within a set time: seven days of travel costs $219; 15 days, $319; 30 days, $419; and 60 days, $589; passes for overseas travelers run about five percent less. Domestic passes are valid from the date of purchase, so it's a bad idea to buy them in advance; overseas visitors, however, can buy passes before leaving home, and they will be validated at the start of the trip.

By car

From Alabama to Alberta, cars trolling through the parks sport license plates from across the US and Canada, proof positive that the region is a prime **road-trip** destination. Driving your own car gives the greatest freedom and flexibility, and if you don't have one, you can **rent a car** by phoning your local branch of one of the major agencies (listed on p.27).

One thing to bear in mind when driving in Yellowstone is that conditions can often be extreme. See p.25 for tips on driving in all conditions.

Approaching the parks

Yellowstone occupies the far northwest corner of Wyoming, overlapping slightly into Idaho and Montana. Two of the park's **five main entrances** are in Wyoming, via I-14/16/20 to the east (**East Entrance**) and I-89/191/189 to the south (**South Entrance**); to reach the South Entrance from Jackson – a distance of 60 miles – you drive through **Grand Teton** and the slim **John D. Rockefeller, Jr. Memorial Parkway**. Driving distance from Cody to Yellowstone's East Entrance is 53 miles.

The park's other three entrances are all in Montana. Busiest is the **West Entrance**, bordering the gateway town of **West Yellowstone**, 90 miles south of Bozeman via Big Sky and 100 miles east of Idaho Falls, Idaho. Nearly as active, the **North Entrance** at **Gardiner** is Yellowstone's historic original entrance, located 50 miles south of Livingston through the Paradise Valley and 85 total miles from Bozeman. The sleepy **Northeast Entrance** is a couple miles west from tiny **Cooke City**, located 70 miles northwest of Cody and 125 miles from Billings, Montana. Yellowstone's sixth entrance – easily the most isolated and least used – is at the **Bechler Ranger Station** in the park's southwest corner, located 20 miles east of **Ashton**, Idaho, final stop on a winding, dead-end road.

Grand Teton, located entirely in Wyoming, has entry points from the north, south, and east. Speedy Hwy-191 is the main artery, shooting north from **Jackson** and spanning the entire park to Yellowstone's South Entrance 60 miles away. From **Teton Village** north of Jackson, the slower Moose-Wilson Road passes through another southern entrance, the **Granite Canyon Entrance Station**, en route to the park Headquarters at Moose. Hwy-26/287 enters the park from the east at **Moran Entrance Station**, located 55 miles from Dubois, Wyoming.

Miles to Yellowstone (West Yellowstone Entrance)

Atlanta 1950 miles (28 hours)
Boston 2500 miles (35 hours)
Chicago 1500 miles (20 hours)
Detroit 1800 miles (24 hours)
Houston 1700 miles (23 hours)
Los Angeles 1000 miles (13 hours)
Miami 2600 miles (37 hours)
New York 2300 miles (33 hours)
San Francisco 950 miles (12 hours)
Salt Lake City 325 miles (5 hours)
Seattle 750 miles (11 hours)
Washington D.C. 2200 miles (32 hours)

Airlines, agents, and operators

Airlines

Air Canada US & Canada ⓣ1-888/247-2262, ⓦwww.aircanada.com, UK ⓣ0871/220 1111, Republic of Ireland ⓣ01/679 3958, Australia ⓣ1300/655 747 or 02/8248 5757, New Zealand ⓣ09/379 3371
Air New Zealand Australia ⓣ13 24 76, New Zealand ⓣ0800/737 000, ⓦwww.airnz.co.nz.
Alaska Airlines US ⓣ1-800/252-7522, ⓦwww.alaska-air.com.
America West Airlines US ⓣ1-800/235-9292, ⓦwww.americawest.com, Australia ⓣ1300/364 757 or 02/9267 2138, New Zealand ⓣ0800/866 000
American Airlines US & Canada ⓣ1-800/433-7300, ⓦwww.aa.com, UK ⓣ0845/7789 789, Republic of Ireland ⓣ01/602 0550, Australia ⓣ1300/130 757, New Zealand ⓣ0800/887 997
British Airways US and Canada ⓣ1-800-AIRWAYS, UK ⓣ0870/850 9850, Republic of Ireland ⓣ1890/626 747, Australia ⓣ1300/767 177, New Zealand ⓣ09/966 9777, ⓦwww.ba.com.
Big Sky Airlines US ⓣ1-800/237-7788, ⓦwww.bigskyair.com.
Continental Airlines US and Canada ⓣ1-800-523-3273, UK ⓣ0845/607 6760, Republic of Ireland ⓣ1890/925 252, Australia ⓣ02/9244 2242, New Zealand ⓣ09/308 3350, International ⓣ1800/231 0856, ⓦwww.continental.com.
Delta US and Canada ⓣ1-800-221-1212, UK ⓣ0845/600 0950, Republic of Ireland ⓣ1850/882 031 or 01/407 3165, Australia ⓣ1300/302 849, New Zealand ⓣ09/379 3370, ⓦwww.delta.com.
Frontier Airlines US ⓣ1-800/432-1359, ⓦwww.flyfrontier.com.
JetBlue US ⓣ1-800/JET-BLUE, ⓦwww.jetblue.com.
Northwest/KLM Domestic ⓣ1-800/225-2525, International ⓣ1-800/447-4747, ⓦwww.nwa.com, ⓦwww.klm.com.
Korean Air US and Canada ⓣ1-800-438-5000, UK ⓣ0800/413 000, Republic of Ireland ⓣ01/799 7990, Australia ⓣ02/9262 6000, New Zealand ⓣ09/914 2000, ⓦwww.koreanair.com.
Northwest/KLM US ⓣ1-800-225-2525, UK ⓣ0870/507 4074, Australia ⓣ1-300-767-310, ⓦwww.nwa.com.
Southwest Airlines US ⓣ1-800/435-9792, ⓦwww.southwest.com.

United Airlines Domestic ⓣ1-800/241-6522, International ⓣ1-800/538-2929, wwww.united.com.
US Airways US and Canada ⓣ1-800-428-4322, UK ⓣ0845/600 3300, Ireland ⓣ1890/925 065, ⓦwww.usair.com.
Virgin Atlantic US ⓣ1-800-821-5438, UK ⓣ0870/380 2007, Australia ⓣ1300/727 340, SA ⓣ11/340 3400, ⓦwww.virgin-atlantic.com.

Travel agents

CIE Tours International Republic of Ireland ⓣ01/703 1888, ⓦwww.cietours.ie. General flight and tour agent.
Educational Travel Center ⓣ1-800/747-5551, ⓦwww.edtrav.com. Low-cost fares worldwide, student/youth discount offers, car rental and tours.
Flightcentre US ⓣ1-866/WORLD-51, ⓦwww.flightcentre.us, Canada ⓣ1-877/WORLD-02, ⓦwww.flightcentre.ca, UK ⓣ0870/499 0040, ⓦwww.flightcentre.co.uk. Rock-bottom fares worldwide.
Flights4Less UK ⓣ0871/222 3432, ⓦwww.flights4less.co.uk. Good discount airfares. Part of Lastminute.com.
North South Travel UK ⓣ01245/608 291, ⓦwww.northsouthtravel.co.uk. Friendly, competitive travel agency, offering discounted fares worldwide. Profits are used to support projects in the developing world, especially the promotion of sustainable tourism.
STA Travel US ⓣ1-800/781-4040, ⓦwww.statravel.com, Canada ⓣ1-888/427-5639, ⓦwww.statravel.ca. UK ⓣ0870/160 0599, ⓦwww.statravel.co.uk, Australia ⓣ1300/733 035, ⓦwww.statravel.com.au, New Zealand ⓣ0508/782 872, ⓦwww.statravel.co.nz. Worldwide specialists in independent travel. Also student IDs, travel insurance, car rental, rail passes, and more.
Travel Cuts US ⓣ1-800/592-CUTS, Canada ⓣ1-888/246-9762, ⓦwww.travelcuts.com. Popular, long-established student-travel organization, with worldwide offers.
Travelers Advantage ⓣ1-877/259-2689, ⓦwww.travelersadvantage.com. Discount travel club, with cash-back deals and discounted car rental. Membership required ($1 for one month's trial).
Travelosophy US ⓣ1-800/332-2687, ⓦwww.itravelosophy.com. Good range of discounted and student fares worldwide.
Trailfinders UK ⓣ0845/058 5858, ⓦwww.trailfinders.com, Republic of Ireland ⓣ01/677 7888, ⓦwww.trailfinders.ie, Australia ⓣ1300/780 212, ⓦwww.trailfinders.com.au. One of the best-informed and most efficient agents for independent travelers.

Tour operators

Adventure World Australia ⓣ02/8913 0755, ⓦwww.adventureworld.com.au, New Zealand ⓣ09/524 5118, ⓦwww.adventureworld.co.nz. Agents for a vast array of international adventure travel companies. One option is TrekAmerica's Northwest Escape tour, a 14-day package spending nearly a week in and around Yellowstone, along with Yosemite in California and Mount Rainier in Washington.
Backroads US ⓣ1-800/GO-ACTIVE or 510/527-1555, ⓦwww.backroads.com. Cycling, hiking and multi-sport tours designed for the young at heart (including families), with the emphasis on going at your own pace. Their Yellowstone options range from a week in the region's best hotels to a week of camping out.
Canada & America Travel Specialists Australia ⓣ02/9922 4600, ⓦwww.canada-americatravel.com.au. North American specialists – accommodation, adventure sports, car and motorhome rentals, escorted tours, independent travel, and more. Week-long packages to Yellowstone in both winter and summer on offer taking in Yellowstone and Grand Teton along the way.
Contiki UK ⓣ020/8290 6777, ⓦwww.contiki.co.uk. Tours and trips for 18–35 year-old party animals. The two-week Parks and Canyons tour, taking in Yellowstone and Cody, starts at US$1700.

Cosmos US ⓣ1-800/276-1241, ⓦwww.cosmosvacations.com. Planned vacation packages with an independent focus. Their 12-day National Parks and Canyon Country package starts in Denver and ends in Las Vegas, spending four days in and around Yellowstone.

Dragoman UK ⓣ01728/861133, ⓦwww.dragoman.com. Australia ⓣ02/8913 0755, New Zealand ⓣ09/524 5118, ⓦwww.dragoman.com. Extended overland journeys in purpose-built expedition vehicles, along with shorter camping and hotel-based safaris. Their seven-week long "ARM" adventure travels from Anchorage, Alaska, to Mexico City, taking in Yellowstone and Grand Teton along the way.

Exodus UK ⓣ0870/240 5550, ⓦwww.exodus.co.uk. Adventure tour operators taking small groups on specialist programs in countries around the world. One Yellowstone option is their 15-day camping loop of the region, beginning and ending in Salt Lake City.

Explore Worldwide UK ⓣ0870/333 4001, Ireland (c/o Maxwell's Travel) ⓣ01/677 9479, ⓦwww.exploreworldwide.com. Big range of small-group tours, treks, expeditions and safaris on all continents, staying mostly in small local hotels. Their 16-day Yellowstone and Western Trails tour takes in plenty of hiking and combines camping with hotel stays.

Inghams UK ⓣ020/8780 4433, ⓦwww.inghams.co.uk. Large and respected ski tour operator with a long menu of ski trip options including Jackson Hole.

Mountain Travel Sobek US ⓣ1-888/MTSOBEK or 510/594-6000, ⓦwww.mtsobek.com. A well-established US-based adventure travel company offering intricately planned activity holidays. Their six day "Wild Wyoming" tour includes two nights of camping on an island on Jackson Lake, along with a float trip down the Snake River.

Trek America US ⓣ1-800/221-0596, ⓦwww.trekamerica.com, UK ⓣ01295/256 777, ⓦwww.trekamerica.co.uk Walking and soft adventure tours all over the US, Canada and Mexico, year-round. offer several tours in the park from 1-4 weeks long.

Wildlife Worldwide UK ⓣ020/8667 9158, ⓦwww.wildlifeworldwide.com. Tailor-made trips for wildlife and wilderness enthusiasts. Their Wolves of Yellowstone program spends a week in and around the park in the winter, tracking wolves and taking snowcoach tours.

Getting around

To fully explore the Yellowstone region, you'll need your own transportation, whether that be a car, RV, motorcycle, or for the heartiest of visitors, bicycle. Public transportation options are basically non-existent, with only Jackson and Cody having anything close to fully realized bus networks. Though bus plans for both parks have been suggested for decades, there has been little funding for such programs, and given both visitor apathy and the overall size of the parks, a major public transportation network remains a pipe dream. Park tours by bus, however, are readily available and vary greatly by subject and length; see Chapter 10 for complete details of the best tours of Yellowstone and Grand Teton.

Driving

Driving is by far the best – and in many cases only – way to get around the parks. Along with the ease of traveling to your own flexible schedule, having a car lets you best explore the region's wide-open landscapes, backcountry roads, scenic vistas and the like. Indeed, for some visitors cruising, windows down, by the Tetons or curving alongside Yellowstone Lake will be a highlight of the trip.

For the most part, **road conditions** are good, save for winter when most of the roads in Yellowstone are closed for the season along with the Teton Park Road within Grand Teton; see Chapter 7 for in-depth details on winter closures. Upon entering Yellowstone or Grand Teton, along with a newspaper and

Road condition hotlines

Grand Teton ⓣ307/739-3682
Yellowstone ⓣ307/344-2117
Idaho ⓣ1-888/432-7623
Montana ⓣ1-800/226-7623
Wyoming ⓣ307/772-0824

map you'll be given a sheet detailing **major road closures**, typically due to construction but sometimes caused by rockslides, floods, or other natural disasters. It pays to check ahead of time either through the parks' websites or road hotlines (see box, above) for any major closings as you may need to plan long detours to avoid them given the dearth of roads in the region.

Gas will cost anywhere between $2 and $3 a gallon (3.8 liters), and service stations are easy to find within the parks and in the gateways towns; you're best off, however, never letting your supply dip below a quarter of a tank as there are some areas with thirty mile long gaps or longer between stations.

Rules of the road

Driving conditions in the parks are good in summer, with the major distractions being attention-grabbing scenery and wildlife wandering onto the roads. While the major roads within **Yellowstone** are paved and as wide as a minor highway, driving requires a fair amount of patience. Along with the omnipresent, slow moving RVs, **bison-jams** caused by the two-ton creatures criss-crossing the road are common, as are **backups** stemming from gawkers pulling over to check out moose, elk and other roadside animals. Due in large part to the animals in the park, the maximum **speed limit** within Yellowstone is 45mph, something worth keeping in mind when route-planning; given frequent back-ups, you're best off giving yourself even extra time to reach your destination. Over a hundred deer, moose, bear, elk and bison are killed each year by drivers within the park, so always obey the speed limit and keep on the lookout for crossing creatures. If the thought of killing an animal isn't reason enough, be aware that police do not hesitate in giving out expensive **tickets** to those caught speeding.

Unlike Yellowstone, maximum speed limits vary within **Grand Teton**. Though not at all unusual, animals cross the park's roads less frequently, and the major north/south **Hwy-191** (also Highways 26/89/287 in spots) is treated, for the most part, like typical highway, with speed limits of 55mph – though drivers breaking the 80mph mark are common. From the northern edge of the John D. Rockefeller, Jr Parkway down to the southern boundary of the park, the Hwy-191 is 55 miles long, and it's possible to make the journey is under an hour and a half in good conditions; note that the 25-mile stretch between the park's southern boundary to the Moran Entrance Station requires no park pass, giving road-trippers a free head-on shot of the Tetons to the west. Speed limits on the rest of the roads range 10–45mph, and, as in Yellowstone, are enforced attentively by police and rangers.

Outside of the parks, the maximum speed limits on interstates in Wyoming, Montana and Idaho is 75mph. On state highways, the maximum is typically 65mph, with lower signposted limits – usually 35–45mph – in built-up areas, and 20mph near schools when children are present. If the **police** flag you down, don't get out of the car, and don't reach into the glove compartment until you're given the OK to do so; simply sit still with your hands on the wheel, be polite and don't attempt to make jokes.

Apart from the obvious fact that Americans drive on the right, various rules may be unfamiliar to **foreign drivers**. US law requires that any alcohol be carried unopened in the trunk of the car; it's illegal to make a U-turn on an interstate or anywhere where a single unbroken line runs along the middle of the road; to park on a highway; and for passengers to ride without fastened seatbelts. At junctions, you can turn right on a red light if there is no traffic approaching from the left; and some junctions are **four-way stops**: a crossroads where all traffic must stop before proceeding in order of arrival.

It can't be stressed too strongly that **Driving Under the Influence (DUI)** is a very serious offence. If a police officer smells alcohol on your breath, he/she is entitled to

Winter driving

If you're unaccustomed to driving in icy conditions, it's best to be very conservative and to avoid driving during snowstorms if possible. Basic equipment for winter driving in the mountains includes snow-tires and/or chains, an ice-scraper for clearing your windshield and a shovel for clearing away built-up snow. It also pays to have warm clothes, blankets, and extra food and water in case you do get stuck, along with a cell phone (provided you get coverage).

If your car has snow tires (you should definitely double-check this when booking a rental car for a winter trip into the mountains) you'll be in good shape for general highway and town driving in winter. Major roads are regularly cleared throughout the winter, as are town and city streets, though you should not rely on smaller county roads and such being cleared every day. At times you may see road signs indicating that drivers are required to carry chains in a certain area.

Even with the best of precautions, you may find yourself on a stretch of road covered in an unbroken sheet of ice. Even snow tires won't help you much, and if you have no alternative but to keep driving, you'll need to be very careful indeed. The reaction to skidding on ice depends on whether your car is equipped with anti-lock brakes (ABS). If it is not, firmly pump the brakes until the car is back under control. If equipped with ABS brakes, your car should automatically pump the brakes after pressing down the pedal, keeping the wheels from locking up.

administer a breath, saliva, or urine test. If you fail, they'll lock you up with other inebriates in the "drunk tank" of the nearest jail until you sober up. Your case will later be heard by a judge, who can fine you a minimum of several hundred dollars or in extreme (or repeat) cases, imprison you for thirty days.

Renting a car

The first order of business for most visitors upon landing at one of the local airports will be **renting a car**. Each of the airports – in Jackson, Bozeman, Cody and, further afield, Salt Lake City – hosts at least a couple of the rental agencies listed below. Renters are supposed to have held a license for at least one year (though this is rarely checked); those under 25 pay a higher insurance premium. A credit card is essential, as rental companies will rarely accept a cash deposit.

4WD vehicles are available, but you'll pay a premium for them and also end up paying more at the gas pump. All the major roads within the parks are accessible in a regular car, meaning a 4WD is only necessary if you're planning to drive lots of backcountry roads – although they are a good choice for winter driving too. Note also that **ski/bike racks** can often be requested as well.

It's worth booking in advance via the Internet to get a good deal on rentals of a week or more. Otherwise you can phone the major firms' toll-free numbers and ask for their best rate – most will try to beat the offers of their competitors, so always haggle. Be sure too to have written confirmation of your booking to present when collecting your vehicle.

One oddity about the rate for car rental is that **cheaper deals** are almost always done by the week; for example, a car rented at $45 per day can often be had for $200 a week. Rental companies' strict adherence to weekly discounted rates can lead to the bizarre situation where it's cheaper to rent a car for fourteen days than for ten.

Important details to check are whether the rate includes free unlimited mileage, and what the insurance cost will be. When looking at some of the cheaper rental firms, keep in mind that there's a big difference in the quality of cars from company to company; industry leaders like Hertz and Avis tend to have newer, lower-mileage cars, often with air-conditioning and decent stereo systems – no small consideration on a long drive through the mountains. Virtually all US rental cars have automatic transmissions.

When you rent a car, read the small print carefully for details on the **Collision Damage**

Waiver (CDW) – sometimes called a Liability Damage Waiver (LDW) or a Physical Damage Waiver (PDW) – a form of insurance that usually isn't included in the rental charge but is well worth considering. Americans may already be covered by their own vehicle insurance (check before you leave home) but foreign visitors should definitely consider taking this option. It specifically covers the car that you are driving, as you are in any case insured for damage to other vehicles. At $10–14 a day, it does add considerably to the daily rental fee, but without it you're liable for every scratch to the car – even those that aren't your fault. Some credit card companies offer automatic CDW coverage to anyone using their card; again, check before leaving home.

If you **break down** in a rented car, you can normally call an emergency assistance number, printed on your rental contract. If you're not carrying your own, you might consider renting a **mobile telephone** from the car rental agency (or from outlets at major airports) If you don't have one – you often only have to pay a nominal amount until you actually use it. Having a phone can be reassuring at least, and a potential lifesaver should something go terribly wrong.

Car rental agencies

Alamo ⓣ1-800/462-5266, ⓦwww.alamo.com.
Avis ⓣ1-800/230 4898, ⓦwww.avis.com.
Budget ⓣ1-800/527-0700, ⓦwww.budget.com.
Dollar ⓣ1-800/800-3665, ⓦwww.dollar.com.
Enterprise ⓣ1-800/726-8222, ⓦwww.enterprise.com.
Hertz ⓣ1-800/654-300 1, ⓦwww.hertz.com.
National ⓣ1-800/962-7070, ⓦwww.nationalcar.com.
Thrifty ⓣ1-800/847-4389, ⓦwww.thrifty.com.

Renting an RV

Besides cars, Recreational Vehicles or **RVs** (camper vans) can be rented starting at around $1000 a week. The idea of traveling with your accommodation may sound liberating, but it's far from cheap. On top of the rental fees, take into account the **cost of gas** (some RVs do twelve miles to the gallon or less) and any drop-off charges, in case you plan to do a one-way trip across the country. Also, keep in mind that although you're traveling with a roof overhead, you'll still need to pay to "camp out" in the parks, with RV sites averaging over $30 per night. Outside of the parks, it is rarely legal simply to park and spend the night at the roadside as well – you are expected to stay in designated parks that start at around $20 per night and can be as expensive as a basic motel room for full-hook ups.

The Recreational Vehicle Rental Association (ⓣ703/591-7130 or 1-800/336-0355, ⓦwww.rvra.org) has an online directory of rental firms in the US and Canada. One of the largest companies offering **RV rentals** is Cruise America (ⓣ1-800/327-7799, ⓦwww.cruiseamerica.com), with rentals out of the Eagle Rent-A-Car office in Jackson (ⓣ307/739-9999).

Cycling

As roads within Yellowstone are fairly narrow and drivers tend to be inattentive as they're busy looking at scenery and wildlife, **cycling** within the park is not the safest way of getting around. Cycling through Grand Teton is somewhat better given the flatter roads and longer straights, but even here many of the roads have narrow to non-existent shoulders and plenty of heavy vehicle traffic – including RVs with their dangerously wide mirrors – to contend with.

That said, scores of visitors each year risk it and cycle through both parks, often on longer trips throughout the Rockies or even cross country. It's important to choose your routes carefully to ensure you don't take on an entirely unrealistic trip through extreme mountainous terrain, and you're best off planning your trip early or better yet later in the season as well, when there's less traffic to deal with.

Both parks do their best to make conditions fair for cycle travellers, and have downloadable **brochures** available on their websites. A limited number of first-come first-served hiking/biking campsites are available at all of Yellowstone's **campgrounds**, save for Slough Creek, but given the distances between campgrounds you may want to book ahead or risk arriving late in the afternoon to a booked campground.

For **long-distance cycling**, you'll need a helmet, bright clothing, maps, spare tires, tools, panniers, and a good quality multi-speed bike. Don't immediately splurge on a mountain bike, unless you are planning a lot of off-road use – good road conditions and trail restrictions in both parks make a touring bike an equally good or better choice. The most pleasant routes are along quieter roads; cycling on interstate highways is illegal (and very dangerous).

For information on tour operators, renting bikes in the region and shorter, non-travel based bike routes, see Chapter 6: Summer Activities.

Health and personal safety

Staying safe while visiting Yellowstone and Grand Teton is mainly a case of common sense. For reasons unbeknownst to rangers and other park planners, some visitors tend to assume that once in a National Park, the rules of the wild are suspended and that they've now entered a realm where all sharp edges have been dulled. This, of course, is not the case. While there are guardrails, warning signs, and similar safety precautions at some of the more heavily trafficked areas, for the most part there is nobody watching over you while in the parks. Emergency call boxes are not dotted throughout the backcountry, the native animals are not trained to be human-friendly, and rangers are not babysitters paid to monitor a visitor's every move.

If you're prepared for the worst, the worst by and large won't happen. Should you have a serious accident in the region, however, emergency services will generally get to you quickly (depending on how remote the location). For emergencies or ambulance, dial ⓣ911. If you're well enough to drive or have someone to drive you, there are clinics and hospitals throughout the region. Those within the parks are listed below, while hospitals in the gateway towns are detailed within their respective chapters.

Most visitors will leave with only sore legs or perhaps a sunburn. As with any other outdoor location, use **sunscreen** and wear a hat when warranted, and work your way up towards the toughest hikes instead of trying to tackle one on the first day. It's also worth carrying insect repellent for **mosquitoes**, which can get amazingly annoying in the woods in summer. Another small nuisance are **ticks**, which can pass on Colorado Tick Fever and Rocky Mountain Spotted Fever. Both have similar symptoms – headaches and muscle aches, nausea, vomiting, skin rash, and abdominal pain. Ticks are most likely to attach themselves to bare legs or feet when walking through brush, forest or grassland. If you find a tick burrowing into your skin, grab it by the head with a pair of tweezers and gently pull it out. If any of the above symptoms occur within two weeks, contact a doctor.

Foreign visitors should bear in mind that many pills available over the counter at home require a **prescription** in the US – most codeine-based painkillers, for example – and that local brand names can be confusing; ask for advice at the **pharmacy** in any **drugstore**.

Animals

When it comes to interacting with **animals** in the parks, tales of incredible foolishness and feats of wanton ignorance abound. From families lining up for a bison-side group portrait to hikers feeding baby bears, there's no limit to the amount of common sense rules

Area clinics and hospitals

Yellowstone

Lake ☎307/242-7241, mid–May through late Sept daily 8.30am–8.30pm; closed rest of the year.

Mammoth ☎307/344-7965. Open year-round 8.30am–5pm; closed weekends in the off-season.

Old Faithful ☎307/545-7325. Open daily May through mid Oct, mainly 8.30am–5pm. Closed weekends during shoulder season and completely during rest of the year.

Grand Teton

Jackson Lake Lodge ☎307/543-2514, late May through Sept, daily 10am–6pm

Cody

West Park Hospital 707 Sheridan Ave ☎307/527-7501, 24hr emergency care.

Jackson

St John's 625 E Broadway ☎307/733-3636, 24hr emergency care.

willing to be broken by visitors entranced by run-ins with wild animals. As the parks note on signs, pamphlets and at Ranger Stations, animals here – from the smallest squirrel to the biggest bear – are not tame and should be viewed with caution. The basic rule of thumb is if an animal reacts to your presence, you are too close, and it's your responsibility to back away, not the animal's.

Actual **dangerous encounters** with animals are rare and not too difficult to avoid. Never surround or block an animal's line of travel, avoid sudden movements in their presence, and do not approach them – a point that visitors with cameras pressed up to their faces seem to forget. As some shutterbugs have learned, a camera makes a pitiful shield against a charging bison. Specifically, you must stay at least 100 yards away from bears and at least 25 yards away from all other animals, including elk, bison, coyote, moose and wolves. Come winter, you should double these distances, as conserving energy during the coldest season is the key to survival for these animals and spooking them can have drastic consequences.

It should go without saying that **feeding** any wild animal is strictly **forbidden**. As is often said, "a fed bear is a dead bear," and this commonly applies to all creatures, large or small. Feeding animals, including birds, causes them to become overly reliant and comfortable around humans, leading to aggressive or dependent behavior, again with drastic consequences.

For in-depth details on **bear encounters**, see the box on pp.118-119

Water safety: lakes, rivers, and thermal features

Water quality is excellent throughout the Rockies and it's quite safe to drink from taps. However, while the streams and lakes may look clean and inviting, water should be chemically treated, boiled, or filtered before you **drink** it to avoid the risk of *giardia* contamination or a similar bacterial disorder; see Chapter 4 for more details.

Aside from car accidents, **drowning** is the most common cause of accidental death within the parks. Given the altitude and long winters in the region, rivers and lakes are extremely cold. Water temperatures in Yellowstone Lake, one of the more extreme examples, average a numbing 45 degrees, giving capsized paddlers less than a half-an-hour survival time. Along with frigid temperatures, rivers, especially in spring and early summer, run swift and strong and can quickly overpower even the most skilled swimmers. In short, you should only swim in designated areas (listed on p.167), and always remain alert when near water, especially when traveling with children. On certain backcountry trails, you may also need to make a **river crossing** to continue onwards; again, see Chapter 4: Day Hikes for tips.

Thermal areas likewise can be dangerous. Always stay on designated trail and boardwalks when in a thermal area. These paths not only keep the delicate formations from being destroyed, but can keep you from breaking through any thin crusts and suffering a severe scalding, or worse. Never travel through thermal areas after dark and note that is illegal to bathe in any thermal waters that are completely of thermal origin, Visitors with children in tow should take time to explain the dangers of hot springs, geysers, mudpots and the like to children, as their bright colors and weird formations can be particularly mesmerizing.

Weather

It's commonly said in Wyoming that if you don't like the **weather**, all you need to do is wait five minutes or travel five miles. Daily temperature swings of fifty degrees or more are common, and thunderstorms and blizzards can swing through with surprising rapidity. With this in mind, hikers should always pack a warm, waterproof layer regardless of the temperature or duration of the hike. For details on exactly what to pack for longer trips, see Chapter 5 "Backcountry hikes".

The most dangerous and possibly deadly threat from being caught unprepared in freezing weather is **hypothermia**, caused by your body losing heat faster than it can be produced. Telltale signs of the onset of hypothermia include slowed or slurred speech, uncontrollable shivering, and intense drowsiness. Anyone displaying signs of hypothermia should get medical attention immediately. If in the backcountry, you can fight the onset of hypothermia by getting the victim into a warm, windless shelter – be it a tent, cabin or, in an extreme emergency, thick stand of trees or hastily dug snow cave – immediately. After removing all wet clothing, the victim then needs to be warmed. Skin on skin warming is often the sole solution, meaning two naked bodies snuggled tight in a single sleeping bag. Warm – but not too hot – drinks can help increase body temperature, but under no condition should alcohol be used (booze actually lowers body temperature).

Another threat in winter is **frostbite**, a loss of feeling and color in body parts exposed to freezing temperatures. Though not as dangerous as hypothermia, anyone displaying frostbite-like symptoms should seek immediate medical attention. If not available, avoid undue pressure on affected areas – i.e., avoid walking, if possible, on frostbitten ten feet and do not rub body parts – and immerse affected areas in comfortably warm water until proper care can be had.

Another danger of the region's unpredictable weather is **lightning**. Should you be caught in a thunderstorm, avoid exposed ground and hustle as quickly and safely as possible to below the treeline. Should lightning be fast approaching, seek out clumps of shrubs or trees of uniform height and get into a crouched position. If in a group, do not clump together, and instead spread out at least twenty feet apart until the danger passes.

Altitude sickness

You should be aware of the possibility of **altitude sickness** within the Yellowstone region, especially if you've traveled high up straight from sea level. The symptoms, including lightheadedness, weakness, headaches, nausea and breathlessness, are brought on by the body having problems trying to process less oxygen at higher altitude. Although there isn't actually less oxygen in the atmosphere, the barometric pressure is lower so you absorb less oxygen from the air.

At the kind of heights attained in the area, altitude sickness is unlikely to bring on serious problems such as pulmonary odema (water on the brain), but if you start to feel any of the above symptoms you should descend as quickly as possible to a considerably lower level if possible, take plenty of fluids (not alcohol), eat well and rest. The problem should sort itself out within 24 hours.

The problem can be exacerbated by pushing it too hard on your first day in the mountains, and by fatigue, poor nutrition and hangovers.

Traveling with children

Families looking to wean their kids off a steady diet of TV, video games, and Internet surfing would be hard pressed to find a better place to do so than the Yellowstone region. The parks go out of their way to cater for the younger set with programs that all but the most hardened PlayStation junkies should enjoy, and the gateway towns similarly lay out lists of options for families to partake in. That said, parents should remember that both parks have their wilder elements and unlike a theme park or zoo, things have not been child-proofed. Kids must be clearly instructed on how to act around animals, be versed in safety precautions in thermal areas, and always be kept close by when near water or heights.

For starters, many of the adult orientated activities in the region are perfectly suited for kids. Most of the fireside **ranger programs** are kid friendly, for example, and supply a free night's entertainment for the family; check park newspapers, or the bulletin boards at visitors centers and campgrounds for the latest schedules. Similarly, the summer shoot-outs in Jackson and Cody are designed with families in mind, as are other events such as rodeos, parades, and cowboy cook-outs.

Many **outdoor activities** – from relaxed float trips and trail rides to skiing and snowboarding in winter – are likewise great for kids, with the added bonus of reduced kid rates. Depending on age, fitness and enthusiasm, most of the hikes listed in Chapter 4: Day Hikes can be taken by families as well.

As for kid-specific fare, a good place to start are the bookshelves at any of the region's visitors centers. Most boast a wide selection of **kid books**, ranging from simple picture and coloring books to Native histories and activities guides based around wildflowers, rocks, animal tracks and more. The parks' **websites** (Ⓦwww.nps.gov/yell, Ⓦwww.nps.gov/grte) also have sections set aside for kids, with plenty of print outs to use while exploring. Best is Yellowstone's "Windows into Wonderland," a large selection of electronic field trips covering the parks animals, natural history and more.

Within Yellowstone itself, kids can join in on the **Junior Ranger Program**, open to children 5–12 years old. Families can sign up at any visitor center within the park, and for $3 receive a 12-page newspaper filled with all manner of activities. Once a child completes all the goals – which include attending a ranger-led program, taking a short hike, and having various pages stamped at a series of visitors centers – they are rewarded with an official Junior Ranger patch. Grand Teton runs a similar program – called **The Grand Adventure** – for $1.

A final, more rewarding (and more costly) option for kids would be to attend an **educational program**, either with the family or alone on a camp-like break. For example, the Yellowstone Institute (see p.203 for full details) offers the Yellowstone for Families tour (kids 8–12), which includes wildlife tracking, photography and even painting. And, just outside of Gran Teton in Kelly, the **Teton Science School** (Ⓣ307/733-4765, Ⓦwww.tetonscience.org; see p.203) has a selection of classes for eight year olds and up, including two to five-week long residential courses for junior high and high school age students.

Travel essentials

Costs

One unavoidable expense in visiting the parks is the **entrance fee**, which runs $10 per person for a single hiker or cyclist, or $20 per vehicle; both are good for seven days. If you're planning on spending more time in the area, the $40 **Parks Specific Pass** gives entry to Yellowstone and Grand Teton for a year. Ten dollars more gets the **National Park Pass**, good for most National Parks for a full year.

Accommodation is likely to be your biggest single expense. Few hotel or motel rooms in the region cost under $40, and hostel accommodation is very limited. It's more usual to pay between $40 and $80 for anything halfway decent in town, while rates for rooms or private cabins in the parks and at the area's ski resorts can go much higher. Camping, of course, is the cheaper way to go, with backcountry sites in both parks requiring only a free permit. Designated car-camping sites within the parks cost $12–17 per night, while the sites dotted about the nearby National Forests range from free to $15 a night.

As far as **activities** go, hiking is the cheapest choice, costing nothing as long as you've got the proper gear. Fishing requires a license (see p.160), while raft and horseback trips average $40–50 for a half day. Come winter, most lift tickets cost at least that much, while a day of snowmobiling will cost double that at the bare minimum.

Electricity

110V AC. Most plugs are two-pronged and rather insubstantial. Some travel plug adapters don't fit American sockets. British-made equipment won't work unless it has a voltage switching provision.

Entry requirements

For years, citizens of the UK, Ireland, Australia, New Zealand, and most Western European countries (check with your nearest US embassy or consulate) visiting the United States for a period of less than ninety days traveled under the **Visa Waiver Program (VWP)**, needing only a valid passport, visa waiver form (supplied on the plane en route) and a return ticket. While the Visa Waiver Program still exists, there have been many updates in the post-9/11 landscape, and before traveling from overseas it's highly recommended that you check both Ⓦwww.dhs.gov and with your local passport issuing agency for any new changes on the United States's rather Byzantine entry requirements.

The majority of updates are centered around new **biometric passports**, featuring digital photos, a computer chip, and other high-tech features aimed at keeping, in the words of the Homeland Security Department, "America's doors open and our nation secure." To qualify for the visa waiver, any passport issued after Oct 26, 2006, must be an "e-Passport." If your passport was issued before that time, you can still travel without a visa as long as it includes a machine-readable zone and digital photograph. In all other cases, you'll need to obtain a visa. See Ⓦwww.dhs.gov for examples of suitable passports as well as information on getting visas.

At this point, **Canadian** citizens do not come under the same set of rules, though it's still highly recommended that you bring along a passport – at the time of writing, it isn't the law, but border agents have been known to treat it as so.

Visitors from countries not mentioned above require a valid passport and a non-immigrant visitor's visa for a maximum ninety-day stay. How you obtain a visa depends on what country you're in and your status on application, so contact your nearest US embassy or consulate. Most travelers do not require inoculations to enter the US, though you may need **certificates of vaccination** if you're en route from cholera- or typhoid-infected areas in Asia or Africa – check with your doctor before you leave.

US embassies and consulates abroad

In Australia

Online ⓦ usembassy-australia.state.gov
Canberra Moonah Place, Yarralumla, ACT 2600 ⓣ02/6214 5600.
Melbourne 553 St Kilda Road, PO Box 6722, Vic 3004 ⓣ03/9526 5900.
Perth 16 St George's Terrace, 13th floor, WA 6000 ⓣ08/9202 1224.
Sydney MLC Centre, 59th Floor, 19–29 Martin Place, NSW 2000 ⓣ02/9373 9200.

In Canada

Online ⓦ www.usembassycanada.gov
Calgary 615 Macleod Trail SE, Room 1000, AB T2G 4T8, ⓣ403/266-8962.
Halifax Suite 910, Purdy's Wharf Tower II, 1969 Upper Water St, NS B3J 3R7, ⓣ902/429-2480.
Montréal 1155 St Alexandre St, Québec, H3B 1Z1, ⓣ514/398-9695.
Ottawa 490 Sussex Drive, ON K1N 1G8,ⓣ613/238-5335.
Quebec City 2 Place Terrasse Dufferin, behind Château Frontenac, Québec, Québec G1R 4T9, ⓣ418/692-2095.
Toronto 360 University Ave, ON M5G 1S4 ⓣ416/595-1700.
Vancouver 1075 W Pender St, BC V6E 2M6 ⓣ604/685-4311.

In Ireland

Dublin 42 Elgin Rd, Ballsbridge, ⓣ01/668-8777, ⓦ dublin.usembassy.gov.

In New Zealand

Online ⓦ usembassy.org.nz.
Auckland 3rd floor, Citibank Building, 23 Customs St , ⓣ09/303 2724.
Wellington 29 Fitzherbert Terrace, Thorndon, ⓣ04/462 6000.

In the UK

Online ⓦ www.usembassy.org.uk.
London 24 Grosvenor Square, W1A 1AE, ⓣ020/7499 9000; visa hotline (£1.50 a minute), ⓣ09061/500590.
Belfast Danesfort House, 223 Stanmillis Road, Belfast BT9 5GR, ⓣ028/9038 6100.
Edinburgh 3 Regent Terrace, EH7 5BW, ⓣ0131/556 8315.

Insurance

Although not compulsory, international travelers should have some form of **insurance**. The US has no national health-care system, and prices for even minor medical treatment can be shocking. Before paying for a new policy, however, it's worth checking whether you are already covered: some all-risks home insurance policies may cover your possessions when overseas, and many private medical schemes include coverage when abroad.

Rough Guides has teamed up with Columbus Direct to offer you **travel insurance** that can be tailored to suit your needs. Products include a low-cost **backpacker** option for long stays; a **short break** option for city getaways; a typical **holiday package** option; and others. There are also annual **multi-trip** policies for those who travel regularly. Different sports and activities (trekking, skiing, etc) can usually be covered if required.

See our website (ⓦ www.roughguidesinsurance.com) for eligibility and purchasing options. Alternatively, UK residents should call ⓣ0870/033 9988; Australians should call ⓣ1300/669 999 and New Zealanders should call ⓣ0800/55 9911. All other nationalities should call ⓣ+44 870/890 2843.

Internet

Public computers with **Internet** access are nearly non-existent in both parks. Should you be toting along a laptop, the main lobby at Grand Teton's Jackson Lake Lodge has free wireless access, though at the time of writing there were no similar options within Yellowstone. Getting online in the gateway towns is much easier – for example, the entire area around Cody's visitors center is a WiFi hotspot – and details are listed in the Directory within each gateway town chapter later in the guide.

Laundry and showers

Self-service, coin-operated **laundries** in Yellowstone include those at the Canyon Village and Grant Village campgrounds, Fishing Bridge RV Park, and Lake Lodge. Within Grand Teton, head for Flagg Ranch or Colter Village. All of the gateway towns have laundries, the locations of which are listed in their respective chapters.

Public **showers** in Yellowstone can be had for a small charge at Canyon Campground,

Fishing Bridge RV Park, Grant Village Campground, Mammoth Hot Springs Hotel, and Old Faithful Lodge. In Grand Teton, head for the Colter Bay or Flagg Ranch RV parks.

Living in and around Yellowstone

Getting **work** in and around Yellowstone is relatively easy for US citizens and those with valid work visas, provided you don't mind working a rather menial job. Both the summer and to a lesser extent winter ski seasons see long lists of jobs needed to help take care of the influx of visitors. Besides students, anyone planning an extended legal stay in the United States should apply for a special working visa at any American Embassy before setting off. Different types of visas are issued, depending on your skills and length of stay, but unless you've got relatives (parents or children over 21) or a prospective employer to sponsor you, your chances are slim at best.

Illegal work is not as easy to find as it used to be, now that the government has introduced fines as high as $10,000 for companies caught employing anyone without a **social security number** (which effectively proves you're part of the legal workforce). Even in the traditionally more casual establishments, like restaurants and bars, things have really tightened up, and if you do find work it's likely to be of the less-visible, poorly paid kind – dishwasher rather than waiter. Making up a social security number, or borrowing one from somebody else, is of course completely illegal, as are **marriages of convenience**; usually inconvenient for all concerned and with a lower success rate than is claimed.

Those with the necessary work visa, or social security number will however, have no problem in finding casual, seasonal work – as long as you apply early. Ski resorts and nearby businesses will start to hire from early November, those looking for summer staff will usually have all vacancies filled from early June. Most of the work available is doing menial work in shops, hotels, or restaurants, although if you have special skills relevant to the service industry or a sport you might find a position in your field. Don't expect to make much more than the minimum doing casual work – but at least you'll get plenty of summer hiking in or perhaps a free ski pass.

Foreign students have a slightly better chance of a prolonged stay in the Rockies, especially those who can arrange a "year abroad" through their university at home – most universities have semester abroad programs to different countries. Otherwise you can apply directly to a university; if they admit you (and you can afford the painfully expensive fees charged to overseas students) it can be a great way to get to know the country, and maybe even learn something useful. The US grants more or less unlimited visas to those enrolled in full-time further education. Another possibility for students is to get onto an **Exchange Visitor Program**, for which participants are given a J-1 visa that entitles them to accept paid summer employment and apply for a social security number. However, most of these visas are issued for jobs in American **summer camps**, which aren't everybody's idea of a good time; they fly you over, and after a couple of months' work you end up with around $500 and a month to six weeks to blow it in.

Local job sources

Along with the traditional routes used for **job searches** – newspaper classifieds, resort websites, bulletin boards, etc – the following sources are tops for finding work in the region.

Coolworks ⓦwww.coolworks.com. Company placing mainly younger workers in seasonal service industry positions in amusement parks, national parks and the like. Links to both Grand Teton and Yellowstone, along with information for foreign workers.

Craigslist ⓦwww.craigslist.org. Both Montana and Wyoming have their own dedicated sections on this all-in-one wonder site, good for not just daily job listings but also apartment rentals, buying/selling gear, and a whole lot more.

Grand Teton Lodge Company ⓦwww.gtlc.com. In charge of most of all lodging and dining facilities at Jackson Lake Lodge, Jenny Lake Lodge, and Colter Bay Village, this company hires more than 1000 employees each summer, and many of these jobs are posted online.

State Job Banks ⓦwww.wyjobs.st.wy.us, ⓦwww.jobs.mt.gov. The official state job banks for both Wyoming and Montana; registrations required for most in-depth searches.

Xanterra ⓦwww.yellowstonejobs.com. The jobs website for Yellowstone's primary concessioner, with positions ranging from housekeepers to mechanics and drivers for the winter snowcoaches. The first place to look if you want to live and work inside the park.

Yellowstone General Stores ⓦwww.yellowstonegeneralstores.com. The concessioner in charge of over a dozen general stores within Yellowstone. Most positions are either in the kitchen or behind the cash register.

Yellowstone Park Service Stations ⓦwww.ypss.com. Yellowstone's smallest concessioner, in charge of seven convenience/gas stations and a handful of automotive repairs shops. Positions include dorm accommodations and two days off each week.

Mail

Post offices, located at all the major park villages and area towns, are usually open Monday through Friday, from 9am to 5pm, although some are open on Saturday from 9am to noon or 1pm. Ordinary **mail** sent within the US costs 39¢ (at press time) for letters weighing up to an ounce, while standard postcards cost 23¢. For anywhere outside the US, airmail letters weighing up to an ounce cost 80¢; postcards and aerogrammes 70¢. Airmail between the US and Europe, for instance, may take a week, and up to two weeks for Australia and New Zealand. Domestic letters that don't carry a **zip code** are liable to get lost or at least seriously delayed; phone books list zip codes for their service area, and post offices – even abroad – should have zip-code directories for major US cities.

Letters can be sent c/o **General Delivery** (what's known elsewhere as **poste restante**) to the larger post offices in the region – including Jackson and Cody – but must include the zip code and will only be held for thirty days before being returned to sender; make sure there's a return address on the envelope. To send a package out of the country, you'll need a green **customs declaration form**, available from the post office.

Maps

The excellent official **map** handed out at entrance stations to either park along with the detailed maps inside this guide should fulfill all your needs while exploring by car. Hikers, however, will want to get their hands on a **topographic map** of the area they plan on tramping through. The best are the series of waterproof maps by Trails Illustrated (National Geographic), available online and at most of the region's visitor centers. The full map of Grand Teton (1:78,000; $10) is fine for the smaller of the two parks, as it includes an even closer look (1:32,000) at the busiest hiking area on the Tetons themselves on the flip side. The overall Yellowstone map (1:168,500; $10, however is too small scale to be of practical use on trails. Instead, choose one or more of the maps splitting the park into four equal size quadrants (1:63,360; $9 each): Old Faithful Area, Mammoth Hot Springs Area, Tower/Canyon Area, and Yellowstone Lake Area.

Money

Regular upheaval in the world money markets causes the relative value of the **US dollar** against other currencies to vary considerably. At the time of writing one pound sterling will buy $1.80–1.90, a Euro $1.25–1.35, a Canadian dollar 85–90¢, and an Australian dollar 70–80¢.

ATMs are pretty easy to find, even in the parks where machines can be found at most general stores. In the gateway towns, banks, supermarkets and most convenience stores have outlets where you can withdraw cash. Seeing as you'll pay a small a small transaction fee for each withdraw a (usually around $1–2), it make sense to pull out a larger amount and budgeting accordingly.

Major banks in Jackson, Cody and West Yellowstone should be able to **change foreign travelers' checks**, but it's unlikely you'll be able to exchange British Pounds, Euros or Australian Dollars. In any case it's far better to take only **US dollars checks** with you, as these can be used as cash in many stores. The most recognized kind are American Express and Thomas Cook, available from their various agencies or from banks in your home country (the usual fee for travelers' check sales is one or two percent).

Credit cards are a very handy backup source of funds, and are often needed to rent gear or reserve a tour or guide. MasterCard,

Visa and American Express are accepted just about everywhere, but other cards may not be recognized in the US.

Wiring money

Having money **wired** from home using one of the companies listed below is never convenient or cheap, and should be considered a last resort.

Money-wiring companies

American Express Moneygram US and Canada ⓣ1-888/269-6669, ⓦwww.americanexpress.com; UK ⓣ0870/600 1060, ⓦwww.americanexpress.co.uk.
Thomas Cook US ⓣ1-800/287-7362, Canada ⓣ1-888/823-4732; UK ⓣ01733/318 922, Belfast ⓣ028/9055 0030; Dublin ⓣ01/677 1721; ⓦwww.thomascook.com.
Travelers Express Moneygram US ⓣ1-800/926-9400; Canada ⓣ1-800/933-3278; UK ⓣ0800/6663 9472; ⓦwww.moneygram.com.
Western Union US and Canada ⓣ1-800/325-6000; Australia ⓣ1800/649 565; New Zealand ⓣ09/270 0050; UK ⓣ0800/833 833; Republic of Ireland ⓣ1800/395 395; ⓦwww.westernunion.com.

Opening hours and public holidays

Both Yellowstone and Grand Teton are **open** 24 hours a day throughout the year. Come winter, however, most of Yellowstone's entrance stations and roads close, as does the Jenny Lake Loop Road within Grand Teton. See Chapter 7: Winter Activities, for more in-depth information on winter closings.

The opening hours of specific visitor attractions, stores, and offices are given in the relevant accounts throughout the guide. **Visitors centers** and **ranger stations** are typically open daily 9am–5pm, with extended hours (often 8am–7pm) throughout the heart of summer. **Shops and services** are generally open Monday to Saturday 8am/9am–5pm/6pm. Many stores are also open on Sundays, and the larger gateway towns have 24-hour supermarkets.

On the national **public holidays** listed below, banks and offices are liable to be closed all day, and shops may reduce their hours. The traditional summer season for tourism runs from **Memorial Day** to **Labor Day**. Attractions throughout the region – from visitors centers to restaurants – follow this timetable, with many closing or drastically reducing their hours outside of these dates. Not surprisingly, the summer season is the busiest time in the parks, though with schools starting as early as mid-August in many places, the late summer season is not a busy a time as it used to be.

January 1: New Year's Day; 3rd Monday: Dr Martin Luther King Jr's Birthday
February 3rd Monday: President's Day
May Last Monday: Memorial Day
July 4: Independence Day
September 1st Monday: Labor Day
October 2nd Monday: Columbus Day
November 11: Veterans' Day; 4th Thursday Thanksgiving Day
December 25: Christmas Day

Park passes

Considering budget cuts and the high cost of upkeep, entrance fees to the parks are a real bargain. The most basic **Park Pass** costs $25 per car, good for seven days in both Yellowstone and Grand Teton; rates drop to $20 for motorcyclists and $12 for bikers and hikers. Be sure to keep your receipt, as you'll need to flash it each time you re-enter a park. For $40, you can get the **Annual Pass**, valid for a full year in both parks from date of purchase. If planning on visiting any other parks within the next year, opt for the **National Parks Pass**, accepted at all National Parks at $50. An extra $15 upgrades this pass to the **Golden Eagle Pass,** opening up most federal fee areas – national forests, wildlife refuges, etc – as well. US citizens or permanent residents 62 years of age or older need only pay $10 for the **Golden Age Passport**, providing lifetime access to all National Parks; the free **Golden Access Passport** does the same for all US citizens and residents who are blind or permanently disabled.

Pets

Visitors are best off leaving **pets** at home, as there's a long list of necessarily strict rules that must be followed when bringing them into the parks: pets are not allowed in the backcountry, on most trails and boardwalks, and must be leashed at all times when out of the car. Pets may not be left in cars alone for any long period of time as well. There are no kennels within the parks; check Yellowstone's website (Ⓦwww.nps.gov.yell) for a list of reputable kennels in the bordering towns.

Phones

There are very few **area codes** in use in the Yellowstone region; Wyoming (Ⓣ307), Montana (Ⓣ406), and Idaho (Ⓣ208) each have just one code. It is always necessary to include the area code when dialing beyond the local area, even though you may be in the same area code. For example, although Ⓣ307 is the code for all of Wyoming, a call from Cody to Jackson is a long-distance call, and so the prefix Ⓣ1-307 must be dialled first and long-distance charges will apply.

Any number with Ⓣ800, Ⓣ866, Ⓣ877, or Ⓣ888 in place of the area code is **toll-free**; most major hotels, government agencies, and car rental firms have a toll-free number, and we've listed these when available throughout the Guide. Numbers with a Ⓣ1-900 prefix are toll calls, typically sports information lines, psychic hotlines and phone-sex centers, and will cost you a variable, though consistently high, fee for just a few minutes of use.

Making telephone calls from **hotel rooms** is always more expensive than from a pay phone; however, some hotels offer free local calls from rooms – ask when you check in. Even with the ubiquity of cell phones, **public telephones** can still be found in most public locations – outside of visitors centers, on street corners, in hotels, bars, and restaurants. They take 5¢, 10¢, and 25¢ coins, and the cost of a **local call** from a public phone is usually 50¢; when necessary, a voice comes on the line telling you to pay more.

Pricier are long-distance calls, for which you'll need plenty of change. Long-distance calls are much less expensive if made between 6pm and 8am – the cheapest rates are after 11pm and at weekends – and calls from private phones are always much cheaper than those from public phones. In virtually all cases, you're best off buying a **pre-paid phone card** – available at convenience stores, gas stations, and supermarkets – allowing for calls to around the world. Sold in increments of $5, $10 and $20, these are reasonably good value and can be used from both private and public phones.

Cell phones

For the most part, visitors with a major provider should find that their **cell phones** work within both parks, at least within the village areas. In the larger gateway towns – Jackson, Cody and West Yellowstone – coverage is even more dependable. If visiting from **overseas** and you want to use your cell

Useful telephone numbers

Emergencies Ⓣ911 for fire, police or ambulance
Operator Ⓣ0
Local directory information Ⓣ411
Long-distance directory information Ⓣ1 +area code/555-1212
Yellowstone Park information Ⓣ307/344-7381
Grand Teton Park information Ⓣ307/739-3300
International calls to Yellowstone:
Dial your country's international access code + 1 for the US + area code + phone number
International calls from Yellowstone:
Dial Ⓣ011 + country code + phone number
Country codes: Australia Ⓣ61, Ireland Ⓣ353, New Zealand Ⓣ64, United Kingdom Ⓣ44. For all other codes, dial Ⓣ0 for the operator or check the front of the local White Pages.

phone, you'll need to check with your service provider whether this is possible, what it will cost and how the call charges will work. Unless you have a tri-band phone, it is unlikely that a mobile bought for use outside the US will work inside the States. They tend to be very expensive to own in the US, too, as users are billed for both incoming and outgoing calls. Calling a US mobile, however, costs no more than making a call to a landline in that area code. Check out ⓦwww.telecomsadvice.org.uk/features/ for further information on using_your_mobile_abroad.

Senior travelers

Yellowstone and Grand Teton cater well to **senior travelers**. As well as the obvious advantages of being free to travel for longer periods during the quieter less expensive seasons, anyone over the age of 62 can enjoy the tremendous variety of discounts available.

Foremost among these deals is the **Golden Age Passport**: with this $10 card, any US citizen or permanent resident aged 62 or over is entitled to free admission for life to all national parks, monuments, and historic sites; it can be issued at any entrance station. This free entry also applies to any accompanying car passengers in their car or, for those hiking or cycling, the passport-holder's immediate family. It also gives a fifty percent reduction on fees for camping and other fees.

Touring both parks is breeze, provided you have your own transportation. A large percentage of sights within the parks can be seen either from the car or a short walk (paved) walk away, and handicap parking spots abound should they be needed.

But before heading out to the Yellowstone region, its worth doing your homework on **health** matters first. The **high-altitude** of the region in general and the mountain passes specifically can aggravate certain conditions: those with heart problems should tread carefully over around 10,000ft – getting advice from a physician before your trip is best if you are in doubt. Respiratory conditions can also be aggravated – those with emphysema should avoid high altitudes completely – and again it's worth checking with your doctor before you go.

Time

The Yellowstone region is on Mountain Time, two hours behind the US east coast and seven hours behind Greenwich Mean Time (GMT).

Tipping

Unless the service is substandard, you shouldn't leave a bar or restaurant without leaving a **tip** of at least fifteen percent and about the same should be added to taxi fares. A hotel porter should get roughly $1 for each bag carried to your room. When paying by credit card you're expected to add the tip to the total bill before filling in the amount and signing. Tour leaders, ski instructors, fishing guides and the like should also be tipped for a job well done.

Tourist information

Upon arriving at either park, you'll be handed over a stack of flyers that includes a handy park **map**, the seasonal park **newspaper**, and any updates on current road detours or delays due to construction. A good read overall, the newspapers are particularly useful for the latest Ranger lecture and walking tour schedules, along with opening hours for everything from visitor centers to restaurants.

Located typically by a major area of interest are the parks' **visitor centers**. Yellowstone is home to nine centers in a range of sizes, including a desk inside the West Yellowstone Information Center just outside of the West Entrance. Along with the soon-to-be-finished visitor center/park headquarters at Moose, Grand Teton runs three more facilities, including the one at Flagg Ranch just outside of the park to the north. Basic contact details for all these centers are listed below, but see the Guide chapters for opening dates and hours, along with explanations on the exhibits and amenities within each.

Visitor Center contact information

Yellowstone

Albright Visitor Center (Mammoth) ⓣ307/344-2263; see p.47.

Canyon Visitor Center ⓣ307/242-2550; see p.58.

Fishing Bridge Visitor Center ⓣ307/242-2450; see p.84.
Grant Visitor Center ⓣ307/242-2650; see p.79.
Madison Information Station ⓣ307/344-2821; see p.68.
Norris Geyser Basin Information Station ⓣ307/344-2812; see p.62.
Old Faithful Visitor Center ⓣ307/545-2750; see p.74.
West Thumb Information Station No phone; see p.79.
West Yellowstone Visitor Center ⓣ406/646-4403; see p.226.

Grand Teton

Colter Bay Visitor Center ⓣ307/739-3594; see p.112.
Flagg Ranch Information Station ⓣ307/543-2372; see p.114.
Jenny Lake Visitor Center ⓣ307/739-3343; see p.107.
Moose Visitor Center ⓣ307/739-3399; see p.95.

Outside of the parks

The **gateway towns** all have visitor centers of vary usefulness, with the two largest and best located in Jackson and West Yellowstone. Details for all of these centers are listed in the respective town chapters toward the end of the Guide.

Beside and beyond the gateway towns, both parks are completely encircled by national forests, equally as scenic in many spots and less regulated. To the north and west of Yellowstone is the **Gallatin National Forest** (ⓦwww.fs.fed.us/r1/gallatin), a 1.8million acre forest preserve established not long after Yellowstone in 1889. The district offices in Gardiner (ⓣ406/848-7375) and Hebgen Lake (ⓣ406/823-6961) near West Yellowstone are the most useful stopovers for park visitors. To the east of Yellowstone is the even larger **Shoshone National Forest** (ⓦwww.fs.fed.us/r2/Shoshone), stretching from the Montana stateline south all the way to Lander, Wyoming. Headquarters for the 2.4 million acre reserve are in Cody (ⓣ307/578-1200), though you'll also pass by the informative **Wapiti Ranger Station** (ⓣ307/578-1200) when driving east of Yellowstone on the Buffalo Bill Cody Scenic Byway.

To the west of southern Yellowstone as well as most of Grand Teton is the **Caribou-Targhee National Forest**(ⓦwww.fs.fed.us/r4/caribou-targhee), three million acres of protected lands dotted around Idaho and the sliver of Wyoming around Grassy Lake Road between Yellowstone and Grand Teton. The two closes field offices are in Driggs (ⓣ208/354-2312) and Ashton (ⓣ208/652-7442), both in Idaho. Finally, circling Grand Teton from the southwest to northeast is the largest of the them all, the 3.4 million acre **Bridger-Teton National Forest** (ⓦwww.fs.fed.us/btnf). Responsible for the Teton and Gros Ventre Wilderness Areas is their office in Jackson (ⓣ307/739-5400), located next door to the town's visitor center.

Useful websites

There are few places to access the Internet within the parks, but the following sites should prove handy while planning your trip or when staying in one of the gateway towns.

General information

National Park Service ⓦwww.nps.gov/yell, ⓦwww.nps.gov/grte. Packed with information – including handy pdfs of most of the newspapers and bulletins handed out at visitor centers – the official sites for Yellowstone and Grand Teton should be the first online stop for anyone looking for all-purpose Information.
Windows Into Wonderland ⓦwww.windowsintowonderland.org. A wonderful kid's site created by the National Park Service. Based around novel "electronic field trips," kids can click through lessons ranging from Yellowstone's history to the modern plight of proghorn in the region.
Wolves in Yellowstone ⓦwww.forwolves.org, ⓦww.r6.fws.gov/wolf, ⓦwww.wolftracker.com, ⓦwww.wolf.org. From official government reports to naturalist blogs, the web is filled with dozens of sites on Yellowstone's wolves. An hour spent clicking thorough this small sampling will bring you up to date on the latest issues and pack formations.
Yellowstone Volcano Observatory (YVO) ⓦvolcanoes.usgs.gov/yell. Homepage for the YVO, a partnership between the park, government Geology Survey, and University of Utah to monitor geologic unrest in the park. Displays literarily up-to-the-minute updates on the latest tremors, along with links to recent stories on volcanic or earthquake activity in the region.

Support groups and organizations

Grand Teton Natural History Association ⓦ www.grandtetonpark.org. Since 1937, dedicated to supporting interpretive and educational activities in Grand Teton, from running the visitor center bookstores to holding historical festivals in and around the park. The online bookstore stocks a great selection of books on the park and around.

Grand Teton National Park Foundation ⓦ www.gtnpf.org. Private non-profit set on raising funds for projects to protect and preserve Grand Teton. One of the driving forces behind the new visitor center at Moose.

Greater Yellowstone Coalition ⓦ www.greateryellowstone.org. A quarter of a century old, this non-profit works to keep the greater Yellowstone ecosystem intact by limiting development and keeping protected areas protected.

Yellowstone Association ⓦ www.tellowstoneassociation.org. Homepage of Yellowstone's major non-profit partner (see p.203). Along with membership information and the latest course schedules, the Park Store stocks dozens of the best books and maps on the region.

Yellowstone Park Foundation ⓦ ww.ypf.org. Founded in 1996, this foundation has quickly become a major force, working to protect Yellowstone's wonders and funding projects ranging from trail improvement to wildlife studies and improved visitor facilities.

Travelers with disabilities

Travelers with **disabilities** are likely to find Yellowstone and Grand Teton – as with the US in general – to be much more in tune with their needs than anywhere else in the world. Both parks have done an admirable job updating their facilities, and continue to do so whenever funding permits. Visitors in wheelchairs will find that most toilets in picnic areas and campgrounds are accessible, as are several self-guided boardwalk trails, fishing areas and even a few backcountry sites. Both parks have accessibility handouts available at entrance stations, visitor centers, and on their respective websites.

Citizens or permanent residents of the US who have been "medically determined to be blind or permanently disabled" can obtain the **Golden Access Passport**, a free lifetime entrance pass to both parks along with all other federally operated parks, monuments, historic sites, recreation areas and wildlife refuges that charge entrance fees. The pass must be picked up in person, and it also provides a fifty percent discount on fees charged for camping, boat launching and parking, and the like.

The major **car rental** firms can, given sufficient notice, provide vehicles with hand controls (though these are usually only available on the more expensive models, and you'll need to reserve well in advance).

Contacts and resources

Yellowstone Park Accessibility Coordinator, PO Box 168, Yellowstone National Park, WY 82190 (ⓣ 307/344-2017, TDD ⓣ 307/344-2386, ⓦ www.nps.gov/yell

Grand Teton TDD ⓣ 307/739-3400, ⓦ www.nps.gov/grte

The Parks

The Parks

1

Northern Yellowstone

Along with the entrance roads from Gardiner to the north and Cooke City to the northeast, **northern Yellowstone** covers the upper half of the park's figure-of-eight Grand Loop Road. If Old Faithful is the star attraction within the park's southern half, then the **Grand Canyon of the Yellowstone** leads the pack of must-see sights within the northern half – even if the region's geysers and hot springs dried up long ago, the canyon would have still earned Yellowstone its national park status. Carved by the Yellowstone River, which makes a dramatic entrance by way of two impossibly picturesque waterfalls, the canyon's steep honey-colored walls are dappled in rusted oranges and reds. The panorama from **Artist Point**, at the canyon's south end is the park's most photographed scene for very good reasons, and it pays to arrive early to beat the crowds and get the best light conditions.

North of the Canyon area, the Yellowstone River flows past the hulking mass of **Mount Washburn** and near **Tower Fall** into the Northern Range, home to some of the country's largest elk and bison populations. Prosaically referred to as "North America's Serengeti" for its abundant wildlife, the **Lamar Valley** here is also home to predators such as grizzlies, wolves, and mountain lions, and many repeat visitors spend much of their time parked roadside here hoping for a sighting of them. The two final highlights of the north loop are major hydrothermal sites. The first, **Mammoth Hot Springs**, stays open to car traffic year round and is an essential stop for both its fascinating travertine terraces and **Fort Yellowstone**, home to the US army from 1886–1918 and now the park headquarters. To the south is the **Norris Geyser Basin**, boasting the world's tallest spouter, **Steamboat Geyser**, along with scores of eerie sizzling pools and steaming vents.

Sights and orientation

The following tour of northern Yellowstone begins at **Mammoth Hot Springs**, the most accessible village within the park with **Gardiner**, Montana, only five miles away. The nearly fifty-mile highway heading east from Mammoth through the wildlife-rich Northern Range to tiny Cooke City is the sole portion of the Grand Loop Road open throughout the year. Just past rustic **Roosevelt Lodge**, the highway splits off from the Grand Loop and leads through the famed **Lamar Valley**, one of the pre-eminent areas to spot the likes of bison, elk, pronghorn, and wolves from the roadside.

South from Roosevelt and back on the Grand Loop, the highway passes narrow **Tower Fall** before climbing past **Mount Washburn** and over **Dunraven Pass** in a thrilling series of tight turns bordered by steep drops. Much of the roadway here runs parallel to the epic **Grand Canyon of the**

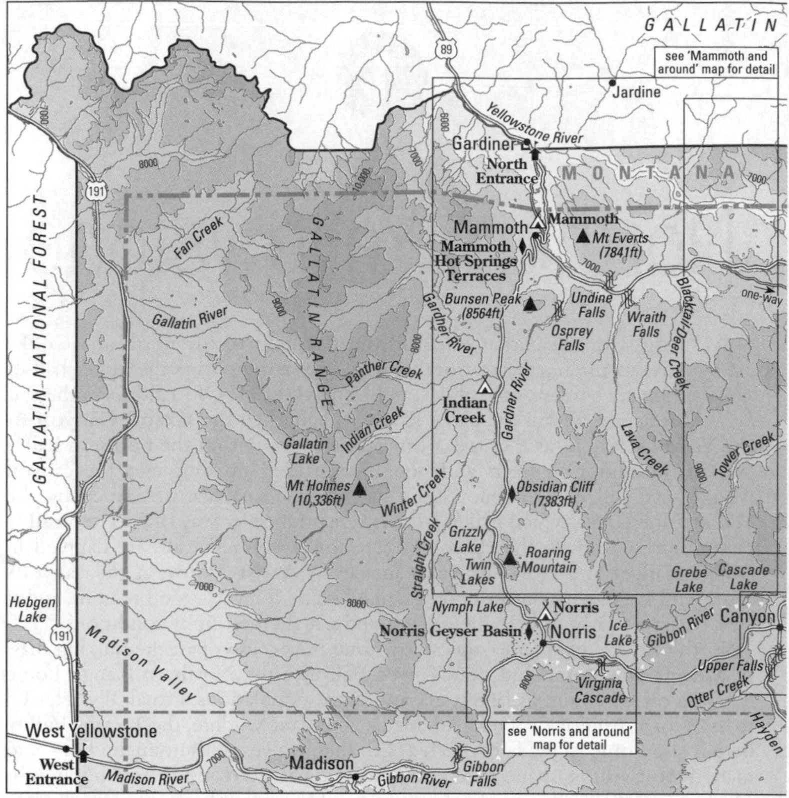

Yellowstone, the multi-colored walls of which can be seen from dramatic side roads edging the north and south rims. After gawking at the powerful **Upper** and **Lower Falls**, visitors can repair to nearby Canyon Village to eat, sleep or check out the new, high-tech visitor center. The area south of Canyon Village, including Hayden Valley, is covered in Chapter 2, while the road west leads to the **Norris Geyser Basin**.

Mammoth Hot Springs and around

Long the entry point for explorers, **Mammoth Hot Springs** has always been park headquarters. Regional visitors were coming to bathe in the allegedly therapeutic waters of the springs since the early 1870s, and within a decade the railroad was ferrying in tourists by stagecoach from a string of steadily approaching terminals to the north, eventually ending at Gardiner's 1903 train station only five miles away. By 1883, when the hastily erected *National Hotel* opened its doors, Mammoth was in full bloom, home to all manner of buildings from stables to the

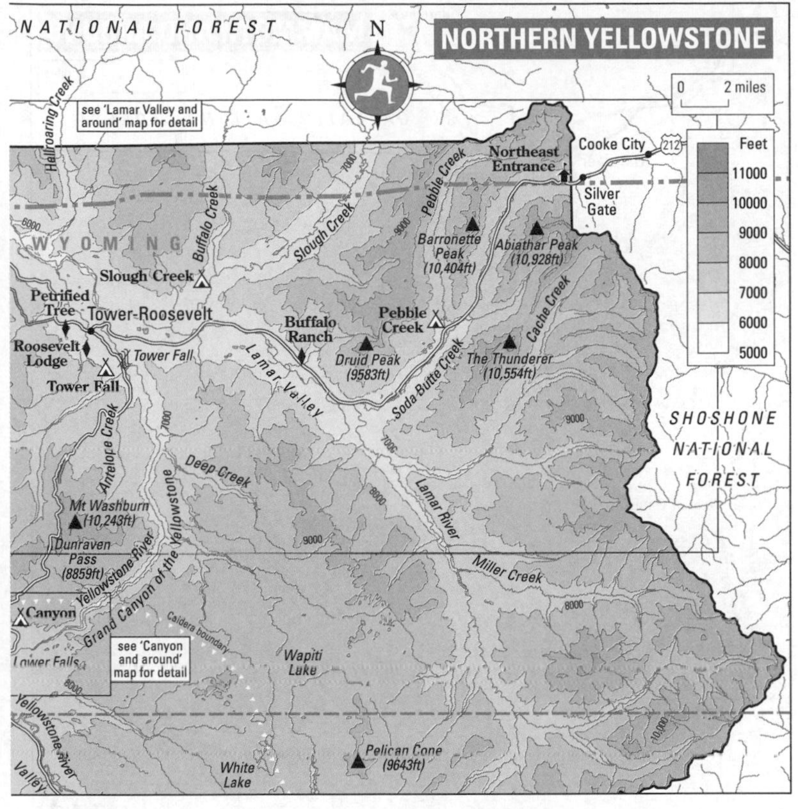

homes of park administrators and the first of Yellowstone's souvenir stands. In desperate need of law and order, the army took over in 1886, setting up camp by the hot spring terraces and eventually building **Fort Yellowstone**, a small town's worth of stone structures than remains standing and fully used today.

Lower in altitude and thus typically warmer than Yellowstone's other visitor hubs, Mammoth remains open to cars year-round. Buzzing with a mix of tourist and administrative activity, the area demands at least a full afternoon's attention. At Mammoth's northern end are the rows of buildings built by the

Mammoth's elk

Particularly around dawn and dusk, it can seem like there are more **elk** in Mammoth than people. Drawn year-round to the area's irrigated grasses, the grazers are a common fixture, to the point that residents must fence in all their trees and flowers to keep them from being nibbled away. Regardless of how comfortable the elk seem they are *not* tame. Cows with calves are particularly irritable in spring, while bulls get more aggressive during the fall rut, but at all times you must keep at least **25 yards distance** – including your car, which bulls have also attacked on occasion.

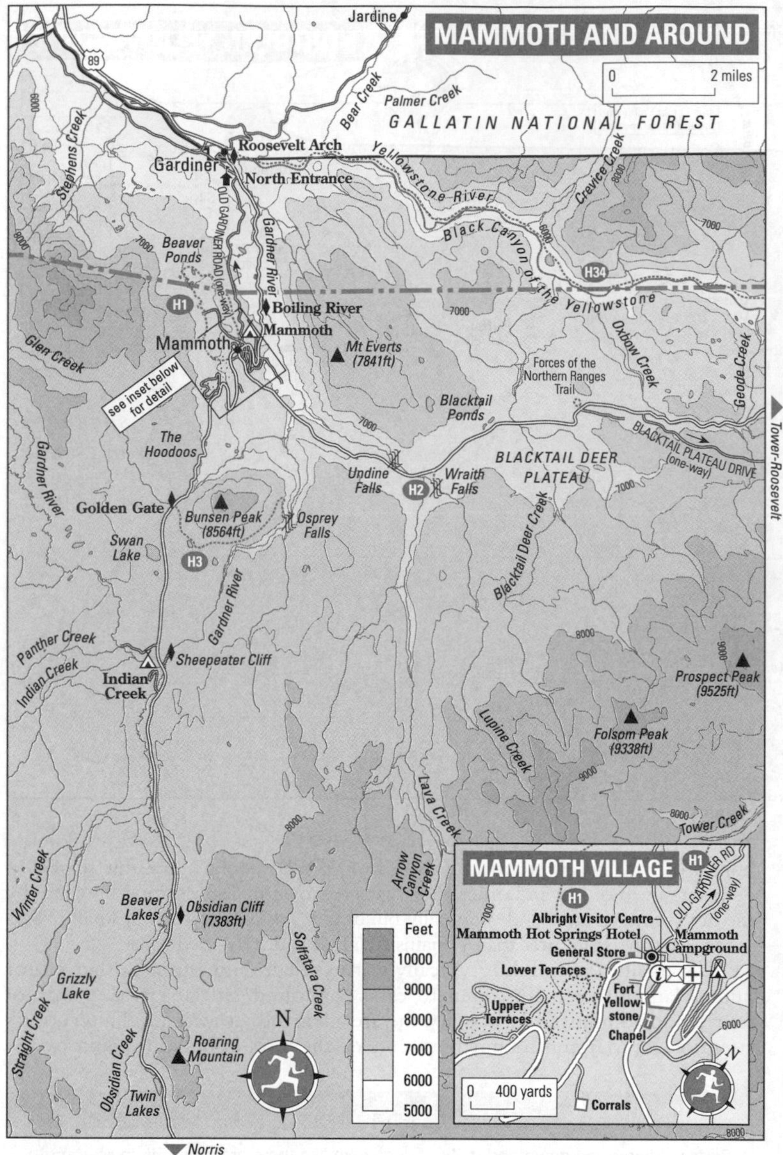

army, including what is now the **Albright Visitor Center**, official park headquarters and the best place to begin a visit. To the west are the visitor amenities, centered around the rather plain **Mammoth Hot Springs Hotel**, built mostly in 1937 over the demolished *National Hotel*. A longer walk south leads to the most popular attraction, unique **travertine terraces** of barnacle-like deposits cascading down a vapor-shrouded hillside.

The Albright Visitor Center and Fort Yellowstone

The first thing most visitors do when touring Mammoth, and often Yellowstone on the whole, is to pay a visit to the **Albright Visitor Center** (late May to early Sept daily 8am–7pm, rest of year approximately 9am–5pm; ⓣ307/344-2263). Housed in what used to be the army's bachelor officers' quarters, the 1909 stone structure marks the northwestern edge of **Fort Yellowstone** and acts as the official park headquarters. Along with an information desk and one of the Yellowstone Association's best-stocked bookstores, **exhibits** inside focus on the park's natural and human history, from the earliest expeditions through the army's 32 years in control and the park service years since.

Of most interest are the glass cases displaying items from the two expeditions that literally put Yellowstone on the map – the Washburn Expedition of 1870 (see p.268) and the Hayden Survey of 1871–72 (see p.269) – including a knife and tobacco pouch used by the gutsy Captain Doane and five pistols belonging to Nathaniel Pitt Langford; both were key members of the earlier Washburn Expedition, with Langford becoming Yellowstone's first-ever Superintendent within a year of their return. Skip the bland 20-minute film in the nearby theater and instead head further back to the rooms lined with works by the artist **Thomas Moran** and photographer **William Jackson**, each brought along on the Hayden Expedition to provide visual evidence of the wonders of Yellowstone to a sceptical public. Until being moved to the temperature-controlled confines of Gardiner's new Yellowstone Heritage and Research Center (see p.241), many of Moran's original field sketches, along with other historical artefacts, were stored in the building's leaky basement, causing a mad ranger rush to evacuate them during downpours. The sole original on display now is an 1892 painting entitled "Lower Falls of the Yellowstone." Jackson's black-and-white photos of the park's geysers and expedition members are worth a similarly long look, as is his massive box camera on display. A final room upstairs has a few bits and pieces from the fur-trapping era and local Sheepeater Indians, along with numerous stuffed animals.

Just around the corner from the center are the Mammoth Clinic and **Post Office** (Mon–Fri 8.30am–5pm), the latter built in 1936 in a style known as French Renaissance Moderne. Painted white with light blue trim, it's one of Yellowstone's most elegant buildings, guarded by a pair of stone grizzly statues and, more often than not, elk grazing on the lawns out in front.

Fort Yellowstone

For fifteen years from its creation in 1872, a succession of five civilian superintendents was put in charge of Yellowstone. Hamstrung by minuscule budgets, these administrations were overwhelmed by a maddening combination of poachers, petty thieves, greedy businesses, and souvenir-stealing tourists willing to chip Yellowstone away one pocketful at a time. A tight-fisted Congress had little choice but to call in the **army**, and on August 13, 1886, **Captain Moses Harris** from Fort Custer in the Montana Territories marched in with 50 men and assumed the title of park superintendent. Harris was the first of a dozen officers to successfully lead the park, with the army staying on until 1918 when the newly formed National Park Service could take over. (For the full story, see the "History" section in Contexts, p.265.)

As the main hub of activity within Yellowstone, Harris immediately set about erecting the temporary **Camp Sheridan** by the base of the terraces to the south. Realizing that the army wasn't going anywhere soon, they began lobbying Congress for more funds, and by 1891 the first series of buildings within the permanent **Fort Yellowstone** were erected; two more major waves of constructions occurred in 1897 and 1909. Most of these buildings remain standing and now function as residences for park employees. They are best seen on a **walking tour** beginning from the Albright Visitor Center. By the front steps, pick up the useful *Fort Yellowstone Tour Guide* (50¢), including a map outlining a 30-minute self-guided tour, or check inside the visitor center for details on the ranger-led hour-long tours (free) run three times each week.

The most appealing of the nearly two-dozen buildings spread along two main streets include the sandstone **Field Officer's Quarters**, a suitably impressive home built in 1909 for the post commander and still the residence of the park superintendent today, and the simple yet elegant **chapel** at the fort's eastern end, the army's final structure built in 1913 using native stone that's now attractively flecked with orange lichen. The chapel's interior can only be seen during one of three weekly services (interdenominational services Sun 8.30 & 10am; Catholic Mass Sat 7pm). A short walk from the chapel is one of the fort's more dejected looking buildings, the **Guardhouse**, built in 1909 and still the park jail to this day. To complete the tour as a temporary inmate might, walk west, past the old barracks and stables that now house park offices and equipment, to the 1903 **US Engineer's Office**, located kitty-corner to the visitor center. Designed by the same architectural firm behind New York City's Grand Central Terminal, the striking green-roofed structure is known locally as both the Pagoda for its triangular roof and the Temple of Truth as it has long housed the park's courthouse.

Mammoth Hot Springs Terraces

Building the boardwalks weaving through **Mammoth Hot Springs Terraces** – a short walk south of Fort Yellowstone – is one of the most thankless jobs in Yellowstone. There's no telling when one of the carefully crafted wooden paths

△ Travertine terraces at Mammoth

Mammoth mementos

A park brochure claims that at Mammoth, "rock forms before your eyes." Certainly that's overstating the case, but only slightly. It's estimated that as much as a dozen tons of travertine are deposited in the area each week, with some terraces growing a foot taller in just a year's time. Taking advantage of this natural feat, Yellowstone entrepreneurs in the late 1880s used the springs for a one-of-a-kind **curio business**. Started by one-time assistant superintendent and then hotelier **George Henderson** and perfected afterwards by Mammoth storeowner **Ole Anderson**, racks were placed under the flowing water at the most active terraces. Before touring the park, visitors would drop off trinkets like pinecones and tin toys to be placed on these racks. It only took a few days for the item to become completely covered in travertine, and when visitors returned they were the proud owner of "**coated specimen**." Before being eventually banned, Anderson began coating a wide range of items – vases, statues, decorative horseshoes – and selling so many that his store became known as the Specimen House. A rare antique today (the era's rough wagon and train rides tended to jar the travertine loose), Gardiner's Yellowstone Heritage and Research Center has a few of Anderson's creations in their collection.

can become obsolete, as the colorful springs and terraces are capable of drying up at any time, evidenced by the remains of long-dormant terraces seen throughout the entire Mammoth area. Be prepared to spend much of your time walking boardwalks leading past little action, and don't be surprised if that colorful terrace you remember from a previous visit is now crumbling away.

That's not to say Mammoth's terraces have all dried out. The overall activity has remained consistent for centuries, and you're guaranteed a weird and wild selection of chalky white terraces tinted a splendid array of greens, yellows, browns, and oranges by various heat-loving thermophiles. These sculpted terraces are composed of **travertine**, a form of limestone which, having been dissolved and carried to the surface by boiling water, is deposited as tier upon tier of steaming stone. The springs may lack the drama of the more explosive geysers, but there is nothing else in the park that looks quite like this alien arrangement, and groups of **elk** often provide a curious photo opportunity as they bask in the middle of them. It takes around ninety minutes to stroll the two sections of boardwalk that traverse the Upper and Lower terraces, with an additional thirty minutes needed to loop Upper Terrace Drive by car. Hour-long ranger **tours** of the terraces departs daily from Liberty Cap at 9am throughout summer.

Lower Terraces

The spider-web of boardwalks spilling across and up the steep hillside of the **Lower Terraces** lead past Mammoth's most famed sights. Towards the flatter, northern end of the terraces looms **Liberty Cap**, the 40ft cone of a dormant hot spring thought to be 2500 years old and named by the Hayden Expedition in 1871 after the peaked hats worn during the French Revolution. At nearby **Palette Spring**, water cascades down the scalloped edges of colorful steps ranging from three inches to three feet in height; another dormant hot spring cone, **Devil's Thumb**, sits here as well. Beyond here, the hillside is covered with large expanses of travertine terraces, some of which have been dormant for well over a decade. Even when dry, however, the likes of **Cleopatra Terrace** and **Minerva Terrace**, the latter aptly named after the Roman goddess of sculptors, are remarkable, colored a near blinding snow white and composed of thousands of tiny terraces facing in all directions. The uphill hike north to the Beaver Ponds (see H1, p.120) also begins beside the Lower Terraces.

Upper Terraces

A long row of wooden steps climb from the Lower Terraces to the **Upper Terraces**, but as many of the sights are strung along a 1.5 mile drive it's worth being lazy this one time and driving a mile up to the start of Upper Terrace Drive. The first stop on the narrow one-way loop is also the finest, with boardwalks leading to a series of viewpoints looking over the Lower Terraces and down to Fort Yellowstone beyond. The most interesting of the rapidly changing hydrothermal features is **Canary Spring**, bubbling up on the edge of an expanse of white limestone dotted with small terraces. The picturesque spring earned its name in the late 1800s due to a preponderance of yellow bacteria, still present today along with brilliant blue and orange tones. Beyond here, many of the named features along the road such as **New Highland Terrace** and **White Elephant Back Terrace** have been dormant for years, leaving little more than crumbling limestone in their wake. A dramatic exception is **Orange Spring Mound**, a giant brain-shaped blob of travertine with steaming water leaking down all of its sides; bracketed by gnarled dead trees and half coated with bright orange bacteria, it's one of Mammoth's most photogenic features.

North to Gardiner

Montana's friendly town of **Gardiner** hugs the park border only five miles north of Mammoth, and the main highway there dips down nearly 1000ft through a dusty, desert-like canyon formed by the **Gardner River** (see p.238 for an explanation of the different spellings). From Fort Yellowstone, the road north leads down past the *Mammoth Campground* and an incongruous suburban-like tract of employee homes before curving alongside **Mount Everts** (7842ft), named after the wayward explorer Truman Everts (see p.51) and layered in fossils from an ancient inland sea. At the two-mile mark, the road crosses into Montana at the **45th Parallel**, meaning you're halfway between the equator and the north pole. Considering temperature extremes range -20 and 100°F here, you'll probably feel far closer to one or the other depending on the season. At the border is the parking area for the **Boiling River**, a popular swimming hole located a half-mile upstream in the Gardner River warmed by thermal waters spilling down travertine terraces. The river is closed in spring and early summer when swollen by snowmelt, but remains open afterwards from late June through winter; bathing suits are required. It's three more miles from here to the North Entrance Station and the **Roosevelt Arch** (see p.241) just beyond; keep an eye out for bighorn sheep clinging to the steep, rocky walls on either side of the highway along the way.

Old Gardiner Road

For a different view of this arid stretch, those in a sturdy car can head north from Mammoth on the one-way **Old Gardiner Road** (4WD recommended; no trailers or RVs), an old stagecoach route starting behind the *Mammoth Hotel*. Unless it's been raining, the bumpy dirt road is open May–Oct, running high above the highway and across sagebrush flats with views down to Gardiner. Pronghorn, elk, and bison are all commonly seen, which make this a popular mountain biking route as well.

Lost in Yellowstone

The second organized party to explore Yellowstone was the 19-man **Washburn Expedition**, who spent a month trudging through the wilderness in the late summer of 1870. There were no battles with natives or bloody grizzly attacks to spice of their tales, and along with nearly starving to death the worst incident to befall the group happened to **Truman C. Everts**. Everts, the oldest explorer at 54, was in-between jobs at the time the expedition left from Helena, Montana, and joined for the adventure. He ended up with plenty more adventure than he bargained for, however, after accidentally splitting off from the party south of Yellowstone Lake. His fellow explorers sent out search parties, but the thick forest and a sudden snowstorm made tracking impossible and they were forced to move on after several days, leaving behind caches of precious supplies in their wake. The near-sighted Everts never did find the trail, and instead camped by Heart Lake, living on little more than roots while hoping to be found. Eventually Everts struck north, and for a total of 37 days, he wandered lost in Yellowstone, misplacing one important item after another – including a lens he used to start precious fires – and slowly wasting away. Though most of Helena's citizens figured Everts to be dead, members of the Washburn Expedition offered a $600 reward for finding him upon their return, and two locals set off in search. They found the shoeless, dirt-covered Everts in the park's northern reaches on October 6 – actually five miles east of what is now know as **Mount Everts** due to a map-making error – and nearly shot him at first, mistaking him for a bear. Frost bitten and emaciated, the near-dead Everts was carried off and slowly nursed back to health. The dramatic experience must not have left much lasting harm, as Everts fathered a son two decades later at the ripe age of 75. A feisty and stubborn man, Everts also refused his saviors their just reward – he claimed he would have made it back so safely without their help – and also complained bitterly until his death at age 85 that the far more grand Mount Sheridan, above his camp at Heart Lake, should have been named after him.

East to Tower-Roosevelt

The 47-mile road east from Mammoth to Tower-Roosevelt junction and beyond to the Northeast Entrance is the only highway in Yellowstone open through the winter. It's only eighteen miles from Mammoth to the key road junction fronting Roosevelt Lodge, but a number of detours mean you can easily spend several hours along this initial section in any season. Keep your camera at the ready, as the road passes through Yellowstone's **Northern Range**, 200,000 acres of open country that hosts some of the park's largest populations of wolves, coyotes, grizzly and black bears, bison, and mule deer. With upwards of 10,000 elk living hereabouts as well, this is also the finest stretch in the park for witnessing bull elks bugling and challenging each other for mates during the September rut.

After crossing over the 200ft **Gardner Bridge** just over a mile from Mammoth, the road leads past two turnoffs with waterfall views. First is **Undine Falls**, where a roadside platform looks over to the falls off Lava Creek, plunging 60ft over three tiers. Several unmarked paths lead down to different views as well as a smaller plunge downstream, but **only go with an expert guide**; several visitors have fallen to their deaths in the area. Far less risky is the short trail out to **Wraith Falls** (See H2, p.122), leading south from the highway a mile further on. Continuing east the highway passes by the marshy **Blacktail Ponds** where bison occasionally get stuck in the quicksand-like mud, soon becoming an easy dinner gift for grizzlies and other local scavengers, to the

Forces of the Northern Range Trail. The half-mile of boardwalk here features exhibits touching briefly on subjects like glaciation and wildflowers; look out for the fascinating casts of wolf tracks as well as the board describing the Huckleberry Ridge Tuff, the first of three supervolcano eruptions to have occurred in the region over the last two million years.

Blacktail Plateau Drive and the Petrified Tree

Halfway between Mammoth and Roosevelt, the one-way eastbound **Blacktail Plateau Drive** cuts off the main highway for a slow seven-mile ramble across the wildlife rich Blacktail Deer Plateau. When accessible – the road is cross-country skiing only in winter and closes whenever muddy throughout summer – it's well worth the scenic detour, passing through rolling sagebrush hills with peaceful panoramic views before eventually meeting back up with the highway just before the narrow half-mile turnoff leading to the **Petrified Tree**. Fenced in to protect it from the fate of the two other trunks that also stood here before they were chipped away by souvenir hunters, the tall and jagged trunk was once a redwood tree that was coated in volcanic ash some 50 million years ago. Additional petrified trunks can be seen in the backcountry on hikes up Specimen Ridge to the east; for details, stop by the tiny **ranger station** a mile downhill to the east at the Tower-Roosevelt junction.

Tower-Roosevelt and the Lamar Valley

Open year-round, the Northeast Entrance Road winds eastward from the **Tower-Roosevelt Junction** through the **Lamar Valley**, the scene of daily life-and-death struggles between predators (grizzlies, wolves, mountain lions) and their prey (elk, bison, pronghorn, mule deer). The valley is where two of the country's most storied wildlife experiments began, namely the restoration of both bison (see box, p.55) and the gray wolf (see *The wolves of Yellowstone* color section). It's also where the park's first gamekeeper, **Harry Yount**, was stationed in 1880 to help stop the illegal slaughter of animals. Yount lasted only one frigid winter, but he's considered the forefather to the modern day ranger. Back at the highway junction, **Roosevelt Lodge** holds a tiny, rustic cluster of amenities and a bustling horse corral, while two miles south a paved trail leads down to the spray-drenched base of **Tower Fall**; it's only a mile or so round-trip, and the best view is from the bottom, not the top. South again looms the largest landmark in the area, **Mount Washburn**, whose lookout tower can be reached by a much longer half-day hike or cycle ride.

The Lamar Valley

We stopped at this place and for my own part I almost wished I could spend the remainder of my days in a place like this where happiness and contentment seemed to reign in wild romantic splendor surrounded my majestic battlements which seemed to support the heavens and shut out all hostile intruders.

Osborne Russell, 1835

As one of the area's earliest explorers, Osborne Russell may have had a different name for the **Lamar Valley** – he called it the Secluded Valley – but his descriptions ring true to this day. The wide-open valley is a real highlight, with wildlife

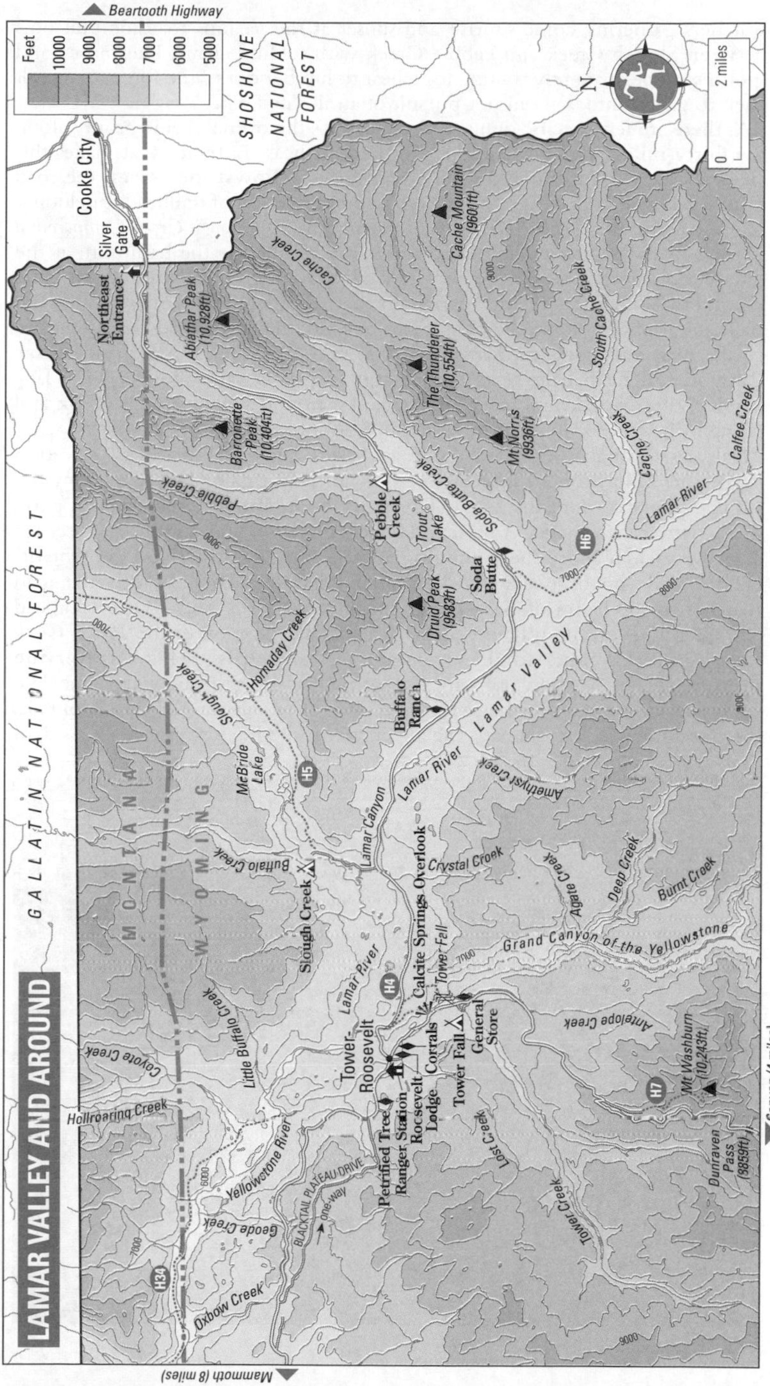

LAMAR VALLEY AND AROUND

GALLATIN NATIONAL FOREST

SHOSHONE NATIONAL FOREST

MONTANA

WYOMING

Feet
10000
9000
8000
7000
6000
5000

Cooke City

Silver Gate

Northeast Entrance

Beartooth Highway

Mammoth (8 miles)

Canyon (4 miles)

Abiathar Peak (10,928ft)

Barronette Peak (10,404ft)

The Thunderer (10,554ft)

Mt Norris (9936ft)

Cache Mountain (9601ft)

Druid Peak (9583ft)

Mt Washburn (10,243ft)

Dunraven Pass (8859ft)

Pebble Creek

Trout Lake

Soda Butte

Buffalo Ranch

Slough Creek

McBride Lake

Lamar Canyon

Lamar River

Lamar Valley

Tower-Roosevelt

Petrified Tree

Ranger Station

Roosevelt Lodge

Corrals

Calcite Springs Overlook

Tower Fall

General Store

BLACKTAIL PLATEAU DRIVE

one-way

Hellroaring Creek

Coyote Creek

Little Buffalo Creek

Buffalo Creek

Slough Creek

Hornaday Creek

Pebble Creek

Cache Creek

Soda Butte Creek

South Cache Creek

Calfee Creek

Oxbow Creek

Geode Creek

Yellowstone River

Lost Creek

Tower Creek

Antelope Creek

Crystal Creek

Amethyst Creek

Agate Creek

Deep Creek

Burnt Creek

Grand Canyon of the Yellowstone

H34

H4

H5

H6

H7

N

0 2 miles

watchers gathering come sunrise and sunset at the various roadside pull-outs between Slough Creek and Pebble Creek with folding chairs, Thermoses, and spotting scopes, patiently waiting for a bear to lumber out of the forest, or a wolf pack to gallop into view in hot pursuit of an ill-fated elk.

As there are few specific sights in the valley, it's the overall scenic beauty along the thirty-miles of highway leading to the Northeast Entrance that makes this an essential tour. After crossing high above the **Yellowstone River**, the road from Roosevelt Lodge leads five miles east past a handful of trailheads (including H4) and across the **Lamar River** to the turnoff for the *Slough Creek Campground* (see H5, p.124). Look out for the mailbox tucked beside the bathroom at the intersection here; it's used by the isolated *Silver Tip Ranch*, tucked into the Beartooth Wilderness on the park's northern border fifteen miles away and accessible only by horse. For ten miles beyond, the main road then dips and curves away and along the Lamar River as it cuts through the narrow **Lamar Canyon** and, further upstream, spills across the grassy valley floor in huge lazy bends. Cottonwood trees line the riverbanks, around which groups of elk and pronghorn weave amongst a huge herd of bison.

Halfway through the valley, the road passes the park's premier education facility, the Yellowstone Institute's Buffalo Ranch (see p.56), before meeting the rushing intersection of the Lamar River and **Soda Butte Creek**. This is good spot to watch hyperactive American Dippers diving in and out of the water for bugs, as well as bighorn sheep clinging to the steep crags of Druid Peak (9584ft) on the road's opposite side. As the Lamar River cuts to the south, the road switches to the banks of Soda Butte Creek, passing the Soda Butte Trailhead (see H6 p.124) on the way out of the Lamar Valley and on to the *Pebble Creek Campground*. En route to the campground, you'll pass a huge **travertine mound** created by a now dormant hot spring that gives the creek its name. The final ten miles to the Northeast Entrance, half of which run through Montana, are most notable for dramatic head-on views of the fortress-like masses of

△ Bison in the Lamar Valley

Bison in Yellowstone

Considering the massive herd usually seen grazing within the Lamar Valley, it's hard to fathom that **bison** were once nearly completely hunted out of the entire Yellowstone region. While the park can proudly claim to be the sole area of the United States where bison have continually lived in the wild since primitive times, their total destruction was only a few poachers' bullets away.

In 1902, Yellowstone's total bison population dipped to as few as two dozen. To protect the remaining creatures – and, it must be said, for the enjoyment of tourists – a pen was built in Mammoth in the early 1900s. In addition to the native population, ranched-raised bison were imported and placed inside, and within five years the herd of nearly sixty bison had outgrown its enclosure. The solution was to move them to the newly built **Buffalo Ranch** in the Lamar Valley in 1907, and gamekeepers at the ranch managed to raise bison numbers to more than a thousand by the 1930s, treating them like domestic cattle and feeding them hay throughout the winter months. A portion of this "tame" herd was even used in filming the 1933 Western, *The Thundering Herd*. By the early 1950s, management practices evolved to more natural approaches, and operations at the ranch were suspended. Bison were free to roam as they pleased, though the park still employed drastic **culling** measures due to mistaken assumptions on over-grazing, and the 1960s saw bison numbers plummet to fewer than three hundred.

Culling was banned in 1968, and afterwards the current practice of letting nature balance out the population was employed. With abundant terrain to graze upon, the bison population thrived, and now more than 4000 bison roam through Yellowstone in **three main herds**: the Lamar Valley's Northern Herd, the Mary Mountain Herd traveling through the Hayden and Firehole valleys, and the Pelican Valley Herd.

Bison and brucellosis

Were bison able to recognize the borders between Yellowstone and the surrounding ranchlands, their rousing success story would perhaps be complete. Without fences holding them back bison tend to roam, particularly during fierce winters when frozen grazing grounds force them to search elsewhere for food. Unfortunately, around half Yellowstone's bison test positive for **brucellosis** (a disease that causes cattle to abort their young), a fact that has spawned one of the region's most heated debates over the past two decades. In the 1980s, cattle ranchers in Montana managed to get their stock certified as brucellosis-free, and they are justifiably weary of losing this vital classification. While it's difficult for bison to infect cattle – transmission is thought to occur only when cattle eat the afterbirth of bison – it's not impossible, and Montana's powerful livestock industry has fought hard to keep bison off their land.

The original solution was a **bison hunt** on Montana land around Yellowstone, instituted in 1985; it wasn't much of a "hunt," considering one can walk directly up to a bison and shoot at point blank range, and public outcry lead to the hunt being banned five years later. The current solution involves "hazing" bison that wander outside of the park boundary back into Yellowstone with gunshots, snowmobiles and even helicopters. Those that don't return are rounded up into holding pens and then shipped off to **slaughter** if they test positive. It's an inelegant solution at best – for one, wild bison don't take kindly to being loaded into trailers and brutally kick and butt each other during the transport phase – and one that few on either side of the issue are content with. Several new plans are afoot, including possible vaccinations and restarting bison hunts, but the issue is sure to remain a contentious one for years to come. Throwing a tricky curve into the controversy as well is the fact that **elk** in the region also test positive for brucellosis, but as hunting plays another vital role in the local economy they are not slaughtered nor targeted similarly. For more information on this complex topic from the conservationist point of view, head to Ⓦwww.buffalofieldcampaign.org.

Barronette and **Abiathar peaks**, as well as late-summer fishing in Soda Butte Creek. For details on the tiny towns of Silver Gate and Cooke City beyond the entrance, see Chapter 14.

The Buffalo Ranch

No longer a working ranch, the **Buffalo Ranch** in the heart of the Lamar Valley is now the park home of the **Yellowstone Association** (see box, p.203). Overlooking the wild valley, the non-profit uses it as a base for naturalist-led field trips and seminars, and it's not that rare for a class to broken up by stampeding bison or wolves chasing an injured prey around the barn and log bunkhouses. Limited accommodation is available for those enrolled in overnight courses, but even if not taking a class at least stop by to visit the small onsite **bookstore**.

Tower Fall and around

Named after one of Yellowstone's most famous visitors and early boosters, **Roosevelt Lodge** was built a year after Theodore Roosvelt's death in 1919. Save for a gas station and small ranger station, there's little reason to stop here unless you're hungry for bbq ribs and chicken or considering a horseback or wagon ride. The **corral** here is the park's best, with a range of rides heading northeast for pretty Northern Range vistas. A short drive south leads to the **Calcite Springs Overlook**, from where you get a clear if vertigo-inducing view of spookily steaming pale slopes alongside the Yellowstone River far below. Osprey are commonly seen swooping about or nesting in the gorge, known properly as The Narrows, and bighorn sheep graze around the rim above the volcanic basalt columns on canyon wall opposite.

Over the next half-mile, several turnouts afford more views into the downstream end of the Grand Canyon of the Yellowstone before reaching the parking lot for **Tower Fall**. An upper platform about a hundred yards past the General Store overlooks the impressive 132ft falls, formed as Tower Creek rushes through a rocky chute before plunging in a long uninterrupted stream between a crown of volcanic stone pinnacles. The view from the bottom is even more dramatic, making the steep half-mile walk down well worth the effort. Known alternately as Little Falls and Lower Falls by early trappers and prospectors, the cascade has long been a busy meeting place, as the **Bannock Trail** used by hunting parties from Shoshone, Nez Perce and other native tribes weaves directly past. Following this trail, the Washburn Expedition camped here and named the waterfall in 1870, but it was Thomas Moran's sketches and subsequent paintings from the following year that fully etched it into the country's conscience.

South to Canyon: Mount Washburn and Dunraven Pass

The highway between Tower Fall and Canyon to the south combines the park's most hair-raising curves with its finest panoramic roadside views. The seventeen-mile stretch, topping out at **Dunraven Pass** (8859ft) due west of **Mount Washburn** (10,243ft), was also less enthusiastically known for its countless potholes and crumbling edges. A major construction project finished in 2005 has revamped all but a section of it, and even with a 25mph speed limit it's a curvy thrill-ride for motorcycles and sports cars. Those in RVs still have a white-knuckle ride ahead of them, and nervous drivers may want to skip the narrow road entirely. Six miles uphill from Tower Fall, the rough **Chittenden Road** leads a mile to a parking lot from which hikers and bikers can head up Mount Washburn (see H7 p.125); the final destination, a three-story fire tower upon the peak, is clearly visible from the road.

From this point to Dunraven Pass four miles away, gale winds are common, and tall piles of plowed snow crowd the roadside through June. The views get increasingly more dramatic – keep a lookout for **bighorn sheep** by the roadside – culminating in a jaw-dropping vista just beyond the pass. Overlooking an untrammeled stretch of wilderness that knows no roads and very few trails, the panorama takes in the Absarokas and the Mirror Plateau – a huge backcountry expanse home to secret waterfalls and abundant wildlife – with the pale patches of both the Grand Canyon of the Yellowstone and Washburn Hot Springs breaking up the sea of deep green in the foreground. It's four miles downhill to Canyon, passing the **Cascade Lake Picnic Area**, starting point for a wildflower-rich hike to Cascade Lake (see H8, p.126), along the way.

Canyon and around

For more than twenty miles, the **Yellowstone River** roars and tumbles between the sheer golden cliffs of the **Grand Canyon of the Yellowstone**, whose width varies between 1500 and 4000 feet and its depth between 800 and 1200 feet; almost the entire length of the canyon actually runs parallel to the road between **Canyon Village** and Tower-Roosevelt on the north loop, but you're too far from the canyon to get any decent views. The best viewpoints are clustered around the busy junction at Canyon Village. The most visited is **Artist Point**, and the moment you glimpse **Lower Falls**, juxtaposed with sheer canyon walls

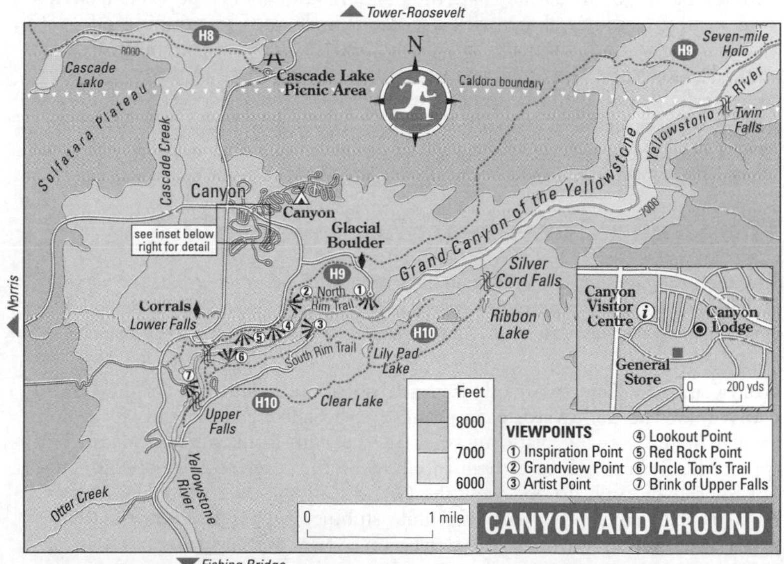

fired with streaks of orange and red, the origins of the name will be only too clear. Painter Thomas Moran was the first to capture the falls on canvas in 1871, and artists still flock to draw what may be the most reproduced painting subject in North America.

The road south of Canyon through picturesque Hayden Valley and past malodorous Mud Volcano is covered in Chapter 2, "Southern Yellowstone."

Canyon Village

Long a popular stopping point for visitors, **Canyon Village** has a storied architectural history. Two rickety hotels had already been built here when the celebrated *Canyon Hotel* began construction in 1910. Designed by Robert Reamer, the man behind the *Old Faithful Inn* the 430-room inn billed itself "a miracle in hotel building" due to it's sheer size and speedy construction, and featured a lounge large enough to host a full orchestra. While successful for decades, the costs of running such a huge enterprise eventually overtook any profits and the run-down building was sold for $25 to a wrecking crew in 1959. It burnt down under mysterious circumstances the following year. Nowadays most of the village's buildings are less inspired, a testament to the National Park Service's "Mission 66" program, a decade-long program to update facilities that ended with the Service's fiftieth anniversary in 1966. Dominating the scene is the **Canyon Lodge**, at park brochures brag is longer than a football field. It's about a charming as well, though considering 5000 guests dine here daily, its size is warranted. Along with a gift shop, the lodge houses a decent restaurant and lounge, a convenient deli, and a workaday cafeteria. Across the parking lot is one of the park's largest general stores (including a diner and coffee/ice-cream bar) and a sporting goods store. Further away in the opposite direction, the huge *Canyon Campground* is fronted by a handy laundry and shower facility.

There is hope for the aesthetic revival of Canyon Village however, as evidenced by the innovative **Canyon Visitor Center** (late May to early Sept daily 8am–7pm; early Sept to early Oct 9am–6pm; ⓣ307/242-2550). Taking inspiration from the burnt down *Canyon Hotel*, the building's designers used stone quarried from nearby Gardiner along with a cedar shingle roof to winning effect. It manages to be both intimate and grand, and the center's opening in 2006 marked Yellowstone's first major visitor center development in thirty years. The geological-themed exhibits inside are suitably state-of-the-art, including a room-sized topographic map of the park's geological history lit with fiber optics, along with a large rotating globe pinpointing other volcanic hot spots around the world. There's also an information desk and bookstore onsite.

The Grand Canyon of the Yellowstone

Here the very ground is changed, as if belonging to some other world. The walls of the cañon from top to bottom burn in a perfect glory of color, confounding and dazzling when the sun is shining...All the earth hereabouts seems to be paint.

John Muir, 1885

From Canyon Village, two roads trace the north and south rims of the **Grand Canyon of the Yellowstone**, accessing over a half-dozen marked viewpoints. Several of the viewing platforms stick to the rim, from where you can best appreciate, in the words of naturalist John Muir, the "prefect glory of color" that tint the canyon walls. To best view the Grand Canyon's two waterfalls – **Lower Falls** tumbles an impressive 308ft, while stubbier Upper Falls travels 109ft – you'll want to head down into the canyon on a series of steep paths and staircases.

Indeed, if you only have the time to explore one Yellowstone area on foot, consider doing so here. Canyon's renowned for it superb **trails network**, and while only one path leads to the canyon floor (the demanding Seven Mile Hole Trail; see H9 p.227), several others weave around the rim and beyond, offering breathtaking views that change dramatically as the sun works across the sky. While it's possible to view both falls along the same trail, a bend in the river prevents seeing both at the simultaneously, unless riding in a plane.

The North Rim

The 2.5-mile **North Rim Drive**, which runs one-way southbound from Canyon Village, provides access to several overlooks on the canyon's north side; you can simply park and take in the view from atop the rim, but it's well worth taking at least one downhill hike to get even with the falls themselves. The eastern most overlook, **Inspiration Point**, is at the end of a mile-long spur road; a series of steps leads to a small, windy platform best for views of the canyon walls, streaked with hourglass-shaped landslides every few hundred yards. En route to Inspiration Point, stop to ponder the immense power of glaciers at **Glacial Boulder** – the enormous chunk of granite, estimated to weigh 500 tons, was brought and deposited here by a passing glacier from the Beartooth Mountains forty miles away. A trailhead by the boulder leads to a view of Yellowstone's tallest waterfall, narrow **Silver Chord Falls** (see H9 p.127), approximately a mile down the trail.

Grandview Point is next on the main drive, and while's there's no view of the falls, it's worth stopping for another angle of the multicolored canyon and to watch for **osprey**, the nests of which are built atop precarious pinnacles inside the canyon. **Lookout Point** beyond the next bend offers the first unblocked view of Lower Falls, and the **Red Rock Trail** here switchbacks down an uneven path and wooden steps to an even better view, where you can watch the falls powerful splash rise up before blowing away. The emerald-green stripe to the side of the falls is deeper water, marking a notch in the lip of the brink. The last and most impressive viewpoint is also the toughest to reach, located down a steep ten-minute walk offering a view of the Upper Falls a short way down. After completing the last of ten switchbacks, take your time to enjoy the **Brink of Lower Falls**, from where you can see close up the awesome power of the 2.2 million gallons of water which go over every minute, and watch the thunderous falls making short work (geologically speaking) of the rock walls below.

South of North Rim Drive, another road leads to the **Brink of Upper Falls**, from where you can walk a short distance for a closer look at the swirling pool created by the thickset Upper Falls. If in a convoy, this is a good spot to park one car before walking the paved three-mile **North Rim Trail** back to Inspiration Point and the second car.

The South Rim

The shorter South Rim Drive has only two viewpoints of note, but both are extremely popular and therefore best visited early or late in the day. The first, **Uncle Tom's Trail**, descends steeply into the canyon to a gently vibrating, spray-covered platform right in the face of Lower Falls. Closed in by rust-red and golden colored canyon walls, all able-bodied souls should make the heart-racing trip down the path's 328 metal steps to soak up one of the most memorable views in the park. Close to a mile downstream, **Artist Point** trades in the intimacy of Uncle Tom's small viewing platform for panoramic grandeur, and virtually everyone who has been to Yellowstone has stopped here for a long look.

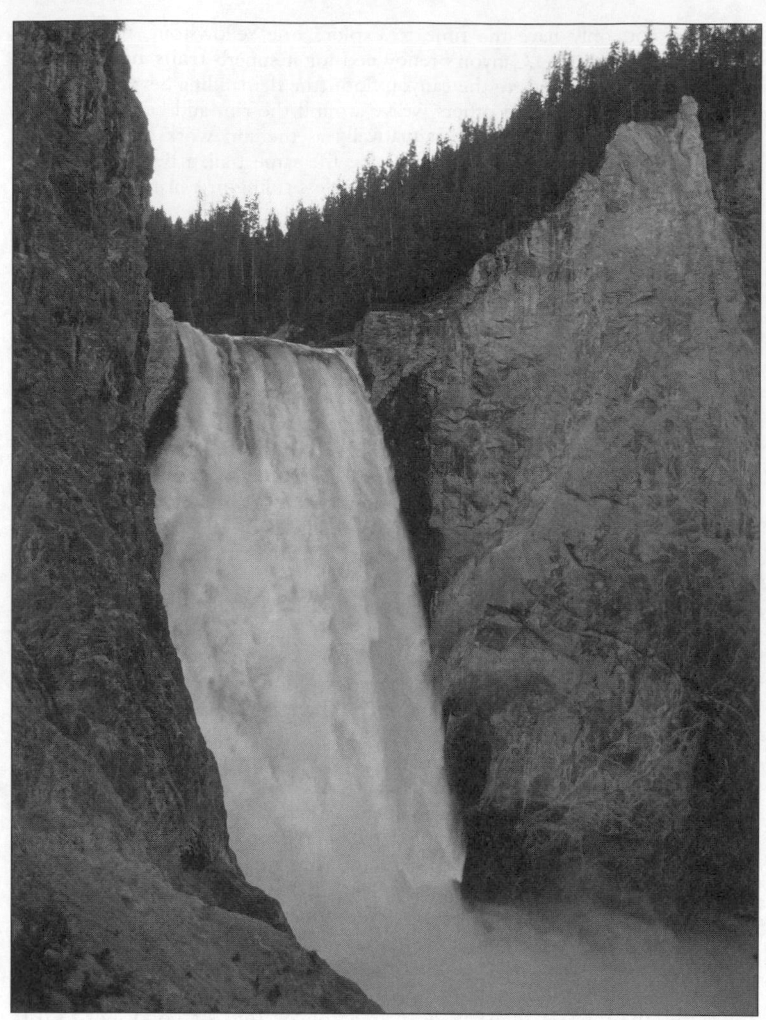

△ Lower Falls from the bottom of Uncle Tom's Trail

The upper and lower decks afford majestic views both towards Lower Falls and downstream into the canyon, and provided the crowds aren't too much to bear it's worth sticking around for one of the 15-minute ranger talks given up to ten times daily. Should the crowds be too much – or if you have time to spare – consider heading downstream into the backcountry from here to Point Sublime and beyond (see H10, p.129).

West to Norris

Forming the waist of the Grand Loop's giant figure-eight highway, the twelve mile road between Canyon in the east to Norris in the west begins by climbing up the **Solfatara Plateau**, a reasonably flat expanse dotted with several of Yellowstone's most accessible backcountry lakes including Cascade, Grebe, Wolf, and Ice lakes. Atop the plateau, wonderful views look west to the rounded masses of the Madison Range, after which the road plunges downhill for a couple of miles en route to the **Virginia Cascades** turnoff. The 2.5-mile one-way side-road (eastbound) hugs the steep northern rim of the Gibbon River Canyon while passing the 60ft sparkling waterslide down the rim of the Yellowstone Caldera, above which the Gibbon narrows to a calm creek as it exits Virginia Meadows. Just before reaching Norris Junction, a **picnic area** makes for a peaceful spot for a nap or to try your luck at fishing the Gibbon.

Norris and around

Yellowstone's **Norris** region is named after the buckskin-wearing **Philetus W. Norris**, the park's second superintendent from 1877–1882 (for more on his story see p.271). Along with Madison Junction fifteen miles to the south, Norris Junction is the only other major intersection in the park without a restaurant, general store, or indoor accommodation. Unlike Madison, however, there's still plenty to see, particularly for dedicated geyser-gazers. The huge **Norris Geyser Basin** is Yellowstone's oldest, hottest, and most dynamic hydrothermal area, and it takes several hours to explore the two large loops here.

North of the geyser basin and guarding the entrance to the wooded *Norris Campground* is the **Museum of the National Park Ranger** (daily 9am–5pm; free), housed in a large log cabin built by the Army as an outpost in 1908. Honoring rangers from across the park system, exhibits and posters inside focus on their varied responsibilities, from law enforcement to fire fighting to search-and-rescue. Another room inside recreates what the conditions were like for the men stationed here, who suffered mightily in winter when only one or two men were posted and ordered to patrol the arctic area on snowshoes. The displays are all minorly interesting, but the cabin itself, fronted by a wide porch with burlwood columns, is the best reason to visit.

South of the geyser basin sits **Gibbon Meadows**, a photogenic expanse where elk frequently graze. A short road here leads east to the **Artist Paint Pots**, where a mile-long loop climbs uphill through burnt forest past an amazing collection of gurgling mudpots and dirty pink puddle-sized pools, seemingly awaiting the dip of a giant paintbrush. The road further south to Madison Junction, including Gibbon Falls, is covered in Chapter 2, "Southern Yellowstone."

Norris Geyser Basin

Norris Geyser Basin is divided into two main sections, **Back Basin** and **Porcelain Basin**, and both are in dramatic contrast with the pretty settings of most of the park's other geyser basins. Partly because the basin sits at the intersection of three faults, temperatures can be incredibly hot – scientists have measured temperatures over 450°F within the ground here – and the boardwalks have had to be moved several times due to intense ground heat. It's particularly important to stick to marked trails in this area at all times.

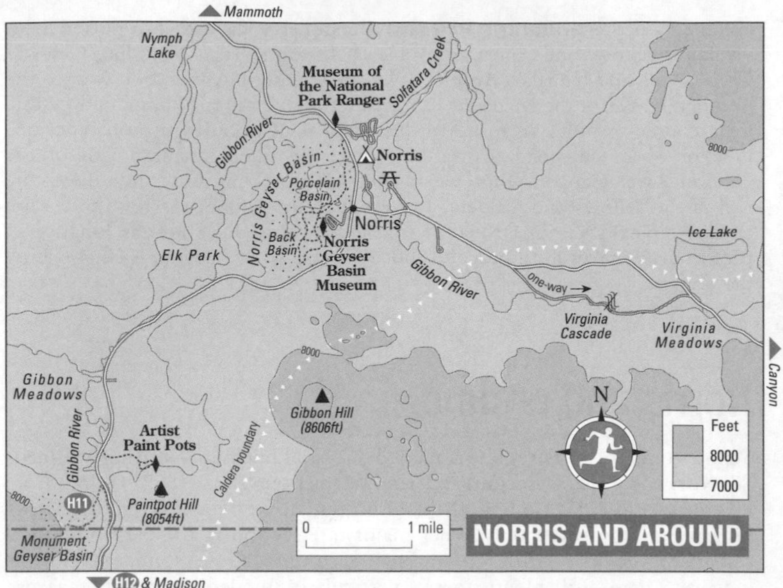

At the intersection of the two loops sits the **Norris Geyser Basin Museum** (late-May to Sept daily 10am–5pm; free), two rooms separated by an open walkway. Built in 1929, the squat log-and-boulder structure houses basic panels detailing hydrothermal geology, including an explanation of the natural plumbing beneath nearby Steamboat Geyser. A ranger mans the **information desk** between the two rooms, and also leads at least one walk, talk, and campfire program daily. There's no posted schedule for geyser eruptions as there are at Old Faithful because the activity here it too unpredictable to forecast. Closer to the parking area in a stand-alone hut is one of the Yellowstone Association's handy **bookstores**.

Back Basin

Patched with forest, an odd-shaped loop snakes around **Back Basin** for 1.5 miles, though a cut-off lets you halve the trip if need be. Starting from the museum, the loop first passes **Emerald Spring**, where yellow sulfur deposits combine with the pool's blue water to form the glorious green color that gives it its name. Just beyond, two viewing platforms look over **Steamboat Geyser**, the world's tallest (on the rare occasions that it does decide to blow). Capable of forcing near-boiling water 380ft into the air, Steamboat eruptions have occurred anywhere between a few days and several decades apart, so you may not wish to sit and wait for the next one. In the meantime its angry main vent tantalizes the crowds with lesser bursts of ten to forty feet a couple of times a day. Further south, **Echinus Geyser**, surrounded by rocky sea urchin-like formations, is the largest acid-water geyser known; every 35 to 75 minutes it spews crowd-pleasing, vinegary eruptions of forty to sixty feet while the eponymous spring next to it sizzles like butter on a hot pan. There are more than a dozen additional named features worth seeking out alongside the boardwalk, including sparkling lemon-lime **Cistern Spring**, which drains to feed Steamboat Geyer's eruptions; **Pearl Geyser**, one the prettiest in the park, rimmed by circle of pinkish mother-of- pearl like rock; and **Porkchop Geyser**, a spring that exploded in 1989, blowing open its vent from mere inches to a span seven feet wide, tossing rocks more than two-hundred feet away in the process.

Porcelain Basin

A tour of fascinating **Porcelain Basin** begins from an overlook on the museum's north side. From here visitors look across a psychedelic swirl of light blue pools, orange streaks of microscopic thermophiles, and patches of deep green lodgepole, all seen through a veil of wispy white steam pouring from the **Black Growler Steam Vent** on the hillside below. A half-mile loop leads downhill past **Ledge Geyser**, capable of eruptions over 125ft high, to the photogenic runoff from the pools of **Whirligig Geyser** and **Pinwheel Geyser**; the hotter water of Whirligig hosts a long mat of heat-loving orange bacteria, while a streak of green algae streams out of the cooler Pinwheel. If short on time, skip the longer western portion of the loop, where the most interesting site is **Crackling Lake**, a large pond sounding like a massive bowl of Rice Krispies.

North to Mammoth

The first four of the 21 miles north from Norris to Mammoth climbs and dips through forest untouched by the fires of 1988, the canopy creeping up to the road's edge. Just past Twin Lakes, **Roaring Mountain** is a barren hillside pockmarked with scores of steaming fumaroles. Much more powerful when named the late 1800s, steam still pours off the face of the mountain, the one-time roar now more of a hiss audible only when there's a break in traffic. Scientists have found that heat-loving microbes known as *sulfolobus acidocaldarius* live on the surface of the mountain, feeding on the gases rising up from below.

△ The Golden Gate leading to Mammoth

Jim Bridger's tall tales

Forced to spend the warmer months trapping in small groups and the winter bivouacked in lonely forts, the mountain men of the fur-trapping era turned to storytelling for entertainment. One of the best tellers of tales was **Jim Bridger**, a talented scout, trapper, and guide from Virginia who roamed the northern Rockies for decades throughout the mid-1800s. Renowned for his exaggeration-laced yarns, several of Bridger's tales were set in Yellowstone, not surprising given both the mind-boggling reality of the park's landscape and the fact he was one of the first white men to explore the region. In one such story, he told of sitting down amongst a forest of petrified trees – a plausible tale, until he reached the part about the petrified birds that landed nearby singing their petrified songs. One of his most outlandish tales was set at **Obsidian Cliff**. As the story goes, Bridger was out hunting one day when he spied large bull elk. After firing a perfect shot, the elk failed to fall and in fact continued grazing as if nothing happened. Bridger crept closer and closer, repeating his shots until he ended up face to face with a wall of glass. He then realized that he'd been shooting not at an elk, but at the image of one reflected through Obsidian Cliff. Not only that, but the cliff's glass face had acted like a telescopic lens and the bull elk was in fact grazing peacefully miles away.

A five-minute drive further north, the road passes another storied mountain (see box, p.64), **Obsidian Cliff**. Created by a lava flow some 180,000 years ago, the ribbed cliff rising upwards of 200ft was of vital importance to native tribes, who came to mine the plentiful black volcanic glass for use as projectile points and other tools; prehistoric artefacts made from this obsidian has been found as far away as Michigan to the east and Mexico to the south. Nowadays, travel on or near the cliff is forbidden, and punishment for taking obsidian is harsh.

From here, the highway north follows alongside Obsidian Creek, through a narrow and past a marshy zone that's one of the better areas in Yellowstone to spot a **moose**. The creek then runs into the Gardner River by the isolated *Indian Creek Campground*, beyond which a turnoff leads to the **Sheepeater Picnic Area** where there's a close of up view of the same type of 500,000 year old basalt columns seen above the Yellowstone River near Tower. More of these columns dot Sheepeater Canyon downstream, as seen on the hike to Osprey Falls (see H3 p.122) beginning from the Bunsen Peak Trailhead a couple miles north across pretty Swan Lake Flat meadows. Past the trailhead, the road cuts through the dramatic **Golden Gate Canyon** on a hanging road originally built for stagecoaches in the late 1800s; the current concrete bridge dates to the 1970s. Predominantly volcanic ash and pumice, the canyon's yellow rocks make up the finest exposure of the earth-shattering Huckleberry Ridge Tuff, which erupted during Yellowstone's first volcanic cycle two million years ago. Past the canyon, the road spirals downhill, passing by the **Hoodoos** – bizarre rock formations suitable for low-key rock climbing – and the staging area for winter snowcoaches before entering into Mammoth.

The wolves of Yellowstone

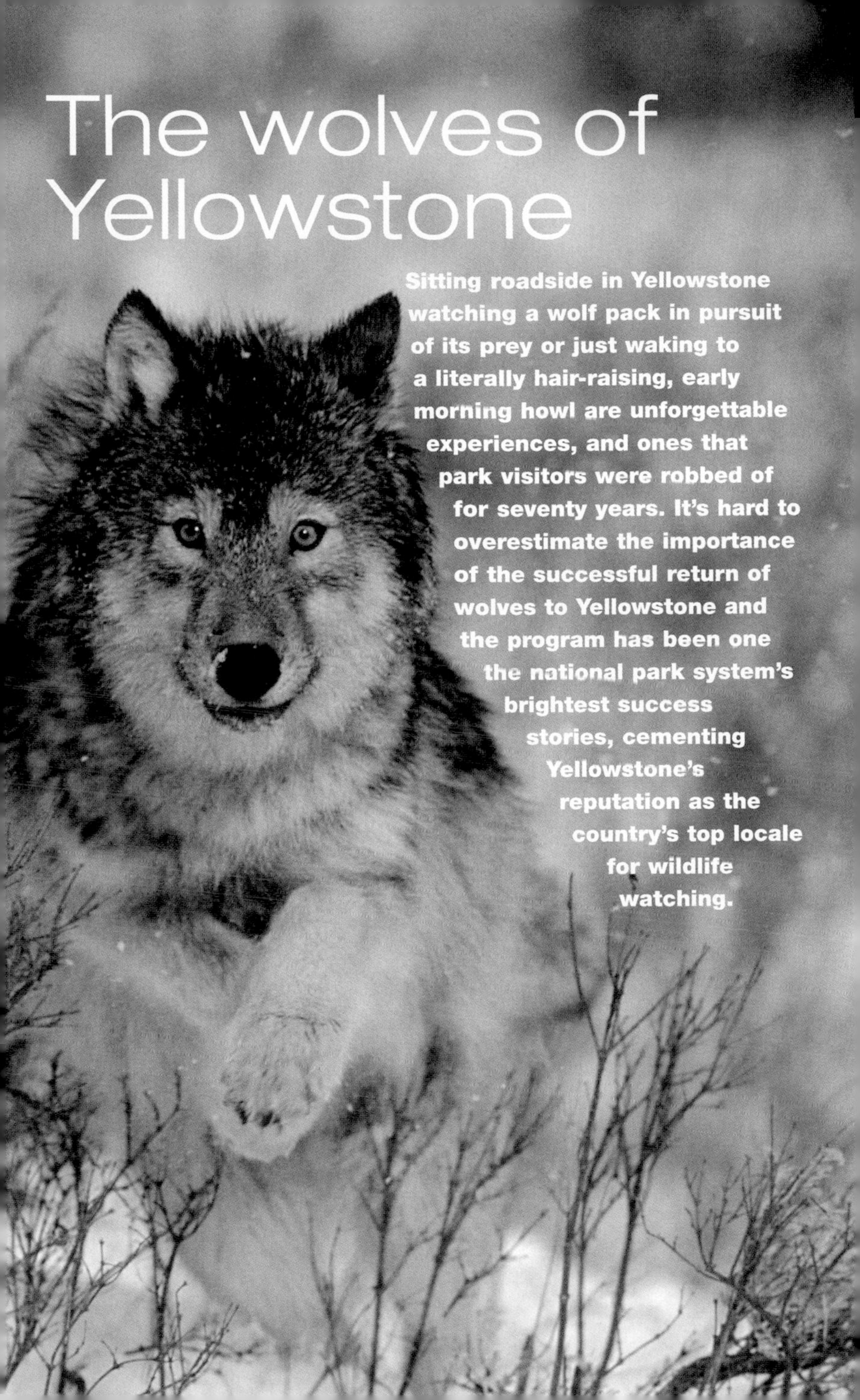

Sitting roadside in Yellowstone watching a wolf pack in pursuit of its prey or just waking to a literally hair-raising, early morning howl are unforgettable experiences, and ones that park visitors were robbed of for seventy years. It's hard to overestimate the importance of the successful return of wolves to Yellowstone and the program has been one the national park system's brightest success stories, cementing Yellowstone's reputation as the country's top locale for wildlife watching.

▲ Biologists track the wolf population with radio collars.

The reintroduction

In Yellowstone's less enlightened days, countless crackpot schemes were employed to protect certain species of wildlife. Rangers in the 1920s stomped on pelican eggs to save cutthroat trout from their natural predator, and wolves – effective cullers of crowd-pleasers like elk and mule deer – were given even less mercy. Until the last native **gray wolf** was exterminated in Yellowstone in 1926, the "devil's dog" was trapped, poisoned, and shot at most every opportunity. As early as the 1940s, forward-thinking biologists like **Aldo Leopold** were lecturing on the importance of bringing wolves back to restore the ecosystem's precarious balance, but it wasn't until 1994, after nearly half a century of heated debate, that the first round of wolves to be transplanted were captured in Alberta. Canadian wolves were chosen, as they were acclimatized to hunting elk, Yellowstone's primary food source for large predators.

On January 12, 1995, fourteen wolves were trucked in under Gardiner's Roosevelt Arch. In the following year, seventeen more wolves, this time from British Columbia, arrived, while ten orphaned pups from northern Montana were added soon after. Due to large numbers of wintering elk and bison in the area, the **41 wolves** introduced all started off in acclimatization pens hidden throughout the **Lamar Valley**. For two months before being released, the radio-collared animals were fed a steady diet of elk, deer, moose, and bison that had died around the park, including roadkill hauled in by volunteers. Several more years of transplants where scheduled, but the program was such a spectacular success from the start that these were quickly cancelled. By 2003, the high-water mark population-wise, 173 wolves were living in Yellowstone.

Gray wolves up close

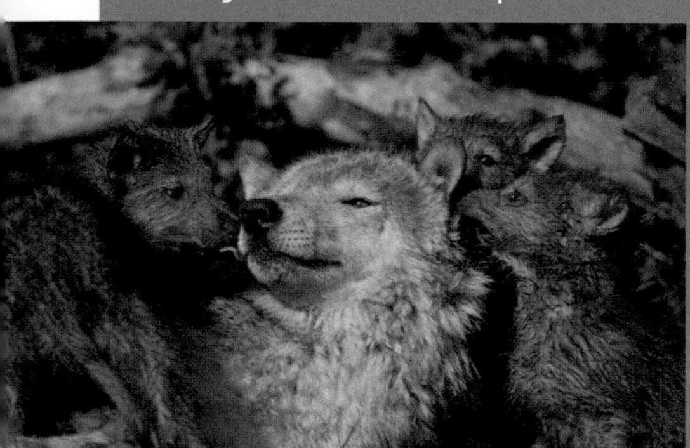

Despite the name, the coat of a **gray wolf** (*canis lupus*) may be any color from snow white to midnight black; males can weigh upwards of 130 pounds, with females topping out at 110. A wolf's life is not an easy one, and fatal wounds earned by taking on much larger prey are common – their **average lifespan** in the wild is only 3–4 years. Typically only the alpha female is allowed to get pregnant, giving **birth** in April to an average of five pups. The entire pack takes turns in caring for the young, and along with bringing food to the den, Yellowstone pack members have been seen carrying back sticks and colorful bits of trash for the cubs to play with. Extremely **territorial**, packs will attack and kill intruding wolves, including renegade Romeos hoping to poach a lesser female to start a new pack.

Friend and foe

The effect of wolves on other animals has been closely studied. More visible before the reintroduction, **coyotes** have certainly been negatively affected, but whether or not their population has decreased is uncertain; it's possible coyotes may have become better at hiding in the face of stronger competition. **Grizzlies**, on the other hand, seem to be benefitting, often stealing a pack's fresh kill and lazily hanging around it for days to finish it off. Perhaps benefitting most of all, **ravens** are a vital friend to wolf and wolf-spotter alike. The birds are present at an amazing 98 percent of all kills, and as many as 135 ravens have been counted around a single dead elk in the Lamar Valley. The winged scavengers have also been seen leading wolves to already dead animals, and some believe they might even point out sick elk that make easier prey.

▲ Ravens at a wolf pack's fresh kill

Yellowstone's wolf packs

At the time of writing, fourteen packs roamed in and out of Yellowstone, with an overall population hovering around 140. Due to the high density of prey, pack **territories** around Yellowstone are small. Where a single pack in Alaska might need 5000 square miles to survive, those in Yellowstone can live with less than fifty square miles, making the park – particularly the elk-rich Northern Range – the most reliable place in the world for watching wolves in the wild. A social creature, wolves live in packs ranging in size from six to more than thirty, led by an alpha male and female who keep everyone in line. Tracking the packs is fascinating, with coups and the natural deaths of alphas leading to splinter groups and lesser packs taking control. The **Druid Peak Pack**, a long park favorite, dominated the Lamar Valley for nearly a decade, rising up to thirty-plus members before losing power to upstarts like the **Agate Creek Pack**.

◀ One of Yellowstone's wolf packs in the Lamar Valley

Along with territory size, pack numbers depend on the main food source, with groups like **Mollie's Pack** and the **Hayden Valley Pack** that hunt bison growing larger in order to take down the massive creatures; up to fourteen wolves have been seen biting and hanging from a bison at one time. Elk are easily the most common **prey**, though mule deer, moose, beaver, and occasionally domestic cattle on neighboring ranchlands are also hunted.

Wolf-watching

Wolf-watching has become a fascinating addition to the Yellowstone experience. Numerous companies and guides lead spotting expeditions, including those run out of the Lamar Valley by the Yellowstone Institute (see p.203). High-powered binoculars or spotting scopes are essential, with wolves more often than not sighted a half-mile away or further. Winter is the best time for wolf-watching, as packs are more active in hunting elk and, to a lesser extent, bison struggling to survive the frigid cold. Also, wolves' coats show up more clearly silhouetted against a snowy background, making them easier to spot. Because as wolves are **crepuscular** – active around dawn and dusk – you'll need to be on their schedule to increase the chances of seeing one; the majority of sightings occur before 8am.

Unless you hear talk of a recently seen pack or fresh kill elsewhere, your best bet is to troll the road east of *Roosevelt Lodge* and through the Lamar Valley, which remains open year-round and cuts through the range of at least six wolf packs. Particularly in winter, you're sure to pass Yellowstone's most hardcore wolf-watchers – some working for the official Yellowstone Wolf Project, others just enthusiasts – and most will happily fill you in on the latest news and perhaps let you use their spotting scopes. Along with roadside spotting parties, other **telltale signs** that wolves might be near include flocks of ravens, herds of elk fleeing in fear, and, most obviously, the howl of a wolf. As with other wild animals, it's your responsibility to not interact with wolves; a fed wolf is a dead wolf, so always take any food scraps or trash along with you. Should a wolf approach – a rare but not unheard-of occurrence – get into the closest car and drive away.

2

Southern Yellowstone

The first explorers to report on Yellowstone's marquee attraction, **Old Faithful**, were the members of the Washburn Expedition, who tramped into the Upper Geyser Basin with spirits sagging on September 18, 1870. Not only had they recently lost fellow adventurer Truman C. Everts (see box, p.50), but they were also running perilously low on food. In just two wondrous days spent marveling at the steaming sights, their mood had risen to new heights and they had named several of the park's big-name geysers, including Giant and Giantess, Beehive and Grotto, and even Old Faithful, named by Henry Dana Washburn himself. Paved paths, boardwalks, and interpretive signs now figure prominently in the geyser basins that dominate **southern Yellowstone**, but the scenes remain just as awe-inspiring as they did nearly 140 years ago.

Encompassing the lower half of Yellowstone's Grand Loop Road along with the roadways leading to the West, South and East entrances, southern Yellowstone's long list of attractions are lead by steady Old Faithful and enormous **Yellowstone Lake** to the east. Its most important feature, however, can't really be enjoyed from a singular viewpoint. In fact, its existence wasn't even known until being uncovered by geologist Bob Christiansen in the late 1960s. With high altitude photos recently taken by NASA in hand, Christiansen was amazed to realize that the ancient volcanic crater that he was searching for was far larger than he ever imagined, spreading out over half of the park's territory. Created by an earth-shattering "supervolcano" eruption 640,000 years ago, this massive basin (approximately 45 miles by 30 miles in length), is now known as the **Yellowstone Caldera**.

Underneath the Yellowstone Caldera is one of the world's most active volcanic hotspots, a massive chamber of magma bubbling perilously close to the surface beneath a thin crust of earth. This molten rock is the furnace stoking the park's hydrothermal wonders, making the caldera's 965 square miles, outlined clearly on park maps, home to the largest concentration of geysers, hot springs, mudpots, and fumaroles in the world. The majority of these are dotted within easily accessed clusters known as geyser basins, including the **Upper**, **Middle**, **Lower**, and **West Thumb geyser basins**, though some areas – such as the **Shoshone Lake Geyser Basin** – are tucked away deep in the backcountry. The northern half of Yellowstone Lake is also within the caldera boundaries, and its murky bottom is home to a myriad of superheated vents, underwater springs, and bizarre spire-shaped geological formations.

Outside of the caldera's boundary in southern Yellowstone lies mainly untrammelled wilderness. Some of the region's best hikes are accessed via the east and southern entrance roads, including a stiff climb up Avalanche Peak or a trip out to Heart Lake respectively. Beyond these roadways are the extremely isolated

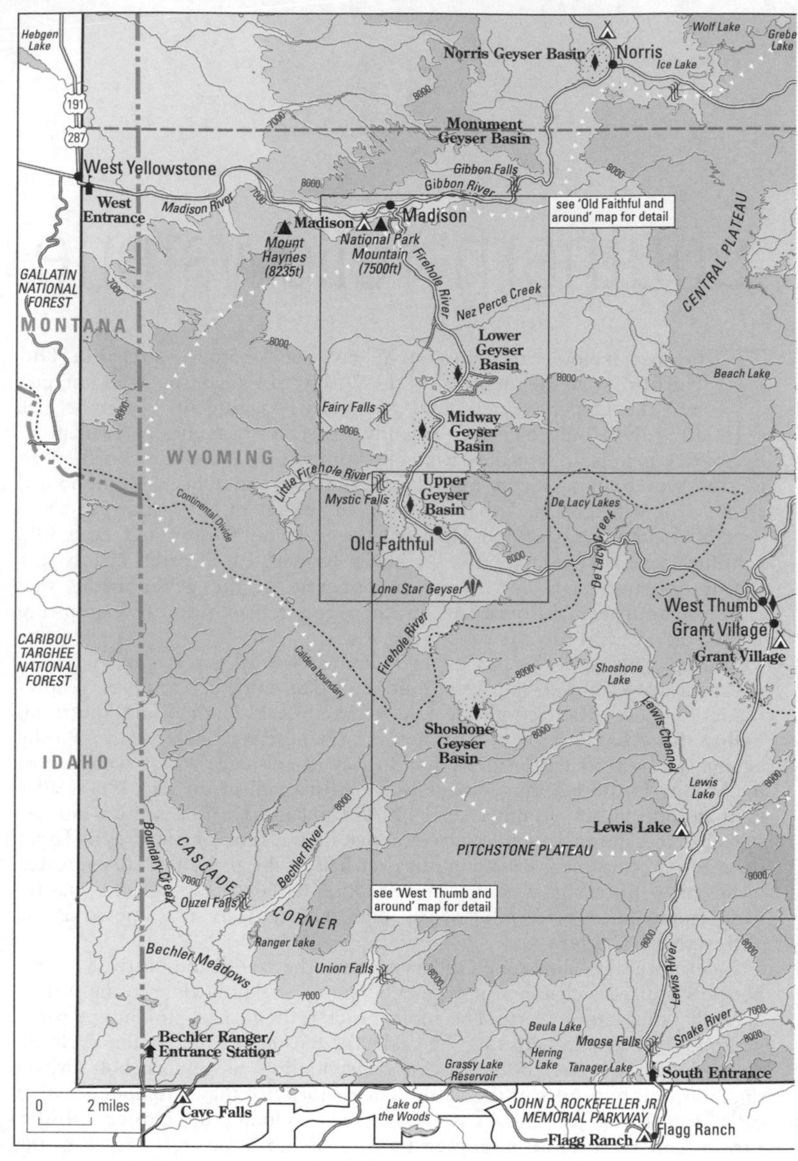

southeast and southwest corners of the park, the latter home to the hard-to-reach **Bechler Ranger Station** at the end of a long dirt road.

Sights and orientation

The following tour of southern Yellowstone begins at **Madison** junction, fifteen miles east of the park's busiest entry point, the **West Entrance**

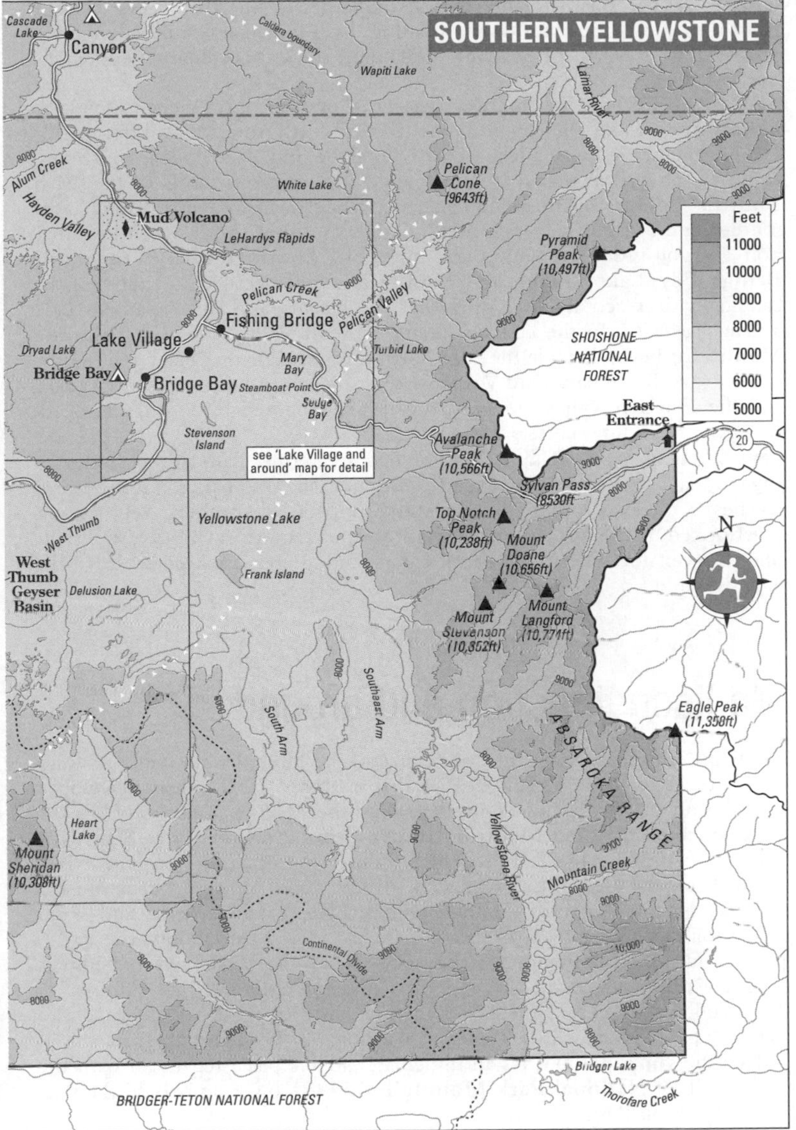

Station. South of Madison, the Grand Loop follows the Firehole River upstream and for fifteen unbelievable miles it weaves through the heart of Yellowstone's geyser country. The northernmost **Lower Geyser Basin** hosts the bubbling mud of the Fountain Paint Pots and the towering eruptions of Great Fountain Geyser, while **Midway Geyser Basin** showcases Grand Prismatic Spring, rung with fluorescent orange and yellow bacteria. The

Upper Geyser Basin to the south is the largest of the three geyser basins, boasting several of the world's most famous hydrothermal features along with a small town's worth of buildings, including the extraordinary *Old Faithful Inn* (see p.75).

From Old Faithful, the highway twists east over the Continental Divide to **Yellowstone Lake**, the largest alpine lake in North America, and the world's second largest freshwater lake above 7000ft behind Lake Titicaca in South America. The views across it from beside the gorgeous pools of the **West Thumb Geyser Basin** are remarkable, while nearby **Grant Village**, the southernmost visitor village, is useful mainly as a spot to fill up on information, gas, and groceries. Lining the shores of Yellowstone Lake to the north, **Bridge Bay**, **Lake Village**, and **Fishing Bridge** together host most of the lakeside visitor activity, including the sole marina and the expansive *Lake Yellowstone Hotel*. To the east lies pretty **Pelican Valley** and the **Absaroka Mountains** beyond, while the road north towards Canyon Village follows the Yellowstone River past **Mud Volcano**, the park's most noxious thermal basin, and the **Hayden Valley**, an immense dale frequented by bison, elk, bears, wolves, and wildlife spotters.

Separated from the Grand Loop Road by more than twenty miles of rugged backcountry, the **Cascade Corner** in the park's southwestern reaches is the only other road accessible portion of southern Yellowstone. Overlooked by the vast majority of visitors, this remote corner is a waterfall-filled heaven for hikers, horseback riders, and anglers looking to leave the crowds behind.

Madison Junction and around

Madison Junction sits at the confluence of the Firehole and Gibbon rivers, which meet to form the mighty **Madison River**. It's the least developed intersection on the Grand Loop, with only the *Madison Campground* to the west and the charming **Madison Information Station** (June–Sept daily 9am–5pm; ⓣ307/344-2831) to the south. As headquarters for the park's Junior Ranger Program (see p.202), this 1929 wood and stone structure is a particularly good stop for families, with a table of animal pelts and skulls inside for kids to handle and half-hour talks offered throughout the day. A plaque outside commemorates the spot where the Washburn Expedition allegedly camped towards the end of their explorations in the summer of 1870 and first discussed the novel idea of protecting the wonderland as a national park. There's little evidence backing up the claim up that this is indeed the same spot, but it's an undeniably idyllic place regardless with the rocky hulk of **National Park Mountain** (7549ft) towering behind the start of the Madison River.

The West Entrance Road

Madison's information station hosts a tiny bookstore, but for food, gas or other supplies, the closest option is bustling **West Yellowstone** fourteen miles to the west. The drive is both pretty and popular, curving alongside the Madison River almost the entire way with over a dozen turnouts accessing the water, a boon for anglers, photographers, and picnickers. From Madison, the road first cuts through the **Madison Canyon** and past several picturesque mountains – including the Three Brothers, Mount Jackson (8276ft), and Mount Haynes (8231ft) – standing sentinel on both sides of the river. After crossing **Seven Mile Bridge**, the landscape opens up considerably, with the Madison River flowing in a wide ribbon across a marshy meadow often dotted with elk and, in spring and fall, bison. Charred tree trunks pepper the scene, a reminder of the devastating fires of 1988. Two miles before passing through the West Entrance Station and into West Yellowstone (see Chapter 12, p.130), the highway crosses into Montana.

North to Norris

There are no major sights on the fourteen miles of road between Madison and Norris to the north, but it's worth budgeting extra time for a short hike and slower driving for roadside photo-ops along the **Gibbon River**. You might not have a choice anyway, as this rough stretch is next in line for major reconstruction once enough funds are collected. From Madison, the highway immediately passes the trailhead for **Purple Mountain** (see H12, p.130) and then **Terrace Springs**, where a roadside boardwalk leads around a trio of steamy pools. The **Tuff Cliff Picnic Area** a mile beyond is more interesting, located beneath a rocky escarpment of light, honeycombed rocks created by a series of spectacular volcanic ash flows. Just over four miles from Madison is the most popular stopover, **Gibbon Falls**, tumbling 85ft over the rim of the Yellowstone Caldera. For the best **photos**, park fifty yards downstream, where you'll be able to frame the horsetail falls in their entirety along with the web of logs smashed together at its base. Upstream, the highway parallels the Gibbon more closely, eventually passing the trailhead for the bizarre **Monument Geyser Basin** (see H11, p.130). Just beyond the road cuts through the elk-rich Gibbons Meadows and past Artist Paint Pots en route to Norris Geyser Basin, all of which are covered in Chapter 1, "Northern Yellowstone."

South to the Lower Geyser Basin

South of Madison, the road towards Old Faithful follows the **Firehole River** upstream. Just over a mile from the junction, **Firehole Canyon Drive** leads one-way (southbound) alongside the river for a couple of miles through its eponymous canyon. The scenic spur road's first section runs along the canyon floor, steep rhyolite cliffs blocking out the sky like pockmarked skyscrapers. Rising up alongside the volcanic rock, the side road then works its way to a head on view of **Firehole Falls**, a squat forty-foot wall of crashing water. If cars are parked alongside the road above the falls, it means the **Boiling River** is open for business. This is one of two spots in the park where swimming in thermally heated river water is openly permitted – the other, also called the Boiling River, is north of Mammoth (see p.50). The popular **swimming area** is accessed via a set of wooden steps, and it's a huge relief on a hot summer's day; there's no lifeguard on duty and bathing suits are required, and it's also a punishable offense to swim here when officially closed (typically from mid-Sept to mid-June). Beyond the riverside swim spot the drive meets back up with the main road at the **Firehole Cascades**, a narrow rocky channel causing the Firehole to pinball violently back and forth. It's a short way south to Fountain Flats Drive, the northern edge of the Lower Geyser Basin.

Old Faithful and around

The heart of Yellowstone's geyser country stretches fifteen miles along the steaming Firehole River, divided up between the **Lower**, **Midway**, **and Upper geyser basins**. The last of these is the largest, home to famed **Old Faithful** as well as the area's numerous amenities. But each of the basins boasts unique charms, and it takes at minimum a full day to properly explore them. It's easy to get overwhelmed by the seemingly endless collection of gushing geysers and gurgling hot springs, so it pays to break up a tour over several days if possible, sprinkling in hikes, a bike ride or fishing trip, or visits to nearby portions of the park not as focused on thermal features such as the Grand Canyon of the Yellowstone. Whether here for a few hours or a full week, your first point of order should be the **Old Faithful Visitor Center**, where the eruption times of six of the park's finest predictable geysers are posted. The Upper Basin's **Grand Geyser** and **Riverside Geyser** are both worth planning a day around, as is the eruption of **Great Fountain Geyser** in the Lower Basin.

The Lower Geyser Basin

The **Lower Geyser Basin** features a trio of diversions. Northernmost is **Fountain Flat Drive**, a mile long road leading southwest along the Firehole River. Used mainly by fly-fishermen, the road doesn't pass any thermal features of note, but dead ends at a **trailhead** from which hikers can tramp west to peaceful Sentinel Meadows and the ruined bathhouse by Queens Laundry (see H13 p.131). **Bikers** can pedal south along flat Fountain Freight Road five miles to the Fairy Falls Trailhead. South of the side road, the highway crosses over narrow Nez Perce Creek and through Fountain Flats, a smooth green expanse dotted with grazing bison throughout the early summer and capped with rising steam from the numerous geysers and springs to the south.

△Great Fountain Geyser

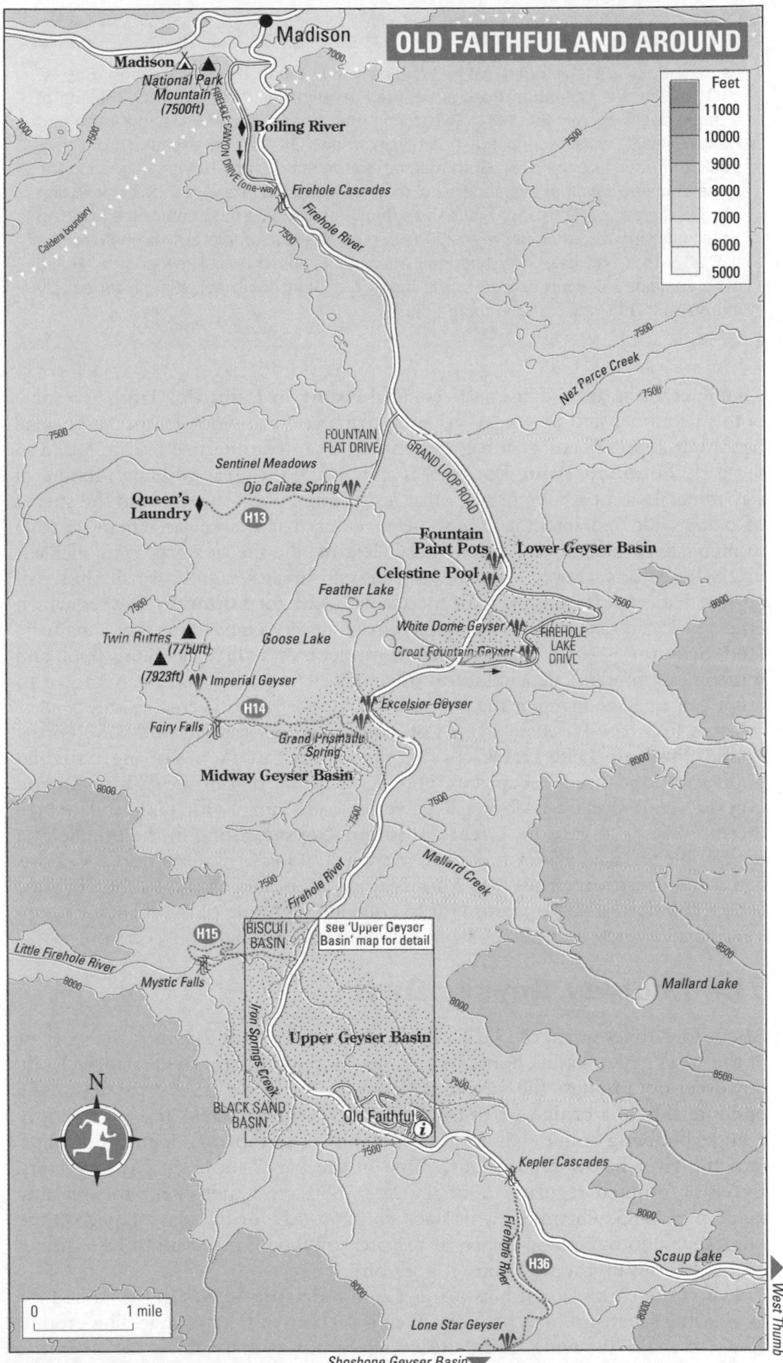
OLD FAITHFUL AND AROUND
Madison
Madison
National Park
Mountain
(7500ft)
FIREHOLE CANYON DRIVE (one-way)
Boiling River
Firehole Cascades
Firehole River
Caldera boundary
Feet
11000
10000
9000
8000
7000
6000
5000
Nez Perce Creek
FOUNTAIN
FLAT DRIVE
GRAND LOOP ROAD
Sentinel Meadows
Ojo Caliate Spring
Queen's
Laundry
H13
Fountain
Paint Pots
Lower Geyser Basin
Celestine Pool
Feather Lake
White Dome Geyser
FIREHOLE
LAKE
DRIVE
Great Fountain Geyser
Twin Buttes
(7750ft)
(7923ft)
Goose Lake
Imperial Geyser
H14
Excelsior Geyser
Fairy Falls
Grand Prismatic
Spring
Midway Geyser Basin
Mallard Creek
Firehole River
BISCUIT
BASIN
see 'Upper Geyser
Basin' map for detail
H15
Little Firehole River
Mystic Falls
Mallard Lake
Iron Springs Creek
Upper Geyser Basin
N
BLACK SAND
BASIN
Old Faithful
Kepler Cascades
Firehole River
H36
Scaup Lake
West Thumb
0
1 mile
Lone Star Geyser
Shoshone Geyser Basin

Celestine tragedy

As detailed by park historian Lee H. Whittlesey in *Death in Yellowstone* (see "Books" in Contexts), the **Celestine Pool** along the Fountain Paint Pot Trail was the site of a tragic death on July 20, 1981. Two young men from California, David Kirwan and Ronald Ratliff, were touring the boardwalk when Ratliff's dog escaped from their truck and dove into the pool. Both men ran to the spring, and Kirwan – ignoring the pleas from several other bystanders not to go in – stepped in and then dove head first into the deeper water to save his friend's dog. It only took a moment for the scalding water, later measured at just over 200°F, to burn Kirwan completely, and he died the day after in a Salt Lake City hospital. After being pulled out of the pool by Ratliff (who sustained second degree burns to his own feet doing so), Kirwan reportedly mumbled: "That was a stupid thing I did."

Some of this steam rises from the essential **Fountain Paint Pot Trail.** Accessible both in summer and in winter via snowcoach and snowmobile, the fairly small boardwalk loop offers a grab bag of every type of hydrothermal feature found in the park. **Fountain Paint Pot** itself is aptly named, a great gurgling mixture of clay minerals and particles of silica that just needs a good stir to blend the streaks of orange and red into the heavy cream color that dominates. There are two stunning, deep-blue pools – **Silex** and **Celestine**, the site of a gruesome incident in 1981 (see box, above) – a couple of hissing fumaroles, and a small cluster of geysers that erupt frequently if not spectacularly, save for **Fountain Geyser** which erupts between ten and fifty feet approximately every eight hours. The enigmatic **Red Spouter** is sometimes a fumarole, sometimes a dirty, bubbling pool, and sometimes a mudpot, depending on its supply of water; it's also been known to erupt like a geyser, giving it the attributes of all four hydrothermal features.

Across from the Fountain Paint Pot Trail is the exit for the one-way (northbound) **Firehole Lake Drive**, curving three miles past a series of angry, sizzling pools and pond-sized hot springs. Highlights of the detour are **White Dome Geyser**, a massive thirty-foot tall gesyerite cone rung with pink and orange thermophiles, and glorious **Great Fountain Geyser**, sitting in the middle of a remarkable terraced platform of sinter on which pools of water reflect sky above. Estimated **eruption times** (9–12 hours apart) are posted at Old Faithful's visitor center, and if possible plan your visit to coincide with one of the dramatic hour-long bursts, which average 100ft but can double that height on occasion.

The Midway Geyser Basin

About four miles north of Old Faithful, **Midway Geyser Basin** is the smallest of the area's geyser basins, home to only two noteworthy thermal features. Both, however, are amongst the largest and most electrifying in the park. On the opposite side of a bridge across the Firehole, **Excelsior Geyser** – now mostly a huge, bubbling crater – disgorges thousands of gallons of superheated water into the river below each minute. One of the park's more eccentric geysers, Excelsior erupted regularly until the late 1880s, and then went inexplicably quiet until 1985, when it blew its stack continuously for two days. Based on the impressive photograph on display at the site, you would not want to be standing on the boardwalk the next time it goes off.

Nearby, the park's largest hot spring, **Grand Prismatic Spring** is named for its amazing spectrum of rich colors, from royal blue to fiery orange. The ground views of the 370ft wide spring are certainly not as dramatic as the overhead

Steam cleaning and cooking

Over the years, Yellowstone's hydrothermal features have been put to numerous uses beyond selling postcards and calendars. Some of these long-gone practices were quickly banned – such as the **soaping** of geysers, which caused them to erupt quickly but also damaged their plumbing – but others were officially condoned. The tradition of coating specimens up in Mammoth is one such example (see box, p.49), while a separate money-making enterprise was started by Henry Brothers, who built the **Brothers Bathhouse and Plunge** by the *Old Faithful Inn* using thermal water from Solitary Geyser to fill a large swimming pool and a half-dozen smaller tubs. A much smaller operation, **Chinese Spring** directly north of Old Faithful was originally named Chinaman Springs after the Asian attendant who used it to clean visitor laundry. Similarly, **Handkerchief Pool** in the Black Sand Basin was used as a crowd-pleasing washing machine; rangers would instruct bystanders to drop a handkerchief inside, and wait as the hot water swirled it downwards and returned it minutes later. Not all made it back, however, and one ranger reported finding dozens of handkerchiefs as well as coins, a horseshoe, and even a spark plug upon trying to unplug the vent in 1929. Perhaps most famous of all was **Fishing Cone** in the West Thumb Geyser Basin, into whose boiling waters anglers dipped fresh-caught trout for decades, cooking a meal on the spot. For the most part, visitors are more respectful these days, though vandalism – from those tossing rocks, sticks, coins, and the like into the geysers – still occurs.

△ Heat and eat fishing in the 1890s

shots you'll see on postcards, but they're still worth the walk for flashes of bright color through the steam and a close up look at the acres of bright bacterial mats that surround it.

Just south of the basin is the **Fairy Falls Trailhead**, the starting point of a popular hike to the eponymous falls and Imperial Geyser beyond (see H14, p.131).

The Upper Geyser Basin

It's not a stretch to say everyone who visits Yellowstone also visits **Old Faithful**, an assertion reinforced by the many facilities and service buildings surrounding it in a giant half-circle. As if by some cosmic plan, the world-famous geyser sits alone at the southern tip of the **Upper Geyser Basin** in a spot that guarantees full attention. To the north, thermal features dot both sides of the Firehole River for two awe-inspiring miles, ending at **Biscuit Basin** on the opposite side of the highway. Alongside Iron Spring Creek, **Black Sand Basin** a half-mile west of Old Faithful completes the Upper Geyser Basin's colossal collection of geysers and pools.

Along with three large lodges, two general stores, and a backcountry ranger station, this is also where you'll find the **Old Faithful Visitor Center** (hours vary, but typically daily: summer 8am–7pm, rest of year 9am–5pm; ⓣ307/545-2750). Unfortunately, until the grand new center is finished in 2009, visitors will have to make due with a basic trailer office. There's little room for more than an information desk and bookstore, but this should be your first stop in any case to scribble down the estimated eruptions times for Old Faithful, Castle,

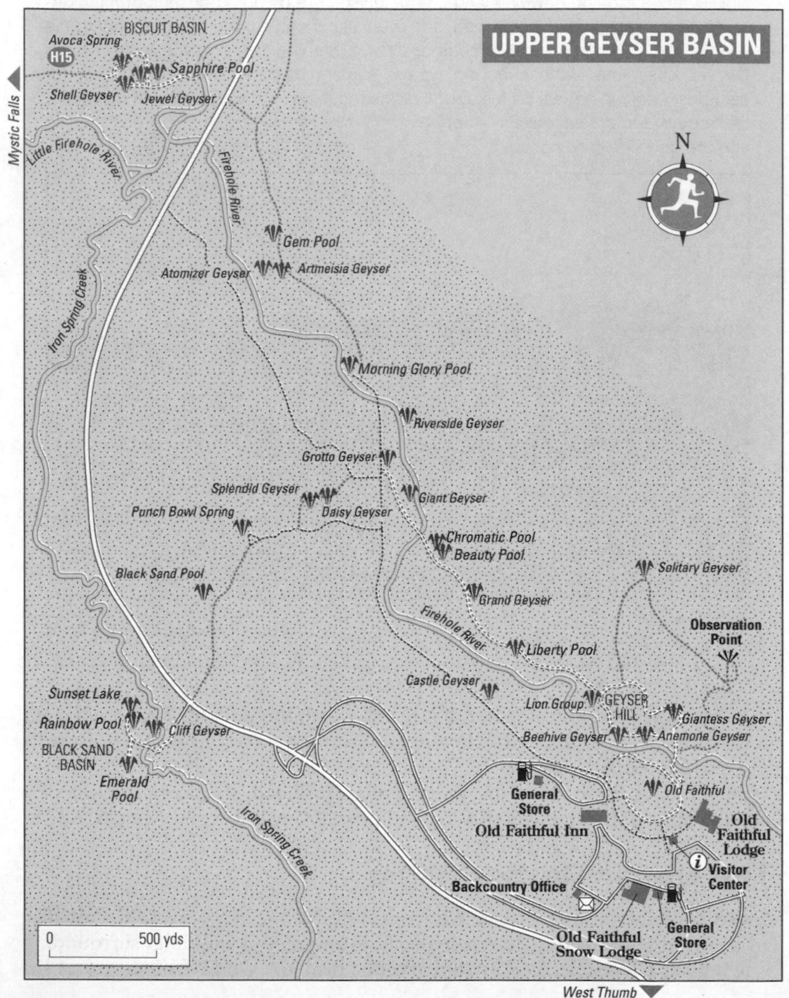

Grand, Daisy, Riverside, and Great Fountain geysers. Rangers also run several programs from the temporary quarters each day, including an hour-long guided walk around Geyser Hill.

The Old Faithful Inn and around

A suitable counterpoint to Yellowstone's most famous natural attraction, the shingle-coated **Old Faithful Inn** is the park's most glorious structure. Said to be the world's largest log building, the inn was built during the bitter winter of 1903–04 to satisfy the growing demand of upscale visitors wanting to spend more time in the Upper Geyser Basin. Architect **Robert C. Reamer** filled the interior with beams, banisters, railings, and other decorative flourishes built from gnarled and twisted branches, in an attempt to reflect the chaos of nature itself. Amidst this forest-like web, the seven-story **lobby** was built around a 500-ton, four-sided **fireplace** pieced together with rhyolite mined within the park. The main building, which features a series of steep roof peaks and is known as the "Old House," has lost none of its charm over the years, though additions of east and west wings have increased the original 140-room capacity to 329.

At the time of writing, the "Old House" was in the midst of a $20 million **renovation project**. A century of wear and tear, along with damage from a 1959 earthquake, had taken its toll on the building, though much of the needed renovation – new electric and plumbing, along with steel beam reinforcements – won't be noticeable when completed. The new architects did, however, spend years studying Reamer's old plans, and whenever possible they restored past changes to their original condition, including the return of the sunken sitting area round the main fireplace along with two guest rooms lost to storage over the years. Unfortunately, there are no plans to restore the upper viewing deck, from which guests used to watch midnight eruptions of Old Faithful illuminated by spotlight.

The *Old Faithful Inn* is one of several historic buildings in the area. The **Lower Hamilton Store**, which actually predates the inn by seven years, is the oldest structure still in use in the Upper Geyser Basin, featuring a one-of-a-kind knotty pine porch from which you watch geysers erupt in the distance. Closest of all to Old Faithful, the **Old Faithful Lodge** was designed in 1923 by another famed national park architect, Gilbert Stanley Underwood. The low log-and-stone lodge remains a rustic space, somewhat lost in the shadows of the *Old Faithful Inn* and modern *Snow Lodge* nearby, though it does have a full wall of windows and a porch facing out onto the great geyser. Inside, the sky can be seen through cracks in the roof, and chipmunks scurry around in search of crumbs from the onsite cafeteria and bakery.

Old Faithful

For well over a century, dependable **Old Faithful** has been the most popular geyser in the park, erupting more frequently than any of its higher or larger rivals. As a result, a half-moon of concentric benches now surround it at a respectful distance on the side away from the Firehole River; they quickly fill with hundreds of visitors in the minutes leading up to an eruption, and empty quicker still in a mad dash back to the parking area once the show ends. For any sense of privacy, you'll need to arrive around sunrise, visit at night when there's a bright full moon, or hike up to nearby Observation Point above Geyser Hill (see p.76).

While the legend that Old Faithful once blew off every hour, on the hour, never held true, the geyser's eruptions did, in fact, once average close to sixty minutes apart. Due to earthquakes rattling its underground plumbing over the years, the geyser now "performs" for the expectant crowds every 92 minutes on average, with a minimum gap of just under an hour and a maximum of three hours; approximate **schedules** are displayed in the visitor center and in the lobby of the *Old Faithful Inn*. The first sign of **activity** is a soft hissing as water splashes repeatedly over the rim. After several minutes, a narrow column of water shoots to a height of 105–185ft, the geyser spurting out as much as 8500 gallons of heated water.

Geyser Hill

A short walk across the Firehole from Old Faithful, **Geyser Hill** contains close to a dozen named hydrothermal features in a tight loop. The stubby **Beehive Geyser** doesn't look like much when inactive, but its tight cone combined with powerful plumbing forces a narrow spray as high as 200ft during its five-minute long eruptions (they occur, on average, twice a day). The nearby **Lion Group** is more active, with four geysers atop a large mound that "roar" when erupting.

Also on Geyser Hill is a mile-long trail leading up to **Observation Point**, from which you can watch Old Faithful and other nearby geysers erupt while sitting high above the action. If you take the stiff uphill hike, be sure to complete the trail by passing the scenic **Solitary Geyser** to the northwest; formerly a hot spring, Solitary began erupting after it was tapped in 1915 to fill the pools within the Brothers Bathhouse and Plunge (see box, p.73) near the *Old Faithful Inn*. Even though both the pipeline and pools are long gone, the geyser continues to erupt 5–10ft every few minutes.

The Upper Geyser Basin: Castle Geyser north to Gem Pool

Old Faithful is certainly the most famous geyser in the Upper Geyser Basin, but it's hardly the most spectacular. A few miles of boardwalk and paved path – much of the latter bike accessible – weave north from Old Faithful past dozens of other geysers, several of which spew higher or have a more attractive setting than their better-known sibling. Though its steamy blasts only reach 75ft, **Castle Geyser** is a must-see for its massive sinter cone, thought to be thousands of years old. The tallest predictable spouter in the park is **Grand Geyser**, located off the boardwalk on the opposite (east) side of the Firehole River. This colossus blows on average twice a day, for twelve to twenty minutes in a series of powerful bursts climbing to 200ft; don't be deterred by crowds – the show is worth waiting for. Further north, **Giant Geyser** may erupt only a dozen times per year, but the hour-long spurts reach as high as 250ft. Less powerful but more picturesque, **Riverside Geyser** is one of the park's most photogenic geyser (see box, opposite). Perched on the banks of the Firehole, the geyser blows for twenty minutes every six hours, spraying a 75ft tall tower of rainbow-streaked water over the river. Few leave the area without taking a snapshot of nearby **Grotto Geyser** as well, featuring a twisted cone that resembles a Hobbit hole carved from alabaster. Uphill from here to the west, **Daisy Geyser** is one of the most predictable geysers in the park, shooting a jet of water 70ft high at a conspicuous angle every three hours.

In this area too are a number of hot springs, with **Morning Glory Pool** the most attractive – it's well worth the 1.5 mile walk or bike ride from Old Faithful to eyeball the pool's yellow-orange outer rings and mesmerizing blue depths. Perfectly named after the funnel-shaped flower, Morning Glory has

Kipling's tour

Decades before becoming the first English language writer to win the Nobel Prize for Literature, British writer **Rudyard Kipling** toured the world as a travel writer, publishing his tales in various newspapers (collected in his *From Sea to Sea: Letters of Travel*). After visiting Burma, China, and Japan, Kipling traveled to the United States, where in 1889 he embarked on a stagecoach tour of Yellowstone National Park. While his acerbic account spends much of its time teasing the park's visitors and soldiers, he also wrote eloquently about the "howling wilderness... full of all imaginable freaks of fiery nature." A bubbling pool was likened to a "goblin splashing in his tub," while the eruption of Old Faithful was "a plume of spun glass, iridescent and superb, against the sky." One of his most entertaining accounts within the "miraculous valley" of the Upper Geyser Basin takes place at **Riverside Geyser**, a description that continues to ring true 120 years later:

"I think they call it Riverside Geyser. Its spout was torn and rugged like the mouth of a gun when a shell has burst there. It grumbled madly for a moment or two and then was still. I crept over the steaming lime – it was the burning marl on which Satan lay – and looked fearfully down its mouth. You should never look a gift geyser in the mouth. I beheld a horrible slippery, slimy funnel with water rising and falling ten feet at a time. Then the water rose to lip level with a rush and an infernal bubbling troubled this Devil's Bethesda before the sullen heave of the crest of wave lapped over the edge and made me run. Mark the nature of the human soul! I had begun with awe, not to say terror. I stepped back from the flanks of the Riverside Geyser saying: "Pooh! Is that all it can do?" Yet for aught I knew the whole thing might have blown up at a minute's notice; she, he, or it being an arrangement of uncertain temper."

lost some of its lustre over the years thanks to vandals tossing vent-blocking objects, including seemingly innocuous stones and branches, into the pool. No bikes are allowed past Morning Glory, but consider hoofing out another half-mile north to stare into the sparkling blue depths of **Artemisia Geyser** and **Gem Pool**.

Biscuit and Black Sand basins

Biscuit Basin, three-miles north of Old Faithful, is named for the biscuit-shaped rocks that used to ring **Sapphire Pool** until an earthquake in 1959 blew them away. The pool is still true blue, moving from bright yellow on its edges to a deep turquoise center. Beyond Sapphire, an easy boardwalk loop leads past several lesser hydrothermal features to the trailhead for Mystic Falls (see H15 p.132). **Black Sand Basin** to the south has its own distinct charms; here a plateau of volcanic black sand is split by gurgling Iron Spring Creek. Attractions include some very pretty hot pools, including the deep-green **Emerald Pool** and gorgeous **Sunset Lake**, whose central geyser sends waves lapping constantly onto vermilion shores, and creekside **Cliff Geyser**, looking like the perfect six-person hot tub until it spurts out boiling water 30ft into the air. You can walk or cycle along paved paths from the Old Faithful area to Biscuit Basin and Black Sand Basin.

East to West Thumb

The highway east from Old Faithful to the West Thumb junction climbs, swoops, and dips as relentlessly as a seventeen-mile-long roller-coaster track.

A couple miles from Old Faithful, a viewing platform juts over the Firehole River for a head on view of the **Kepler Cascades**, a 125ft-long streak of whitewater tumbling down three separate steps. The nearby Lone Star Trailhead is the entry point for a flat roadbed along the Firehole River to **Lone Star Geyser** less then three miles away (see H36 p.154); it's a popular route with both joggers and bikers in summer, and cross-country skiers come winter. After climbing steeply east to Craig Pass (8262ft) and over the Continental Divide for the first time (it crosses again south of Grant Village), the highway passes the **Delacey Creek Trailhead**. The popular trail here is the shortest path to **Shoshone Lake**, considered the largest backcountry lake in the contiguous United States, three miles due south.

West Thumb, Grant Village, and around

It takes a creative mind to picture it on current maps, but early explorers drew **Yellowstone Lake** in the shape of a left hand, hanging downwards as if ready to pinch **Heart Lake** to the south. Thanks to this bit of anthromorphic cartography, the lake's westernmost extension became known simply as **West Thumb**. Connected by a narrow neck, the "thumb" is actually a caldera within a caldera, created by a powerful volcanic explosion 160,000 years ago that eventually filled with water. These underground forces are plenty visible today at the **West Thumb Geyser Basin**, easily the largest collection of hydrothermal features on Yellowstone Lake. South of the geyser basin is humdrum **Grant Village**, the park's southernmost base and best visited for its visitor center.

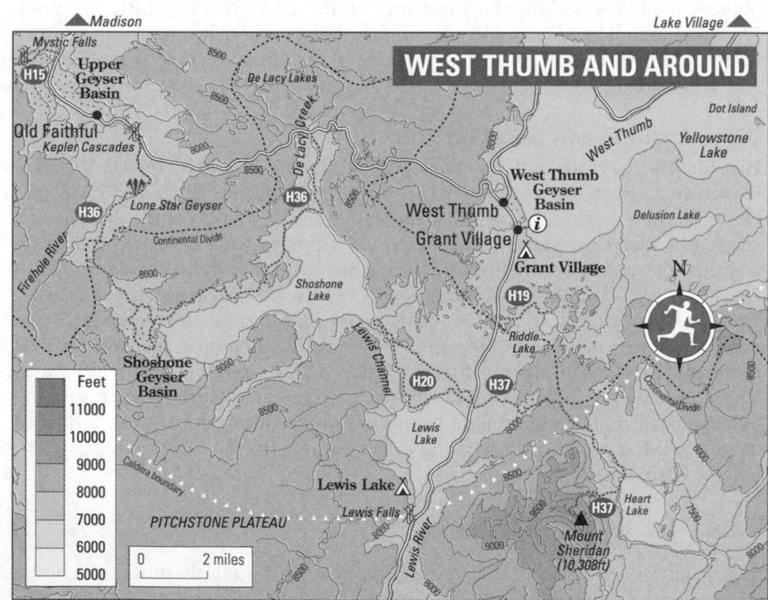

West Thumb Geyser Basin

Although it lacks the explosiveness of the geysers in the Old Faithful area, **West Thumb Geyser Basin** boasts an astonishing setting, perched right on the edge of Yellowstone Lake, with the Absaroka Mountains clearly visible far across the eastern shores. A string of hot pools empty right into the tranquil waters and fizz away into nothing, and it's easy to see why early tourists made use of the so-called **Fishing Cone** hot spring on the lake's edge by cooking fresh-caught fish in its boiling waters. Fishing by the now-dormant cone, which is covered by rising waters until mid-summer, was banned after a fisherman was burnt by an eruption in the 1920s. A half-mile of boardwalk loops around the geyser basin, starting near a log hut built in 1925 as a backcountry ranger station (now a bookstore in summer and warming hut in winter; daily ranger tours depart from here 10am and 4pm in summer). From the hut, the path leads past a string of pools and springs and around the lake's edge. One of these, the eye-catching **Abyss Pool**, does indeed look bottomless; it's actually 53ft deep – one of the park's deepest – and has been known to erupt as high as 100ft. The boardwalk curves right up to the edge of **Black Pool**, letting you peer down into its formerly dark 40ft depths that now sparkle green, indicating lower water temperatures than bright blue pools. Elsewhere in the basin, a set of mud pots bubble away contentedly while fumaroles blow a steady stream of steam into the air. While there have been no regular geyser eruptions in recent years, the collection of otherworldly-colors and the stunning lake vista make this basin unmissable – try early morning for a breathtaking sunrise over the water.

Grant Village

In part to protect encroaching thermal features, the marina, cafeteria, and cabins that were once located at the West Thumb highway junction were torn down in the early 1980s and the action was moved to **Grant Village**. The unsightly development is named after Ulysses S. Grant, the eighteenth president of the United States, who signed the bill creating Yellowstone National Park in 1872. The former Civil War hero also has a picturesque peak by Frost Lake on the park's eastern border named after him, a more fitting tribute.

While handy for its general store, backcountry office, and post office, there's little order to the hodgepodge collection of buildings strung along the drive leading down to the waterside *Lake House* eatery. The restaurants and indoor accommodations are some of the least inspired in the park, though to be fair the sites at the large campground are pleasantly wooded. The main reason to visit is the **Grant Village Visitor Center** (daily: late May to early Sept 8am–7pm, early Sept to late Sept 9am–6pm; ⓣ307/242-2650). The park fires of 1988 are chronicled here (see box, p.80), with video footage and an account of the fierce debate about the role of fire in regeneration that has not entirely subsided since. Look out for the display dedicated to the amazing **lodgepole pine**, Yellowstone's most common tree. Though not true of all lodgepoles, many of the female trees of this species sprout serotinous cones that open to spread their seeds only after being blasted by the heat of a forest fire, a major reason why these trees are so common in recently burnt areas.

The South Entrance Road

There are really no major sights on the twenty miles of road from Grant Village south to Yellowstone's **South Entrance**, but there's certainly plenty to do as several

The Fires of 1988

The now infamous **summer of 1988** started off like most others in Yellowstone. Rainfall had been slightly above average through April and May, and while lightning started a few forest fires, there was little reason to be concerned and most burnt themselves out as expected. June, however, brought near drought conditions, and the moisture content of trees and grasses dipped to dangerously low levels. The hope that July would bring rain never came to pass, and by the middle of that month it was obvious the park's natural fire program would need to be suspended.

By the end of July, firefighters were called in to battle the many fires burning throughout the park. It was an impossible fight, however, as high winds combined with low humidity and the already dry wood to cause a firestorm of epic proportions. All in all, **51 separate fires** – nine caused by humans, the rest by lightning – raged, some burning as high as 200ft and leaping across chasms as wide as the Grand Canyon of the Yellowstone. Several of the park's villages, including Old Faithful and Grant Village, had to be evacuated, as did outlying towns. All in all, some 25,000 people were employed in battling the blazes at a cost of $120 million, and miraculously only one life was lost. Thanks to both a bit of luck and the heroic efforts of the firefighters, historic buildings like the *Old Faithful Inn* were saved. Snowfalls in September finally tamed the blazes, but not before 36 percent of Yellowstone – some 800,000 acres – had burned, with even more razed in the surrounding national forests.

The sight of the country's flagship national park in flames was broadcast as a public relations disaster. Park authorities correctly insisted the burn was a natural part of the forest's eco-cycle, clearing out 200-year-old trees to make way for new growth, but a long list of **dire predictions** were nonetheless made. Some argued the mass of downed and dead trees would lead to another major fire, or claimed visitor numbers would drop precipitously and never climb back. There's no doubt that Yellowstone's ecosystem has changed, including a major decline in the moose population and the fact that slow-growth trees like whitebark pine and Engelmann spruce will require decades to return. But twenty years later it's abundantly clear the ecosystem is still alive and well, thanks in part to this dramatic and necessary burst of new growth.

important trailheads branch both east and west off the highway. The first of these, just beyond the sign indicating the Continental Divide, is the **Riddle Lake Trailhead**, from where it's an easy stroll out to its eponymous lake (see H19, p.135). Just two miles further south, the highway passes the **Shoshone/Dogshead Trailhead** (see H20, p.136) and the **Heart Lake Trailhead** (see H37, p.155), with **Mount Sheridan** (10,308ft) towering over Heart Lake to the east. Combining a small backcountry geyser basin, an appealing isolated lake, and stupendous panoramic views, the latter is one of the finest hikes in Yellowstone. From here, the highway hugs the eastern shore of **Lewis Lake** for two miles, giving roadside fishermen a chance to cast for a variety of trout. The lake's southern end is home to the wooded *Lewis Lake Campground*, as well as a boat dock giving paddlers a chance to explore backcountry Shoshone Lake via the Lewis Channel.

South of the campground turnoff, the road meets up with the **Lewis River** by **Lewis Falls**, where tour buses stop to let visitors arriving from the south snap photos of the rather underwhelming 30ft cascade. The road progressively gets higher above the sparkling blue band, with viewpoints looking across the steep **Lewis Canyon**. It's a dramatic scene, not the least because most of the area is still heavily scarred with fire damage from 1988; look out for the interpretive sign explaining how 50mph winds allowed the fires to hopscotch across the 500-yard wide canyon. A mile from the South Entrance Station, the road crosses over Crawfish Creek. A parking area to the northeast accesses a short path to pretty **Moose Falls**, a 30ft plunge bracketed on both sides by moss-covered rocks dotted with wildflowers. Fishermen often stop here, as do swimmers and sunbathers on the hottest of summer days. At the boundary, the highway meets up with the **Snake River** and enters the John D. Rockefeller Parkway, covered in detail in Chapter 3.

Lake Village and around

It takes only a moment's glance to realize a simple fact about **Yellowstone Lake** (7732ft) – it's massive. According to famed mountain man and storyteller Jim Bridger (see box, p.64), the lake was so big that just before going to sleep he could yell "wake up!" across the water and then doze blissfully while the echo crossed the water, eventually returning to rouse him from his slumbers hours later. The lake's actual figures need no such exaggeration: it boasts a **surface area** of 132 square miles with a shoreline 141 miles in length. Completely natural – the Yellowstone River flowing in from the south and out to the north is the longest undammed river in the continental US – the average depth is around 140ft, with the deepest known underwater canyon stretching a whopping 430ft downward. And it used to be even bigger, at one point reaching 200ft higher and covering ground as far north as the **Hayden Valley**.

Despite its size and central location, there's actually not a great deal of activity on the water itself. Yellowstone Lake doesn't suffer fools gladly, nor does it take

△ Yellowstone Lake

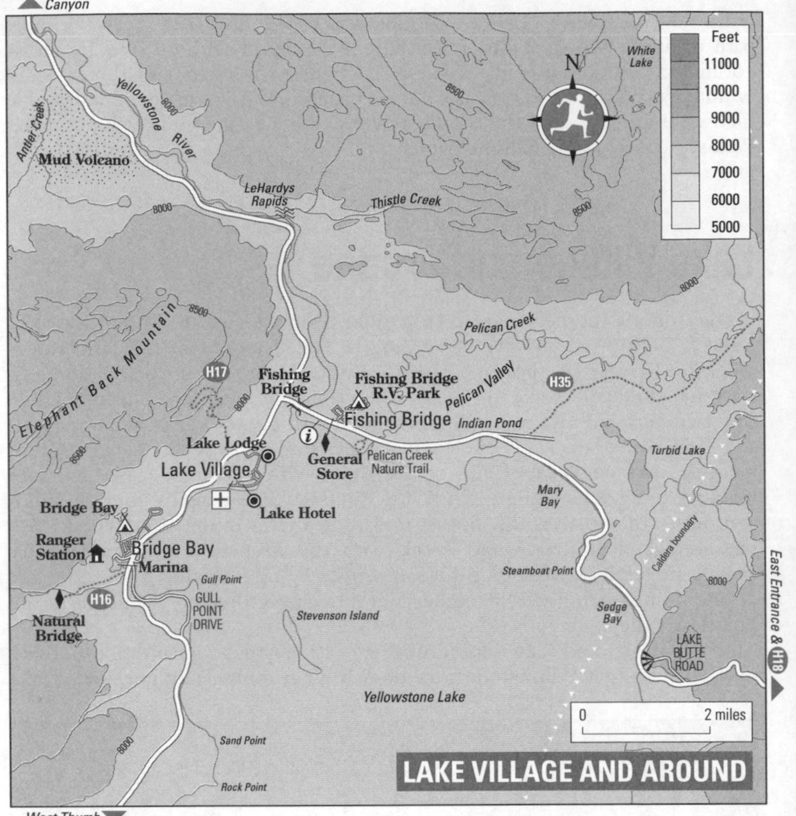

all that kindly to even the most knowledgeable rowers and sailors. It only takes a few minutes for the wind to churn the calm surface into six-foot waves, and by late August the **surface temperature** peaks at a still uncomfortable 65°F. Typically frozen for half the year (late Dec to late May), average water temperatures are closer to 45°F, meaning a paltry survival time of only 15–20 minutes if forced to swim. Plenty of fishermen do head out to try their luck with cutthroat trout and the invasive lake trout (see box, p.84), and canoers and kayakers hit the water to camp overnight at one of forty backcountry campsites lining the shore. It's highly recommended that first-timers only attempt these activities with a knowledgeable guide.

Still, there's plenty to do around the lake, from hiking and biking to wildlife watching or simply gazing across it towards the Absaroka Mountains marching along the eastern shore. The busiest hub is **Lake Village**, home to the swanky **Lake Yellowstone Hotel** as well as the more rustic **Lake Lodge**. To the south, **Bridge Bay** is where you'll find the lake's sole marina, while north is **Fishing Bridge**, at one time an exceedingly busy junction but now more relaxed after the park service moved many facilities from here to protect bear habitat. The highway north from Fishing Bridge passes by both **Mud Volcano** and the picture perfect Hayden Valley en rout to Canyon

Village, while the road east climbs up and over the Absarokas to the **East Entrance** and Cody beyond.

Bridge Bay

For most of the way, the twenty miles of highway between West Thumb north to **Bridge Bay** stick to the shores of Yellowstone Lake. Around a half-dozen designated picnic areas line the road, but there are few sights in particular to look out for save for **Gull Point Drive**, just before Bridge Bay itself. The two-mile side road hugs the lake even closer with a straight on view of **Stevenson Island**, just over a mile offshore and named after James Stevenson, second in command on the Hayden Expeditions (1871–72) and possibly one of the first men to climb Grand Teton (see the box on p.108 for more on this controversial claim). Across from the northern entrance to Gull Point Drive, the trailhead for the **Natural Bridge** is a span of rock under a mile away (see H17, 133). Bridge Bay itself is a gem of a sheltered bay that's home to Yellowstone Lake's sole **marina**, a small store (bait available), and rangers station, along with the park's largest campground. Motorized and non-motorized boats can be rented, and both fishing trips and pleasure cruises are charted as well; see Chapter 6, "Summer activities," for full details.

Lake Village

Located between Bridge Bay to the south and Fishing Bridge to the north, **Lake Village** is centered around the sprawling **Lake Yellowstone Hotel**. With a section dating back to 1889, the buttercup-yellow inn is the oldest standing building in Yellowstone. The original eighty-room hotel was much more basic, built by the Yellowstone Park Association, a front for the Northern Pacific Railroad. Guests would often arrive via steamship across the lake from West Thumb, one of the reasons the hotel's frontside faces the lake and away from the road leading in. When architect Robert Reamer began the *Old Faithful Inn* in 1903, he was also asked to expand the *Lake Yellowstone Hotel*, and the grand Southern-mansion style building seen today is mostly his creation. The tall ionic columns and fifteen false balconies Reamer added created a structure a world apart from the overgrown log cabin at Old Faithful, a testament to the architect's wide-ranging aesthetic. Thanks to a ten-year renovation begun in 1981, the wooden hotel has aged gracefully, and it remains one of the finest places to stay in the park. Even if not staying or eating at one of the park's best dining rooms, the hotel is worth quick tour or, better yet, an evening drink in the airy "Sun Room" looking over the lake.

Also fronting the grassy expanse on the lakeside of the hotel are the **Lake Clinic** (see p.29), a small general store, and the **Lake Ranger Station**, built in 1923 soon after the army left Yellowstone. Designed in part by then Superintendent Horace Albright, the log cabin features an octagonal community room built around a stone fireplace where rangers could exchange stories after a day in the field. Further away but within walking distance, the **Lake Lodge** was built two years earlier to accommodate the new influx of car-driving visitors. A much larger yet still cozy and intimate log building, it's a handy stopping point for the onsite cafeteria and laundry, as well as for the roaring fireplaces and comfortable couches that make for particularly welcome respite on cold and rainy days.

Just north of Lake Village en route to Fishing Bridge a mile north, the road passes by the trailhead for **Elephant Back Mountain** (see H17 p.134); it's a moderately stiff hike that rewards visitors with good views over the *Lake Hotel* and the vast lake beyond.

Fishing Bridge

The Yellowstone River flows north out of Yellowstone Lake at **Fishing Bridge**. The outlet is a major spawning ground for native **cutthroat**, who swim here in great numbers starting in early June to lay eggs in the river bottom's gravel bed. The actual Fishing Bridge spanning the neck of the river was a popular fishing spot dating back to its original construction in 1902, with anglers lined up pole to pole along its length. Fishing has been banned from the existing bridge (erected in 1937) since the early 1970s to protect the native trout, but you can still linger on it to observe fish swimming below along with their predators, including grizzlies and bald eagles.

The tiny cluster of amenities east of the bridge consist of a gas station, the *Fishing Bridge RV Park*, and the most pleasantly atmospheric **General Store** in

Paradise recovered… for now

A haven for fly-fishermen, Yellowstone's **fisheries** were nearly paradise-lost decades ago and remain a fragile ecosystem today, with new threats present or poised to arrive soon. By the 1960s, nearly a century of rampant overfishing and poor management practices forced officials into the unpopular move of banning the sport from some of the most well-liked areas, including Fishing Bridge where visitors used to line shoulder-to-shoulder throughout the summer. As more fishermen arrived, regulations got increasingly strict, leading to a **complete ban** on keeping native sport fish caught within Yellowstone in 2001. These rules have certainly helped the local cutthroat, arctic grayling, and mountain whitefish populations, but the biggest problems plaguing the region's rivers and lakes stem from **invasive and non-native species**, a much tougher foe to conquer.

Stocking no longer occurs within the park, but managers had run major stocking programs from the park's inception through the 1950s. **Brook**, **brown** and **rainbow trout** were all introduced into the park's rivers, while Shoshone and Lewis lakes were filled with **lake trout**. It's uncertain just how lake trout got into Yellowstone Lake –some believe it was the work of a single self-interested individual – but soon after the first one was reeled up in 1994, it was clear that the lake's cutthroat population was in mortal danger. A single adult lake trout eats 50–60 cutthroat a year, and this is more than just bad news for anglers. The loss of cutthroat would be devastating to the local bear and eagle population, just two of more than forty mammals and birds who rely on cutthroat as part of their diet. Lake trout are now *piscis non grata* in Yellowstone, and officials are doing all they can to reduce, if not eliminate the invader. Gill nets have been used to catch hundreds of lake trout at a time, and there's no creel-limit on lake trout while fishing on Yellowstone Lake; in fact, all lake trout caught in the lake and its tributaries must be killed on the spot. The fight to protect local cutthroat – split into the Yellowstone, Westslope, and Snake River subspecies – is being waged in local rivers as well, where non-native trout are overpowering them. Attempts to place the fish on the endangered species list have repeatedly been blocked, but both park officials and dedicated non-profits have pressed on with heroic plans. In one such example, a strategy to restore Westslope cutthroat to creeks in Yellowstone's northwest corner was approved in 2006; miraculously, a stream of previously unknown genetically-pure Westslope were found in an isolated stream the summer previous, and it is hoped these fish can kick-start a revival of pure cutthroat. For more information or to get involved, check Ⓦ www.greateryellowstone.org.

the park, with a diner tucked into the back. Opposite all of this is the historic **Fishing Bridge Visitor Center** (daily: late May to early Sept 8am–7pm, early Sept to late Sept 9am–6pm; ⓣ307/242-2450). Built in 1931 by Herbert Maier, who created the similar structures at Norris and Madison, the arresting native rock and log building looks like the lakeside vacation home of Snow White's seven dwarves. There's a relaxed information desk and bookstore inside, along with a room full of exhibits dedicated to the birds of Yellowstone. The display cases holding stuffed models nearly eighty years old include sandhill cranes, osprey, and a particularly ferocious bald eagle fit in perfectly with the antiquated mood of the building. On Yellowstone Lake behind the visitor center is a long stretch of sandy **beach**. As the water here is some of the shallowest and warmest in the lake, the beautiful beach is a great spot to picnic and even soak in the sun on hot summer days.

North to Canyon

The highway north from Fishing Bridge follows alongside the Yellowstone River, which is flat and wide for the most part as it flows towards the chaos of Upper and Lower Falls at Canyon, fifteen miles away (covered in Chapter 1, "Northern Yellowstone"). The most animated stretch of water en route is **LeHardys Rapids**, where a short boardwalk follows the riverbank. During June and July it's possible to see cutthroat trout leaping upstream on their way to spawn near Fishing Bridge three miles south. There's no fishing allowed around the rapids themselves, but the river on either side is popular with anglers once the season opens on July 15.

Mud Volcano

You will have already visited a geyser basin or two before arriving at **Mud Volcano** a few miles north, and if you thought the outpouring of sulphurous gases was an intense olfactory experience you're in for a real treat here. Thanks to a higher level of acidity, this collection of mudpots and cauldrons make up the moodiest and ugliest of the park's thermal regions; a one-mile boardwalk winds through gurgling pools of sickly grey and yellow mud, past trees that have been steamed to death, to the bleak, barren shores of **Sour Lake** – the perfect set for a horror movie. Joining a free ranger led tour (June–Aug daily 1pm) here gives you the chance to get off the boardwalk and into the backcountry, where the **Big Gumper**, which blew into existence in the 1970s, bubbles with big gray globs of smelly mud.

Across the road from Mud Volcano is a single, isolated feature simply called **Sulphur Cauldron**. It won't surprise you to learn that sickly yellow arrowhead-shaped bubbling pool is thought to be the most acidic in the entire park, with a pH equivalent to that of battery acid. Groups of bison often congregate in the Mud Volcano area, and bison-jams may hold up traffic for some minutes.

The Hayden Valley

After the terrors of Mud Volcano, the sight of **Hayden Valley** due north is literally a breath of fresh air. Indeed, there may not be a more sudden change in the landscape anywhere else in region, from pallid stinking mudpots to a vast, blue-sky valley that is one of the finest habitats for bear, bison, and elk in the country. The Yellowstone River winds its way north across the wide open plain of the valley floor, a patchwork of dusty green grasses, silvery gray sagebrush

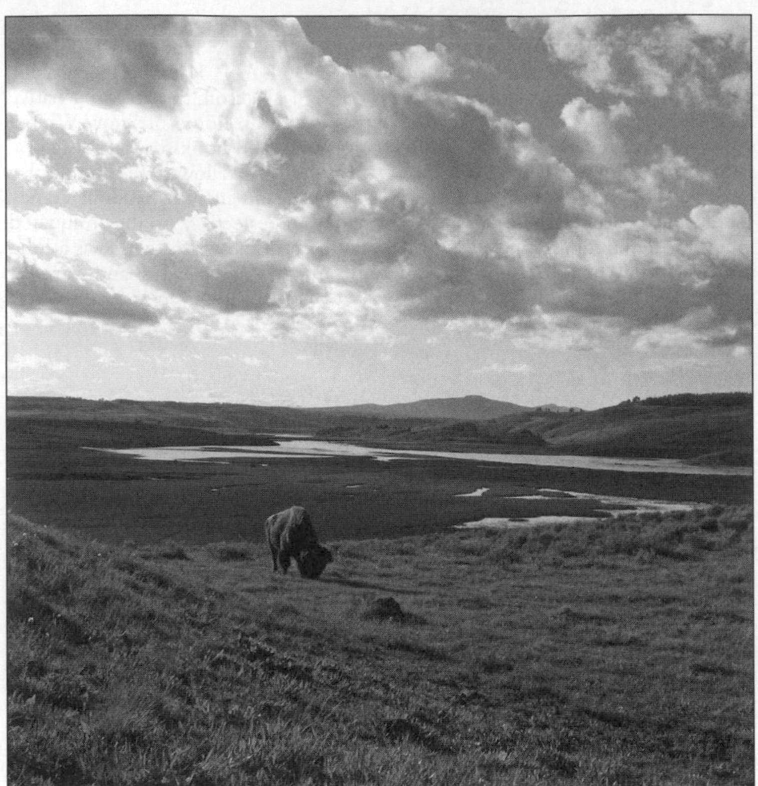

△ Hayden Valley

and the crystalline blue waters of Trout, Elk Antler, and Alum creeks. Only the Lamar Valley to the north is more popular with **wildlife spotters**, and during the sunrise and even more spectacular sunset hours the roadside turnouts fill with spectators. It's not unusual to look over literally hundreds of bison and elk grazing peacefully, while numerous waterfowl and even beaver can be scoped swimming on the rivers and creeks below. The biggest crowd-pleasers, grizzly bears and wolves, roam through the valley as well; at the time of writing, the **Hayden wolf pack** had become particularly active, hunting and killing both bison and elk in full view of the crowds.

The East Entrance Road

The highway east from Fishing Bridge bends around the northeast shores of Yellowstone Lake before working up and over Sylvan Pass on the way to the **East Entrance**, 27 miles away. Even if not heading to Cody, at the very least head a mile east of Fishing Bridge to view one of the finest sights along the entire stretch, the **Pelican Valley**. Shifting from wet marshlands in May and early June to a meadow of dusty yellow grasses dotted with grazing bison by late August, the valley is of vital importance to area wildlife, including grizzly bears who have historically flocked here in spring to hunt for spawning trout.

Whirling disease and lake trout (see box, p.84) have wrecked havoc on the native cutthroat in **Pelican Creek**, however, and fishing is now banned throughout the entire valley. To further protect wildlife, overnight camping is forbidden though there are still some very worthwhile trails here. When bison are present, visitors park at the bridge over Pelican Creek to take photos of the tranquil scene, while just west the half-mile **Pelican Creek Nature Trail** is worth a stroll to the lakeshore when dry later in summer. Past the bridge, a side road across from **Indian Pond** leads to the popular **Pelican Valley Trailhead** (see H35, p.153); Indian Pond itself was formed by a hydrothermal blowout that created a crater in which water eventually pooled.

Beyond here the highway rounds pretty **Mary Bay** – a particularly good spot for grizzly-spotting in spring and early summer – and past numerous thermal features puffing away near the lake's edge, including **Steamboat Springs**. Plenty of lakeside pullouts line the curvy road, giving drivers a chance to enjoy the views safely. After cutting away from the lake, the highway leads through a mile of heavily burnt forest to **Lake Butte Road**, a top spot for photographers and hopeless romantics at sunset; heading uphill for a mile, the side road leads to a superb **viewpoint** over the lake from which the jagged Tetons can be seen, with the rounded hump of Mount Sheridan in the foreground.

At the time of writing, the final third of the highway beyond Sylvan Pass closed nightly 8pm–8am for major **road construction**, with frequent half-hour long delays throughout the day. Check the park's website or call ahead (T307/344-2117) for the latest updates.

Avalanche Peak and Sylvan Pass

Along with travelers heading to Cody via the surreal Wapiti Valley (covered in Chapter 15), peak-bagging hikers should continue east towards the park boundary. For seven twisting miles from Lake Butte Road, the highway climbs up the **Absaroka Range** to narrow Sylvan Lake, where the serrated pinnacle of Top Notch Peak (10,245ft) looms in background. Just beyond, opposite tiny Eleanor Lake, is the trailhead for **Avalanche Peak** (10,566ft; see H18, p.134), one of the best peak hikes in Yellowstone. After cresting at Sylvan Pass (8530ft), the roadside views get even more stunning, the north side dominated by immense cliffs while a heavily forested canyon formed by **Middle Creek** lines the south side. Descending some 1500ft from the pass, the road eventually passes through the isolated East Entrance Station at Middle Creek itself, together leading east to meet with the North Fork of the Shoshone River.

Cascade Corner

At any given time, Yellowstone's isolated **Cascade Corner** has about as many miles of trails as it does visitors. Known alternatively as the **Bechler** (Beck-ler) area, the southwest corner of the park is unconnected by road to any other portion of the park, and is reachable only by trails heading down from the north or via the dirt Cave Falls Road from Ashton, Idaho, to the west or the even bumpier Grassy Lake Road from Flagg Ranch to the east (see p.114). The only permanent sign of occupation is around the **Bechler Ranger Station**, a cluster of small buildings including the Bechler River Soldier Station erected by the army in 1911 as an outpost to curtail poaching in the area.

Named for its wealth of **waterfalls** – most of which spill off of the **Bechler** and **Falls rivers** – the Cascade Corner is rustic, rugged and quite scenic, with very little in the way of amenities or roadside sights. The five thousand or so visitors who come here each summer to hike, horseback, and fish are rewarded with plenty of peace and solitude.

The drive in ends at **Cave Falls**, which drops only 20ft but is Yellowstone's widest at 250ft across. The rest of the fifty-plus waterfalls must be seen either on foot or on horseback, including **Union Falls**, a 250ft plunge widely considered Yellowstone's prettiest waterfall (see H22, p.137). Equally memorable is the **Bechler Meadows**, a vast ocean of grass with the backside of the Tetons visible to the south (see H21, p.137). While only these two hikes have been listed in the guide, there are dozens of other options, including an unforgettable three-night trip starting from Old Faithful in the north and covering thirty miles, mainly along the Bechler River Trail, to the Bechler Ranger Station.

Bechler practicalities

Due to heavy snowpack, plenty of rain, and marshy meadows, travel within the Cascade Corner is not recommended until mid-July. Even if you don't mind the knee-deep mud, most of the rivers will be too swift and deep to ford regardless before this time, limiting your travel options immensely. While the many waterfalls are at their strongest earlier in the summer, the best time to visit is between mid-August and mid-September, when trails are dry (or drier) and the plentiful bugs are at their least ferocious. The park doesn't run any drive-in camping facilities, though the Targhee National Forest's **Cave Falls Campground** directly south of the Yellowstone boundary rarely fills up. A quick drive from Cave Falls, the campground has 23 well-spaced sites, most spread along the Falls River, for only $8 a night. There are numerous **backcountry sites** strung along the area trails, and permits can be organized at the Bechler Ranger Station, where you should check in even if day-hiking. You'll have to bring along all food and drink, as the closest supermarket is an hour's drive west in tiny Ashton, Idaho.

3

Grand Teton

The majesty of the peaks within **GRAND TETON NATIONAL PARK** has always left wide-eyed onlookers searching for ways to best describe them. Native tribes had numerous names for the jagged spires, from the Three Brothers to the evocative Hoary Headed Fathers, the seemingly age-old peaks commonly dusted in silvery snow. The Shoshone knew them as the *Teewinot* ("many pinnacles"), while early white explorers called the range the Pilot Knobs, sky-high lighthouses used to navigate the surrounding wilderness. The designation that stuck, *Les Trois Tetons* (literally "The Three Breasts"), was bestowed in the 1830s by imaginative, if sex-starved, French-Canadian fur-trappers as they approached the mountains from the west.

The mountains themselves are so much the dominant feature of Grand Teton's 485 square miles that it's just as well to be able to identify the major summits before describing much else. While the forty-mile-long Teton Range comprises twelve main peaks over 12,000ft, there are six clearly dominant points; in order from south to north, these are **Nez Perce** (11,901ft), **Middle Teton** (12,804ft), **Grand Teton** (13,770ft), naturally the tallest of the bunch, **Mount Owen** (12,928ft), **Teewinot Mountain** (12,325ft), and the hulking mass of **Mount Moran** (12,605ft) looming apart from the rest. The mountains are an obvious magnet for both hardy hikers and skilled climbers, along with the subject of countless photographs – the Tetons are reputedly listed third behind Mount Fujiyama and the Matterhorn as the most photographed mountains on earth.

The string of peaks, however, occupies only the western third of the park, which was created in 1929 and expanded two decades later. Attracting a comparable share of attention from the 2.5 million annual visitors are the lakes and rivers to the east along the floor of Jackson Hole. The ribbon of pretty glacial lakes, including gem-like **Jenny Lake**, hugging the range's base are largely the scene of idyllic gazing and the occasional chilly swim, while larger **Jackson Lake** – essentially a reservoir created by Jackson Lake Dam – buzzes with sailboats, row-boating fisherman, and motorboats towing waterskiers throughout the summer. And the somewhat tamed **Snake River**, known by early explorers as the Mad River for its ferocious pre-dam run-off, draws fly-fisherman and float-trips down its grand southern flow.

As the flat valley floor of Jackson Hole hosted settler homesteads for decades before being turned into a national park – even today chunks of privately owned land remain within the boundaries – there are also several **historical attractions** worth visiting, from the photogenic remains of ranch buildings to a restored ferry crossing manned by a docent in period dress. And **wildlife**, while not as bountiful as in Yellowstone to the north, is still plentiful; indeed, you're more likely to spot a moose chomping willows around Jackson Lake and the Gros Ventre River than anywhere in Yellowstone.

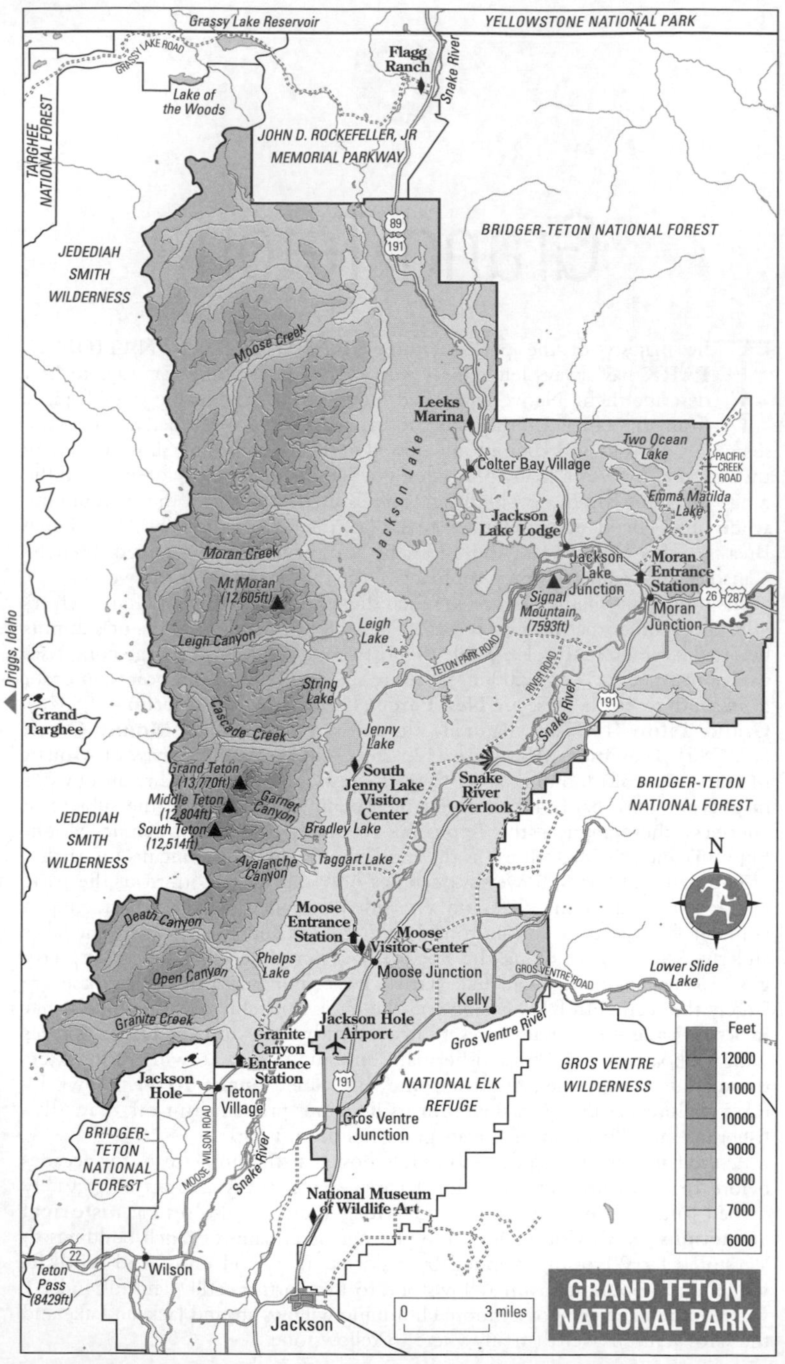

Grassy Lake Reservoir
YELLOWSTONE NATIONAL PARK
GRASSY LAKE ROAD
Flagg Ranch
Snake River
Lake of the Woods
TARGHEE NATIONAL FOREST
JOHN D. ROCKEFELLER, JR MEMORIAL PARKWAY
89
191
BRIDGER-TETON NATIONAL FOREST
JEDEDIAH SMITH WILDERNESS
Moose Creek
Leeks Marina
Jackson Lake
Colter Bay Village
Two Ocean Lake
PACIFIC CREEK ROAD
Emma Matilda Lake
Jackson Lake Lodge
Moran Creek
Jackson Lake Junction
Moran Entrance Station
Mt Moran (12,605ft)
Signal Mountain (7593ft)
26
287
Moran Junction
Leigh Lake
Leigh Canyon
TETON PARK ROAD
RIVER ROAD
Driggs, Idaho
String Lake
Snake River
Grand Targhee
Cascade Creek
191
Jenny Lake
South Jenny Lake Visitor Center
Snake River Overlook
BRIDGER-TETON NATIONAL FOREST
Grand Teton (13,770ft)
Middle Teton (12,804ft)
South Teton (12,514ft)
Garnet Canyon
Bradley Lake
Taggart Lake
Avalanche Canyon
N
Death Canyon
Moose Entrance Station
Moose Visitor Center
Phelps Lake
Moose Junction
Open Canyon
GROS VENTRE ROAD
Lower Slide Lake
Kelly
Granite Creek
Jackson Hole Airport
Gros Ventre River
Feet
12000
11000
10000
9000
8000
7000
6000
Granite Canyon Entrance Station
GROS VENTRE WILDERNESS
Jackson Hole
Teton Village
191
NATIONAL ELK REFUGE
Gros Ventre Junction
BRIDGER-TETON NATIONAL FOREST
MOOSE-WILSON ROAD
Snake River
National Museum of Wildlife Art
22
Wilson
Teton Pass (8429ft)
0
3 miles
Jackson
GRAND TETON NATIONAL PARK

Photogenic vistas

For the classic photograph of the Tetons, an hour or two past sunrise is best; the **Snake River Overlook**, roughly halfway between Moose and Moran Junction, is generally considered the top spot. **Willow Flats Overlook**, just south of *Jackson Lake Lodge*, is another beauty, as is the viewing deck at the lodge itself. Towards Moran Junction is the **Oxbow Bend** turn-out, another excellent position; the view from here is dominated by Mount Moran, while the craggy pinnacle of Grand Teton is just visible to your far left. Oxbow Bend is also a pretty spot to take out your folding chair and binoculars and settle in to watch for beaver, moose, and bird activity early or late in the day. Another popular spot is the top of the five-mile **Signal Mountain Summit Road**, 800ft above the valley floor, for a panoramic view. The five-mile **Jenny Lake Scenic Loop** is one-way southbound from String Lake at the north end of Jenny Lake (it's two-way northbound), and affords tantalizing glimpses through the trees of the mountains towering above the lake's southwest shore.

Park orientation

Save for the shuttles from *Jackson Lake Lodge* and Colter Bay to Jackson, there is no useful public transport within the park, and you'll ideally want a car (or bike) to get around. No road crosses the Tetons inside the park boundary, but those that run along their eastern flank were designed with an eye to the mountains, affording stunning views at every turn. It's possible to drive the length of the park and back in a day, but to take in a quick look at the best sights along with a hike or two, budget at least two days for exploration.

Grand Teton splits easily into **three main divisions**: a southern third, encompassing Moose Junction and the Gros Ventre River area, along with the two approaches from Jackson; the park's center, aligned along the popular Teton Park Road and its speedier twin Hwy-191 across the Snake River to the east; and the northern third, home to the busy visitor hubs of *Jackson Lake Lodge* and Colter Bay Village. In this later third we've also included the **John D. Rockefeller, Jr. Memorial Parkway**, a bridge of land connecting the park to Yellowstone named after Grand Teton's patron saint.

Southern Grand Teton

Two roads head north into Grand Teton from Jackson – the more frequently used and faster **Hwy-191** and the narrower **Moose-Wilson Road** through Teton Village to the **Granite Canyon Entrance**. Both lead to **Moose Junction**, home to park headquarters along with a cluster of appealing historic attractions and amenities. Whichever route you choose, try to loop back down to Jackson on the other road when you leave the park, to see what you missed. Similarly, time permitting, take a couple hours at least to explore the park's southeastern corner, crisscrossed by a series of dusty roads accessing the town of **Kelly** and the **Gros Ventre Slide** – both reachable in winter as well – along with the beautiful barns lining **Mormon Row** prominently featured on postcards across the region.

Hwy-191 north to Moose

Many visitors first lay eyes on the Tetons from this stretch of highway, both because the regional airport is located here and because day-trippers from

A brief history of Grand Teton National Park

Ranching and farming in **Jackson Hole** – originally known as Jackson's Hole after trapper Davey Jackson – date back to the 1880s, when homesteaders and cattle first began colonizing the valley. That the mostly smaller homesteads managed to eke out a living on the brutally tough lands here for a few decades is a testament to the perseverance and hard-working nature of the settlers, but a major drought beginning in 1918 along with calf and crop prices plummeting at the end of World War I led many farms and ranches to the brink of bankruptcy. Into this scene stepped **Horace M. Albright**, Superintendent of Yellowstone, who had long wanted to extend Yellowstone south to cover the **Tetons** (as did several of his predecessors, dating back to Army Superintendent S.B.M Young in 1897). In 1923, Albright met with local ranchers and business owners inside **Maude Noble's cabin**, by the Snake River, for a historic meeting to discuss protecting the valley. Albright endorsed the idea of protecting the valley as part of Yellowstone, with the ranchers being compensated for the loss of their land by the government. Skeptical of any form of federal control, many of the attendees agreed with the overall idea, realizing it was their best hope out of a tough situation, but refused on the principal of federal control. Sensing the end was near, these ranchers began circulating a petition to consider selling their land to other interests in order to turn the valley into a privately run but still protected recreation area.

During same period, Albright introduced the National Park idea to **John D. Rockefeller, Jr.** while taking the wealthy philanthropist on a twelve-day tour of the region in 1926 (see p.111 for more on their historic stop at **Lunch Tree Hill**). Blown away by the mountain scenery and dismayed by the hodgepodge of commercial interests invading the valley, Rockefeller quickly latched onto the plan, creating the **Snake River Land Company** the following year to begin purchasing ranches throughout the valley with the eventual hope of donating the land to the government for parkland. Ever the businessman, Rockefeller tried to keep his association with the company silent, knowing that if word of the actual buyer got out, ranchers would double or triple the selling prices of their land. Commercial aspirations were not entirely absent from the process, as one condition was that the **Grand Teton Lodge Company**, which Rockefeller then owned, ended up having to run the hotels and tourists amenities that were purchased, making it the exclusive operator of park concessions. This, however, was born more out of necessity than of some sinister plan to control the tourist trade, with little, if any, profit being made.

In 1929, **Grand Teton National Park** was officially created. The park – pieced together from parts of the already federally controlled Teton National Forest, created much earlier in 1897 – was much smaller than today's version, containing only the mountain range itself along with the string of smaller glacial lakes at its base (and not Jackson Lake). Local opposition was minimal, as little useable ranching and timberland was included. However, when word got out the following year that Rockefeller was the man behind the Snake River Land Company, locals felt betrayed and tempers flared. Angered by the apparent conspiracy and ever distrustful of East Coast interests, residents refused to accept any land donated by Rockefeller, forcing the hand of **President Franklin Delano Roosevelt**, who created the **Jackson Hole National Monument** in 1943, a neighboring parcel to the park that included nearly 35,000 acres of land donated by Rockefeller, along with Jackson Lake and more acreage from Teton National Forest. By 1950, local anger and distrust had subsided enough to finally combine the National Park and National Monument, cementing the present day boundaries of Grand Teton.

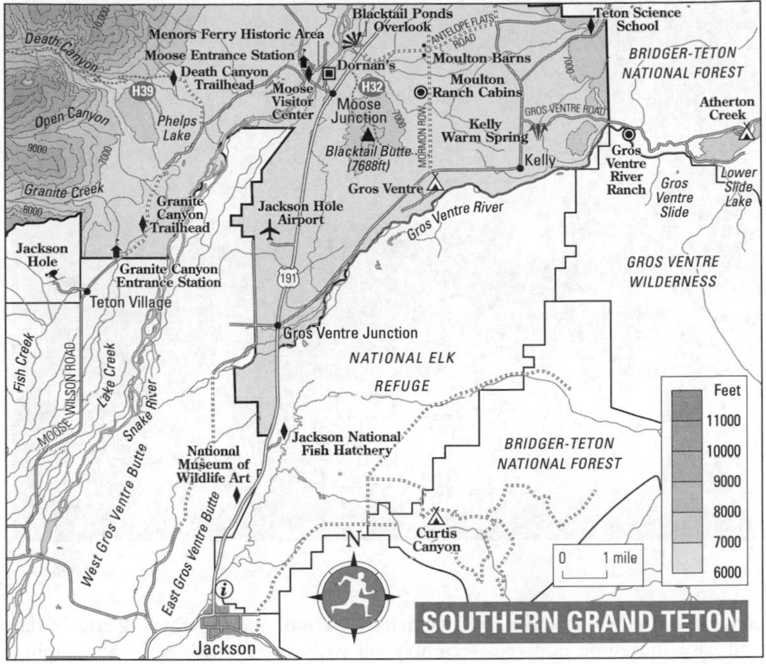

Jackson can drive 25 miles north to Moran Junction without having to pay an entrance fee. A few miles past the National Wildlife Museum and just past the turnoff for the Jackson National Fish Hatchery – each covered in detail in Chapter 11 – the highway enters Grand Teton, a moment commemorated with a roadside pullout. It's worth a stop for photo with the iconic national park sign in the foreground and the Tetons falling away into the horizon, but this is only the first of many such dramatic views to come.

Soon after, the highway speeds over the **Gros Ventre River** and its eponymous road junction to the entryway for **Jackson Hole Airport**, some five miles from the park entrance. Open since the 1930s, it's the only commercial airport located within a national park in the US and one would be hard pressed to find a landing strip with a more spectacular view. Continuing north, between the airport and Moose Junction three miles away is the **Albright View Turnout**. Named after Horace Albright, former head of both Yellowstone and the National Park Service and a major catalyst in the creation of Grand Teton National Park, the stunning view focuses in on Albright Peak (10,552ft), an easy climb in summer and an experts-only backcountry skiing descent throughout winter.

The Granite Canyon Entrance Station north to Moose

Just under 1.5 miles north from Teton Village, the Moose-Wilson road enters Grand Teton National Park at the **Granite Canyon Entrance Station**, open year-round save for a couple weeks during November and December for maintenance (no trailers or RVs). The road beyond the gate, however, is not

△ Moose crossing the Gros Ventre River

plowed and closes to motorized vehicles in winter, making for a relatively flat and easy snowshoe and cross-country ski path. After a half-mile of winding though attractive stands of Aspen and brush, the road turns bumpy as the pavement ends for a two-mile long stretch. Within this unpaved section is the **Granite Canyon Trailhead**, the entry point for hikes through Granite and Open canyons.

Back on pavement again, the Moose-Wilson road soon meets the turnoff for the **Death Canyon Trailhead**, reached via a rocky 1.5-mile road; a 4WD vehicle with high clearance is recommended. Several worthwhile hikes head out from here (including H39, p.157), but if you don't have time for those longer trips budget an hour to tramp a mile uphill on a well-marked trail to the **Phelps Lake** overlook. You'll be rewarded with an impressive view of the greenish-blue waters of the park's fourth largest lake, its northern edge lined with natural beach. While here, raise your water bottle to the philanthropic spirit of the Rockefeller clan, who until recently still owned the 1100 acre JY Ranch ringing the southern shores of the lake. Willing to give up the sole right to motorboat on the lake as his family had for decades, Laurance S. Rockefeller (1910–2004) donated the former dude ranch to the park shortly before his death. Now known as the **LSR Reserve**, at the time of writing the park was busy building a small welcome center on the Moose-Wilson road with exhibits on this new addition. Past the Death Canyon Trailhead entrance, the Moose-Wilson Road weaves close to four more miles to Moose, passing by the **Sawmill Ponds** and some prime **moose** habitat en route.

Moose

The heart of activity in Grand Teton's southern third is **MOOSE**, a dusty spread of buildings and side streets divided by the **Moose Entrance Station**, where you'll need to pay the $20 entrance fee or prove that you've already done so in order to head north on Teton Park Road. Just beyond the tollbooth, a portion of this fee goes into maintaining a small historic zone – the Menor's Ferry Historic District – delving into the lives of early homesteaders.

East of the entrance station, the park's headquarters are located within the **Moose Visitor Center** (daily 8am–5pm; until 7pm June to early Sept; ⓣ307/739-3399). Rangers are on hand to give advice, and the exhibits inside cover mountaineering, glaciation, and animal migration. The center is also the meeting place for a variety of Ranger-led programs, and home to a small gift shop with a great selection of kids books plus the regular selection of maps and guides. A few steps away is a **post office** (Mon–Fri 9am–5pm, Sat 10–11.30am), where you can mail off letters sporting a Moose postmark, along with a small and private neighborhood of homes used by park employees.

Menor's Ferry Historic District

Towards the Tetons is the **Menor's Ferry Historic District**, a collection of buildings providing the region's finest peek into the lives of early Jackson Hole settlers. As one of the few spots in the valley where the Snake River consistently sticks to a single, narrow channel, the banks here made for an ideal spot for a bridge or ferry. Learning of this soon after arriving in 1894, **William D. Menor** squatted on 150 acres off the western side of the Snake River to begin his homestead, which along with a small home evolved to include a store, ice house, blacksmith shop, and, most importantly, a **ferry crossing**. Menor – pronounced "Mean-Or," or as his brother Holiday was apt to say: "I may be mean, but my brother's Menor" – was certainly no saint, and his ferry was run to make a profit. It quickly became one of the most important crossings in all of Jackson Hole, with rates ranging between 25 cents per foot passenger up to $4 for a wagon and team of four horses, playing a key role in transporting both settlers and vacationers coming to local dude ranches. By 1918, Menor had tired of the business and sold out to neighbors Frederick Sandell and Maude Nobel. The new partners promptly doubled the crossing rates; locals were undoubtedly overjoyed when a steel bridge was built south of the crossing in 1927, ending the ferry's necessity.

Following the interpretive loop clockwise from the parking lot, the first building of note is Menor's original **homestead cabin**, open for viewing and frequently attended by a docent dressed in period clothing (daily mid-May to late Sept 9am–4.30pm). The whitewashed cabin was built in three obvious sections, with the western third – constructed of rough, horizontal logs – tossed up in 1894. The middle section was added a year after as a kitchen, perhaps even built around the still functional, massive iron stove inside. A decade later, Menor added the taller final third as a general store, selling tobacco, coffee and sugar to settlers using his ferry; today you can buy cold drinks, old-fashioned candy, and assorted knick-knacks. As rickety an affair as it seems, the cabin was a veritable mansion for an unmarried homesteader, including such creature comforts as a wooden floor and glass windows. A few steps away from the cabin is the spot where Menor launched his ferry, a clever contraption consisting of two pontoons with a plank platform laid on top. Attached to a system of cables and steered with a pilot wheel, the current of the river itself would propel the ferry across the water – a not always accident-free undertaking, and in at least one recorded case a tree trunk drifting down stream slammed into the ferry hard enough to snap the cables, beaching it and a hopping mad Menor on a gravel bank downstream. When the budget allows for it, the Park Service runs a **replica ferry** across the river, an experience well worth lining up for.

Past the landing, the **transportation shed** houses a random collection of wagons dating back to the late 1800s, but the **Maude Noble Cabin** beyond is of more interest. Moved here from nearby Cottonwood Creek in 1918 after Noble purchased Menor's homestead and half-interest in the ferry, this was the sight of a momentous meeting between local residents and Yellowstone's Superintendent Horace Albright that helped breakdown local opposition to protecting the Tetons as a preserved park (see the box on p.92 for more details). Inside is a collection of faded though still fascinating black-and-white photos of local interest, divided into subjects like dude ranching, hunting and elk preservation.

On the opposite side of the parking lot is the **Chapel of Transfiguration** (Episcopal services every Sunday Jun–Sept at 8 and 10am). Built in 1925, the interior is simple, with a few pews cut from local Aspen and a wooden cross fronting a large picture window framing a heavenly view of the Tetons, Grand Teton standing guard at the center; only the equally small Soldier's Chapel facing Lone Mountain in Big Sky (see p.232) comes close to having such a dramatic altar view in the region.

Dornan's

Across the river banks from the visitor center, **Dornan's** (Ⓣ307/733-2415, Ⓦwww.dornans.com) is effectively a park concessionaire. The private in-holding has been owned by the same family since Evelyn Dornan established a small 15-acre homestead here in the 1922. Nowadays amenities strung along the short drive includes Dornan's Trading Post, a small but wellstocked grocery and deli; Will Dornan's Snake River Angler, a fly shop and float trip operator; Moosely Seconds, an outdoor goods store; the *Spur Ranch*, offering cabins year-round; and a gas station. Best of all is the *Pizza and Pasta Co* and the attached **wine shop**, the latter boasting one of the largest selections in the region. You can bring a bottle to the popular upper deck of the relaxed restaurant and watch the sun set over the Tetons as the Snake River's golden shimmer turns inky black.

East of Moose

Save for **Mormon Row**, the area east of Moose is an undervisited corner of Grand Teton, crisscrossed by a series of flat roads popular with bicyclists for both light traffic and terrific wildlife spotting. Two notable geological formations stand out here, the closest being **Blacktail Butte** (7688ft) sprouting up from the sagebrush plains just east of Hwy-191. Visible for miles in all directions, the large, broad-shouldered hump is popular with both climbers and hikers (see H32 p.145). Along the park boundary further east are the foothills of the **Gros Ventre Range** (pronounced "Grow Von"), framing the eastern side of Jackson Hole and home to Sheep Mountain, where the staggering **Gros Ventre Slide** occurred in 1925. Sheep Mountain is also known locally as **Sleeping Indian**, as from the valley floor it appears to form the shape of a Native chief, complete with headdress, laying flat on his back. Some claim the name of the range itself (meaning "Big Belly" in French) comes from this giant imaginary chief's stomach, but the more plausible explanation comes from yet another bout of miscommunication between French fur trappers and natives. In an attempt to tell the trappers that the Indians living in these mountains were always hungry, members of the Plains tribes to the east rubbed their hands over their bellies. The trappers – perhaps the same group who came up with the fantastical *Les Trois Tetons* – mistook this to mean the mountain dwellers had large bellies, and thus the name Gros Ventre was born.

Gros Ventre Junction and Kelly

When entering Grand Teton from the south on Hwy-191, the first worthwhile side-trip begins at **Gros Ventre Junction**. Heading northeast from this intersection, a road follows the sparkling **Gros Ventre River**, dotted with stands of cottonwood trees, to the *Gros Ventre Campground* about five miles away. Keep your eyes peeled for cyclists – this is a particularly popular stretch with local tour groups – and wildlife. This is one of the best areas in Grand Teton for animal watching, with the sagebrush flats to the northwest being where the park's **bison** herd spends much of its time. On the road's opposite side, short paths access the river, lined with spots perfect for setting up a tripod to take photos of the **bald eagles** that perch waterside high upon cottonwood branches. Make plenty of noise when approaching the water, as **moose** are commonly found streamside as well.

A half-mile beyond the entrance to the large **Gros Ventre Campground** (reviewed on p.193), the road passes a poorly signed turnoff cutting due north to Mormon Row en route to **KELLY**, a tiny village dating back to the 1890s that was once one of Teton County's largest, narrowly losing out on the county seat to Jackson by only a few votes in the early 1920s. Save for a post office, there's little here besides a rambling spread of homes and a lingering hippie vibe that belies the multi-million dollar real-estate deals made here in recent times. Several miles north of town and tucked into an attractive wooded valley is the **Teton Science School**, hosting short and long courses and seminars along with day-long wildlife tours; see p.203, for details.

Mormon Row

A short drive east of Moose is the area's most popular attraction, **Mormon Row**. This stretch of historic barns can be reached from the south along a dirt

△ Mormon Row

road east of the *Gros Ventre Campground* or, more easily, via **Antelope Flats Road**, connecting to Hwy-191 north of Moose Junction. Clustered around the intersection of these two side roads are a series of old wooden structures in various states of disrepair, including two proud buildings – known as the **Moulton Barns** – that might just be the most photographed barns on earth, framed by the shark-toothed Tetons in the background and surrounded by grazing bison and blooming wildflowers throughout summer. Now maintained by the Park Service, the structures were built by homesteaders in the early 1900s, most of whom were Mormons escaping drought conditions in modern day Utah. All of the homesteads that weren't already sold by the 1920s were scooped up by Rockefeller's Snake River Land Company, save for an acre in-holding still owned by descendents of the barn-building Moultons and home to the *Moulton Ranch Cabins* (see p.192 for a review). Even if you're not staying the night, stop by the front gate, where the friendly proprietors have posted a **map** detailing the original settlers and their plots from 1918, including the phonetically spelt "Grovont" homestead.

Past Mormon Row, Antelope Flats Road continues east across pancake flat terrain that's part of the migratory path of **pronghorns** to an intersection with **Shadow Mountain Road**; south leads towards Kelly and the Gros Ventre Slide, while to the north the winding road turns to gravel and snakes in and out of the Bridger-Teton National Forest, giving stupendous views over the Tetons, before eventually dumping out by the *Triangle X Ranch* near the historic Cunningham Cabin towards the park's center.

The Gros Ventre Slide and around

A few miles north of Kelly sits the **Gros Ventre Road** junction in the midst of working cattle fields. Heading east and out of Grand Teton, the meandering road leads up to the area's most intriguing sight, the Gros Ventre Slide just under five miles away. Less than a half-mile from the turnoff, the road passes **Kelly Warm Spring**. The small, spring-fed pond is a popular spot with local citizens and bison for a quick dip in the squishy bottomed warm water; no more than three feet, it's most fun for kids, who can splash about trying to catch the tiny minnows swimming about. Less than a mile and a half onwards, the road passes by a popular sight for Western buffs, a **cabin** used in the filming of *Shane*; while an entire town set was built west of here on Antelope Flats, this dilapidated frame is one of the few remaining structures still left from the Oscar-winning movie.

After passing the cabin, the road leaves Grand Teton, entering into the **Bridger Teton National Forest**. As if on cue, the landscape begins to change as the road meets back up with the Gros Ventre River and climbs steadily past progressively redder bluffs. Tiny turnouts every few hundred yards give views into the dramatic river valley below, much of it home to the *Gros Ventre River Ranch*, a working dude ranch with space for forty guests (see p.190), before reaching the **Gros Ventre Slide Geological Area**. The view here looks straight across the river valley to the wide scar across Sheep Mountain caused by an earth-shaking landslide in 1925 (see box, p.99). Dramatic as the reddish gash may be, the true power of the massive slide is best appreciated on the half-mile loop starting below the parking area. Ramshackle signs along the **interpretive trail** point out local flora, but it's the head-on view of the slide and flood area, where the remains of bleached tree trunks and large boulders are scattered about like tossed playing cards, that demands attention. At the loop's far end is a pretty view of **Slide Lake**, created by the slide itself. Should you want to explore the actual slide, follow nearby Taylor Ranch Road to the bridge-side parking area and scurry up one of the untended trails to the scar on the mountain. The terrain is

Coming down the mountain

On June 23, 1925 a rancher living at the foot of **Sheep Mountain** heard a noise that he couldn't explain. It had been a very wet spring, and water had seeped into the layers of rock above his ranch. What he experienced over the next two minutes was the **Gros Ventre Slide**, one of the largest landslides witnessed in history. A nearly mile-long slump of the mountain – estimated to be 50 million cubic yards of rock, sandstone and shale – had broken free, tumbling into the valley below and sliding as far as 300ft up the opposite slope. Witnesses likened it to a massive tidal wave rushing down the mountain, and within minutes the debris blocked the Gros Ventre River and **Slide Lake** began to form behind a huge natural dam. Engineers debated the strength of the earthen dam, which measured more than 200ft in height, and determined it would hold. And it did... until May 18, 1927, when the earth gave way and the lake spilled out, virtually washing away the town of Kelly – only the church and a handful other buildings survived the torrent – and killing six people. A flood of biblical proportions, the wall of cascading water was a mile wide in some places, and it drenched towns along the Snake River drainage for days, leaving deposits of mud upwards of three feet high in Jackson more than ten miles away.

challenging, and there is considerable bear activity in the area, so be cautious. There is also great swimming and fishing at this location, so bring a picnic and make a day of it.

Beyond the slide area, the landscape continues to meld into the red and orange bluffs that local **bighorn sheep** call home. Towards the center of Slide Lake is the dusty, shade-free *Atherton Creek Campground* (23 sites; $12). Beyond here the road worsens considerably, leading five miles to another pair of national forest **campgrounds** (*Red Hills, Crystal Creek*). Stay slow, as this stretch is used by local mountain bikers looking for a bumpy road ride; trailheads along the way lead up Horsetail, Redmond and Miners creeks, all good for isolated treks into the Bridger-Teton National Forest. Beyond the campgrounds, the road continues to meander for another ten miles or so before petering out, passing **Upper Slide Lake** along the way.

Central Grand Teton

The heart of Grand Teton stretches from Moose Junction in the south to Jackson Lake Junction to the north, spanning all of the major peaks in the Teton Range along with most of the park's glacial lakes, including **Jenny Lake** and the southern end of **Jackson Lake**. Two major roads cover the area, forming an epic 45-mile loop dotted with turnouts and side roads boasting the park's best views, along with numerous trailheads and points of historic interest. The more celebrated of the two is **Teton Park Road**, hugging the base of the peaks and accessing both the popular **Signal Mountain Summit Road**, with panoramic views 800ft above the valley floor, and the **Jenny Lake Scenic Loop**, a one-way road affording memorable views of the trees of the mountains towering above the lake's southwest shore. To the east, further away from the peaks and on the opposite side of the Snake River, the views from speedy **Hwy-191** are more panoramic, and best timed to be seen around dawn or dusk.

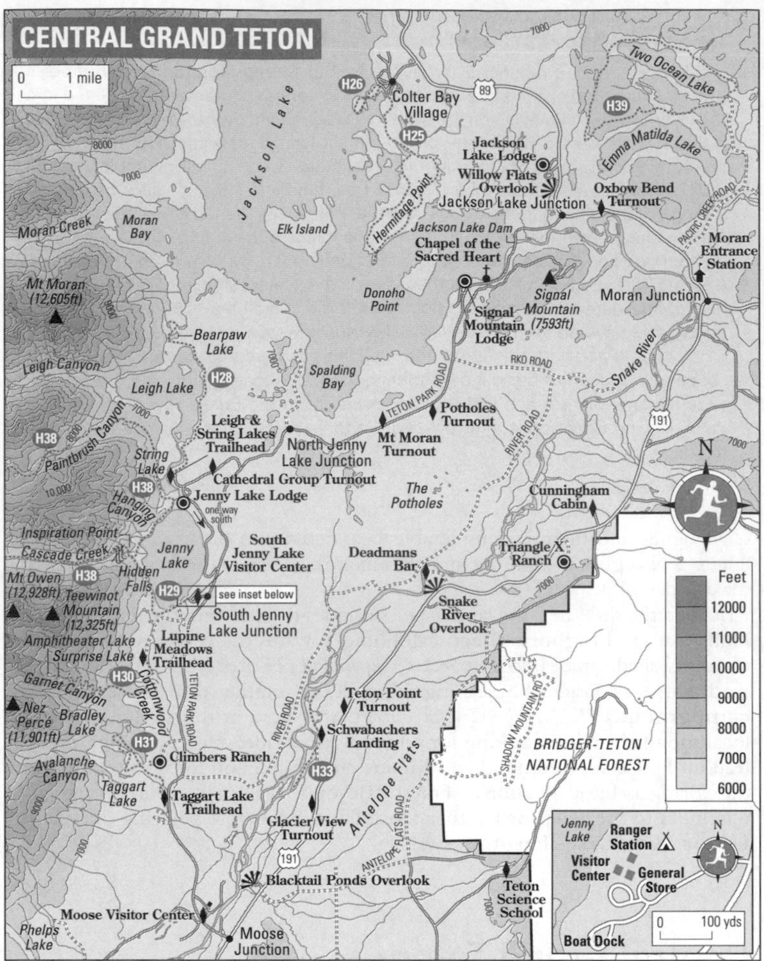

Hwy-191: Moose to Jackson Lake Junction

Directly north of Moose Junction, a parking lot at **Blacktail Butte** accesses a set of rough steps leading up to some popular climbing routes. Just beyond the Antelope Flats Road turnoff leading to Mormon Row, the highway then passes the **Blacktail Ponds Overlook**. From the overlook, a steep, rocky slope leads down through the ponds themselves, once prime beaver habitat; today it's fishermen who visit the most, cutting across the marshy meadow to fish along the banks of the Snake River (Aug–Oct only).

A couple miles ahead is the **Glacier View Turnout**, with a head-on view of Grand Teton fronted by the cottonwood and Engelmann spruce lined path of the Snake River and, closer still, several hundred yards of sagebrush flats. It's a neat encapsulation of the park's varied landscapes, capped off by **Teton Glacier** itself, the largest of a dozen still active glaciers flowing down shaded mountain pockets inside the park; note the glacial debris piled up beneath it, looking like scoops dropped off by a giant size bulldozer. The park's current glaciers are not remnants of the last major ice age, known as the Pinedale Period, but instead formed approximately 1000 years ago, and they've been shrinking since the "Little Ice Age" ended around 1850; global warming has sped up the process, and most scientists now predict Teton Glacier will be completely gone within fifty years.

The next turnoff from the highway accesses **Schwabacher Landing**, located a mile down a gravel road and of most interest to boaters. The area around the landing, however, also makes for a lovely picnic spot, where you can spot trout facing upstream, snagging bites of their own lunch as you eat yours. Afterwards, considering taking a stroll along the riverbank as detailed in H33, p.146; head north for the finest photo opportunities. Past the landing's entrance is the **Teton Point Turnoff**, with another awesome head-on view of the peaks and more interpretive signs explaining the region's unique geology.

Snake River Overlook to the Cunningham Cabin

Hwy-191 within the center of Grand Teton is book-ended by two of the park's most celebrated scenic viewpoints. The more southerly of the two is the **Snake River Overlook**, three miles north of the Teton Point Turnoff across the flat, grey-green expanse of Antelope Flats. Crowded with photographers at dawn and dusk, the Tetons are at their most angular here, broken shards of glass cutting into the sky. The Snake River bends widely in the foreground, and from this vantage point it's easy to note the steep, 200ft high banks marking the course of the ancient river that once flowed through the valley. To try to get two bends

Dead man walking

While the area around **Deadmans Bar** is perfectly peaceful today, it was the sight of a bloody incident in 1886. In the summer of that year, only two years after settlers first began arriving in Jackson Hole, four Germans, including a man by the name of **John Tonnar**, set up a claim on the Snake River hereabouts to take up placer mining. They hoped to extract gold from the riverbed, as the gravel here was reputed to be rich with gold. The precious metal was indeed present, but separating it out quickly and profitably proved to be a near impossible task. Perhaps this complication is what led to arguments within the group, or perhaps, as Tonnar later claimed, it was the fact that the other miners ganged up on him, roughing him up in an attempt to scare him off and keep his share of the gold after the hard work of digging was completed. Whatever the cause of fighting, Tonnar murdered his three companions – one by gunshot and the other two he bludgeoned with an axe – then weighed the bodies down with rocks and threw them into the river. The crime may have gone unnoticed had he done a better job in disposing of the bodies, but soon after a group of vacationers floating down the Snake made the gruesome discovery of the dead men floating just below the surface. A posse was quickly formed to track Tonnar down, which they did with surprising ease – perhaps in a state of shock still, he had not traveled far and was found working on the ranch of local homesteader Emile Wolff cutting late summer hay. Sent to jail in Evanston, a county seat in the Wyoming Territory, he was put on trial the following spring and pleaded not guilty. His story of abuse at the hands of the other miners must have struck a chord with the jury, as he was – much to the surprise of the judge and local populace – found not guilty. Directly after the trial, Tonnar smartly boarded the first train out of town and was never heard from again.

of the river in your shot – as Ansel Adams did in his iconic photo *The Tetons – Snake River* from 1942 – take a short walk past the northern end of the turnout and look back.

After the overlook, Hwy-191 immediately spills downhill, cutting through a patch of thick forest to the turnoff for **Deadmans Bar**. After a very steep entry, the side road turns to gravel, leading under a mile to a popular put-in spot named after one of Jackson Hole's most grisly tales (see box, p.101). While the story makes for great campfire fodder, there's little to see here today, and continuing further north Hwy-191 squiggles for a couple miles over more glacial plains and past **Hedrick Pond** to the well-known **Triangle X** dude ranch, offering week-long stays and guided fishing/float trips throughout the summer and snowmobiling in winter; see p.190 for details.

North of the dude ranch on the other side of the highway is the historic **Cunningham Homestead**, known as the Bar Flying U Ranch when established by J. Pierce Cunningham in the late 1880s. Cunningham, who arrived in Jackson Hole in 1885, already had a ranch closer to Jackson, but staked out a new homestead and a new bride for himself here as the soil, filled with sediments left behind by an ancient glacier lake, was better than most other spots in the valley. Though the scene of a macabre shoot-out in its early days (see the box below), the homestead evolved into one of the region's most successful, eventually expanding to over 500 acres. Cunningham likewise became one of the valley's leading citizens, but by the mid 1920s even he was feeling the combined pinch of drought and plummeting agricultural prices, leading him to sell the ranch to Rockefeller's Snake River Land Company in 1928.

Once home to several buildings including a comfortable ranch house, all that stands today is a long and low-slung **cabin**. The first building Cunningham built to "prove up" his homestead claim, the "dog-trot" style structure – actually two small cabins connected by an open breezeway – is maintained in its original condition, its horizontal logs chinked with dirt mortar and the roof sporting a carpet of grass. You can enter the sagging three-room cabin, peering through

Gunfight at the Cunningham Cabin

As with nearby Deadmans Bar, the **Cunningham homestead** played a major role in one of Jackson Hole's earliest violent dramas. Contrary to the myths promoted by the Hollywood-backed Westerns filmed in Jackson Hole decades later, the homesteading period here was really a peaceful time, with gun battles nearly non-existent and poachers, not villainous bandits, playing the role of major scoundrels. In the fall of 1892, however, Cunningham was approached at his first ranch on Flat Creek, closer to Jackson, by two men looking to buy hay for a group of horses they had in tow. Along with selling them hay, Cunningham agreed to let the men winter in his cabin twenty miles to the north. Throughout the snowy months rumors that the two men were **horse thieves** swirled about, and when a posse of riders from nearby Driggs, Idaho, arrived in April of 1893 looking for the culprits behind a recent theft of horses, they were pointed in the direction of Cunningham's cabin. In total, 16 armed men – including several residents of Jackson who joined the posse in town – rode to the homestead in the middle of the night and announced their presence at dawn. A gunfight quickly ensued, and when the smoke cleared both of the alleged rustlers had been killed. The posse had originally set out to arrest the men, not kill them, and without a trial or even concrete evidence that the two were the actual thieves to begin with, the incident of vigilantism was quickly hushed over, and even today it remains one of the region's darkest, most secretive chapters.

windows boasting million-dollar views above a dirt-packed floor. Afterwards, walk the half-mile loop crossing the property, littered with reminders of the homestead like postholes, narrow irrigation ditches, and the foundations of several other buildings. The overall spread provides an evocative backwards glance into the hardscrabble existence of homesteaders in the late 1800s and early 1900s, who had to figure out how to scratch out a living raising cattle and crops like hay, alfalfa, and oats in a valley averaging a slim 60 frost-free days a year; indeed, a popular saying amongst settlers in Cunningham's times went "If summer falls on a weekend, let's have a picnic."

Moran Junction to Oxbow Bend

Six miles north of the Cunningham Homestead, **Moran Junction** is the end of the line for visitors taking a free tour of Grand Teton via Hwy-191. If driving north towards this junction around dawn or dusk, pull over for a moment to listen for a random howl; the park's eastern corner around **Uhl Hill** (7443ft) has become a favorite hunting ground for **wolves** travelling south from Yellowstone.

A geological primer

The Rockies on the whole, including the nearby Snake River and Gros Ventre ranges, are made up of mountains formed between forty and eighty million years ago. The **Teton Range**, however, is the baby of the system, dating back only around nine million years when two massive blocks of the Earth's crust along the **Teton Fault** began pushing against one another. Movement along the fault, running roughly along the same lines as Teton Park Road, started to release the intense stress caused by the stretching and thinning of the earth's crust. As the blocks along the fault grinded against one another, the mass to the west rose as the block on the east sank. The most commonly used example to illustrate the action is a trap door, one side lifting upwards to create the Tetons, the other falling downwards to form **Jackson Hole**. Standing on the flat valley floor, it's easy to think the block forming the Tetons did all the work; however, geologists estimate the Jackson Hole block has actually fallen four times the depth that the Teton block has risen. This dramatic faulting and lifting is only part of the story. As soon as the mountains and valley floor began forming, **erosion** kicked in with its sculptural work. Wind and rain both played their role, but **glaciers** created the most spectacular effects. The three most recent glacial advances are known as the **Buffalo Period**, the oldest at around 200,000 years; the **Bull Lake Period**, covering the region close to 140,000 years ago; and the **Pinedale Period**, at its peak only 25,000 years ago. Created by years of continual snowfall followed by minor or no snowmelt, glaciers up to several thousand feet thick formed during these periods. Gravity and their own massive size forced them into movement, and as these seas of ice flowed downhill and through Jackson Hole they carved away at rocks, transporting incredible amounts of debris with them along the way. Evidence of their handiwork can be found virtually everywhere throughout the park, including spectacular **U-Shaped canyons** like Cascade Canyon. At the base of these canyons, deposits of glacial debris known as **moraines** formed natural dams, leading to the creation of the **piedmont lakes** – Jenny, Phelps, Taggart, Bradley, String, and Leigh – at the range's base. Both **cirque lakes**, such as Lake Solitude high up above Paintbrush Canyon, and **kettle lakes**, like the Potholes west of the Snake River, were created by glaciers as well. Even the flat valley floor owes its current existence to glaciers, which scraped the plains flat. The dozen glaciers that remain within the park today are not leftovers from these major periods, but instead formed several thousand years ago during a minor ice-age; they're all disappearing at a steady pace today.

From Moran Junction you can continue north within the park, passing through the **Moran Entrance Station**, or leave Grand Teton heading east over Togwotee Pass (9658ft) towards Dubois, Wyoming, 55 miles away. En route, Hwy-26/287 east crosses back over the **Buffalo Fork** of the Snake River and past the scenic **Buffalo Valley Road**, to the Bridger-Teton National Forest's *Hatchet Campground* (9 sites; $10) eight miles away. Just beyond is the forest's Buffalo Ranger District office, where information on the area's many outdoor activities, including superb trout fishing on the Buffalo Fork, can be found.

From the Moran Entrance Station, it's five miles to Jackson Lake Junction. A third of the way, **Pacific Creek Road** splits off to the north, accessing trails leading around **Emma Matilda Lake** and **Two Ocean Lake** (H27, p.141). It's certainly not an essential detour, and the road itself is rough and slow going (4WD recommended), taking as long as a half hour to drive the four miles to Two Ocean Lake. There is a pretty **picnic area** around the lake, and as one of the few spots in the park not dominated by a view of the Tetons, the area does make for a refreshing change of pace.

Past Pacific Creek Road is the second of the two finest viewpoints on Hwy-191, **Oxbow Bend Turnout**. A loop in the Snake River cut off from the main channel, the big bend hosts plenty of **wildlife** in and around its calm waters, from river otters and moose to osprey, great blue heron and pelicans, and folks line the banks throughout the day in search of the perfect photo. Mountain wise, the massive bulk of **Mount Moran** (12,605ft) is the star of the show, and on particularly clear days Skillet Glacier on its front face shows up clearly in the river's mirrored reflection.

Teton Park Road

Known also as the "inner-loop road," **Teton Park Road** stretches twenty miles from Jackson Lake Junction to Moose. A more leisurely route than the "outer-loop" Hwy-191, the road unveils one spectacular view after another as it curves around Jackson Lake and then hugs the Tetons by their base. The highlights are **Summit Mountain Road**, a five-mile drive up to Jackson's Hole most dramatic viewpoint, and beautiful **Jenny Lake**. Named for the Shoshone wife of famed Jackson Hole trapper and guide "Beaver Dick" Leigh – Jenny and their children all died tragically of smallpox in 1876 – the lake is dramatically set at the mouth of Cascade Canyon, reflecting the peaks towering upwards of 7000ft above; in fact, there's more distance from the alpine lake's surface to Grand Teton than there is from lake level to sea level.

Jackson Lake Dam and around

From Jackson Lake Junction, Teton Park Road cuts south along the edge of Willow Flats before crossing **Jackson Lake Dam**, the lake to the right and the controlled flow of the Snake River to the left. Parking lots on both sides of the dam allow for a closer look at the 60ft high concrete structure, originally built in the early 1900s and refurbished in the 1980s (see the box on p.105). Pretty as Jackson Lake looks from atop the dam in early summer, it's easy to forget that the visible body of water is in truth a reservoir, dammed to impound the Snake River and irrigate farms in Idaho's Snake River Valley. This reality comes into focus by late August, when the drained lake shrinks and leaves behind wide, muddy banks. Sitting forty feet beneath the water's surface when the reservoir is full, the original Jackson Lake was nearly 10,000 acres smaller than today's lake.

One the lakeside of the road a short way from the dam is the **Chapel of the Sacred Heart**, a popular summer wedding spot. Built in 1937, two years before

The damming of Jackson Lake

"Let me pause to lay my ineffectual but heartfelt curse upon the commercial vandals who desecrated the outlet of Jackson's Lake with an ugly dam to irrigate some desert land away off in Idaho... There is more beauty in Jackson's Hole than even such a beastly thing could kill; but it has destroyed the august serenity of the lake's outlet forever; and it has defaced and degraded the shores of the lake where once the pines grew green and dark. They stand now white skeletons, drowned by the rising level of water."

Owen Wister, *Harper's Magazine*, 1936

The battle over **water** in Jackson Hole is but one small chapter in the sordid tale of irrigating the arid West. Skirmishes began almost immediately after settlers arrived, as homesteaders dug ditches off the Snake River and its tributaries to water their plots, and continue on today, with issues over taxation and the rights of neighboring states to local water remaining hot button issues. Much of the drama centers on the federal government's **Reclamation Service**, established in 1902 to oversee water development projects throughout the western states.

Immediately after being formed, members of the Reclamation Service began to survey and make plans in the greater Yellowstone area, starting with the Shoshone Dam – known now as the Buffalo Bill Dam – outside of Cody in 1904. In 1907, they built the first **Jackson Lake Dam** out of logs. After failing soon after, construction began on a larger concrete structure in 1910. There was little local opposition as this new dam was being built, as construction flooded the local economy with money and there was still an overall sense that rugged valley could only benefit by being tamed. Within a few years of its completion in 1916, however, opinions began to change dramatically. The dam had bloated Jackson Lake into a caricature of its former self, destroying acres of forest and surrounding the lake with an unsightly ring of dead trees that took decades to clear. Even more insulting locally, the new dam did nothing to benefit farmers within the state, as potato and beet farmers downstream in Idaho received all the rights to the pent-up water; rights that they still retain today. The Reclamation Service's dominating management style angered residents as well, to the point that plans for damming Jenny Lake and several other rivers and lakes within Grand Teton and Yellowstone were all shouted down in subsequent years.

The role Jackson Lake Dam has played in limiting more dams in the region is arguably its most lasting legacy. A less comforting future legacy has been suggested by the recent warnings of **earthquake** experts. Though reinforced in the late 1980s, these experts believe the dam, located less than ten miles from the Teton Fault, would be destroyed by a major quake – something the fault, geologically speaking, is due for anytime. It's hard to forecast the exact effects a wall of water six stories high ripping down the Snake River, but devastation would certainly ensue.

Grand Teton was created, the log-cabin chapel hosts Catholic services from June through September (Sat 5.30pm, Sun 10am; ⓣ307/733-2516). Inside is a lovely piece of purple and gold stained glass with the sacred heart at its center, and behind the chapel is a serene lakeside **picnic area**, featuring a terrific view of Mount Moran across the water.

Signal Mountain Lodge and Road

Up next on Teton Park Road is **Signal Mountain Lodge**, once an exclusive fishing resort and now a mainly privately operated cluster of amenities. While the lakeside setting is splendid, the fading facilities themselves are a time warp back to the 1970s; along with motel rooms, cabins, and a park campground, they include a gas station, grocery/sporting goods store (May to mid-Oct daily 8am–10pm), and a pair of restaurants and bars. If you're not spending the night or grabbing a meal, the chief reason for pulling in is Jackson Lake. The lodge's **marina** (mid-May to mid-Sept hours vary; ⓣ307/543-2831) rents all manner of watercraft, from canoes and kayaks to motorboat and flat-bottomed deck cruisers, and runs private fishing and sailing tours as well; see Chapter 6, p.166 for details.

Of more interest to non-boaters is nearby **Signal Mountain Road**, a five-mile road leading 800ft up to the summit of Signal Mountain (7593ft). Laced with plenty of curves (no trailers or RVs), the ride up can be painfully slow – the speed limit is 20mph – but the trip is well worth it, especially to view a sunrise or sunset. Separate parking lots access two summit **viewpoints**: the first, Jackson Point Overlook, faces west towards the mountains, while the second, Emma Matilda Overlook, faces northeast towards its namesake lake. The views from both are jaw dropping, with the Teton Range at its most majestic and Jackson Hole looking impossibly flat, the clusters of forest on the valley floor looking like continents adrift on a dusty ocean plain; ringing the valley to the east you can also spot the Gros Ventres range along with the Absarokas in Yellowstone to the north. If you'd rather earn the view, a nine-mile round-trip **trail** from Signal Mountain Lodge leads up to the summit, passing lily-pad rich ponds and wildflower filled meadows.

South to Jenny Lake

Less than a mile south of the Signal Mountain Road turnoff is **RKO Road**, named after the Golden Age Hollywood studio that used the area's dramatic backdrop to film an assortment of Westerns. Unpaved, the heavily rutted road is slow going, crossing sagebrush flats with wonderful wide-open views east for 3.5 miles to a small parking area by the Snake River. Fishermen frequently use the route, but anyone can park by the water and hike the trails along this peaceful stretch of the river; it's a good elk spotting area, as well as a simple way to experience the solitude of a float trip without actually getting onto the water. If driving a 4WD, it's possible to follow the southern branch of the RKO Road (also known as **River Road**) about a dozen miles along the western shelf of the Snake River – an exceedingly rocky route also open to **mountain bikes** – to where it eventually meets back with Teton Park Road by the picnic area north of the Taggart Lake Trailhead. Come October, the entire road closes until spring to protect the migratory path of local pronghorn.

Between the RKO Road entrance and North Jenny Lake Junction are two stellar viewpoints. The **Potholes Turnout** focuses in on the pockmarked plains to the south, dotted with the tiny depressions created by stagnant blocks of ice left by retreating glaciers. Nearby is the **Mount Moran Turnout**, from which the fourth-tallest peak in the chain looms across Jackson Lake. Aptly named Skillet Glacier, one of five still clinging to the flat-topped peak, is clearly visible on the front face, as is a vertical scar at the peak; called a diabase dike, the black stripe is made of hardened magna some 775 million year old. The mountain is named after artist Thomas Moran, whose sketches and subsequent paintings from the Hayden Expedition of 1871 helped spur Congress to create Yellowstone National Park. Hayden named the peak in 1872, several years before Moran himself got a chance to return to paint the Teton Range for the first time. South again, past a dirt road leading north to a secluded **boat ramp** at Spalding Bay on Jackson Lake, is **Mountain View Turnout**, the final pull-off along this stretch.

Jenny Lake Scenic Loop

At **North Jenny Lake Junction**, the road splits, with Teton Park Road continuing its march southward and a four-mile scenic loop branching off towards the mountains. This latter route is justifiably one of the most popular drives in the park, accessing a string of glacial lakes – **Leigh Lake**, **String Lake** and **Jenny Lake** – that each merit a look on foot. Before reaching them, the wooded branch-road cruises by the **Cathedral Group Turnout**, a good place to brush up on the geological forces that created the scene before you. Boards explain the naming of the Cathedral Group – Teewinot Mountain, Mount Owen and Grand Teton, forming a single massive, multifaceted fortress from this view – and locate the five-story tall **fault scrap** visible beneath nearby Rockchuck Peak, clear evidence of the dramatic rising and falling that continues to occur along the Teton Fault.

There's little to see at the high-end *Jenny Lake Lodge* south of here, but visitors with an hour or so to spare should take the road across from it to the **Leigh and String Lakes Trailhead**. From the picnic area beside String Lake, an easy, scenic trail leads a mile alongside the narrow lake through woods to a picturesque view across the greenish waters of Leigh Lake; if you have more time, continue on to Bearpaw Lake as detailed in H28 (see p.142). One-way south of *Jenny Lake Lodge*, the road next skirts the eastern edge of Jenny Lake before meeting back up with Teton Park Road. An **overlook** en route gives superb views across the lake into Cascade Canyon, along with the option to scramble down the moraine ridge to soak your feet in the crystalline waters.

South Jenny Lake

Back to a single highway, Teton Park Road quickly passes the entrance to **South Jenny Lake**, a buzzing hub of activity around lake's southern shores. The main parking lot fills up fast during peak season, and most visitors hustle straight for the boat dock, where you can rent canoes or hop on the charming pontoon **ferry** across the lake (May 15–30 & Sept 16–30 daily 10am–4pm, June to mid-Sept daily 8am–6pm; ⓣ307/734 922; $7.50 round-trip, $5 one-way). Taking off every fifteen minutes, the ride drops off at the mouth of Cascade Canyon, from where the park's most popular trail leads to nearby **Hidden Falls** and, more strenuously, **Inspiration Point** high above Jenny Lake. Long lines form at both docks in the afternoons, so either plan on completing the round-trip in the morning or skip the boat and tack on a couple extra miles by hiking to or from the far boat dock along the moderate two-mile trail circling the lake (see H29, p.143 and H38, p.156).

Back near the parking lots are two handy information centers. The **Jenny Lake Visitor Center** (June–Aug daily 8am–7pm, Sept daily 8am–5pm; ⓣ307/739-3343) is housed in the cozy Crandall Studio, built in 1925 as a gallery and store by local photographer/painter Harrison Crandall; it was moved here from its original setting by String Lake in 1995. Along with the information desk and a fireplace that's a welcome windfall on frosty mornings, an exhibit inside details local geology. A few steps away, the **Jenny Lake Ranger Station** (May–Sept; hours vary; ⓣ307/739-3343) dispenses backcountry permits along with climbing information. The rangers here are responsible for search and rescue missions, and a simple exhibit inside describes the most common causes of climbing accidents; according to the rangers, 93 percent of accidents are due to human error as opposed to gear failure or acts of nature. Should you want to try climbing, headquarters of the highly regarded **Exum Guides** service is a short walk south across Cottonwood Creek (see Chapter 6, p.171 for details). Also in the South Jenny Lake area is the popular

A "Grand" debate

In 1872, **Ferdinand Hayden** returned to Yellowstone with his band of cartographers, guides, artists and soldiers for a second exploratory tour of the region. Months earlier, President Ulysses S. Grant officially declared Yellowstone the world's first national park, and Hayden's expedition party spent the summer mapping close to 10,000 square miles of terrain. To cover the huge expanse, his group split into northern and southern divisions, with Hayden's second in command, **James Stevenson**, leading the Snake River Division south down along Shoshone and Lewis lakes and into Jackson Hole. Tagging along with this group was **Nathaniel "National Park" Langford**, a former member of the Washburn Expedition (see p.268) and Yellowstone's first Park Superintendent. On July 28, fourteen expedition members set out to climb **Grand Teton** (13,770ft). Half of the group made it as far as the peak's Lower Saddle (11,200ft), and Langford and Stevenson certainly made it as far as the Upper Saddle (13,160ft), as they were the first to officially report on a man-made rocky enclosure found there, thought to be a native spiritual site built at some unknown time. Both claim to have continued onwards a further 600ft up extremely technical terrain to the summit. Weeks later, an elated Langford gave a speech to the entire gathered expedition, proposing that the Grand Teton's name be changed to Mount Hayden. Hayden proudly accepted, and so in a span of about two weeks Grand Teton was successfully conquered and also renamed.

Or so it seemed. Momentum for the name change quickly fizzled out, and before the turn of the century so did Langford-Stevenson's bold claim. In August of 1898, six members of the Rocky Mountain Club began climbing Grand Teton. Two stopped at the Upper Saddle, but the remaining four – **William Owen**, **Franking Spalding**, **Frank Peterson**, and **John Shive** – continued on, picking their way carefully to the top. Their path, known now as the **Owen-Spalding Route**, remains heavily used as the easiest, albeit still tricky, way up. Atop the peak, the four members could not find any signs of prior human visitation; as per custom, they chipped their names into boulders and left behind a cairn as proof of their visit. Soon after, Owens published a story in the *New York Herald*, describing his group's adventures and claiming that they were in fact the first to reach the peak. A public battle quickly broke out, with Langford defending his claim. Inconsistencies in some of his previous accounts – Langford wrote, for example, that the enclosure was actually on the summit, and not well below as is the case – plus any lack of physical proof weakened his case, and Owens eventually won the war of words and his group is now considered to be the first to officially climb Grand Teton. (Of course, whomever built the lonely rocky enclosure in the Upper Saddle decades or even centuries earlier could very possibly have completed the climb, without official credit being given.)

As for other documented firsts, **Eleanor Davis**, vice-president of the Colorado Mountain Club, became the first woman climber to top Grand Teton in 1923. And in June of 1971, **Bill Briggs** climbed to the summit of Grand Teton, clicked into his skis, and became the first maniac to ski down Grand Teton. Briggs now runs the ski school on the somewhat less death-defying terrain of Jackson's Snow King ski resort only a few miles to the south.

tent-only **Jenny Lake Campground**, and **Jenny Lake Store**, best for a coffee and free copy of the *Jackson Hole Daily* newspaper.

South to Moose

Save for a pair of trailheads, there's not a whole lot of reason to stop on Teton Park Road south from Jenny Lake to Moose. The views along the entire eight-mile stretch are stupendous, however, with nothing between the road and towering Grand Teton directly to the west but flat sagebrush plains. The **Lupine Meadows Trailhead**, 1.5 miles down a well-maintained side road, one of the top trailheads for climbers to set off from (see H30, p.143). Some of these mountaineers stay at the **Climber's Ranch** a few miles further south on Teton Park Road, a set of rustic cabins run by the American Alpine Club. The nearby **Taggart Lake Trailhead** is the starting point for hikes to Taggart and Bradley lakes (see H31, p.144), both hidden behind the forested moraines viewable from the roadside parking lot, bumpy islands of green floating on the dry outwash plains.

Northern Grand Teton

Along with its scenic viewpoints and handful of outstanding hikes, the northern third of Grand Teton is most notable for the amenities clustered around two main stopovers, **Jackson Lake Lodge** and **Colter Bay Village**. Both are located a short way north of Jackson Lake Junction, from where it's 24 miles on Hwy-191 to Yellowstone's southern border, the final third leading through the **John D. Rockefeller, Jr. Memorial Parkway**. The area's main draw is Jackson Lake, humming with all manner of watercraft throughout summer. Boat ramps are located at Colter Bay Village and **Leeks Marina** further to the north until late-August most years, by which time the insatiable water diet of farmers downstream has drained the lake-cum-reservoir to levels unsafe for docking and cruising.

Jackson Lake Lodge and around

Just north of the **Willow Flat Overlook** – one of the best spots in the entire Yellowstone region for moose spotting – **Jackson Lake Lodge** is the park's swankiest public area. *Jenny Lake Lodge* is more expensive, but there's nothing for the regular visitor to see or do there. On the contrary, *Jackson Lake Lodge* has plenty beyond its hotel rooms and cottages. Built by Rockefeller's Grand Teton Lodge Company, the main lodge was considered an eyesore by many upon completion in 1955. It's certainly not as memorable as some of Gilbert Stanley Underwood's finest creations, including Yosemite's *Ahwahnee Hotel*, but the architect's blocky design has survived its critics well, occupying a bluff above Willow Flats with simple, Modernist grace. Closer to the main road, the complex is also home to the **Grand Teton Medical Clinic** (mid-May to Sept daily 10am–6pm; ⓣ307/543-2514), and a **corral** with trail and wagon rides from late-May through September (ⓣ307/543-2811).

Jackson Lake Lodge warrants a stopover for the second floor **lobby**. Famous guests like Presidents Kennedy, Nixon, Reagan, and Clinton have all been photographed in front of the centerpiece, a series of massive picture windows lining the western wall, perfectly framing the Teton skyline beyond. Along the other three walls are wildlife prints by painter Carl Rungius – some of the originals hang in Jackson's National Museum of Wildlife Art (see p.215) – and nearby is the table where US and Soviet diplomats signed a statement of peace in 1989, helping end the Cold War. With plenty of couches, two corner fireplaces, free wireless Internet, and a newsstand downstairs, the common area makes for a relaxing spot to sip on a coffee while plugging back into the world.

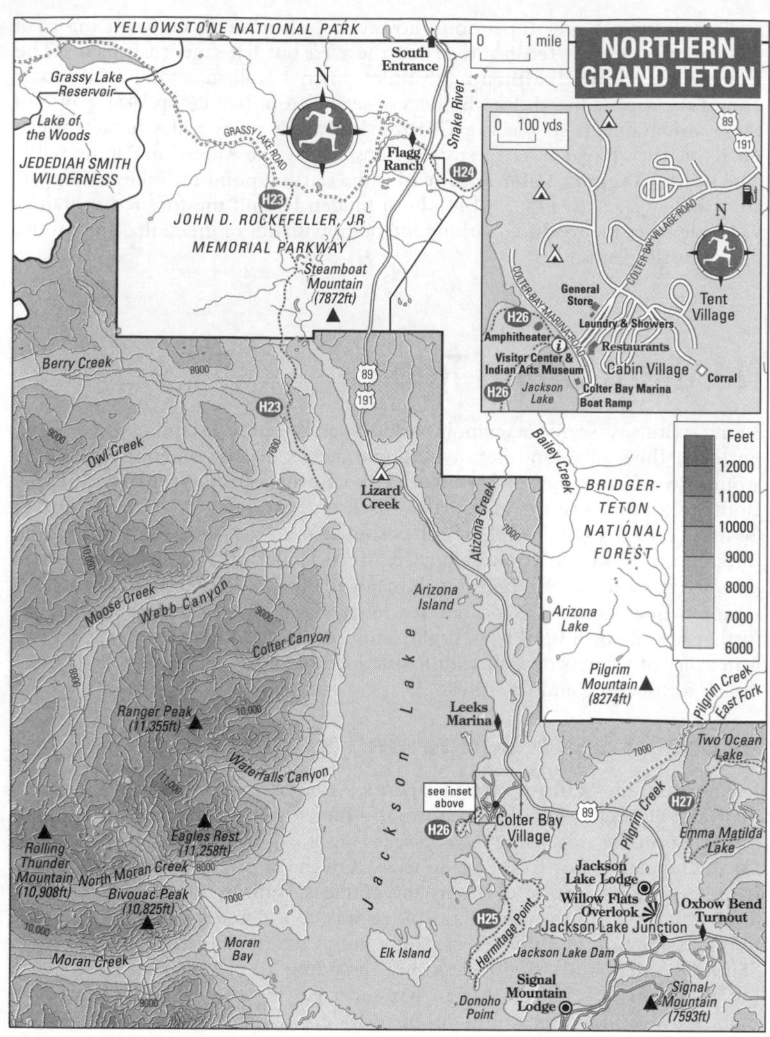

For more substantial fare, two of the park's top **restaurants** – the diner-like *Pioneer Grill* and more upscale *Mural Room* (both reviewed on p.199) – are just steps away.

Accessed from the same room, the lodge's large back **deck** has a stupendous view over Willow Flats. It's the best place in Grand Teton to come socialize while watching the **sunset**. A ranger is posted here in the evening to answer questions and help scope out moose in the marshy meadows ahead; typically at least one of the gangly creatures are spotted nightly. The deck's *Blue Heron Lounge* also does a roaring trade, letting revellers mix in a huckleberry margarita with the view.

Lunch Tree Hill

An interpretive **trail** north of Jackson Lake Lodge's massive deck leads up historic **Lunch Tree Hill**. Legend has it that during a picnic upon this hill in 1926, Yellowstone Superintendent Horace Albright helped convince John D Rockefeller, Jr. – who had hiked up this same hill two years earlier with his sons – of the need to protect the mountain and surrounding valley as a national park (see box, p.92). Thanks to the work of these two men, you don't need to be a millionaire to enjoy the unfettered hilltop view today. The first half-mile of the trail, which leads eventually north to Colter Bay, is lined with placards detailing how features throughout Jackson Hole earned their names. It's a short, **essential hike** to the top of the hill, particularly at dusk when Willow Flats' population of tiny sparrows come alive to swoop drunkenly about for insects while the Tetons, looking lit from within, radiate with evening alpenglow.

Colter Bay Village and around

Though named after John Colter, a Lewis and Clark expedition member and daring trapper widely considered to be the first white man to explore Yellowstone, there's nothing particularly adventurous about **Colter Bay Village** at first glance. A few miles north of *Jackson Lake Lodge*, the sprawling development is the place to run errands in the park. Dotted around several large parking lots are a fairly well-stocked grocery and sporting goods store (late May to Sept daily 6.30am–9.30pm), laundry room, public showers, and two gas stations.

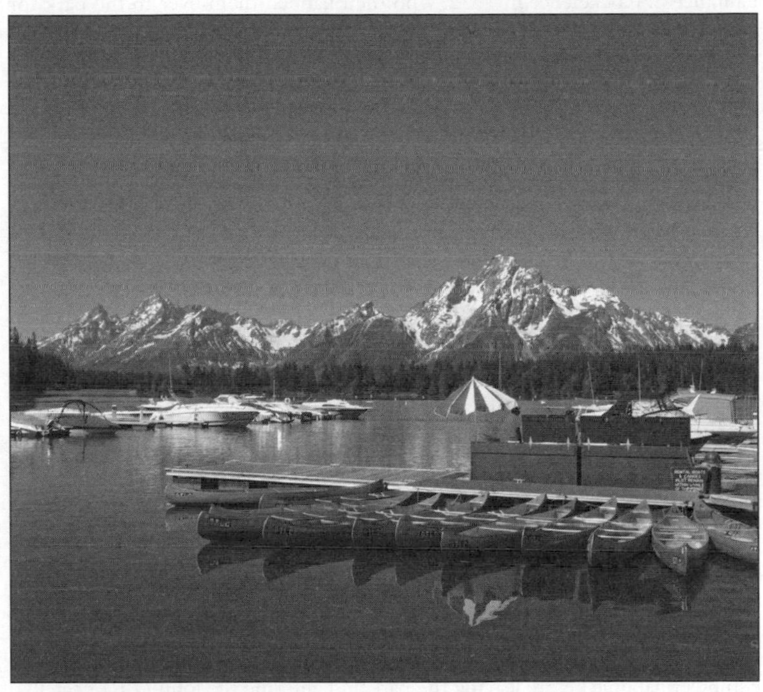

△ Colter Bay Marina

Further out on the village edges are tent, RV, and cabin accommodations, and two bland restaurants.

Unappealing as the village area looks, there are several worthwhile things to do here. Foremost is a tour of the **Indian artifacts** in the visitor center's museum. After that, outdoor options start with the series of well-marked lakeside **trails** leading off from behind the visitor center and south of the marina at the Hermitage Point trailhead. You shouldn't leave the area without stretching your legs on one of the flat paths, for superb mountain views and some waterside wildlife-watching – moose, osprey, and an assortment of colorful ducks (see H25, p.140 and H26, p.141). Provided water levels are high enough, rental boats and tickets for a lake cruise can be gotten at the nearby **marina** or horseback rides head our from the **Colter Bay Corral**; for details, see "Summer activities", p.170.

Colter Bay Visitor Center and Indian Arts Museum

Along with dispensing general information and backcountry permits, the **Colter Bay Visitor Center** (daily: May & mid-Sept to mid-Oct 8am–5pm; June to mid-Sept 8am–7pm; ⓣ307/739-3594) is the meeting place for a handful of ranger-led walks and lectures, both inside and in a pleasant amphitheatre nearby, throughout the week. The center also shelves an impressive array of books on native cultures, a great primer for the **Indian Arts Museum** (free) beginning one room over, a welcome surprise both for the quality of its collection and for its atmospheric layout. Spread over several moodily lit levels, the works were purchased from collector David T. Vernon (1900-73) by Laurance S. Rockefeller in 1972, who then handed them over to the park for display. Not limited to regional tribes, the overarching theme is the utilitarian nature of native art; it's not enough for an item to look good, but it must also serve a function. This ideal comes to life in the display case filled with impossibly intricate beaded sashes, pipe cases, and tomahawk sheaths, along with the dozens of worn yet still beautiful moccasins shown nearby. Equally transfixing are the feathered Crow coup sticks, used by braves as the ultimate test of courage by getting close enough to enemies to tap them with the stick – known as counting coup – before retreating. The lower level hosts a studio where a rotating cast of native guests artists work on and sell original pieces.

Leeks Marina to the northern border

Hwy-191 follows the eastern shore of Jackson Lake as it steadily climbs north towards Yellowstone. A string of picnic areas along with a marina and single campground line the route, which gets more forlorn as the summer season progresses and Jackson Lake recedes, leaving behind wide, muddy flats. **Leeks Marina** is officially open from mid-May to mid-September, but the docks close earlier in dry years. Sheltered in Pelican Bay and guarded by Moose and Cow islands, the marina is named after pioneer Stephen Leek (see box, opposite). With no rentals or campground, there's not a whole lot for the visitor without a boat in tow, though the **pizzeria** here makes a decent pie (11am–10pm daily when marina open).

From the marina, Hwy-191 continues north through thick forests dotted with the occasional meadows. Across the lake to the west, the forest around **Waterfalls Canyon** still clearly displays the effects of a fire that raged through in 1974. Past **Lizard Creek**, Grand Teton's northernmost campground, the road climbs a final mile before leaving the park and entering the John D. Rockefeller, Jr. Memorial Parkway.

Father of the Elk

Stephen Leek, one of the most intriguing but least renowned of Jackson Hole's early settlers, arrived in the valley in 1888. Unlike most of his fellow transplants, Leek didn't take up homesteading but instead set up shop as a hunting and fishing guide, expanding his operations over several decades from a humble tent by the Snake River to a large hunting lodge, complete with tourist cabins and gas station, near where Leeks Marina sits today. Eventually run with the help of his two sons, what was known as **Leek's Camp** is considered by some to be Jackson Hole's first dude ranch.

As is often the case with experienced hunters, Leek respected his prey, and he was one of the first local citizens to sound the alarm over the valley's dwindling **elk** population. By the early 1900s, several elements were working in tandem to destroy the elk's long-standing way of life. Ever-expanding Jackson and the surrounding homesteads were cutting off migratory paths and taking over important elk wintering grounds. And without any federal oversight, poachers were running rampant, including the particularly devious **tuskers** who slaughtered elk solely for their eye teeth – an item that in a sad irony Elks Club members across the country paid good money for to use as ivory pendants. Outraged local citizens, including Leek, eventually managed to run the tuskers out of the valley, but they could do little when the brutal **winter of 1908-09** blew through. The intense cold combined with the decline of good grazing lands led to a gruesome mass starvation, with skeletal elk walking the streets of Jackson in search of anything green. Even after settlers woke to the extent of the tragedy and began feeding the starving creatures hay, thousands of elk died off. Throughout the winter, Leek lugged about his camera – given to him by one of his wealthy customers, George Eastman of Kodak fame – and photographed the carnage.

The following spring, he toured with the **photos** and gave lectures on the need for elk preservation, earning him the nickname "Father of the Elk" and leading Wyoming to authorize $5000 for the purchase of winter feed. Soon after, the federal government got involved, creating the **National Elk Reserve** on the outskirts of Jackson in 1912. Pieced together from public and purchased private lands, the refuge not only helped protect wintering elk, but also promoted the positive side of turning private lands over to the government for preservation, an idea that culminated in the creation of Grand Teton National Park nearly two decades later.

The John D. Rockefeller, Jr. Memorial Parkway and around

Connecting Grand Teton to Yellowstone, the **John D. Rockefeller, Jr. Memorial Parkway** is essentially an eight-mile stretch of highway surrounded by nearly 25,000 acres of forest. The parkway was established in 1972 to recognize the work of the famed conservationist, who a played a role in the creation of not only Grand Teton but several other national parks including Acadia in Maine, Shenandoah in Virginia, and the Great Smoky Mountains in the Appalachians. Save for a turnoff explaining the still evident **Huck Fire** of 1988, a massive blaze caused by a tree blowing across a powerline, there's little reason to stop as the road climbs until reaching **Flagg Ranch** (Ⓣ1-800/543-2861, Ⓦwww.flaggranch.com) a couple miles from Yellowstone's South Entrance Station. Named after the banners that flew at the tiny military fort established here by the US Army, then in charge of Yellowstone's safekeeping, in the early 1900s, the resort was run as dude ranch throughout much of the twentieth century. Today it's a family resort, most useful for its gas station and convenience store. Along with cabins and a campground (for reviews, Chapter 8), the resort runs horseback rides ($30 per person) and has a restaurant open to the public. Unless you're planning on rising early to drive Grassy Lake Road or are looking to hike alongside or fish in the Snake River – there's a good trout hole just upstream of the bridge due south of Flagg Ranch – there's little reason to spend the night, however. The **Flagg Ranch Information Station** (June to early Sept 9am–4pm; ⓣ307/543-2327) by the main lodge is most useful for getting directions to Polecat and Huckleberry Hot Springs. Come winter, Hwy-131 ends at Flagg Ranch, once a buzzing launching point for **snowmobiles** in Yellowstone but now, thanks to stringent regulations, a veritable ghost town throughout the colder months with only the occasional group or snowcoach pulling in.

Grassy Lake Road

From Flagg Ranch, **Grassy Lake Road**, also known as Reclamation Road, meanders 47 bumpy miles west to Ashton, Idaho. Along the way, the road cuts through the Caribou-Targhee National Forest and alongside the 10,000-acre **Winegar Hole Wilderness** on Yellowstone's southern border. Taking at least two hours to complete in dry conditions, the heavily-rutted, dirt road is best driven with a 4WD vehicle. While there are a few sights (and campsites) a short drive from Flagg Ranch, Grassy Lake Road is mainly used by those visiting Yellowstone's secluded **Cascade Corner** (see p.87) from the south.

One mile west of Flagg Ranch sits the tiny parking area for a trail leading to the meadow-side **Polecat and Huckleberry Hot Springs**, clothing-optional dipping spots used mostly by locals; some dedicated soakers even snowshoe to the springs in winter. Completely undeveloped, these natural springs are best visited with a knowledgeable local in tow as you could get scalded by dipping in the wrong spots. Past Polecat Creek, the road turns to dirt, soon passing the first of several rustic **campsites** and the trailhead for H23 see p.139, and remains unpaved for more than thirty miles. Along the way you'll pass through patches of woods, large marshy areas, and attractive open meadows. The Winegar Hole Wilderness to the north was created in 1984 to protect **grizzly habitat**, but other creatures to watch out for include black bear, moose, fox, elk, and waterfowl like sandhill cranes and loons; the area is also renowned for **wildflowers**, which thrive in the plentiful wet zones. At **Grassy Lake** itself, eleven miles from Flagg Ranch, the road crosses over a dam built in the 1930s as part of a compromise to appease those who wanted to dam Yellowstone Lake. Three separate trailheads just north of the lake lead to some of Yellowstone's most isolated attractions, including stunning Union Falls (see H22, p.137). Approximately 15 miles further west from Grassy Lake is the road's prettiest sight, **Indian Lake**; covered in a blanket of lily pads, it's a wonderful picnic area where bald eagles and moose are commonly seen.

Continuing west, the road turns back to pavement within a few miles. If heading to Yellowstone's Bechler Corner, look out for signs pointing towards **Cave Falls Road** soon after hitting the paved stretch. Beyond the turnoff, the road races through rolling Idaho farmland, with the sloping backside of the Teton Range clearly visible all the way to **ASHTON**, a small town of just over 1000 residents dominated by pair of grain elevators. From Ashton, it's fifty miles northeast on Hwy-20 and over Targhee Pass (7072ft) to West Yellowstone (see Chapter 12, p.224).

4

Day hikes

Beyond the parking lots and boardwalks lies the parks' greatest feature, the wilderness itself. There are nearly **1500 miles of trails** weaving through Yellowstone and Grand Teton, and no trip is complete without at least a long ramble or two. Regrettably, only a small percentage of visitors head out for a hike of any length, perhaps due to a mistaken assumption that mysterious gear and a secret set of backcountry skills are needed. Whatever the cause, buck the trend and dedicate as much time as possible to hiking; you'll be rewarded by some stellar scenery and welcome solitude away from the crowds.

The shorter **interpretive trails** – like the boardwalk loops through the main geyser basins – have been detailed within the park chapters of the Guide. The forty hikes discussed within this chapter and the next cover only a portion of the options in both parks, but are a great start for both first-time and veteran visitors. Picking out the "best" hike within either park is impossible as the spectrum of choice is just too vast. Certain hikes are better for wildlife or dramatic vistas, however, and we've included a short **comment** at the start of each hike to help narrow down your choice. Generally speaking, you're best off picking a trail that's close to where your day begins or en route to your evening's destination. Virtually every trailhead leads past something memorable, and there's little point in wasting an hour or two in the car heading to a different area before striking out.

If you follow the basic rules, hiking one of the less strenuous trails in this chapter should be quite easy, regardless of age or experience. If you want a **guided hike**, however, several of the local non-profits and tour operators listed in Chapter 10 offer them; these aren't only for novice hikers, as visitors looking for information on specific subjects ranging from bear behavior to geology can gain from them as well. More **experienced hikers** may feel restricted by the day-hiking recommendations and can flip to Chapter 5, "Backcountry hiking and camping."

Hiking practicalities

A backcountry use permit is not required for a day hike. That doesn't mean, however, that hikers should head straight out without certain **prerequisites**. Along with a map, you'll want to be wearing suitable shoes, have plenty of water and some food in case of emergency, and – most importantly – pack warm and waterproof clothing. Fierce thunderstorms are common throughout summer and it can snow any month of the year, so always be prepared for the worst. For full details on footwear, clothing and what equipment to lug along with you, see pp.150–152 in Chapter 5, "Backcountry hiking and camping."

Hiking and backcountry guidelines

- **Stay on the trail** Walk single file, avoid cutting switchbacks, and limit track-broadening by walking through any wet areas. Avoid injury or worse in hydrothermal areas by sticking to boardwalks and designated trails.
- **Pack out all trash** If you pack it in, pack it out. Some hikers even carry a plastic bag and pick up stuff dropped by less considerate souls.
- **No souvenirs** Leaving no trace also means leaving all as you found it. Fallen antlers, wildflowers, driftwood, and the like are not fair game and should be left untouched.
- **Bury bodily wastes** Use the vault toilets found at most trailheads, but if you get caught short, bury waste at least six inches deep and over forty paces away from any stream or river.
- **Pack out toilet paper** Attempts to burn toilet paper have caused wildfires.
- **Stand aside for horses** Horses and mules are common on many trails – stop on the side of the trail to let them pass.
- **Purify drinking water** Either use a *giardia*-rated filter or boil the water for 3–5 minutes.
- **Camp away from water and trails** Wherever you camp, make sure you are over forty paces away from lakes and streams, and out of sight of nearby trails.
- **No "improvements"** Don't build windbreaks or new fire rings, dig trenches, or cut vegetation for bough beds.
- **Follow fire rules** Never light a fire where banned, and when allowed use only existing fire rings. If you must have a fire, burn only dead and down wood.
- **Wash clean** Avoid putting anything in the water. Carry washing water away from lakes and streams. Even biodegradable soap pollutes.
- **Be bear-safe** See the box on p.118.

Staying on track

For the most part, trails throughout both parks are well maintained, with clearly posted **signs** detailing directions and distances at most intersections. The majority of trailheads likewise have posted directions and any necessary trail updates, and free **trail maps** are available at visitor centers, providing a basic sketch of recommended day hikes. However, for any trip into the woods over a mile or two in length, you should bring along a detailed **topographic map**. Signs can get blown down, knocked over by bison, or simply vandalized, and it's not uncommon to follow an animal track mistakenly or somehow get turned around and need geographic landmarks for guidance. A variety of options are sold in the region's visitor centers and most ranger stations. Highly recommended are the series of waterproof maps by Trails Illustrated (National Geographic). The overall map of Grand Teton (1:78,000; $10) is fine for the smaller of the two parks, but the Yellowstone map (1:168,500; $10) is really too minute of scale to be of much use. Instead, chose one or more of the maps splitting Yellowstone into four equal-size quadrants (1:63,360; $9 each): Old Faithful Area, Mammoth Hot Springs Area, Tower/Canyon Area, and Yellowstone Lake Area.

Safety

Hiking alone is not recommended, and even when hiking with a group you should ideally let someone know what your plans are and when you expect to return. Heed the advice of rangers, and sign in at all trailheads wherever you're

Hospitals and clinics in and near both parks are detailed in Basics; see on p.29.

expected to do so. The most common **safety issues** come down to errors of judgment rather than natural disasters, and most can be averted simply by making sensible decisions based on your level of backcountry experience. There are lots of fantastic hiking opportunities available in well-traveled areas with clearly marked trails, so you're better off sticking to these if your experience is limited. Remember too that a detailed topographic **map** and **compass** are only helpful if you know how to use them.

Mountain weather is notoriously unpredictable, and hail and snowstorms crop up at any time of the year. **Hypothermia** is a serious threat and the number-one cause of hiking deaths; regardless of conditions when setting out, always pack a warm, waterproof layer and put it on before you get wet or cold. When hiking above the treeline you'll be completely exposed to the sun, in which case a lightweight long-sleeve shirt is a very good idea, in addition to a hat. If **lightning** becomes a potential threat, head back down below the treeline; if stuck in the open, crouch between a couple of boulders, or hunker down on top of some insulating material such as a foam sleeping mat. **Altitude sickness** is also of concern; see Basics, p.30 for more information and for tips on adjusting more quickly to the region's elevation.

Thermal areas also demand caution. When in a geyser basin, always stick to marked trails to avoid burns (or worse) by breaking through any thin crusts covering boiling water. Never travel through thermal areas after dark – even park employees have been fatally burnt doing so – and remember that it's illegal to bathe in any thermal waters that are completely of thermal origin (see p.167 for legal places to dip). Certain trails, especially in the wilder Bechler area, require a **river crossing**. For this, bring along a pair of sturdy sandals or old sneakers – you should never cross barefoot and you'll regret it if your boots get wet – and lock arms with a partner or use a walking stick for balance. Also unstrap your pack so you can slip out quickly should you fall. If a crossing seems particularly perilous or is over thigh-deep, turn around and head back.

Encounters with large **animals** such as bears, elk, bison, and moose demand awareness and respect (for details on bears, see p.118). As park rules state, you must stay at least 100 yards away from bears and at least 25 yards away from all other animals. You're far more likely to be bothered by such things as **mosquitoes** and **ticks**, for which a strong repellent and long pants are your best defenses. When hiking through brushy areas, always end the day with a thorough body search for ticks. Lyme disease has yet to arrive in these parts, but ticks here can pass on Colorado tick fever and Rocky Mountain spotted fever. While rare, both have similar symptoms – headaches and muscle aches, nausea, vomiting, skin rash, and abdominal pain. If you find a tick burrowing into your skin, grab it by the head with a pair of tweezers and gently pull it out. If any of the above symptoms occur within two weeks after contact with a tick, see a doctor.

Always take caution when **eating** or **drinking** in the wild. All water not taken from a tap, regardless of how clean the source appears, should be boiled for a few minutes or pumped through a *giardia*-rated filter. And unless you are absolutely sure of your abilities to pick out edible berries, plants, and mushrooms in the wild, do not eat them. There are at least a half-dozen varieties of poisonous mushrooms in the parks, and water hemlock – a member of the carrot/parsnip family – is responsible for two known deaths in Yellowstone's recorded history.

Bear awareness

Being **bear aware** within the Yellowstone region is of vital importance, to both humans and the local ursine population. There are an estimated 600 **grizzly bears** and 500–600 **black bears** within Yellowstone alone, and you don't want to meet any of them up close. In both parks, sightings are monitored and posted at ranger stations and trailheads, and the risks of running into a bear are pretty low on heavily tramped trails. Regardless, it's still essential when hiking and camping to be vigilant, obey basic rules, know the difference between a black bear and a grizzly (the latter are bigger and have a humped neck), know how to avoid dangerous encounters, and understand what to do if confronted or attacked.

The first thing to remind yourself of is not to be overly afraid. Attacks are very **rare** and you should not let the following warnings cancel your plans. Play by the rules, and your trip should work out as smoothly as planned. Popular misconceptions about bears abound – that they can't climb trees, for example (they can, and very quickly) – so it's worth picking up the National Park Services free bear country leaflets, which cut through the confusion and lay out some occasionally eye-opening procedures.

The cardinal rules

Be prepared by following the **cardinal rules**: store food and garbage properly, make sure bears know you're there, don't approach or feed them, and, if you find yourself approached by one, don't scream and don't run. When hiking, walk in a group – bears rarely attack more than four in a group – and make noise, lots of it, as you traverse the wilderness; bears are most threatened if surprised, so warning of your approach will give them time to leave the area. Many people shout, rattle cans with stones in or carry a whistle; be warned though: the widely touted hand-held tinkling bells are not loud enough. Be especially alert and noisy when close to streams, in tall vegetation, or when traveling into the wind, as your scent won't carry to warn bears of your approach: move straight away from dead animals and berry patches, which are important food sources. Watch for bear signs – get out quick if you see fresh tracks, diggings, or droppings – and keep in the open as much as possible. Report any sightings to a ranger as soon as possible.

As for **camping** do so away from rushing water, paths, and animal trails, and keep the site scrupulously clean, leaving nothing hanging around in the open. Lock food and trash in a car, or hang it well away from your tent between two trees at least 15 feet above the ground (many campgrounds have bear poles or steel food boxes). Take all rubbish away – don't bury it (bears will just dig it up) and certainly don't store it in or near the tent. Avoid smelly foods, all fresh, dried, or tinned meat and fish, and never store food, cook, or eat in or near the tent – lingering smells may invite unwanted nocturnal visits. Aim to cook at least 150 yards downwind of the tent: freeze-dried meals and plastic-bag-sealed food is best. Likewise, keep food off clothes and sleeping bags, and sleep in clean clothes at night. One technique worth considering is stopping to cook and eat dinner on the trail before arriving at your backcountry site, thus keeping the scent of food away from your overnight area.

Close encounters and attacks

Bears are unpredictable, and experts can't seem to agree on the best tactics after an **encounter**: there's no guaranteed life-saving way of coping with an aggressive bear.

One final factor likely to give pause is Grand Teton National Park's **hunting season** for elk (roughly mid-Oct through Nov). Reflecting the shortage of large predators in Grand Teton, the park opens sections of the grassy lowlands alongside the Snake River between Moose and Moran junctions, and also further north towards Flagg Ranch, to hunters. Assuming that a bright orange vest is not part of your regular hiking apparel, it's best to avoid these areas when the shooters are about.

Calm behavior, however, has proved to be the most successful strategy in preventing an attack. Bears don't actually want to attack; they simply want to know you're not a threat. Bears in the act of feeding and mothers with cubs are particularly dangerous and prone to suspicion. When a bear makes woofing noises, snaps its jaw, puts its head down and ears back or moves toward you, it generally means that it has picked you as a target. A bear raised on its hind legs and sniffing is trying to identify you: if it does it frequently, though, it's getting agitated. Ideally, on first encounter you want to stand stock still, never engage in direct eye contact (perceived as aggressive by the bear) and – absurd as it sounds – start speaking to it in low tones. Whatever you do, don't run, which simply sets off an almost inevitable predator–prey response in the bear (a bear can manage 35mph – easily faster than the fastest Olympic sprinter); instead, back away quietly and slowly at the first encounter, looking downward and speaking gently all the while to the bear. If the backing off seems to be working, then make a wide detour, leave the area or wait for the bear to do so – and always leave it an escape route.

If **attacked**, things are truly grim. With grizzlies, playing dead – curling up in a ball, protecting your face, neck, and abdomen – is the most effective response. Fighting back will only increase the ferocity of a grizzly attack, and there's no way you're going to win. Keep your elbows in to prevent the bear rolling you over, and be prepared to keep the position for a long time until the bear gets bored. You may get one good cuff and a few minutes' attention and that's it – injuries may still be severe but you'll probably live. With a black bear the playing dead routine won't wash, though they're not as aggressive as grizzlies, and a good bop to the nose or sufficient frenzy on your part will sometimes send a black bear running; at any rate, it's worth a try. Don't play dead with either species if the bear stalks or attacks while you're sleeping in your tent. In these cases, the bear would rather make a meal out of you instead of toss you around for amusement, so fight back with abandon – people who have survived such attacks have often had a brave companion who has attacked the bear in return with something big and heavy.

Bear spray

The one anti-bear measure sold in stores throughout the region is **bear spray**, a mace-like pepper spray designed to be blasted into the face of an attacking bear. In no way does carrying a canister substitute for the rules and precautions detailed above, but as a last-ditch resort to avoiding an attack it can be effective and we recommend carrying a can. Expect to pay $40–50, and be sure to purchase the kind with a shotgun-cloud pattern spray as opposed to a thin stream. Of course, for the spray to be effective it needs to be handy, so do not store it in your pack while hiking; keep it either holstered on your hip or in a pocket that's immediately reachable. Rumors abound of some users spraying the deterrent on themselves and their gear, as one would bug spray; don't – besides the embarrassment of explaining why you've spent the last hour having your eyes hosed out, studies have shown the spray's scent might actually attract curious grizzlies. After purchasing, read all the enclosed instructions, and be sure to test out the spray with a quick downwind blast at the start of each year.

Hikes within Yellowstone

Busy as Yellowstone's roads can be, the more than one thousand miles of trails weaving through the park are often secluded and quiet. Certainly the further one travels from the roads, the more isolated the terrain becomes; on routes like the Thorofare Trail and those within the Bechler area, it's easy to hike for a full

How tough is the hike?

All of the hikes in this guide have been given a difficulty rating in one of four categories:

Easy: Generally a walk of up to a couple of hours on relatively smooth surfaces across flat or gently sloping ground.

Moderate: A hike with some gradient but on well-maintained trails, taking up to several hours.

Strenuous: A tougher proposition on fairly steep and occasionally rough ground, usually consuming several hours if not more.

Very strenuous: A trek of at least eight hours negotiating steep terrain on uneven ground.

day without spotting another soul. But, even on the shorter and most popular paths, moments of seclusion are plentiful along with scenes of idyllic beauty and virtually guaranteed opportunities for wildlife spotting.

Mammoth Hot Springs and around

The steamy travertine terraces of **Mammoth Hot Springs** are the main roadside attraction in the northwest corner of Yellowstone, but the hikes here actually pass few thermal features. With several rivers and small ponds in the area, the featured backcountry attractions hereabouts are wildlife and wildflowers, along with some attractive waterfalls. North of Mammoth, several trails line the dusty road to Gardiner, including the terminus of the narrow path within the **Black Canyon of the Yellowstone** (see H34), ending in the affable town itself.

H1 Beaver Ponds

Difficulty Moderate
Distance 5.2 mile loop
Estimated time 2.5–4.5 hours
Season May–Oct
Trailhead location Map p.46, between Liberty Cap and the private stone-house at the northern end of the Lower Terraces.
Comments An easy to follow hike from Mammoth great for both wildflowers and elk spotting.

You almost certainly won't spot any beavers on **Beaver Ponds Trail** – they're thought to be gone from this area – but you will pass a collection of pretty ponds while cutting through fields renowned for their impressive wildflower displays. An added bonus, this is one of Yellowstone's rare loop hikes that can be walked in a single morning or afternoon.

Starting from the northern end of Mammoth's Lower Terraces, the first several hundred yards of the hike are the steepest, climbing close to 400ft up Clematis Gulch along **Sepulcher Mountain Trail**. At about the three-quarter mile point, you'll branch off to the north at a signed junction, following Beaver Ponds Trail as it heads due north from a couple miles before looping back towards Mammoth. Should you be here in early summer, you'll probably already have walked past hundreds of yellow **Arrowleaf Balsamroot** in dense clumps at this point, particularly on hillsides. Wildlife paths branch off in all directions on the main trail; if the main trail isn't evident, look for the orange blazes nailed high up on tree trunks. As you approach the ponds at the loop's northern end, the trail dips in and out of shady woods – look for the scars left

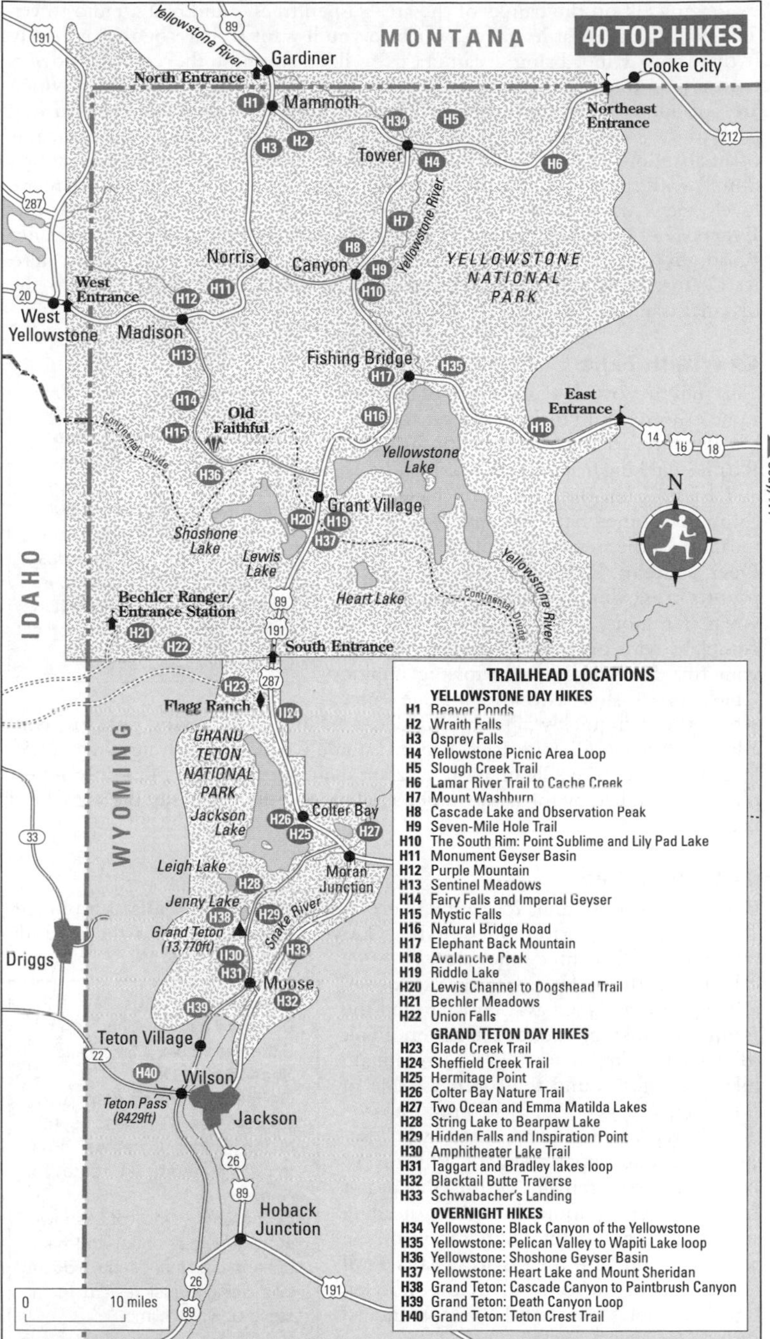

40 TOP HIKES
MONTANA
IDAHO
WYOMING
YELLOWSTONE NATIONAL PARK
GRAND TETON NATIONAL PARK
Yellowstone River
Gardiner
North Entrance
Mammoth
Cooke City
Northeast Entrance
Tower
Norris
Canyon
West Entrance
West Yellowstone
Madison
Fishing Bridge
East Entrance
Old Faithful
Continental Divide
Yellowstone Lake
Grant Village
Shoshone Lake
Lewis Lake
Heart Lake
Bechler Ranger/ Entrance Station
South Entrance
Cody, WY
N
Flagg Ranch
Jackson Lake
Colter Bay
Leigh Lake
Moran Junction
Jenny Lake
Grand Teton (13,770ft)
Snake River
Moose
Driggs
Teton Village
Wilson
Teton Pass (8429ft)
Jackson
Hoback Junction
0 10 miles
TRAILHEAD LOCATIONS
YELLOWSTONE DAY HIKES
H1 Beaver Ponds
H2 Wraith Falls
H3 Osprey Falls
H4 Yellowstone Picnic Area Loop
H5 Slough Creek Trail
H6 Lamar River Trail to Cache Creek
H7 Mount Washburn
H8 Cascade Lake and Observation Peak
H9 Seven-Mile Hole Trail
H10 The South Rim: Point Sublime and Lily Pad Lake
H11 Monument Geyser Basin
H12 Purple Mountain
H13 Sentinel Meadows
H14 Fairy Falls and Imperial Geyser
H15 Mystic Falls
H16 Natural Bridge Road
H17 Elephant Back Mountain
H18 Avalanche Peak
H19 Riddle Lake
H20 Lewis Channel to Dogshead Trail
H21 Bechler Meadows
H22 Union Falls
GRAND TETON DAY HIKES
H23 Glade Creek Trail
H24 Sheffield Creek Trail
H25 Hermitage Point
H26 Colter Bay Nature Trail
H27 Two Ocean and Emma Matilda Lakes
H28 String Lake to Bearpaw Lake
H29 Hidden Falls and Inspiration Point
H30 Amphitheater Lake Trail
H31 Taggart and Bradley lakes loop
H32 Blacktail Butte Traverse
H33 Schwabacher's Landing
OVERNIGHT HIKES
H34 Yellowstone: Black Canyon of the Yellowstone
H35 Yellowstone: Pelican Valley to Wapiti Lake loop
H36 Yellowstone: Shoshone Geyser Basin
H37 Yellowstone: Heart Lake and Mount Sheridan
H38 Grand Teton: Cascade Canyon to Paintbrush Canyon
H39 Grand Teton: Death Canyon Loop
H40 Grand Teton: Teton Crest Trail

by grazing elk on the trunks of the area's aspen trees – and past a radio tower. The path passes by at least five ponds, so you'll want to have bug spray handy if there's no wind; bring a camera as well, as amongst the colorful flowers typically spotted are the delicate **Rocky Mountain Iris** (the roots of which are poisonous) along with the gorgeous **Yellow Columbine**. After turning back to the south, the trail skirts the final, largest pond, home to the remnants of an abandoned beaver dam. Past here, the trail crosses mainly high meadows dotted with sagebrush and, often enough, elk; take your time, as the there are lovely views down to the town of **Gardiner** to the north and dusty **Mount Everts** (7842ft). Towards trail's end, you'll walk alongside the Old Gardiner Road, dipping down to its entrance behind the *Mammoth Hotel*. From here, it's a short walk past the hotel and Yellowstone General Store back to the original trailhead to complete the loop.

H2 Wraith Falls

This trail to **Wraith Falls** is one of Yellowstone's shortest, and makes for a great, quick break while driving the Mammoth-Tower Road. Switching from dirt path to boardwalk and back again, the trail starts by cutting through somewhat marshy sagebrush meadows at the western end of the **Blacktail Deer Plateau**. Even on this brief jaunt, it pays to bring along your bear spray, though you're far more likely to spot a bull elk, complete with his majestic antlers. You get your first view of the falls crossing Lupine Creek on a short wooden bridge, after which the trail quickly zigs up a moderate incline to a viewing platform with a head on view of Wraith Falls. Fed by Lupine Creek and rushing down a 95ft long rocky slide, the falls are more pleasant than powerful, and must only appear ghostly as implied by the name under a full moon. After enjoying the view, head back the way you came.

Difficulty Easy
Distance 0.7 mile round-trip
Estimated time 30 minutes
Season May–Oct
Trailhead location Map p.46. 5 miles east of Mammoth en route to Tower, a half-mile past the Lava Creek Picnic Area.
Comments An extremely short trail leading to the base of a cascade nearly 100ft long.

H3 Osprey Falls

Only those with stamina to spare will get to witness **Osprey Falls** as it plunges 150ft within the narrow **Sheepeater Canyon**. Beginning from the roadside trailhead, the first three miles are easy – the calm before the storm, as it were – following a bumpy service road as it curls around the southern flanks of rounded **Bunsen Peak** (8564ft); the dirt road is open to mountain bikes as well. Around the southeast side of the peak, you get your first view into the deep Sheepeater Canyon, named by Yellowstone's second superintendent Philetus W. Norris after the remains of the Sheepeater Indian shelters he found here. After heading steeply downhill about a hundred yards, the road meets up with the **Osprey Falls Trail** leading down the canyon. As the wooden sign here notes, the trail beyond is indeed

Difficulty Strenuous
Distance 9 miles round-trip
Estimated time 3.5–6 hours
Season May–Oct
Trailhead location Map p.46. Bunsen Peak Trailhead, south of the Golden Gate five miles from Mammoth en route to Norris.
Comments One of Yellowstone's top bike-and-hike options, with thundering, hidden falls being a just reward for a steep downhill climb.

"steep and narrow," and if you've biked in you'll have to dismount and lock up at this point.

Before beginning the long switchback descent to the **Gardner River** some 500ft below, the trail leads south along the canyon rim for about a quarter of a mile, affording views of the bands of volcanic pentagonal columns protruding from the canyon walls. You'll know when the trail begins heading down as the incline instantly turns steep and rocky; take your time on the more than mile-long climb, giving your knees plenty of breaks. As the canyon is so narrow, you don't get a view of the mighty falls until turning a corner down by the banks of the river. Awe-inspiring, the falls thunder down a fifteen-story drop, causing several hundred yards of whitewater downstream early in May and June; it remains impressive throughout the summer. If you're confident in your footing you can climb past the falls' spray for a rocky perch only a few arm's lengths from the rushing water. The walk back up is no picnic, so be sure to rest plenty before tracing your steps back to the trailhead more than four miles away.

Tower-Roosevelt and the Lamar Valley

Taking in Yellowstone's northeast quadrant, these hikes cover the stupendous **Lamar Valley**, trout-rich **Slough** and **Pebble creeks** to the north, and the northern reaches of the **Yellowstone River**. While there are few thermal areas of note, wildlife abounds and the fishing along most rivers and creeks is superb. We've also included the popular hike up **Mount Washburn**, located just about equally between Tower-Roosevelt and Canyon to the south.

H4 Yellowstone Picnic Area Loop

Difficulty Moderate
Distance 3.7 miles
Estimated time 2–3 hours
Season May–Oct
Trailhead location Map p.53. The Yellowstone River Picnic Area on the Northeast Entrance Road, one mile east of Roosevelt Junction.
Comments A family-friendly loop hike with impressive canyon views that are easy to reach.

Starting from the **Yellowstone River Picnic Area**, this looping path affords grand views down into the park's longest, strongest river around **Calcite Springs**, plus opportunities for spotting osprey and bighorn sheep. It's not a perfect loop – the final stretch back to the trailhead requires a walk alongside the Northeast Entrance Road – but the hike's second half away from the river leads through a landscape varied enough to make it worthwhile.

The trail begins by climbing steeply uphill, parallel to the road out to the Lamar Valley, to the east rim of an area known as the **Narrows of the Yellowstone**. For the next 1.5 miles, the trail sticks close to the canyon's edge, the sulphuric smells of Calcite Springs on the opposite side of the river a constant companion. Another steady trail mate are scores of **yellow-bellied marmots**, which dart amongst the rocks by the canyon edge and often approach hikers; resist the temptation to feed the cute critters. Along with peering into the canyon to check out the rows of **volcanic basalt columns** and possibly the nests of **osprey** and **peregrine falcons**, keep a sharp eye on the trail ahead for **bighorn sheep**; if they spot you first, they'll scamper further down the canyon and out of sight. As the trail nears the two-mile point, it turns east away from the river, giving a final view towards the towers guarding Tower Falls (no view of the falls, however). The next mile leads mainly downhill, weaving through fragrant sagebrush meadows and past a small stand of Aspen trees; **pronghorn** are commonly spotted grazing in the area, and **black bear** sightings are not infrequent. Upon reaching the Northeast Entrance Road, it's an unexciting 0.7-mile walk back west to the starting point.

H5 Slough Creek Trail

Difficulty Moderate
Distance 4–20 miles round-trip
Estimated time 2–12 hours
Season May–Oct
Trailhead location Map p.53. Just before *Slough Creek Campground*, a couple miles down the gravel road off the Northeast Entrance Road five miles east of Roosevelt Junction.
Comments Superb angling opportunities and a broad, attractive valley make this a very popular trail.

One of the finest backcountry trips for anglers in Yellowstone, the **Slough Creek Trail** is equally popular with backpackers, particularly late in the season for fall colors and plenty of elk-spotting opportunities. The wide path weaves its way more than ten miles from the trailhead to Yellowstone's northern border, across which sits the private **Silvertip Ranch**, which runs frequent pack and wagon trips down the trail. Should you want to hang around overnight to explore further, seven backcountry sites line the trail; all need to be booked far in advance as fishermen tend to scoop them up quickly.

The trail's first half-mile is all uphill, weeding out the unfit; that is unless they chose to ride horses in, of which there is ample and odorous trailside evidence. After flattening out, the trail leads through a lightly forested zone before dipping slowly down to Slough Creek, just under two miles from the trailhead. The attractive, broad valley area is known as the **First Meadow**, and the wagon trail, passing the Buffalo Fork Junction and then the dilapidated Slough Creek Patrol Cabins, cuts through this, with smaller paths across the tall grasses giving access to the river. Five miles from the trailhead is the **Second Meadow** and the first set of backcountry campsites, while three miles further on is the **Third Meadow**, also complemented with a set of sites and arguably the finest fishing destination. There's no real goal for day-trippers, so hike out as far as you wish, then follow your footsteps back. A second option, seven miles from the trailhead, is to take the **Bliss Pass Trail** six strenuous but stunning miles east over Bliss Pass (9250ft) to switchback down to the **Pebble Creek Trail** and back south to the Northeast Entrance Road. This makes for a very rewarding 21-mile trip, though you'll need to arrange a pick-up or hitch a ride back to the Slough Creek trailhead.

H6 Lamar River Trail to Cache Creek

Difficulty Moderate
Distance 6 miles round-trip
Estimated time 2–4 hours
Season May–Oct
Trailhead location Map p.53. Soda Butte Trailhead (also known as the Lamar River Trailhead), 16 miles east of Roosevelt on the Northeast Entrance Road
Comments Get away from the roadside wildlife watchers and into the famed, wildlife-rich valley.

Camera and scope-toting visitors flock to the roadside pullouts within the **Lamar Valley**, but few actually get out onto the valley floor for a proper hike. This relatively flat trail lets you do just that, giving hikers a bison-eye view of the valley known as "North America's Serengeti." Along with **bison**, you might see **coyote**, **pronghorn** and **mule deer**, and if you visit soon after dawn you could get lucky and hear a wolf pack howling in unison.

From the trailhead's parking lot, the hiking path immediately crosses over **Soda Butte Creek** on a simple wooden bridge; horses cannot make this crossing, which is why the **Soda Butte Stock Trailhead** is located a short drive to the west. Past the bridge, game trails lead off in multiple directions, so stick to the most clearly defined path following the flow of the creek. After hoofing up the ridge forming the edge of the creek's ancient river bed, you'll cross onto the sagebrush floor of the Lamar Valley; don't be surprised if a bison blocks your path at some point, necessitating a wide looping detour around the trail. Just over a mile in, you'll meet up with the stock trail and quickly after the first Y-junction. A right turn leads southwest on the **Specimen Ridge Trail** to a ford of the Lamar River a half-mile away; head left instead, sticking to the southeastern **Lamar River Trail** (which doesn't actually reach the Lamar until four miles later) as it traces the lower shoulder of Mount Norris (9985ft) to the east. For nearly two miles, the trail leads uphill at an easy angle, through the grassy lower end of the Lamar Valley that roadside spotting scopes cannot reach; the opposite hillsides here may be heavily fire scarred, but it's still an equally beautiful and, away from the roads, more peaceful stretch of the valley.

Soon after passing high above an obvious, white thermal stretch tucked into woods off the Lamar River, the trail reaches the second Y-junction. To the left is the **Cache Creek Trail**, which heads east then northeast along the creek for more than twenty miles, eventually crossing Republic Pass (10491ft) and dipping into the Shoshone National Forest and Cooke City beyond. Head right instead, sticking to the Lamar River Trail that leads south and down an often-muddy slope to **Cache Creek** itself. The creek's rocky riverbed is a perfect place to break for a picnic or a couple of hours fishing, with plenty of washed up logs to relax on before returning the way you came. The first of more than a dozen backcountry campsites (3L1) along the Lamar River Trail is here as well, though the rest are located across the creek, a 30-foot ford not recommended until late June at the earliest.

H7 Mount Washburn

Difficulty Strenuous
Distance 5 miles round-trip
Estimated time 3–5 hours
Season June–Sept
Trailhead location Map p.53. 1.4 miles up the Chittenden Road, located 6 miles south of Tower Falls on the Tower-Canyon Road.
Comments Stupendous views, bighorn sheep, and a central location make this one of the park's top hikes.

Rangers often rate the trip up **Mount Washburn** (10,243ft) the best bet for those who have time for only one hike, and it's hard to argue with them. A 1500-foot uphill trek the entire way, hikers are rewarded with some of the best **panoramic views** of the park, plus **bighorn sheep** are frequently seen. Two paths lead up the peak from the Grand Loop Road between Canyon and Tower, one leaving from the **Chittenden Road Trailhead** on Mount Washburn's north side, the other leaving from the **Dunraven Pass Trailhead** on the south side. We've chosen to cover the former as it's mountain-bike-accessible and slightly shorter, but details are similar should you choose the mile-longer Dunraven Pass Trail. If in a group with more than one car, consider leaving a ride at both trailheads and hiking up one and down the other.

Named after Henry Dana Washburn, surveyor-general of the Montana Territories and leader of the 1870 Washburn Expedition (see p.268), the peak, tallest in the Washburn Range, is a remnant of an extinct stratovolcano. From the end of Chittenden Road, the wide 2.5-mile trail (actually a service road) up the

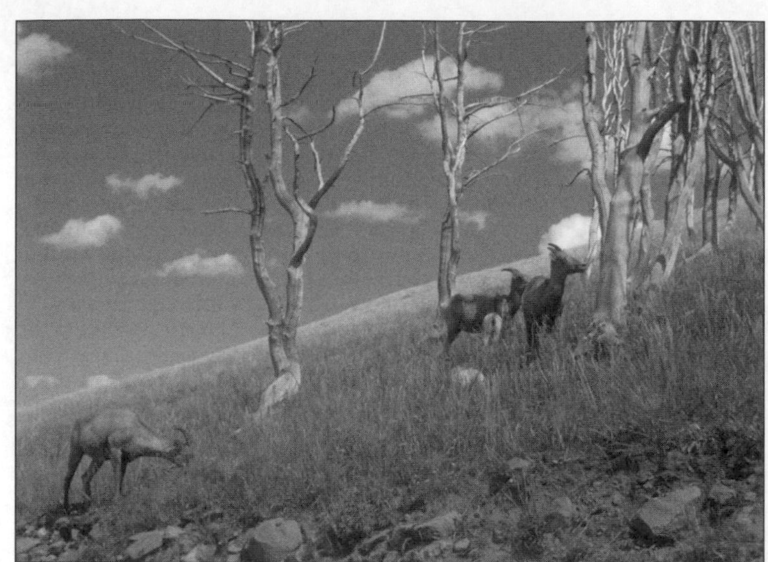

△ Female bighorn sheep (ewes) on Mount Washburn

ancient volcano's north side never gets overly steep, and with frequent breaks groups with kids and less fit hikers should find the journey manageable. As with any other alpine zone, the **flora** hereabouts is particularly delicate – look out for blue lupines, pink monkey flowers, and violet shooting stars – so always stay on trail. As the route up is exposed, pack warm and waterproof gear, and start heading down at the first sign of a storm. Atop the peak sits a three-story **fire tower**, complete with bathrooms, payphone, and indoor/outdoor viewing platforms. Diagrams here point out the major sights, including mighty Grand Teton, visible 75 miles to the south.

Canyon and around

The **Canyon** area lays claim to the finest compact cluster of trails within the park. South of the **Grand Canyon of the Yellowstone**, a tight trail-network gives the option of creating a variety of loops varying from an hour in length to a full day or more, while the canyon's north side includes hikes to **Mount Washburn** (see H7 for a shorter route) and the excellent trail to **Seven-Mile Hole**. Furthermore, trailheads located north towards Tower and west towards Norris lead to several **backcountry lakes**, include Cascade (H8), Grebe, Ice, Wolf and the Cygnet Lakes.

H8 Cascade Lake and Observation Peak

Starting a mile north of Canyon Village, this hike has nothing to do with the Yellowstone River or the surrounding canyon area; instead, it's a journey tailor-made for **wildflower** lovers, along with peak-baggers looking to crest **Observation Peak** (9397ft), a steep uphill climb starting from **Cascade Lake**. Beginning from the edge of the Cascade Picnic Area, a flat trail leads straight west into scrubby woods, where a sign-in box awaits a hundred yards in. Check the recent postings: **grizzlies** are known to forage trailside, and should previous hikers that day mention a spotted bear, it's advisable to skip the trail and head elsewhere. Just beyond, the trail cuts alongside a large circular meadow where hawks circle overhead and moose are sometimes spotted nibbling on willow growing alongside tiny creeks. After hopping over a few of these small streams, the trail intersects with the **Cascade Creek Trail**, which leads 1.7 miles south to the Canyon-Norris Road. Turn right to continue west to Cascade Lake, crossing through a tangle of new growth and burnt lodgepole creaking in the wind before entering a second, narrower meadow. If it's rained lately, things can be pretty muddy from here to the lake, as the meadow turns marshy and the trail crosses over crystal clear Cascade Creek on a short footbridge. The lake itself can be a bit of a letdown, particularly if it's cloudy out as it's southern half is rung by a forest of dead trees; however, there are typically several types of wildflowers in bloom throughout summer, including the yellow glacier lily and the purple, bell-shaped sugarbowl.

Difficulty Moderate to strenuous
Distance 5 miles round-trip to lake, 11 miles round-trip to summit
Estimated time 2–3 hours lake, 7–9 hours summit
Season May–Oct
Trailhead location Map p.57. Cascade Picnic Area, a mile north of Canyon Village on the Canyon-Tower Road.
Comments An easy hike to a little lake through attractive, wildflower-filled meadows, with the option of tacking on a stiff peak hike.

There are also three **backcountry sites** by the lake, useful if you're planning on trying some fishing (the little lake holds grayling and cutthroats, as does **Grebe Lake** a four-mile hike west) or plan on making a more leisurely climb up Observation Peak. Starting from the north end of Cascade Lake, the trail up takes in 1650 vertical feet in just three miles, meaning it's a steady climb the entire way; bring plenty of water as well, as there's no dependable source en route. The panoramic views from atop the aptly named peak are stupendous, with the southern view of the Hayden Valley particularly enchanting.

H9 Seven-Mile Hole Trail

The steep hike down the **Grand Canyon of the Yellowstone** to **Seven-Mile Hole** is another top-candidate in the "if you only have time for one hike" category, provided you have the stamina for the steep, long uphill climb required on the way back out. Along with passing two of the park's longest waterfalls, the trail leads by a pretty high-altitude meadow, through an active thermal area, and down to the banks of the trout-rich Yellowstone River, with views of the canyon's gorgeous multi-colored walls along the way.

Difficulty Strenuous
Distance 10 miles round-trip
Estimated time 5–8 hours
Season May–Oct
Trailhead location Map p.57. Glacier Boulder Trailhead, by Inspiration Point on the one-way North Rim Drive.
Comments Tough on the knees, this steep downhill slog passes two epic waterfalls en route to an idyllic spot by the Yellowstone River.

The trail starts by weaving through the woods for a quarter-mile before reaching the north rim. There's no view of Lower or Upper Falls, both hidden a few bends upstream, but the canyon walls are spectacular enough on their own. Continuing alongside the canyon edge, the trail takes just over a mile to reach a clear view across the canyon to **Silver Chord Falls**, the tallest waterfall in Yellowstone. (Its length is listed between 800–1000ft, depending on whether or not one includes the rocky waterslide at its base). The thin falls lives up to its name later in the day, when the afternoon sun turns the narrow stream into a metallic arrow shooting down through the smallest of gaps. Past here, the trail – dotted with pieces of volcanic obsidian – dips back into the lodgepole forest for a peaceful, if a bit dull stretch, where your sole companion will be the creaking of trees; you'll more than likely have to crawl under or hop over recently fallen trees across the trail. Just before reaching the junction with the **Mount Washburn Trail** at the 2.7-mile point, the path parallels a pretty grassy meadow with views of the peak to the north. Continuing towards Seven-Mile Hole, the trail reaches the canyon edge again in about a half mile.

Now the real work begins, as the trail heads downward nearly 1500ft in just over two miles. The trail doesn't switchback much, instead leading steeply downhill across plenty of crumbling rocks. Unlike the bare walls upstream, the sides of the canyon here are heavily forested, with large swathes of green reaching down to the riverbank. There are still signs of thermal action though, beginning with a fifteen-foot tall **sinter cone** tucked prettily amongst the trees trailside. And a couple minutes further on, you'll cross straight through a shadeless, bright-white **thermal zone** featuring a handful of small bubbling springs and steaming vents. Past the thermal area is a backcountry site (4C1), by the river on its own path, and soon after photogenic **Twin Falls** can be seen across the canyon, a streak of white water and attendant green plant life cascading 135ft between pink and rust-red canyon walls. After passing a second backcountry site (4C2) located trailside, the trail spills out onto **Seven-Mile Hole** itself. It's an idyllic spot for a riverside picnic or an overnight stay, with the trail ending across tiny **Sulphur Creek** at the best of the backcountry sites (4C3), spectacularly located on a flat spot 100ft above the roaring river. As fishing is allowed downstream of Silver Chord Falls, the

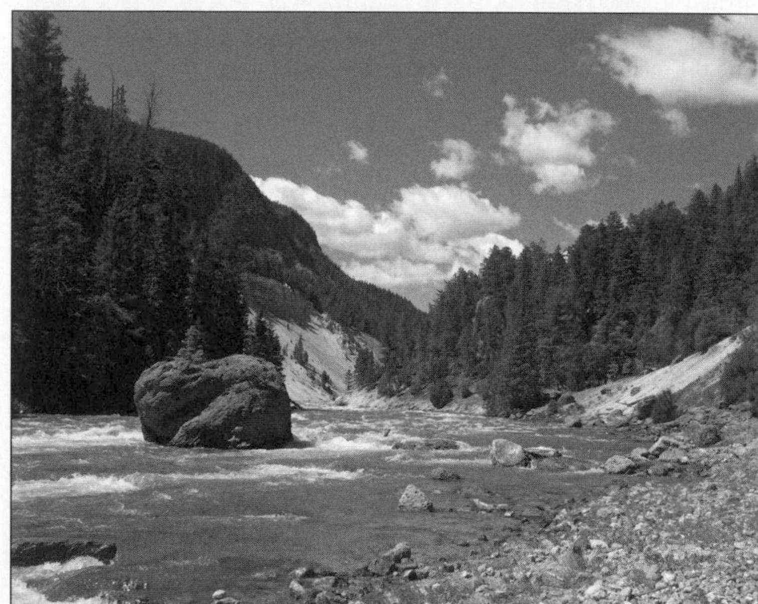

△ Seven Mile Hole

area boasts superb fly-fishing for native cutthroat, which can sometimes be spotted clustered in Sulphur Creek's bathtub-sized pools.

Once you're done hanging out, you'll have to return the way you came; don't forget to fill up on filtered water in the creek or river beforehand.

H10 The South Rim: Point Sublime and Lily Pad Lake

Difficulty Moderate
Distance 2.5 miles round-trip
Estimated Time 1–2 hours
Season May–Oct
Trailhead Location Map p.57. The Ribbon Lake Trailhead, accessed from the Artist Point parking area.
Comments One of many worthwhile trips along the scenic south rim.

This hike along the **Grand Canyon of the Yellowstone** is only one of several great options within the spider web of trails along the canyon's south rim. Some worthwhile detours have been noted, and if you have the time we recommend walking the entire **South Rim Trail**, starting from the Wapiti Trailhead near the Chittenden Bridge and looping back via the Clear Lake Trail. The following route takes in the South Rim Trail's unpaved eastern half, beginning from bustling **Artist Point**. After enjoying the renowned vista and perhaps one of the frequent ranger talks held here, leave the crowds behind by heading up the trail to the east. For the next mile, the path rolls up and down short but steep terrain, alternating between forest and the canyon edge before reaching **Point Sublime**, marked by a rough fence post defining the trail's end. There are several superb, unobstructed views of the canyon along the way, its walls streaked in dramatic pink, orange and rust-reds and dotted with ridges atop which lodgepole pines cling to life on the narrowest of knife-edges. As the trail literally forms the canyon edge at points (a slide off of which would be tragic indeed), this hike is not recommended for visitors with children.

After relaxing at Point Sublime – a pretty, if less spectacular look east at the forested walls of canyon downstream – start heading back. This time, however, when passing the junction with the **Ribbon Lake Trail** at the halfway point, turn south to at least visit pretty **Lily Pad Lake** less than five minutes down the trail. Just before reaching it, you'll pass a sign-in box; there's no need to register if just going to Lily Pad Lake, but check anyway for any recent wildlife reports. The lake itself is more of a pond, attractively topped with hundreds if not thousands of pads; you'll probably not want to linger however, as the mosquitoes can be ferocious. From here, either return the way you came, or expand the hike by heading further east to **Ribbon Lake** and the brink of **Silver Chord Cascade** beyond (better viewed across the canyon on H9), or west to green-tinged **Clear Lake**. If heading to the latter, you'll pass through a large thermal area featuring large **mudpots** along the way.

Norris and Madison junctions

Norris and **Madison** are the two most low-key junctions on the park's Grand Loop Road, both with campgrounds but no commercial services. There are very few marked hiking trails between them as well, and the two most popular are listed below. More trails can be reached heading west from Madison towards West Yellowstone, including a short jaunt to **Harlequin Lake** and the relatively flat **Gneiss Creek Trail**, starting along the Madison River and cutting northeast through the Madison Valley to a trailhead on Hwy-191, fourteen miles away; crossing several creeks along the way, it's a good option for anglers seeking solitude, though there's only one backcountry campsite (WA1) along the entire stretch.

H11 Monument Geyser Basin

Difficulty Moderate
Distance 2 miles round-trip
Estimated Time 1–2 hours
Season May–Oct
Trailhead Location Map p.62. Due south of the Gibbon River Bridge, around 5 miles south of Norris and 8 miles north of Madison.
Comments Take a short break to head to this small backcountry geyser basin, found atop a short but steep climb south of Gibbon Meadows.

Starting south of the Gibbon River Bridge – around which several thermal features puff away – this short and worthwhile ramble leads to a bizarre backcountry geyser basin. The trail begins by following the river upstream for a quarter-mile, passing pockets of lily pads floating in the stream's calmest corners. Once the trail breaks from the river, the path begins a moderately sharp zig-zagging route up to the geyser basin. Along the way, you'll earn pretty views of **Gibbon Meadows** due north – the river looking like a twisted blue ribbon as it lazily floats through its namesake meadows – and snow-capped Mount Holmes in the background. Up top the trail flattens out as you enter into the **Monument Geyser Basin**, located a mile from the trailhead. A narrow, chalky strip 200 yards long, the basin features steaming vents and small sizzling pots, along with a series of bizarre, chimney-shaped sinter cones that has earned it its name. It all seems transported from another planet, or better yet, some monochromatic book by Dr. Seuss. While most of the skinny cones have been sealed, the biggest, known as **Thermos Bottle Geyser**, still manages to let off steam, though it will also soon close itself. Do not travel beyond the basic log and stone boundaries set up at trail's end as you could easily break through crust and burn your foot. Once done poking around, return the way you came.

H12 Purple Mountain

Difficulty Strenuous
Distance 6.5 miles round-trip
Estimated Time 3–4 hours
Season May–Oct
Trailhead Location Map p.62. Small roadside parking area 100 yards north of Madison Junction.
Comments Great views across Yellowstone's west entrance area.

This hilltop hike certainly isn't one of Yellowstone's finest trails, but views from the top are nonetheless worth the effort and it's handily located within walking distance of campers at nearby **Madison Campground**. Starting from the Madison-Norris Road due north of Madison Junction, the trail immediately snakes into a new growth forest and travels alongside a dry ravine (bring plenty of water, as there's no reliable trailside source throughout). For more than three miles, the trail climbs 1500ft up **Purple Mountain** at a remarkably consistent pace through a "lodgepole desert" landscape supporting the tall and narrow trees and little else. At least you'll get plenty of shade, and the trail is smooth throughout, meaning running shoes or sturdy sandals are suitable should you want to jog up. From the peak of the tall hill, park views include the Gibbon Valley to the north and the Firehole Valley, streams of steam rising from the many geysers and pools, to the south. Further off are clear shots of regional mountain ranges, including the Absarokas, Madison, and on the clearest of days, even the Tetons far to the south.

Old Faithful and around

The hikes in this section cover the 33-mile stretch of road from Madison southeast to West Thumb, with **Old Faithful** located at the halfway point. The area is home to the world's greatest collection of thermal features, and hikes here access notable backcountry geysers and springs that many visitors never get to see. All of the mainly boardwalk-based geyser basin trails, including the entire **Upper Geyser Basin**, are covered in detail in Chapter 2, while the popular **Lone Star Geyser Group** is described as part of a longer hike to the backcountry **Shoshone Geyser Basin** (H36) in Chapter 5.

H13 Sentinel Meadows

Difficulty Easy to Moderate
Distance 4 miles round-trip
Estimated Time 2–3 hours
Season May–Oct
Trailhead Location Map p.71. Trailhead located at the end of the Lower Geyser Basin's Fountain Flat Drive.
Comments Walk attractive meadows where bison roam early in summer, plus the chance to visit the remains of a historic bathhouse.

Starting from the parking lot at the end of **Fountain Flat Drive**, this relaxed hike kicks off by following an old gravel road; biking is allowed along this stretch all the way to the Fairy Falls Trailhead (H14), though you'll likely see more anglers walking the road on the way to fishing spots on the Firehole River, which the road crosses 0.3 miles from the start. Sizzling nearby and constantly discharging the rivers is **Ojo Caliente Spring**, surrounded by a stone circle intended to keep people away; as the name implies, the boiling spring is hot indeed (200°F).

Just past the bridge across the river, the **Sentinel Meadows Trail** (no bikes) breaks off to the west, heading downstream alongside the river through a grassy field carpeted with purple, yellow, and white wildflowers in June and July. After cutting away from the river, the trail begins its path through **Sentinel Meadows**, a favorite grazing spot of bison through mid-July before most migrate to their summer habitat in the Hayden Valley. Some of the best views of the beautiful meadow are just past a pair of backcountry sites (OG1, OG2), as the trail crests a small hump. Looking across the green expanse from here, the obvious focal points are three massive thermal mounds known as **Flat Cone**, **Mound Spring**, and **Steep Cone**, each puffing away like a steam engine. From the hump, it's just over a half-mile, partly through patches of new growth forest, to the spring known as **Queen's Laundry**. The bubbling, blue pool was officially named by Superintendent Norris in 1880 after the brightly colored clothes early park workers hung in the nearby bushes while "gambolling like dolphins in the pools." The roofless **log hut** that stands nearby is actually a National Historic Site; built by Norris in 1881 as a bathhouse, the unassuming ruin has the distinction of being the first building constructed for public use in any national park. Swimming is no longer allowed hereabouts, so after taking a break, follow your footsteps in back to the trailhead.

H14 Fairy Falls and Imperial Geyser

This hike makes for an easy trip out to one of the region's prettiest and tallest falls, with the option of tacking on an extra 1.5 miles round-trip to visit one of Yellowstone's most beautiful backcountry geyser pools. From the roadside trailhead, the hike begins by crossing the **Firehole River** on a steel bridge

Difficulty Moderate
Distance 5 miles round-trip to Fairy Falls, 6.5 miles to Imperial Geyser
Estimated Time 2–4 hours
Season May–Oct
Trailhead Location Map p.62. Fairy Falls Trailhead, just south of the Midway Geyser Basin
Comments Graceful falls and a stunning backcountry geyser make this a must-do hike in the Old Faithful area.

and then follows an old road for a mile. This section is open to bikes as well, allowing for a **bike/hike** option to shorten the overall trip time. As the road passes to the south of the Midway Geyser Basin, you get a good view of colorful **Excelsior Geyser** along the way. At the one-mile point, the trail to **Fairy Falls** branches off to the west (no bikes allowed), leading 1.5 miles through a forest of naturally reseeded lodgepole pines, varying in height from 4 to18ft and proving the fires of 1988 were but a temporary setback. Halfway to the falls is a **backcountry site** (OD1) that's one of the closest such sites to a trailhead in the park. The last few hundred yards approaching the falls are the most dramatic, with charred tree trunks standing guard over a green-carpeted forest floor, the steep, craggy edge of the Madison Plateau looming to the south. It's off this rocky-face that Fairy Falls itself plummets, a wispy yet plenty dramatic 197-foot plunge between white-grey rocks and forming a calm, perfect pool at its base.

While many visitors snap their photos and begin heading back, it pays to continue onwards to a series of geysers 0.7 miles further ahead. If it's been raining recently, be prepared for plenty of mud and bugs, but **Imperial Geyser**, the biggest of the bunch, is worth the effort. Framed by the rounded humps of **Twin Buttes**, the geyser first became active in the mid 1920s, spouting as high as 80ft into the air. It quickly became a visitor favorite, even earning its name in a newspaper contest to drum up publicity for Yellowstone. However, the geyser went dormant soon after, and hibernated for nearly four decades before erupting again at smaller heights. Still active, the geyser continues to change dramatically, and at the time of writing it consisted of a large, beautiful green and blue pool, spouting up in five-foot boiling bursts towards the center. Also look for a hot-tub sized gurgling mudpot and several steaming nearby vents that have erupted in the past. From Imperial it's possible to head north several miles to visit the **Queens Laundry and Sentinel Meadows** (H13), a side-trip that can be turned into a long loop or, better yet, a one-way hike if a second car is left at the end of Fountain Flat Drive. If neither is an option, head back the way you came, past Fairy Falls again, to the original trailhead.

H15 Mystic Falls

Difficulty Easy/Moderate
Distance .7 miles one way to the falls; or 3-mile loop
Estimated Time 1.5 to 2.5 hours
Season Late May to early Oct
Trailhead Location Map p.71. West end of Biscuit Basin boardwalk, about 2 miles north of Old Faithful.
Comments A short jaunt to spectacular steaming falls, with an optional high-climbing loop that gives a great overview of Biscuit Basin.

Spectacular **Mystic Falls** is a reward for those willing to depart the visitor clogged boardwalks of the Biscuit Basin. After viewing the geysers and pools here, find the trail to the falls at the west end of the boardwalk. A half-mile walk through a low coniferous forest (re-growth from the 1988 fires) lands hikers at a fork. To continue the easy hike to the seventy-foot-high falls, take a left along the Firehole River and follow the rumble of the water for another 0.2 miles.

Heartier hikers should take a right at the fork for a great view of **Biscuit Basin**, climbing the steep switchbacks of a deeply carved cliff. Lined with raspberries and huckleberries, the path is as sweet in berry season as it is steep. Grey jays, tiny chipmunks, and fat golden-mantled ground squirrels are trailside companions. From the top, the scattered debris of the sapphire pool 500ft below is visible; this geyser exploded violently in 1959, four days after a 7.5 magnitude earthquake, which disrupted numerous thermal features in the vicinity. In the distance the buildings around Old Faithful can be seen along with various jets and steam clouds from every part of the valley. The loop eventually begins to drop in altitude on a less-steep set of switchbacks just above the falls; watch for loose gravel along the steep drop-offs.

To extend this hike, the Mystic Falls loop connects with trails to **Summit Lake** (7.2 miles) and **Fairy Falls** (9.2 miles one-way; see p.131).

Lake Village, Fishing Bridge, and the East Entrance

These hikes cover a large swathe of the park around Yellowstone Lake's northern and eastern shores, from the area around Lake Village east to Fishing Bridge and along the twisting East Entrance road. Much of the area is prime **grizzly country**, particular the narrow and beautiful **Pelican Valley** and the nearby shores of Lake Yellowstone around **Mary Bay**; trail closures due to bear activity are possible, so keep an eye out for signs. See the box on p.118 for details on necessary precautions.

H16 Natural Bridge Road

Difficulty Easy
Distance 3 miles round-trip
Estimated time 1–1.5 hours
Season May–Oct
Trailhead Location Map p.82. Bridge Bay Campground.
Comments An easy stroll ending at the delicate, fun to explore Natural Bridge.

The **Natural Bridge Trail**, leading to a 29-foot-span, 51-foot-high natural arch, begins on the north side of the Bridge Bay boat launch parking area (Bridge Bay campers can also access the path from their campground). The well-maintained trail traces the curve of the marina's bay, eventually leading west through a mature coniferous forest. The path then merges with a closed road that once allowed cars direct access to the fragile bridge. Now this blacktop is an easy walk for families with strollers or for less sure-footed travelers.

The road forks into a loop, with the rock bridge at its far end. The feature formed when **Bridge Creek** meandered into underground cracks in the volcanic soil; frost and freeze cycles loosened debris, letting the stream carry away the rubble over the years, leaving the isolated strip of rock above. It was discovered in 1871 by the Hayden survey party and was opened to the public ten years later when a trail was constructed across the top of it. A later proposal to build a narrow road on the bridge would have made for palm-sweating fun for early car tourists, but was never acted upon. Today signs encourage visitors to stay off the frail volcanic rock altogether.

For a different look at the geological oddity, a rocky trail leads energetic hikers to zigzag up the steep cliff about 60ft. At the top, pastoral carved stairs give access to the shallow creek that runs through the arch; straddling the trickle allows a great photo op for those who stayed at the bottom to capture their friends, high above and framed by the bridge.

H17 Elephant Back Mountain

> **Difficulty** Moderate to strenuous
> **Distance** 4-mile loop
> **Estimated time** 2–3 hours
> **Season** May–Oct
> **Trailhead location** Map p.82. Between Lake Village and the Fishing Bridge junction.
> **Comments** A rewarding loop that'll make you work to earn pleasing views over Yellowstone Lake.

As Lake Village is a short walk away, this loop up the slopes of **Elephant Back Mountain** is particularly popular early in the morning and after dinner with both overnight guests and workers staying there. If not spending the night at Lake Village, there's space for a handful of cars on either side of road at the trailhead, along with a sign-in box. Though you'd have to try pretty hard to get lost off this trail, stop to sign in and check for any **bear** updates; they've been known to frequent the area, and the trail sometimes closes late in the season as a result. From here, the trail briefly starts uphill before flattening out for around a third of a mile through a thick lodgepole pine forest. It's a nice preamble to the strenuous loop that begins at the intersection ahead. Head left at the junction for a slightly shorter uphill slog, following the trail as it cuts back and forth uphill some 800ft, giving the occasional peek out to Yellowstone Lake along the way. After sweating it up to the top, the trail flattens and leads to an open 180-degree **viewpoint** complete with a pair of rustic benches. Directly below is the *Lake Yellowstone Hotel*, while to the east the Absarokas mountains march alongside the tremendous lake to the horizon. Once you've finished enjoying the scenery, the trail loops further back into the woods, before circling back down to the junction and the trailhead beyond.

H18 Avalanche Peak

> **Difficulty** Strenuous
> **Distance** 4.5 miles round-trip
> **Estimated time** 3–4 hours
> **Season** June–Oct
> **Trailhead location** Map p.82. Across the road from Eleanor Lake on the East Entrance road 20 miles east of Fishing Bridge.
> **Comments** A tough slog, but rewarding with some of the best panoramic views of Yellowstone and beyond.

Though out of the way for all save those heading to or from Yellowstone's East Entrance, this tough trail basically leads straight up close to 2000ft to the top **Avalanche Peak** (10,566ft). The peak can boast some of the park's finest views, making it – along with Mount Washburn (see H7) and Mount Sheridan (see H37) – an essential trip for peak junkies. As the final ascent is completely exposed, do not attempt this hike in foul weather; to avoid the frequent summer afternoon storms, head out as early as possible. Futhermore, although the once-plentiful whitebark pines hereabouts have fallen prey to mountain pine beetles and blister rust disease, the remaining purple-brown cones are still a bear's favorite snack, making this **grizzly country** come September and October. Check at the trailhead sign-in box for updates and be prepared for possible trail closure.

The first mile climbs steadily but easily through a pleasant forested landscape before dipping through a cleared avalanche slide area strewn with wildflowers into early autumn. Past here, the trail gets progressively tougher, first granting good views of the aptly named **Top Notch Peak**, then swinging back for the long climb up Avalanche Peak, bare as a newborn's backside from its countless eponymous slides. The last quarter-mile is the toughest, much of it leading

△ One of the estimated 600 grizzlies in Yellowstone

directly across a scree slope littered with lopsided, loose rocks. Work your way carefully along the ridgeline to the peak, where stunning 360-degree views of the park and Wapiti Valley to the east await. For those confident with their **off-trail** skills, it's possible to drop down the northeast side of the peak's bowl and swing back around to the trail, but most hikers should chose to follow their original path back out.

West Thumb and the South Entrance

Covering the 22-mile stretch of road between **West Thumb** to the north and Yellowstone's **South Entrance**, the following hikes lead to Yellowstone's largest, most dramatic backcountry lakes. Along with the hikes detailed below, energetic hikers should check out the superb overnight hikes to the **Shoshone Geyser Basin** (H36) and **Heart Lake/Mount Sheridan** (H37) in Chapter 5; at 20 miles and 23 miles respectively, either one can be completed in a *very* long day.

H19 Riddle Lake

Crossing the Continental Divide, this undemanding there-and-back trail leads to pleasant **Riddle Lake**, whose name comes from a fur-trapper myth about a body of water that flowed into both oceans. On early maps, several different bodies of water throughout the region were named Riddle in honor of this puzzling feat, but by the 1870s only this lake remained officially Riddle. In reality, the lake drains eventually in the Atlantic Ocean by way of its outlet named, of course, **Solution Creek**.

Difficulty Easy
Distance 5 miles round-trip
Estimated time 2 hours
Season mid May to Oct
Trailhead location Map p.78. 2.3 miles south of Grant Village, just past Continental divide sign on east side of road.
Comments An easy ramble to the shores of a little backcountry lake; best hiked in a group, however, due to frequency of bears.

Closed until mid-July due to grizzly activity, the trail leads northeast into the woods from its roadside start, heading through lodgepole forest dotted with large patches of burnt trees and the occasional clearing. For the first couple of miles, the trail marches uphill ever so slightly, with signs of post-fire renewal all about. Before reaching the lake, the trail cuts across and then along a beautiful meadow that bleeds into marsh by the lake's northwestern shore. This is prime area for **moose and bird spotting** (including sandhill cranes), so don't forget a camera. You can continue along the lake's northern edge, however the trail soon peters out and rangers typically forbid travel any further east of the lake due to the prevalence of bears in the area. You're best off sitting down – or even splashing in the shallow waters on hotter days – to take in the serene scene, complete with broad shouldered Mount Sheridan framing the background.

H20 Lewis Channel to Dogshead Trail

Difficulty Moderate to strenuous
Distance 11-mile loop
Estimated time 5–7 hours
Season mid-May to Oct
Trailhead location Map p.78. Five miles south of Grant Village, due north of Lewis Lake on west side of road.
Comments A loop with good views of both Lewis Lake and Shoshone Lake.

One of the park's few true loop hikes, this route takes in Lewis Lake, the scenic Lewis River Channel, and Yellowstone's largest backcountry lake, Shoshone Lake, all within a half-day's journey. From the trailhead, the first mile and a half of the Lewis River Channel Trail heads flatly northwest through woods battling back from the 1998 fires before crossing a sandy wash – wet early in the season – and turning southwest to hook up with **Lewis Lake**. Next, the trail rises up and down along the lake's northern shore, the towering Tetons clearly visible to the south, before cutting inland to hook up with the mouth of the **Lewis River Channel**. For nearly four miles, the trail follows the channel upstream to the north, leaving it only to round the occasional marsh. It's an idyllic stretch of water, popular with fishermen and kayakers, and also a good place to watch osprey and eagles dive-bombing for trout.

The channel ends (or, more truly, begins) at **Shoshone Lake**, where the trail ends as well at an intersection; turning left (west) leads to the Shoshone Geyser Basin 8.5 miles away (see H36). Instead, head right for the **Dogshead Trail** and the second half of the hike. Before heading back, however, stop to visit the shores of Shoshone Lake via the path to backcountry campsite 8S1 (boat only). The passage leads to a rocky beach perfect for a picnic, while just a few steps away sits an A-frame cabin that's home to the Shoshone Lake **Ranger Station**. The lucky rangers who get stationed here patrol the area on kayak. Once break time ends, the Dogshead Trail heads southeast along a portion of the Continental Divide Trail, cresting several good size hills for the next 3.5 miles. There's very little shade about as most of the forest is young re-growth from the 1988 fires, so bring sunscreen and a hat. After crossing Dogshead Creek – dry by late-July – the final 1.3 miles is the hike's least interesting leg, following a flat gravel service road back to the trailhead.

Cascade Corner

Isolated and with few roadside sights, there's not much to do in Yellowstone's Cascade Corner but hike. The two most popular trailheads are the **Bechler Ranger Station** and **Cave Falls**, though several worthwhile hikes start north of **Grassy Lake Road** as well. Wetter than the rest of the park, trails here remain soggy and bug-infested throughout most of summer, meaning the best hiking is to be had from mid-August through September when the meadows dry out and the insect populations die down. River crossings, required on many trails, are also less dangerous at this time.

H21 Bechler Meadows

Difficulty Moderate
Distance 15 miles round-trip
Estimated time 6–8 hours
Season Late July to early Oct
Trailhead location Map p.66. Cave Falls parking area at end of Cave Falls Road
Comments A superb hike along the Bechler River to a loop through the Bechler Meadows.

It would be a sin to visit the Cascade Corner and not visit the **Bechler Meadows**. This long but flat route not only loops through the meadows, but also passes a couple of small waterfalls en route. Indeed, the hike starts at wide **Cave Falls** (see p.88), then heads upstream along the western bank of the raging **Bechler River**, which tumbles down rocky chutes, tossing logs about like matchsticks, up to the confluence of the Bechler and Falls rivers. Past this river junction, the trail heads by the small but fierce **Bechler Falls** about a mile from the trail's start. Above the falls, the river calms greatly, its surface still as glass. In less than a mile, the trail comes to the first of many intersections; turn right (east) and stick to the riverside trail, hugging the Bechler for another two miles to the intersection with the **Rocky Ford Cutoff**. Turn right (east) again, fording the ice-cold river at a spot around fifty-yards wide; this crossing should not be tried until the river calms (typically late July). Past the ford, the trail leaves the river and cuts through an open grassy meadow, a small taste of things to come, to a junction with the **Mountain Ash Creek Trail** a mile onwards. Turn left (north) and continue on the Bechler River Trail for another three miles, hopping across a couple of small creeks, then up and down a series of wooded hills to another junction.

This junction, nearly eight miles from the start, is the gateway to the Bechler Meadows, meaning it's time to leave the Bechler River Trail behind by turning left (southwest). (Should you head northeast and stick to the later in the Bechler Canyon, it's 3 miles to Colonnade Falls, 7.4 miles to Three Rivers Meadows, and 24.3 miles to Old Faithful.) The Bechler River at the junction is all but unrecognizable from the frothy torrent at the hike's start, and just past backcountry site 9B2 is a shorter, but just as icy, river crossing. You're now into the majestic meadows themselves, following a narrow path over two miles through a waving sea of knee-to-waist high grasses. Keep your eyes peeled for moose, herons, and sandhill cranes, but even without any **wildlife** spotting the wide meadows are breathtaking, **Ouzel Falls** faintly visible to the north while the **Tetons** arc into the southern horizon. Towards the southern end of the meadows, past a few islands of trees, you'll cross over wobbly **suspension bridge** and soon after head back into the woods. At the next intersection, head left (east) onto the Rocky Ford Cutoff, which leads just under a mile back to the day's first river crossing and the trail back to where you came from.

H22 Union Falls

This trail to **Union Falls** is perhaps the finest hike in the Bechler area. At 250ft, the waterfall is the one of the highest in the park and a leading candidate for the most breathtaking, formed by the explosive confluence of two streams that happen to join at the top of a massive cliff. The effect is loud, dramatic, and exceedingly photogenic.

Difficulty Moderate
Distance 16 miles round-trip
Estimated Time 7–9 hours
Season Late July to early Oct
Trailhead Location Map p.66. The picnic area on the west side of the Grassy Lake Dam, ten miles west of Flagg Ranch along bumpy Grassy Lake Road.
Comments A long day hike or leisurely overnight trip showcasing one of Yellowstone's most stunning waterfalls.

There are several approaches to the falls, with the following being the most direct. From the trailhead, the **Mountain Ash Trail** cuts through a marshy zone, reaching **Falls River** at the 1.2-mile mark. You'll need to carefully ford the river, which will be swift even when shallow. Just past the ford is a junction with the Pitchstone Plateau Trail, but continue hiking northwest on the Mountain Ash Trail, climbing steadily for several miles. This old roadbed, once referred to as **Marysville Road**, was used by Mormons as they settled within Jackson Hole a hundred years ago. Look closely and you will find wagon ruts carved into the stone. This was a better alternative to the more treacherous crossing of Teton Pass, which required settlers to drag a tree behind their wagon to keep the crate from descending faster than the horses.

Four miles from Falls River, a steep decline leads to a ford across **Proposition Creek**, questioning how difficult it will be to climb up that ridge on the way back. At mile five, take the spur trail northeast to Union Falls, on which you must wade through **Mountain Ash Creek** a few minutes later. There are two backcountry campsites near the trail junction between the creek and the Morning Falls tributary (9U4 and 9U5). A side trail to **Morning Falls** can be explored by following the maintained path from the campsite for about 0.5 miles along the tributary. The trail then becomes unmaintained and can be muddy as it follows several small falls and cascades to Morning Falls. If planning an overnight trip, the **campsites** here are ideal spots to pitch a tent, provided they haven't been taken over by the Boy Scouts, who have a large camp nearby at the Grassy Lake Reservoir. Explore the final two-mile trail to Union Falls at your leisure. At the very end of the trail is a rewarding overlook of Union Falls.

Hikes within Grand Teton

It seems the **Teton Range** was designed for hiking – a tight clutch of stunning peaks, ribbed with canyons sheltering picturesque creeks and bird-filled forests. Trailheads such as the Colter Bay Nature Trail, Hermitage Point, and Hidden Falls/Inspiration Point are tourist-frequented must-dos, but many excellent trails, like the Blacktail Butte Traverse, are virtually empty, save for abundant wildlife.

The north: John D. Rockefeller Jr. Memorial Parkway

Most visitors simply race over the **John D. Rockefeller Jr. Memorial Parkway** and through the thin strip of protected land that connects Yellowstone and Grand Teton. The area, however, is more than just a divider between the parks on a map – the parks' ecosystems merge here, too. Driving through, visitors will notice a climb in altitude from Teton to Yellowstone, with an increase in the pine-to-aspen ratio of trees. The most striking transition, however, is the lush Jackson Lake area melding into the heavily burned wreckage of Yellowstone's 1988 fires.

H23 Glade Creek Trail

A great trail for those exploring the **John D. Rockefeller Jr. Memorial Parkway** area, this path allows hikers to view wildlife and interesting topography at the northern end of Jackson Lake. The trailhead has no amenities, so be sure to make a pit stop at **Flagg Ranch Resort**, which has camping, lodging, and eateries, as well as a gas station and convenience store. The trail begins in a burnt stand of aspen trees that are magnificent with their Dalmatian-like charring pattern. A gentle trail leads hikers closer to the Snake River plain, dropping in elevation to about 50ft above the wetlands below. The main river channel is still a half-mile to the east, but the wildlife viewing (everything from bald eagles to black bears) from this elevation is excellent. Three miles along the trail you will cross the unmarked border into Grand Teton National Park. About five miles in, the trail climbs and strays inland from the lake to intersect with the **Owl Creek Loop Trail**, which can be accessed by kayak or canoe for those seeking a multi-sport adventure. Two and a half miles further south is a good turn around point (and access to Jackson Lake) at the Patrol Cabin. Expect heavy mosquitoes along this trail until the weather turns cold and the bears become more of a deterrent.

> **Difficulty** Easy to moderate
> **Distance** Up to 16 miles
> **Estimated time** Varies
> **Season** August to early Oct
> **Trailhead Location** Map p.110. At Flagg Ranch, take Grassy Lake Road 4 miles west. Trailhead is on the south side of the road.
> **Comments** An isolated trail following the bench of the Snake River to the north tip of Jackson Lake.

H24 Sheffield Creek Trail

The **Sheffield Creek Trail** winds through the wreckage and re-growth of the 1988 Huckleberry Fire, climbing steadily to the Forest Service Lookout Tower high atop Huckleberry Mountain. This area is part of the **Teton National Forest**, and though the trail is maintained with some regularity, the number of dead trees that have fallen across the path since the last chainsaw crew visited may be daunting for hikers not in the mood to play "over and under".

The fire, which started when high winds blew a tree across a power line, has allowed for a unique trail, as the views from this high area are spectacular and not blocked by branches. The first hour of the hike is a steep 1200ft climb through low and thick new-growth forest. As the elevation rises, the number of gnarled and sculpture-like burned trees still upright also increases. The crest of the mountain was untouched by the fire, offering a

> **Difficulty** Strenuous
> **Distance** 10.6 miles round-trip
> **Estimated time** 7–9 hours
> **Season** June to early Oct
> **Trailhead location** Map p.110. John D. Rockefeller Jr. Memorial Parkway, .6 miles south of Flagg Ranch turnoff at the 'Sheffield Creek' sign. Follow road .5 mile across concrete bottomed stream to camping/parking area.
> **Comments** A steep, rugged climb through burned area leading to the Huckleberry Mountain Lookout Tower.

completely different variety of beauty as you walk through a thick forest in the prime of its life.

There are upwards of twenty small runoff streams and several ecozones along the trail, making it ideal for animal spotting. Below the teetering Lookout Tower, the lush, rolling meadows make for great moose and elk habitat. Grouse and other birds are plentiful in the new growth, and deer and bear signs can be found on all parts of the trail. If time allows, be sure to summit the final climb to the **Lookout Tower**, which is perched tentatively upon a spectacular outcropping of weathered rock. The forest service does not usually allow access into the building, but the near-panoramic view from its porch is well worth the climb.

Jackson Lake, Colter Bay, and around

In many ways, **Jackson Lake** is as much of a centerpiece of the park as is Grand Teton itself. Speed boaters, sailors, and kayakers flock here in droves, and the low-lying areas around Jackson Lake offer activities for landlubbers, too. The Hermitage Point, Two Ocean/Emma Matilda Lakes, and Colter Bay Nature Trails all have top-notch valley floor vistas of the majestic Teton Range, provide hiking options that vary in length and topographic challenge, and offer the option of getting away from the crowds.

H25 Hermitage Point

Difficulty Easy to moderate
Distance 9.4 miles
Estimated time 4–5 hours
Season Open year round
Trailhead location Map p.110. Colter Bay, south end of parking area.
Comments A serene walk through the woods of the Hermitage Point peninsula, with wonderful lakeside views of the Teton Range.

Escape from nearby RV traffic by slinking away to Colter Bay and this lovely series of trails. After checking out the incredible native artifacts inside the Colter Bay Visitor Center, lace up your hiking boots and experience what makes this area so special: **Hermitage Point**, extending south from Colter Bay into the southeast part of Jackson Lake. Beginning at a maintenance road at the southern end of the parking area, the series of Hermitage Point hiking trails allow for a half-hour jaunt to a full-day trip, and you can pick and choose your own route. The trail suggested here, a 9.4 mile hike, sticks to the Jackson Lake shoreline.

Since the trailhead is near the Colter Bay stable area, there is much horse traffic on the trails nearest the parking area. Families find that the small loops at the trail's beginning make for good driving intermissions, so also expect lots of foot traffic in the first half-mile of the hike. But as the trail enters the thick forest and passes the beaver lodge in Heron Pond, the crowds quickly thin out.

Deposits left behind by receding glaciers created the Hermitage Point peninsula, which has several ponds where small ice fields continued to settle after the glaciers dissipated. The trail follows a single contour line (save a small climb or dip here and there) above the shore of Jackson Lake, but leads hikers through quite different ecozones. Thick coniferous forests, filled with red squirrels, comprise most of the area, but the southern end is home to sagebrush meadows and Unita ground squirrels. The trail also explores a low wetland meadow and fantastic swan ponds on the east side of Hermitage Point.

For a treat, take a dip in chilly **Jackson Lake** at the southern-most tip of Hermitage Point, which is a perfect lunch spot. The photographic opportunities here are unparalleled. Mount Moran and the Grand Teton tower above the lake's western shore, and the cobbled beach is great to explore.

H26 Colter Bay Nature Trail

Behind the **Colter Bay Visitor Center**, a paved trail strikes off to the northwest, soon becoming a well-marked dirt path leading past an amphitheater hosting a variety of events, including ranger talks, evening gatherings, and Sunday morning religious services. Joggers seeking a short run will like this option as there's little elevation change and is hard-packed without a lot of ankle-twisting glacial till. Consider starting out early to beat the many tourists that claim this accessible walk later in the day. In the morning, there is also less noise from the nearby marina and noisy speedboats on the lake, so the chances of seeing wildlife are high. Past the amphitheater, the trail follows an isthmus to what is an island in high-water years, creating a figure-eight path. One of the fun features of the Colter Bay Nature Trail is that along the way, there is easy and frequent access to **Jackson Lake**. Families can explore stretches of beach, examining splendid driftwood sculptures deposited on the shore, and there are well-placed picnic tables at the northern-most part of the trail for a scenic snack. Bring a camera, as the views of the Grand Teton and Mount Moran looming straight ahead are marvelous as well.

Difficulty Easy
Distance 2-mile loop
Estimated time 45 min to 1.5 hrs
Season Open year round
Trailhead Location Map p.110. Colter Bay Visitor Center.
Comments A quick figure-eight stroll through the woods along the Jackson Lake shore.

H27 Two Ocean and Emma Matilda Lakes

Buzzing with activity at the trailhead, this hike past **Two Ocean Lake** is a good choice for those looking to wear away a winter's worth of rust. There are a series of trails in the area, and the path suggested here is a loop around Two Ocean Lake that climbs to a high lookout at the half-way point, then cuts past Emma Matilda Lake back to the trailhead.

The well-marked trail begins alongside mile-long Two Ocean Lake, which earned its unusual moniker from the belief that its position atop the continental divide caused runoff to flow from one egress to the Pacific and from another exit to the Atlantic. In reality, the lake drains entirely into the Snake River, which dumps into the Pacific. Beginning on a **bridge** spanning the eastern outlet of the lake, expect the first stretch to be clogged with families. The easy trail along the lake's northern shore weaves through small stands of aspens, coniferous patches, and grassy meadows overlooking the lake, with Mount Moran visible to the west.

Though sporadically closed to protect nesting **Trumpeter Swans**, it's possible to complete the loop back around the southern shore an equal distance to the trailhead. For a strenuous challenge, continue from the western tip of Two Ocean Lake to **Grand View**. The mile-long trail heads uphill on switchbacks through coniferous forest sporting dozens of species of birds, including chickadees, yellow warblers, and the

Difficulty Easy to moderate
Distance 9.5 miles
Estimated time 4–6 hours
Season June–Oct
Trailhead location Map p.100. 1 mile northwest of Moran Junction, take Pacific Creek Road to Two Oceans Road.
Comments Two pretty lakes and grand views along with excellent wildlife viewing opportunities.

occasional raven. Make it to the top and you're rewarded with two viewing areas with **360-degree vistas**, including the photogenic Teton National Forest to the east and the Teton Range to the west. The rocky outcroppings here make for prime picnic spots.

After resting, head downhill for 1.7 miles to a junction of trails leading to Jackson Lake Lodge (west), Christian Pond (south), and the southern shore of Emma Matilda Lake (also south). The latter choice loops back to the trailhead, now just 2.7 miles away. The trail slowly gains back most of the altitude lost on the hike down from Grand View, placing hikers on a bench overlooking crescent-shaped **Emma Matilda Lake**. The lake is named for the wife of William Owen, one of the men sharing the controversial honor of making the first recorded ascent of the Grand Teton in 1898 (see the box on p.108).

While the lake looks enticing, the trail never diverges to allow access to the water. Atop the bench, there is little topographic change, and the trail leads through a lighting fire area known for its bear activity; be sure to take precautions. As the trail drops back down toward Two Ocean Lake, it leads through lovely meadows. With one mile left, the trail splits; following it to the right leads hikers around the other side of Emma Matilda Lake, and to the left is your vehicle.

The southwest: Teton Park Road and Jenny Lake

The inner-loop road of Grand Teton delivers visitors to the base of the immense peaks above **Jenny Lake**, itself located just about at the mid-point altitude-wise between sea level and the crest of the Grand Teton. Some of the finest, most enjoyable hiking in the park can be found on the trails weaving around the Jenny Lake area, with hikers feeling ridiculously tiny in this sublime landscape.

H28 String Lake to Bearpaw Lake

> **Difficulty** Easy
> **Distance** 8 miles
> **Estimated time** 3.5 hours
> **Season** May–Oct
> **Trailhead location** Map p.100. Leigh and String Lakes Trailhead.
> **Comments** An easy but still scenic lakeside trail leading to several campsites at the base of the Tetons.

Hiking high up into the Tetons is an experience not to miss, but you don't have to embark on a Herculean hike to enjoy the park's scenic wonder. One of Grand Teton's finest flat hikes begins at the **String Lake Picnic Area** on the Jenny Lake Scenic Loop. String Lake itself is a family favorite as it's shallow enough to actually warm up by mid-summer, and has several small beaches. The trail is busy for the first mile with families exploring the eastern shoreline while looking out for moose and grouse. At the one-mile point, the flat path divides; take the Portage Trail, then veer toward the Leigh Lake Trail/Bearpaw Lake at the next marker. You may well find the trail is all yours the rest of the way in its panoramic glory the soaring mountains act as a backdrop for kayaks and canoes on both String and Leigh Lakes.

Continue along the eastern shore of **Leigh Lake**, dotted with forested islands and duck-topped boulders exposed in the sometimes white-capped water. You'll mainly see expert paddlers here, as the portage from String Lake weeds out the recreational canoeists, and the trail passes directly through three campsites (two small sites and one group site). The north end of Leigh Lake was burned in a fire in the early 1980s and the smaller pines are very dense here, obscuring the lake from sight for the first time. Eventually the path enters a large meadow and splits in three directions: a right turn leads to a campsite on the eastern shores of **Bearpaw Lake** (at a beach bordering a playland of boulders scattered in shallow water); a left turn toward the tip of Leigh Lake and the volunteer-staffed patrol cabin; and straight goes to additional campsites on the western shore of Bearpaw Lake. Take the latter option and continue about a half-mile past the campsites to the Trapper Lake campsite, set back from the trail under tall trees. Just when it seems the trail has ended without ever offering a peek at **Trapper Lake**, a beaver pond spillway appears, splashing noisily into the tiny, very private lake; a favorite of fisherman, trout rise hungrily to the surface when a hatch is on. Spend some time poking around the shore and climbing in the boulders scattered literally at the base of the mountains, then return the way you came, four miles back to the picnic area.

H29 Hidden Falls and Inspiration Point

Difficulty Moderate
Distance 2 miles round-trip; 4.5 with extra leg
Estimated time 1–3 hours
Season June–Oct
Trailhead location Map p.100. West Boat Dock on Jenny Lake
Comments The most popular hike in Grand Teton; ride the boat across Jenny Lake to find yourself right in the Tetons.

This is the most popular hike in Grand Teton, and with good reason – within a short journey into the Tetons, you can take in a boat trip, a photogenic waterfall, and a spectacular overlook of **Jenny Lake**. To begin, the majority of hikers take the **Jenny Lake Ferry** (see p.107) from the East Boat Dock across the water to the trailhead; should you wish to add distance to the short hike, consider the hour-long jaunt around the lake's southern point, saving the boat trip for the way back. From the Jenny Lake Ferry parking area, this easy 2.4-mile addition hugs the lake's southern shore, diving in and out of the sun and past thickets of edible thimbleberry bushes.

From the West Boat Dock, a gentle climb leads to **Hidden Falls**. Despite exposed roots and tricky rocks, most can make the walk without too much trouble. The falls, cloaked by forest on their approach, are spectacular, as is the view to the peaks above. Keep your packs closed, however, as this area is frequented by bears, and the Park Service has deemed it a picnic-free zone. As well as looking out for bears, scan the nearby cliffs for red and white helmets – Exum Mountain Guides use the area as a practice space. From the falls, it's a strenuous .4-mile uphill slog on a rock-strewn trail to **Inspiration Point** (a 500ft gain in altitude). It's well worth it, however, for the spectacular overlook of Jenny Lake, the valley floor, and the Gros Ventre Range (including the Gros Ventre Slide to the south). The trail continues into the mountains as the Cascade Canyon Trail (see H38), but to return to the boat dock you'll need head back the way you came.

H30 Amphitheater Lake Trail

Built in the 1920s by two Jackson Hole businessmen years before the Civilian Conservation Corps constructed the bulk of the Park Service paths, this trail from Lupine Meadows to **Amphitheater Overlook** is one of the oldest and best in the park. You'll feel it for days – the trail gains more than 3000 feet of elevation in just over four miles – and remember it forever. Just don't make this your first hike at this elevation, as you'll want a few days to adjust before you take on steep challenges.

> **Difficulty** Very strenuous
> **Distance** 10 miles round-trip
> **Estimated time** 6–8 hours
> **Season** July to early Oct
> **Trailhead location** Map p.100. Lupine Meadows Parking Area, south of Jenny Lake Junction
> **Comments** An arduous climb up to the treeline, earning you fantastic views.

Throughout much of the summer, wildflowers will greet you at the start at the **Lupine Meadows Parking Area**, and get denser as the trail winds through an upwardly sloped moraine to the junction with the **Valley Trail** (1.7 miles). From here, the switchback trail begins to seriously climb, reaching a second junction – **Garnet Canyon Trail** – after an additional 1.5 miles. Stick to the original trail by veering right, climbing upwards two final miles on nineteen shade-less zigzags. Boulder-lined **Surprise Lake** sits at the 9500ft mark, tucked in a cirque at the base of **Disappointment Peak**. You can expect to see some ice during most of the year, so a refreshing dip won't cross your mind, but there are designated camping spaces here (get a permit ahead of time). **Amphitheater Lake** is another 198ft higher, and is reached by taking the trail on the north side of Surprise Lake around the tree-covered slope dividing the lakes. At the trail's end is Amphitheater Overlook, which looks out at Delta Lake, Teton Glacier, Grand Teton, and Disappointment Peak.

H31 Taggart and Bradley lakes loop

Not quite a perfect loop, this hike is an accessible, straightforward ramble past two of the attractive glacial lakes – **Taggart** and **Bradley** – that dot the Teton's eastern escarpment. From the trailhead parking lot, the dusty trail starts flat, cutting under a row of power-lines to the first of several well-marked intersections. Turn right for the quickest route to Taggart Lake, a mile-and-a-half away. As elsewhere in the park, the region's geological history quickly makes itself known as you head up the **moraine** separating the lake from the russet sagebrush flats to the east. An oasis of green, the moraine's rich soil is home to stands of Engelmann spruce, lodgepole pine, and aspen. Scars from a major fire in 1985 abound as well, however, with charred trunks shooting pencil straight up into the sky as you approach the second fork in the trail. Head left for the final half-mile to Taggart Lake (6902ft), named after a member of the Hayden Survey part of 1872.

> **Difficulty** Moderate
> **Distance** 5-mile loop
> **Estimated time** 2–4 hours
> **Season** June–Oct
> **Trailhead location** Map p.100. 2 miles north of Moose Entrance Station, directly off Teton Park Road
> **Comments** An instructive hike to two glacial lakes, highlighting the region's glacial history and post-fire landscapes.

Following the lake's eastern edge, the trail next heads north uphill just over a mile to Bradley Lake, giving great views en route into the mouth of **Avalanche Canyon**, through which the glacier that scooped out Taggart Lake's basin once traveled. After cresting the moraine separating the two lakes, the path leads down through thick forest untouched by fire to Bradley Lake (7022ft), smaller than Taggart and also named after a subordinate of the Hayden Survey. Several paths lead directly down to the striking lake at the foot of **Garnet Canyon**, many secluded enough for a quick skinny dip on the hottest of days. It's possible to continue heading north around the lake to hook up with the **Amphitheater**

Lake Trail (see H30) 1.5 miles onwards, but to complete the loop it's a mostly downhill mile-long hike south on the Bradley Lake Cutoff back to main trail intersection. From here, you'll retrace your steps just over a mile back to the trailhead.

The southeast: Moran Junction to Moose Junction

While the high, dry southeast section of the park may pale in comparison to the peaks and lakes in terms of dramatic landscapes, there are still plenty of great trails well worth setting out on. One of the best heads up **Blacktail Butte**, rising from the sage east of Moose, while another memorable path drops down from the flats to the river bottoms where you can see what the local beaver and osprey are up to.

H32 Blacktail Butte Traverse

Difficulty Moderate
Distance 4.5 miles one-way
Estimated time 2 hours
Season June to mid-Oct
Trailhead location Map p.100. Mormon Row.
Comments An overlooked gem in the heart of Jackson Hole.

This hike is best if you exploit a shuttle system to save major backtracking. Leave one car at trail's end at the **Blacktail Butte** climbing wall, the first major parking area north of Moose on the east side of Hwy 191/89 – then drive the second car east at Gros Ventre Junction to the junction leading north to Mormon Row. Head north five miles to the gate (which is sometimes closed) and park off the road here.

The trail up Blacktail Butte begins at the gate through meadows lined with aspen trees. Due to a preponderance of bison trails, things can get a bit confusing, but shoot for the trail heading straight up the spine of the butte to the right. The rocky uphill trail gives good insight into the geologic history of the butte. An ice age anomaly, the butte is an outcropping of rock so hard that glaciers divided around it. Much of the slope up is glacial till, left behind when the ice scraped off its earthen luggage, rocks ground down into fist-sized cobbles. Follow the steep course up an 800-foot **climb**. When you stop to catch your breath, use it as an excuse to gaze at the scene to the east of you: the town of Kelly, the Sleeping Indian behind it, and the Gros Ventre Slide at his feet. Beyond the slide are the aptly named Red Hills, which follow the contour of the Gros Ventre River. From this high vantage point try to spot the historic fields of Mormon Row to the north and east of the Butte: the irrigation ditches and patterns of old fields contrast with the land that was not cleared of sagebrush and native vegetation by the settlers. These days the inhabitants consist mainly of bison (the black spots in the fields below) and antelope (grey spots).

At the **summit** of the butte the trail flirts with thick deep woods and moves into quiet meadows. The top features roads once used by ranchers, watering holes for their cattle, an unmarked cowboy grave, and even a rumored airplane crash site. Sightings of the re-introduced grey wolf are also becoming common up top. The trail cuts northwest across the top of the butte, depositing hikers on the west side at large vertical slabs of rocks where climbing fanatics gather. A few yard more, and the trail again reaches the valley floor. From here it is a short jaunt north to your vehicle.

H33 Schwabacher's Landing

Not every hike needs to be a workout; sometimes they can be pure exploration, like this choose-your-own-adventure hike at **Schwabacher's Landing**. A popular fishing spot, Schwabacher's features an ecosystem not represented in other Grand Teton hikes. The Snake River is rarely one channel – in fact, historically it has been difficult for engineers to place bridges along the river because it divides and braids in unpredictable ways each season, and these changes also make a detailed hiking itinerary all but impossible.

Difficulty Easy
Distance Varies
Estimated Time Varies
Season June to early Oct
Trailhead Location Map p.100. Take Hwy 191/89 4.1 miles north of the Moose turnoff to Schwabacher Landing. Follow gravel road to parking areas near river.
Comments A rare, unscripted foray into the river bottoms of the Snake River drainage.

Angler trails provide pathways to exploration here. Follow a trail to the north and you may come across giant **beaver lodges** and remnants of various dams they have constructed. As high water frequently washes away their old engineering projects, the beavers are always busy, and many of the downed trees sport fresh gnaw marks. Though generally nocturnal, beavers can occasionally be spotted in broad daylight, so keep your eyes - and ears – peeled; if they see you first the beaver may loudly slap a flat tail against the water as a warning to others in the vicinity.

While exploring the river bottoms, you're likely to see a **bald eagle**. Once ravaged by DDT and other human-related perils, these birds have made an impressive comeback. Another flying predator hereabouts is the **osprey**. Smaller than an eagle, it is certainly as avid a fish-catcher. Brown above and white below, osprey are often seen flying aerodynamically with a fish facing forward in their talons. Also evident is the area's volcanic history, as rhyelite and obsidian are found mixed in with the other stones, washed down from the Yellowstone region. Remember that rocks, along with driftwood, belong to the park, and cannot be taken home.

5

Backcountry hiking and camping

An undoubted highlight for adventure-seeking visitors will be a night or more spent out in the wilds, waking early on a frosty morning to the echoing sounds of howling wolves or bugling elk. Only a slice of Grand Teton and even less of Yellowstone can be seen from the road and short interpretive trails, and leaving this so-called "frontcountry" behind to enter into the **backcountry** is a thrilling trip that all able bodied souls should consider. From isolated thermal areas like those in Yellowstone's Shoshone Geyser Basin to a high-altitude traverse along the spine of the mighty Tetons, some of the region's finest highlights require a long, rewarding trip to view them.

While the idea of heading off into the hills with your tent may sound appealing, keep in mind that there are certain **responsibilities** you take on when you do so. The reason that so many clichéd backcountry camping mantras – "good campsites are found, not made" and "leave only footprints behind" – exist is that the advice they give continues to be ignored. Few things are as disheartening as spending a full day laboring under a heavy pack only to find that your backcountry site resembles a landfill. When camping rough, always **pack out what you pack in** (or more if you come across someone else's litter), and avoid the old advice to burn rubbish; wildfires have been started in this way. Always check before departing to see if **fires** are permitted at your backcountry campsite; if they are, only use deadwood and fallen wood. Similarly, never move or take anything you find in the backcountry as a souvenir, whether it be a rock, wildflower or shed antler.

Backcountry hikers should also read the introduction to Chapter 4: Day hikes, beginning on p.115, for details on **maps**, hiking **safety**, and more.

Backcountry information and practicalities

The top source for **backcountry information** in the region are the rangers of Yellowstone and Grand Teton national parks. Loaded with the latest information, most will gladly share choice bits of insider knowledge to inquisitive visitors. If things aren't too busy at the ranger station or backcountry office where you can stop to pick up a required backcountry **permit**, feel free to linger and ask the attending ranger for his or her advice on your trails of choice. Before leaving, be sure to let the ranger know where you're heading and when you intend to return. Also check for the latest weather forecasts and any potential hazards along the way, such as bear sightings or rivers that may need to be forded.

Remember that black bears and grizzlies can be encountered virtually anywhere in the backcountry; see the box on pp.118–119 for advice on being **bear aware** throughout your travels.

Yellowstone: backcountry camping and permits

Dispersed camping within Yellowstone's backcountry is prohibited; however, with over 300 **designated backcountry sites**, you should have little problem finding the perfect place to pitch a tent. A free **permit** specifying your assigned sites and nights is required, and these can be obtained from the ranger stations and backcountry offices listed in the box below. Permits can be collected no earlier than 48 hours in advance of your camping trip, and the rangers on-site can often help narrow down your choices with their personal picks. As relatively few people venture into the backcountry, it's rarely a problem to get a **reservation**. However, for the most popular sites – around Yellowstone and Shoshone lakes and the northern half of the Lamar Valley in particular – you may want to make reservations in advance; these cost $20, and are made by post beginning on April 1 for the upcoming season; reservation sheets with mailing addresses can be downloaded from the park's website (Ⓦwww.nps.gov/yell) or you can call the main backcountry office to request one (Ⓣ307/344-2160). Reserved permits must be collected in person by 10am on the day of your trip's start and you'll also have to watch a half-hour video on backcountry safety.

Grant Teton: backcountry camping and permits

The backcountry policy in Grand Teton is slightly different from Yellowstone's. Free **permits** are likewise required for any overnight trip into the backcountry, and there are a couple dozen **designated backcountry sites** around the park's lakes, including Jackson, Leigh, Phelps, and Holly. Unlike Yellowstone, however, the remaining permits are issued for **camping zones**, trailside regions high up in the Tetons where dispersed camping is allowed. As long as you follow the rules – which include camping at least 200ft from lakes and streams and staying out of sight from the trail whenever possible – you can pitch a tent wherever you'd like within each zone. These high-altitude areas are often used by climbers and scramblers sticking close to their rocky routes, but hikers are welcome to overnight as well. Throughout summer, permits can be picked up at the Moose

Yellowstone's backcountry permit offices

As Yellowstone covers such a large area, you're best off picking your **permit** (and the handy advice that goes with it) at the station closest to where your trip begins. That said, all of the following offices can issue backcountry permits when open. During the off-season, call (Ⓣ307/344-2160) to get issued a permit.

- Bechler Ranger Station
- Bridge Bay
- Canyon Ranger Station
- Grant Village Backcountry Office
- Mammoth Ranger Station
- Old Faithful Ranger Station
- South Entrance Ranger Station
- Tower Ranger Station
- West Entrance Ranger Station

and Colter Bay visitor centers (see p.95 and p.112) or the Jenny Lake Ranger Station (see p.107). In the off-season, only the Moose Visitor Center doles them out. One-third of regular campsites and all group sites can be **reserved** in advance, and with fewer spaces than Yellowstone to choose from you may want to consider this option during the high summer season. Reservations are taken January 1–May 15 for the year ahead and cost $15. They can be made in person, via fax (Ⓕ307/739-3438), or by post (Grand Teton, Permits Office, PO Drawer 170, Moose, WY 83102). For more information, call Ⓣ307/739-3309. Reserved permits must be picked up by 10am on the first day of camping out or spots may be given out to others.

Campfires, cooking, and food storage

Open **fires** are only permitted in fire-rings at designated sites. If sitting before a fire is key to your camping experience, work with a ranger to find such a spot, as a good percentage of backcountry sites in the more popular areas of Yellowstone are fire-free; fires are likewise prohibited at many of the designated sites and banned within all of the alpine camping zones in Grand Teton. **Backpacking stoves**, however, are permitted at all sites, and they are easily the quickest, most efficient way to cook your meals. The most common fuel sold in the area, including the parks' general stores, fit Coleman stoves; limited supplies of other butane/propane canisters are sold, but its wise to stock up in one of the gateway towns to be sure.

Upon arriving at your backcountry camping area, one of the first orders of business should be **hanging your food**. Look around for the food storage pole – typically a log lashed high up, parallel to the ground between two trees – provided at most campsites around 100 yards from the tent area. If there's not one, search out a sturdy branch at least fifteen feet off the ground and five feet out from the trunk to hang your food from. You'll need to bring your own rope and stuff-sack to hang food in, and you must also hang all odorous personal items, such as toothpaste, sunscreen and deodorants. Note that all cooking and eating should be done in this area as well to keep food scents away from your sleeping area. Never eat or store food in or by your tent.

Water and waste disposal

Before leaving on any hike of distance, talk to rangers and study maps to get the scoop on accessible **water**. On some hikes, you'll pass creeks and springs every few hundred yards, while on others – particularly late in the season, when run-off has dissipated – you'll need to conserve greatly or pack an extra bottle or two. Regardless of how fresh and clean water in the backcountry looks, it should be boiled for a couple minutes or processed with a *giardia*-rated water filtration system available from camping and sports shops. **Giardia**, a water-borne protozoan leading to chronic diarrhea, abdominal cramps, fatigue, and loss of weight, is a growing problem. To avoid catching it, **never drink** directly from rivers and streams (you never know what unspeakable acts people – or animals – further upstream have performed in them).

As for **garbage**, it's simple: if you pack it in, pack it out. Some of the more popular backcountry areas have very basic pit toilets, but where there are none be sure to **bury human waste** at least six inches into the ground in so-called catholes, a hundred feet minimum from the nearest water supply and camp. Similarly, you should urinate far from the trail and any water source, preferably on rocky ground to avoid damage from animals digging about after you leave. Used tampons should packed out. Finally, don't use **soaps or detergents** (even special ecological or biodegradable soaps) anywhere near lakes and streams; folk using water purifiers or filters downstream won't thank you at all. Instead, when cleaning yourself, dishes, or clothes, carry water at least a hundred feet (preferably two hundred) from the water's edge before washing.

Backcountry equipment and packing

Balance is the crucial element when deciding what **equipment** to take on a trip into the backcountry. Take too much and your back might never forgive you, too little and a trip can be ruined by hunger, sleep deprivation, weather, or some similar minor to major disaster. You'll have to figure out via trial and error the tricky balance between weight and what's essential, but help yourself out by sticking to dried foods and avoiding cans, paring down your clothes to the bare minimum, and leaving behind your laptop and collected works of Shakespeare.

What to wear

It's not uncommon to have breakfast while temperatures are below freezing, only to eat lunch under the sun a few hours later at close to 80°F. You'll therefore want to pack a full complement of **layers**, starting with long underwear. Convertible pants that unzip into shorts are a good choice for your next layer (especially if you'll be fording rivers), along with a couple of T-shirts. You should also have a **waterproof jacket**, **fleece top**, and lightweight **winter hat** and **gloves** on hand in case the weather turns nasty. Though more costly, you will be most comfortable in layers made from polypropylene or similar synthetic, as these don't absorb water and stay dry even as you sweat. Many hiking enthusiasts go so far as to insist that "cotton'll kill ya"; certainly damp cotton clothing will quickly chill you to the bone in a cold breeze at high altitude. For the same reasons, avoid cotton **socks** and splurge on a couple pairs of wool or synthetic wool-like socks instead.

As worthy of a spending spree are sturdy **hiking boots**. The main considerations when purchasing them are whether to get heavy-duty ones or something lightweight, and whether they need to be waterproof or just water-resistant. If you don't plan on spending days on end scrambling about in the backcountry, it may be best to go for a fairly light, flexible boot. If you're heading on a longer expedition and plan on carrying a heavy pack, you will need a high-cut waterproof boot with a good quality sole. In either case, it's well worth being choosy before making a decision; only purchase boots from a reputable store with a staff that will run a series of tests to make sure the boot is right for you. Most importantly, break in the boots by walking in them for a few weeks before beginning your trip to avoid the scourge of all hikers: **blisters**. Broken in boots or not, include a piece of blister-covering moleskin in your first aid kit just in case (though a strip of well placed duct-tape works nearly as well).

Duct tape

If you hike with a Nalgene-brand or similarly sturdy water bottle, carefully wrap several feet of **duct tape** around it. Cliché it may be, but duct-tape is useful in the extreme, from mending broken straps to covering up blisters, and you'll be glad you took time to wrap your bottle the first time you tear off a piece to use in a pinch.

What gear to take

It's worth investing some thought and financial resources to ensure that you have the basic **hiking equipment**, and that you know how to use all of it. First up is a sturdy **backpack** in which to store and transport your gear. Outdoor stores typically stock a wall full of choices, ranging from basic daypacks to extended trip packs large enough to store a week's worth of necessities. Once you've narrowed down the size you're after, concentrate on fit, making sure the pack's maze of straps is properly explained in order to maximize its efficiency. Taking up the most room in your pack will be a **tent**, available in an equally bewildering array of choices. For most, a three-person, three-season tent in the five-pound range will be the handiest, most economical choice. Again, don't wait until the trail to figure out how it works. As for a **sleeping bag**, anything that can't stuff down to the size of a basketball or smaller is likely too bulky. Unless you're winter camping, however, there's no need to blow a couple of hundred dollars on a space-age, sub-zero design. For around a $100, you should

Hiking gear guide

Personal preferences dictate exactly what you'll need to take on a hiking trip, but the following checklist should point you in the right direction. For an overnight trip, you'll need at least the "Day hiking" and "Essential" items listed below; you may want to pack a few from the "Additional" selection too.

Day hiking

- Map
- Bear spray
- Strong hiking shoes or boots
- Wool or synthetic-wool socks
- Waterproof coat
- Sturdy water bottle(s)
- Sunscreen
- Sunglasses
- Hat
- Water
- Snacks and emergency food
- Camera (optional)
- Binoculars (optional)

Essential overnight gear

- Backcountry permit
- Waterproof tent
- Sleeping bag
- Food (including emergency supply)
- Water purifier
- Stove and fuel
- Pots, pans, and utensils
- Pocket knife
- Long-sleeved shirt
- Warm, long pants
- Fleece or down jacket
- Light but warm hat and gloves
- Long underwear
- First aid kit
- Waterproof matches or lighter
- Flashlight/lantern
- Garbage bag
- Toilet paper
- Fifty feet of rope/nylon cord
- Stuff sack (to store food for hanging outside)

Additional overnight gear

- Sleeping pad
- Bug spray
- Small trowel
- Soap / toiletries
- Toothbrush and paste
- Small towel
- Tarp/ground cover
- Journal
- Field guides
- Entertainment: books, playing cards, etc.
- Camp shoes (sandals work best)
- Fishing gear (and license)
- Flask

be able to get a good backpacking bag rated to twenty degrees. Lastly is a **sleeping pad**: inflatable pads stuff down to a small size, while the traditional foam rolls are cheaper and easier to use. Whichever you choose, take one along; not only will they supply a more comfortable night's rest, but by keeping you off the ground you'll also stay warmer. We've listed the remaining items you'll want to lug around in the "Hiking gear guide" box on p.151.

Overnight hikes

The following **overnight hikes** add up to a great introduction to the region's vast backcountry, covering everything from the deep, desert-like Black Canyon in north Yellowstone to the snowy alpine reaches along the highest ridges in the Tetons. Most of the hikes listed can be completed in a few days, as the region's longest hauls – like the 75-mile one-way Thorofare Trail along the eastern shores of Yellowstone Lake south the park boundary – would need an entire chapter to be properly described. Backpackers looking for more options should note that most of the day-hikes in Chapter 4 can be strung together or taken deeper into the untrammeled wilderness for additional overnight trips.

H34 Black Canyon of the Yellowstone

This one-way trip in the northern reaches of Yellowstone tracks the mighty **Yellowstone River** as it flows northwest out of the park through the colorful, desert-like walls of the **Black Canyon of the Yellowstone**. The entire stretch could be tackled in a long, sweat-soaked day, but we've stretched it out into a three-day hike giving plenty of time for wildlife watching (best early in summer) and relaxing in the shade; this area is the hottest in the park, making it a good early or late season choice when snow covers trails elsewhere. The ample opportunities for catching trout in the Yellowstone and its tributaries add yet another great excuse for taking the slow road.

The Continental Divide Trail

An idea born in 1978, the 3100-mile **Continental Divide Trail** (CDT) stretches from the Canadian border at Glacier National Park south to the Mexico border at Antelope Wells, New Mexico. It's far from a straight shot, squiggling like a child's drawing as it traces the path of the Continental Divide through five states (Montana, Idaho, Wyoming, Colorado and New Mexico). It's also far from complete, with a full quarter of the CDT still unmarked, requiring plenty of backcountry navigation skills to complete. Few hikers attempt the entire stretch at once as it takes on average six months to complete, though some speed hikers have completed the span in less than ninety days (presumably they didn't stop for many photos). Far more enthusiasts take it one section at a time, the same strategy used on the Appalachian Trail and the Pacific Coast Trail, the US's other celebrated long-distance trails. The CDT enters **Yellowstone** along the park's western border from Idaho's Caribou-Targhee National Forest and exits nearly 70 miles later via the south border into Wyoming's Bridger-Teton National Forest; sights along the way include Old Faithful, the Shoshone Geyser Basin (see H36), and Heart Lake (see H37). If considering tackling more of the trail from Yellowstone, south is the direction to choose as after heading east of Grand Teton the trail cuts through Wyoming's Wind River Range, home to some of the finest mountain scenery in all the Rockies. For more information, check both www.cdtrail.org and www.cdtsociety.org.

Difficulty Strenuous
Distance 22 miles one-way
Estimated time 3 days
Season May to early Oct
Trailhead location Map p.53. Hellroaring Creek Trailhead, 15 miles east of Mammoth and 4 miles west of Roosevelt.
Comments Save for thermal features, this trip takes in nearly all of the park's different landscapes, from high plains to deep forests and river valleys.

The first day covers seven miles, giving ample time to pick up backcountry permits as well as arranging transportation from Gardiner; you'll either need to leave a second shuttle car in town or arrange a ride to the **Hellroaring Creek Trailhead**. From the trailhead, the path leads steeply down 500ft in a mile to a suspension bridge crossing high above the Yellowstone; black bears are commonly spotted hereabouts, so be bear aware. Beyond the bridge, you'll pass the Coyote Creek Trail and then another junction with the **Hellroaring Creek Trail**. It's possible to continue straight to ford the Yellowstone, but the crossing is exceedingly dangerous. Instead, head northeast on the Hellroaring Creek Trail to the stock bridge 1.8-miles away. Once across, you'll loop back down alongside Hellroaring Creek, past a small ranger **patrol cabin** and pretty duck-filled pond, to backcountry site 2H1, a mile detour off the main trail at the confluence of Hellroaring Creek and the Yellowstone River; it's a great place to spend the night, with a sandy beach nearby.

Day two's hike covers around twelve miles, starting with a climb into a beautiful high meadow; the numerous shed antlers strewn about prove elk enjoy the area as well. As you climb, you're afforded great views down to the river below, with snowcapped peaks on the horizon. Three miles in, the path crosses **Little Cottonwood Creek** (filter more water here) and then **Cottonwood Creek** a mile onwards; trout can be easily spotted in both. You're now within the Black Canyon proper, its dark walls looming across the opposite shore. Three miles further, after crossing over into Montana from Wyoming, the trail passes a junction with **Blacktail Deer Creek Trail** and past pretty **Crevice Lake** and over **Crevice Creek** on a sturdy footbridge. A short way onwards is **Knowles Falls**, a squat and powerful rush of the river dropping some 15ft. Another mile west are two pretty campsites; 1Y2, tucked up against a near vertical canyon wall, and 1Y1 on a big bend in the river, boasting another sandy beach area.

Day three takes in five miles of hiking beside and above the river, cutting through a semi-desert environment surrounded by beautiful "painted" canyon walls. Unlike anywhere else in Yellowstone, it's like you've been transported to one of Utah's national parks for the hike's final stretch. Be sure to stock up on water in the morning, and also keep an eye out for rattlesnakes sunning themselves on the trail. Upon reaching **Gardiner** the trail dumps out by the *Rocky Mountain Campground*, from where it's a half-mile to a true post-hike reward: a burger and chocolate shake from *Helen's Corral Drive-Inn* (see p.242).

H35 Yellowstone: Pelican Valley to Wapiti Lake loop

An excellent choice for fit wildlife watchers, this long overnight trek weaves through the heavenly **Pelican Valley** before cutting north along a loop cresting at **Wapiti Lake** deep in the backcountry. Host to meadows and forest, lakes, and numerous rivers, the area is a magnet for wildlife, and wolves, bison, moose, elk, osprey, and sandhill cranes have all been spotted in and around the valley. Of most interest (and concern) are **grizzly bears**, of which there are many. Indeed, the Pelican Valley makes up some of the finest grizzly habitat in the country, and is therefore heavily managed; the valley is **closed** to hikers until early July to give bears the liberty to hunt spawning trout in peace, and travel within the valley proper is banned between 7pm–9am through November. Though not required, rangers also *strongly* recommend hiking in groups of four or more and never hiking solo.

Due to the presence of bears, there are no backcountry campsites within or just out of the Pelican Valley, necessitating a long trek out to the first series of sites. While day-hikers can travel out as far as they feel comfortable before returning, overnighters must cover close to fifteen miles to reach a site; this isn't an exceedingly difficult task, however, as the trail remains relatively flat throughout.

Difficulty Strenuous
Distance 30 miles round-trip
Estimated time 2 days
Season Early July–October
Trailhead location Map p.32. Pelican Valley Trailhead, down a gravel road 3 miles east of Fishing Bridge.
Comments A long and flat journey through some of the finest grazing and hunting grounds for mega-fauna in the park.

From the trailhead, the hike begins by cutting through patches of forest and past the Turbid Lake Trail, three miles to the winding, blue ribbon that is **Pelican Creek** (no fishing allowed). To continue north, you'll need to ford the shallow creek (the footbridge was washed out last time visited) before tramping 1.6 miles through pretty, grassy meadows to the start of the **Astringent Creek Trail**. This trail forms the western half of a long and narrow creek-side loop, and from here it's eight miles due north to Wapiti Lake, the first two-thirds on the Astringent Creek Trail and the last third on Broad Creek Trail; along the way you'll cut through numerous narrow meadows and pass by **White Lake** and then **Tern Lake**, both worth a quick detour to look out for moose and plentiful waterfowl. Sitting at the top end of the loop, Wapiti Lake itself is rather plain, but it's a convenient overnight spot with two backcountry sites (4W2 and 4W3; wood fires allowed). Should these two sites be booked, there are several more sites back to the south and west.

On day two, 9.5 miles out of a total 15.5 miles are spent heading south on the **Upper Pelican Creek Trail**, paralleling the previous day's route a mile to the east. The first four miles up to the turnoff for the **Fern Lake Patrol Cabin** are nearly identical, crossing through a mix of burnt and old growth forest. Afterwards, however, the focus changes a good deal as the trail follows (and fords several times) Pelican Creek downstream past numerous thermal areas; the biggest of the bunch, **The Mushpots**, includes large bubbling cauldrons of mud alongside springs and steaming vents. A little over a mile south of The Mushpots, the trail intersects with the Pelican Creek Trail, from where it is 1.7 miles southwest back to the junction with the Astringent Creek Trail. Follow your previous day's footsteps home just over four miles to complete the trip.

H36 Yellowstone: Shoshone Geyser Basin

One of the first places that grabs the attention of long-haul hikers as they pore over park maps is **Shoshone Lake**; far enough from the roads to be tantalizing but close enough to hike to inside of a day, this is the largest lake in the Lower 48 that doesn't have any direct road access. The following hike targets one of its highlights, the **Shoshone Geyser Basin**. Sitting at the farthest point from a road by the lake's far western edge, the collection of pools, small geysers, and mudpots make up the largest

Difficulty Strenuous
Distance 20 miles round-trip
Estimated time 2 days
Season mid-June to Sept
Trailhead location Map p.78. Lone Star Trailhead, 3.5 miles east of Old Faithful.
Comments Take in both the biggest backcountry lake and backcountry geyser basin in Yellowstone.

backcountry thermal area in the park. There are several routes to it, with the following overnight hike beginning to the north at the **Lone Star Trailhead** and finishing to the northeast at the **DeLacy Creek Trailhead**. This loops lets you cover fresh ground on the return, but to complete it you'll either need to shuttle a second car or hitch a ride between the two trailheads, located six miles apart on the road between Old Faithful and West Thumb.

From the Lone Star Trailhead just upstream from the narrow **Kepler Cascades**, it's 2.5 miles to the **Lone Star Geyser Group**; this is the hike's easiest portion, following a flat roadbed popular with bikers and joggers as well. Sporting a tall, steep cone, Lone Star Geyser itself is a firm favorite of geyser gazers, erupting regularly every 3–4 hours upwards of 50ft. To witness one of the 30-minute long eruptions, check either the logbook at the trailhead or with the visitor center in Old Faithful for a rough timetable and plan accordingly. Past the geyser, the now narrow trail crosses a footbridge over the Firehole River and weaves though a combination of pretty meadows and sparse woods for 3.5 miles to **Grants Pass**; though not a particularly steep climb, snow can be knee-deep here through mid-June. From here, the trail tumbles down at an easy pace for two miles, passing junctions with the Bechler River Trail and then a stock trail looping around the Shoshone Geyser Basin, to the north end of the thermal area itself. There are more than a hundred thermal features and not a single boardwalk or sign. You'll often have the entire area to yourself, but always stick to solid ground, tread lightly and watch your step – you're a long ways from help should you burn yourself.

An **advanced reservation** is recommended to spend the night at one of the three backcountry sites in the area; closest is 8R5, while similarly lakeside 8T1 is to the south and 8G1 is in a meadow below Grants Pass to the north. After re-exploring the geyser basin in the morning light, you'll trace the northern shores of Shoshone Lake for nearly nine miles on the **North Shoshone Trail**; the first half of the trail is mainly through forest, while the latter half, after passing the backcountry **ranger cabin**, opens up to pretty views across the lake. There are nine backcountry sites along this stretch, but the majority are saved for boat access only. Near the trail's end, you'll have to hop across or ford tiny DeLacy Creek, before reaching the **DeLacey Creek Trail**; from here it's an easy three-mile hike north alongside the creek (look out for plentiful waterfowl, along with the occasional moose) back to the main road and civilization.

H37 Yellowstone: Heart Lake and Mount Sheridan

This there-and-back hike to **Heart Lake** and up nearby **Mount Sheridan** (10,305ft) is a fantastic first choice for an overnight trip into Yellowstone's backcountry. The distance covered is reasonable – indeed, hikers in top shape can make it in a very long day – and the rewards are great, with plentiful wildlife, backcountry geysers, lakeside campsites, and stupendous views from one of Yellowstone's finest peaks. The entire area is closed to hikers until July as a bear management area, so take all necessary precautions, including carrying bear spray.

The first several miles are flat and easy, shooting through forest half-burnt in 1988. Signs of new growth abound in the form of 4–10ft tall Lodgepole pines, and squirrels

> **Difficulty** Strenuous
> **Distance** 23 miles round trip
> **Estimated time** 2 days
> **Season** July–Sept
> **Trailhead location** Map p.78. Five miles south of Grant Village, north of Lewis Lake on the east side of road.
> **Comments** A memorable overnighter, taking in backcountry hot springs, a delightful lake and arguably the park's finest panoramic viewpoint.

dart amongst the scattered logs. At the three-mile point, the trail skirts around the charred hulk of **Factory Hill** (9601ft), which remains bare as the pre-fire stands of Engelmann spruce that covered the slopes take much longer to rebound than other native trees. At this point you'll also begin smelling the telltale scent of sulphur, and soon enough you'll pass the first of many bubbling springs on and just off **Witch Creek**. The trail follows the flow of the creek all the way to Heart Lake, located 7.5-miles from the trailhead. The final mile or so is mainly downhill, crossing over warm Witch Creek several times and past a collection of pretty, greenish-blue pools. At the lake's northern end, the trail splits at the **Heart Lake Ranger Station**. A left turn heads east and around the lake to a series of trails leading deeper into the backcountry. Instead, turn right towards Mount Sheridan to walk along the rocky beach rimming the lake's northwestern shore. Six **backcountry campsites** are strung just off the water here; best are 8H2 and 8H3, the only two that allow wood fires.

One of the hike's selling points is that you can now set up camp, leaving your heaviest gear behind before hoofing it up Mount Sheridan. It's best to save the ascent for the morning to avoid the chance of an afternoon thunderstorm. Whatever the time, it's an extremely tough slog, taking just under four miles to climb 3000ft; there's no dependable water source on the trail, so take plenty along. The trail switchbacks up mainly out in the open, with the reward of progressively better views. At the quarter-way point, turn to appreciate the wooded peninsula jutting into Heart Lake, which indeed resembles a child's drawing of a heart (though some historians maintain the lake's name actually comes from **Hart Hunney**, a hunter who tracked game here in the mid-1800s). Halfway up, massive **Yellowstone Lake** comes into view, giving an extra boost for conquering the peak's final alpine leg, consisting of several hundred yards of crumbling rocks and a narrow ridge crossing. Along with patches of snow that usually stick around through the summer, there's a **fire lookout tower** atop the peak, built in 1932 and restored in the 1990s. Should the attendant be in a chatty mood, he might be willing to point out some of the highlights from the panoramic view (including Grand Teton to the south, Mount Washburn north), and discuss the day-to-day details of fire-spotting. After regaining your energy, the return trip is back the way you came.

H38 Grand Teton: Cascade Canyon to Paintbrush Canyon

Difficulty Strenuous
Distance 19.5 mile round-trip
Estimated Time 2 days
Season June–Oct
Trailhead Location Map p.100. West side of Jenny Lake.
Comments A popular loop with an alpine lake to overnight by.

This classic Teton hike makes for a great overnight jaunt into the alpine wilds. The loop leads from the mouth of Cascade Canyon, forks north to Lake Solitude, and then returns down Paintbrush Canyon via a night at Holly Lake. The first portion of the trip follows Grand Teton's most popular hike to **Hidden Falls** and **Inspiration Point** beyond, reachable via the Jenny Lake Ferry should you wish (see day H29 for complete details).

At Inspiration Point, you've actually gained half of the hike's total elevation as the rest of the trail is a gradual climb. Happily, you'll also leave much of the crowd behind as Cascade Creek ushers you through the canyon. Note the many rockslides, or talus slopes, created by the expansion and contraction from frost, which works the boulders free throughout the year. This nearly five-mile long stretch of the trail leads through the canyon's bottom, with Mount St John (11,430ft) to the north and Teewinot Mountain, Mount Owen, and the Grand

Teton to the south. At trail's end, head north from the T-junction on the **Teton Crest Trail** (also called the North Fork Cascade Canyon Trail) for a steady 1200-foot elevation gain over the next three miles toward the incomparably beautiful **Lake Solitude** (9035ft), rung with thick necklace of alpine fir and whitebark Pine. Due to the shadow cast by the cirque surrounding it, ice stays on the lake well into July. Should you want to turn this hike into a lazy two-nighter, the North Fork Cascade Canyon backcountry camping zone is due south of the lake.

Leaving Lake Solitude, the trail steeply climbs up Paintbrush Divide; at 10,720ft it is the highest point on the Teton Crest Trail. From here it is all downhill, and peaceful **Holly Lake** is a perfect point to set up a tent after a long day of mostly uphill hiking; camping is relegated to three designated sites lakeside, though there are large backcountry camping zones (Upper Paintbrush Canyon and Lower Paintbrush Canyon) along the trail to the west and east. From Holly Lake, follow the trail down Paintbrush Canyon, 4.5 miles east through thick woods, and veer south for 1.3 miles along String Lake to the northern tip of Jenny Lake. Trace the shoreline path to the southeast for a little over two miles to the Jenny Lake Parking Area.

H39 Grand Teton: Death Canyon Loop

Difficulty Very strenuous
Distance 26 miles round-trip
Estimated Time 2–3 days
Season July–Aug
Trailhead Location Map p.93. Death Canyon Trailhead, southeast of Moose on Moose Wilson Road.
Comments A long and steep trail hitting several of Grand Teton's backcountry highlights plus several backcountry camping zones to choose from.

Death Canyon is the second largest canyon within the Tetons, trailing only Webb Canyon at the range's northern end. Its glacially eroded U-shape and 2.5 billion year-old walls make it not only a physical challenge, but a mental one as well as hikers attempt to comprehend the magnitude of time represented in the surrounding rock. For two to three days on this hike, you can ponder the epic scale of the geological timeline amongst the scenic grandeur of the canyon.

Starting from the popular Death Canyon Trailhead, the hike's first mile heads up to the **Phelps Lake Overlook**, as detailed on p.94. From the scenic viewpoint, a 400-foot descent lands hikers in bear and moose territory as they follow the trail into Death Canyon. Inside, the towering walls reveal their layers of Precambrian gneiss, schist and pegmatite, while huge Engelmann spruce shade the canyon floor in a protective canopy. At close to the four-mile mark sits a small log **patrol cabin**, originally constructed during the Civilian Conservation Corps years as a shelter for the men constructing trails and still used today by backcountry rangers. Provided there are no approaching storms, continue the counter-clockwise loop by climbing up **Static Peak** (11,303ft), named for the propensity for lighting to strike it. This switchback trail challenges all with a quick ascent of 3000ft in just four miles, cresting at the highest point on any trail in the park (10,800ft).

The trail continues from the summit of Static Peak along the Alaska Basin Trail; 0.8 miles northwest of Static Peak the trail dips steeply before gently climbing to the cluster of tiny **Basin Lakes**. Just north of the lakes is one of the trail's major junctions; turn left and head west on the **Teton Crest Trail**, scaling the **Sheep Steps** switchbacks to the pass by **Mount Meek** (10,681ft) and on to the renowned **Death Canyon Shelf**, a stretch of trail with stunning mountain views and a thankfully negligible elevation change. Surrounded by

△ The Teton Crest Trail

wildflower-covered meadows, the shelf is a 3.5-mile long, bumpy limestone bench, dotted with crevices and caves created by millions of years of acidic runoff dissolving areas of soft rock. Dispersed backcountry camping is allowed along the entire stretch, making for some of the most memorable campsites in the entire region (sunsets cast a warm, alpenglow on nearby Grand Teton). From Fox Creek Pass, at the southern end of the shelf, you'll turn off Teton Crest Trail and onto **Death Canyon Trail**, heading downhill 5.4 miles east through the upper canyon back to the patrol cabin to complete the loop. The upper Death Canyon area is also zoned for backcountry camping, and has easy access to water in the creek that runs next to the trail.

H40 Grand Teton: Teton Crest Trail

The epic **Teton Crest Trail** runs from Teton Pass, west of the tiny outpost of Wilson, north to Paintbrush Canyon, covering the southern half of the Teton Range. The trail is composed mainly of the western portions of several loop trails that lead deep into the mountain, utilizing the range's canyons as gangplanks on which to march into the highlands. The official length of the trail is just over 35 miles, but a seemingly endless combination of connecting trails lets hikers add on routes to their heart's content (and, possibly, their lungs' discontent).

> **Difficulty** Very strenuous
> **Distance** 35.4 miles one-way
> **Estimated Time** 5 days
> **Season** Late June to early Oct
> **Trailhead Location** Map p.90. Ski Lake Trailhead on Teton Pass (south to north); String Lake Picnic Area (north to south).
> **Comments** Explore the alpine highlands of the Teton Range on one of the country's best destination trails.

Choosing to travel from **north to south** gets the toughest parts of the trail out of the way soonest, and also covers the most awe-inspiring scenery at the get-go. Conversely, a **south to north** route lets hikers ease into the hike with more of a warm-up on the first day out. Either way you travel on this rugged path, you'll want to establish a **shuttle** system, with cars left at either end, or a buddy ready to pick you up at an appointed time. Don't rely on a mobile phone at the end of the trail for contacting your ride, as reception is notoriously inconsistent in this mountainous area.

Most hikers spend four nights on the trail, aiming for about eight miles per day; considering the weight of a full pack and the often-steep trails, it's a reasonable goal for experienced, acclimated hikers. Traveling south to north, start at the **Ski Lake Trailhead**, just downhill of the **Glory Slide** on Hwy-22 halfway up Teton Pass. A gentle climb up Phillips Pass (8932ft), tracing the west side of Jackson Hole Mountain Resort's **Rendezvous Mountain**, lands hikers at the Middle Fork of **Granite Canyon**, a good spot for the first night's camp at 7.8 miles. Zigzag past the North Fork and back uphill to Marion Lake, then past Spearhead Peak (10,131ft) to Fox Creek Pass, where trails from Death Canyon and Fox Creek converge. Continue north across the fantastic **Death Canyon Shelf** and camp at the northern end on night two (see H39).

On the third day, start out hiking up **Mount Meek Pass** and zigzag on the Sheep Steps following the curve of **Alaska Basin**. Heading north from the **Basin Lakes**, the next landmark is **Sunset Lake**, a little jewel to the east of the trail. Heading up and over **Hurricane Pass,** don't miss **Schoolroom Glacier** at just past the 20-mile mark; having received its name as a "textbook" example of an alpine glacier, Schoolroom Glacier features a perfect moraine, where rocks and debris have been pushed by the glacier, and around which an eroded outlet spills out a glacial stream. After descending into the South Fork of Cascade Canyon look for a place to pitch a tent in the backcountry camping zone for night three. Day four is the last strenuous day of hiking. Follow the trail through the North Fork of Cascade Canyon to the substantial **Lake Solitude**, crowned by an embrace of rocks towering 1000ft above (see H38). Take a rest at the lake, as the next leg of the trail ascends to the highest point of the Teton Crest Trail, **Paintbrush Divide** (10,720ft). Dig in for one last night on the downhill slope at one of the camping areas near Holly Lake. Your final day's journey is an easy six-mile descent down the gorgeous **Paintbrush Canyon** to the String Lake Picnic Area.

6

Summer activities

Driving around the parks in **summer**, you'll pass by dirt-encrusted cars and trucks so overloaded with gear they look like modern-day prairie schooners. Kayaks and canoes hug roofs, while bikes hang from trunk racks and fishing poles dangle out open windows. These visitors have the right idea, as Yellowstone and Grand Teton offer a wealth of **outdoor activities**. **Hiking** is the most popular pastime, with day and overnight options covered in detail in chapters 4 and 5. Close behind and steadily growing in popularity, **fly-fishing** in the region's celebrated rivers is a dream come true for many. The largest lakes within the parks draw spin-fishermen to their depths, as well as **boaters** and **paddlers** on hour-long to extended overnight backcountry expeditions. Grand Teton's Snake River is the only major waterway in either park open to float trips, but thrilling **whitewater-rafting** trips can be taken just outside the parks in all directions. **Swimming** is another option in some of the calmer waters, including two popular swimming holes in Yellowstone heated by surges of thermal runoff.

On firmer ground, long-distance **bicycling** on Grand Teton's less congested minor roads makes for a scenic and sweaty workout, while Yellowstone is home to numerous service roads and paths leading bikers past the likes of backcountry geysers and photogenic rock formations. As most hiking trails are open to stock animals as well, the opportunities for **horseback riding** are far greater; guided backcountry trips into the most isolated corners of the parks can be arranged, though most visitors opt for short trail rides leaving from one of several park-run stables. Most adventurous of all, **rock-climbing** in Grand Teton draws mountaineers from across the globe, and courses are offered by two of the finest climbing schools in the country.

Fishing

Yellowstone alone has more than 200 fishable streams, and a roll call of the park's most famous is enough to get **fly-fishers** everywhere running for their waders. Best known are the Yellowstone and Madison **rivers**, with Slough Creek and the Lamar and Firehole rivers leading a secondary pack of at least a dozen equally eminent streams. In Grand Teton, the **Snake River** takes top honors, while more of the country's finest "blue-ribbon" trout streams await only a short drive from either park, including a collection of "**forks**" that could alone justify a week-long fishing trip: the Henry's Fork west in Idaho, the Clark's Fork north of Cody, the Buffalo Fork east of Moran Junction, and the South Fork south of Jackson. Not only are these rivers impossibly scenic – nowhere else can one fish surrounded by steaming geysers, within a long cast of grazing bison, or in the shadow of the Tetons – they're also home to vast

Hydrothermal Yellowstone

The massive Yellowstone Caldera, a volcanic crater created by an epic explosion some 640,000 years ago, outlines one of the planet's most active volcanic hotspots. Upwards of 3000 annual earthquakes attest to the forces bellowing below, but it's Yellowstone's incredible array of hydrothermal features – more than 10,000 at last count, including half of the world's geysers – that best prove the vigour of the area's volcanic muscle. As for the next eruption, most geologists predict the chamber of magma bubbling mere miles beneath the surface won't likely blow for thousands of years at least. Until then, Yellowstone's wonderland of sparkling hot springs, gravity-defying geysers, and other assorted hydrothermal oddities will remain to mystify and amaze.

▲ Lower Geyser Basin

Hot springs

Yellowstone's most common and visually splendid hydrothermal features are its **hot springs**, often called pools. Hot springs are sourced from underground by boiling water heated by magma located only a few miles beneath the surface. Unlike geysers there are no constrictions in the spring's underground plumbing, meaning the superheated water can circulate via convection, cooling off before reaching an eruptive level. Along with the numerous springs bubbling by the park's busy boardwalks, pools ranging from deep puddles to giant-sized hot tubs are dotted throughout the backcountry. Keep your distance, tread cautiously around them when forced to, and forget about taking a dip as these pools are scalding at best, deadly at worst.

Colorful wonders

◄ Morning Glory Pool

The most distinctive feature of hot springs and other hydrothermal features is the amazing range of **colors** they exhibit. The brilliant shades of blues are caused by the refraction of sunlight off particles in the water, while the remaining palette of colors – reds, oranges, yellows, browns, purples – that ring springs and collect in runoff channels are brightly colored algae and bacteria known as **thermophiles**. The range of color indicates a specific temperature range. Green, brown, and rust-red colors typically specify cooler water, while brighter pinks, yellows, and oranges indicate hotter water, with some thermophiles living in temperatures over 170°F. A bizarre and fascinating micro-culture, these heat-loving microorganisms are being studied by scientists for everything from potential medical use to the possibility of finding life on other seemingly inhospitable planets.

Mudpots, fumaroles, and travertine terraces

Rudely burping and plopping away, you'll find children of all ages in the midst of giggle fits when standing by **mudpots**. These are hot springs with a limited but highly acidic water supply that continually breaks down the surrounding rock into muddy clay. Ranging from a weak soup-like consistency to thick pools of melted tar depending on the water available, mudpots have been known to expel dollops of hot mud onto bystanders, so be prepared to high tail it should one get particularly raging. The bubbling within mudpots is caused by escaping gases – the reason they typically stink – not boiling temperatures.

Similar to mudpots, **fumaroles** are short on water, meaning they have to be content with hissing steam through their underground fissures reaching deep down towards the molten rock below. Fumaroles are the hottest of the hydrothermal features, measuring as high as 280°F, and they typically appear on higher ground above geysers or hot springs such as those puffing away above the Porcelain Basin in Norris.

Though not classified as a distinct hydrothermal feature, the **travertine terraces** found at Mammoth make up the park's most alien landscape. Unlike other areas where rhyolite is dominant, limestone is the primary surface rock at Mammoth. Beneath Mammoth is a massive web of fissures and tunnels forcing hot water up from the magma-heated underworld. On the way up, the thermal waters pick up dissolved carbon dioxide to create an acidic solution that dissolves the calcium carbonate found in limestone, depositing it in chalky white mounds and terrace-like formations spilling down hillsides. As with hot springs, thermophiles thrive in the heated waters, adding psychedelic layers of brown, green, yellow, and orange streaks to the travertine formations.

Geysers

There are more than 300 active **geysers** in Yellowstone, by far the largest concentration of them on the planet. Plainly speaking, geysers are hot springs that erupt both water and steam. In order to form a geyser there must be a constriction within the spring's plumbing that prevents the superheated water from reaching the surface to cool off. These geysers erupt when the groundwater, held down by fissures and narrow channels, forms bubbles that literally blow the water through vents at the top. Yellowstone's geysers appear in two basic forms: fountain geysers, which typically bubble up into a pool and then shoot water all over the place before subsiding, and cone geysers, which shoot a single jet upwards through a cone or nozzle formed by a steady accumulation of mineral deposits.

▲ Lone Star Geyser

Must-see hydrothermal features

Hot springs

- **Abyss Pool** The 53ft deep Abyss Pool and the Black Pool steps away, both a stone's throw from Yellowstone Lake, make a trip to the West Thumb Geyser Basin essential. See p.79.
- **Cistern Spring** A lemon-lime pool in the Norris Geyser Basin made all the more dramatic by tiny terrace-like formations on its edges and a stark necklace of dead lodgepole pine. See p.62.
- **Grand Prismatic Spring** Yellowstone's largest spring and also its most vivid, a fierce blaze of near neon blues, reds, yellows, and oranges. See p.72.
- **Sapphire Pool** Star of the Biscuit Basin, this bright blue pool lives up to as name as well as any feature in the park. See p.77.

▲ Sapphire Pool

Mudpots, fumaroles, and travertine terraces

▲ Fountain Paint Pots

- **Fountain Paint Pots** A flatulent pool of bubbling mud that's watery in spring and thick towards summer's end. See p.72.
- **Orange Spring Mound** This brain-shaped mound of travertine off of Mammoth's Upper Terrace Drive sports a coating of orange wherever water continues to seep down. See p.50.
- **Palette Spring** A steep series of rounded travertine steps that earns its name as one the most colorful formations within Mammoth's Lower Terraces. See p.49.
- **Roaring Mountain** Named after the growl of sulphurous steam pouring out if it, the face of Roaring Mountain is pockmarked with dozens of fumaroles. See p.63.

Geysers

- **Great Fountain Geyser** Spectacularly situated in the midst of a massive sinter terrace, this fountain geyser's noisy eruptions splash between 100 to 200ft. See p.70.
- **Lone Star Geyser** It's a five-mile round-trip hike or bike ride to Lone Star, which sports a dramatic cone and picturesque eruptions that make it the most popular backcountry geyser. See p.78.
- **Riverside Geyser** One of writer Rudyard Kipling's favorite spouters, this crowd-pleaser perched on the banks of the Firehole River erupts every six hours on average. See p.70.
- **Steamboat Geyser** You might have better odds winning the lottery than witnessing the world's tallest geyser blow – the 300ft eruptions can occur decades apart – but it's worth a look just in case. See p.62.

▲ Great Fountain Geyser

populations of trout, including the prized native cutthroat, strictly catch-and-release within Yellowstone (see box, p.84).

A wide range of hatches on these rivers requires a well-stocked fly box, and as conditions depend greatly on seasonal variables your best bet upon arrival is to stop by one of the many superb local **fly-fishing outfitters** (see box, p.162). Even if you already have everything needed for a day out on the water, it pays to purchase a couple of flies or a spool of tippet; spending just a couple of dollars frees up the knowledgeable staff to answer questions on current hot spots and which flies to try first. Hiring a **guide** for the day may be pricey, but being taken straight to some of the best locations along with being able to pepper a local expert with questions is well worth the expense; a successful strategy is to hire a guide for the first day or two of fishing, then head out solo afterwards with newly gained know-how. Guides can also be hired at the main **marinas** in both parks for fishing in Yellowstone and Jackson lakes.

Within Yellowstone

Save for a few major exceptions, Yellowstone's **fishing season** runs from the Saturday of Memorial Day weekend (typically the last weekend in May) through the first Sunday in November. A **Yellowstone National Park fishing permit** is required; Wyoming or Montana licenses are *not* valid. Permits can be purchased at all ranger stations, visitor centers and general stores and they cost $15 (3-day), $20 (7-day) and $35 (season). Each permit comes with an 18-page guide listing the numerous fishing regulations, and it's vital that you read and understand them all. Some of most important rules include no lead sinkers or barbed hooks (pinch down barbs with pliers); only artificial lures and flies, meaning no minnow, worms, or foodstuff allowed; and all native fish, meaning cutthroat trout, artic grayling, and mountain whitefish, are strictly **catch-and-release**.

For the most part, if you can reach a **river** in Yellowstone, you can fish it; however, a good place to look for easy access are the numerous riverside picnic areas, where you'll be able to find a shady place to park as well. For a detailed review of Yellowstone's rivers and hatch cycles, *The Yellowstone Fly-Fishing Guide* by Craig Mathews and Clayton Malinero (Lyons Press) is comprehensive, concise, and highly recommended. Early in the season, the finest fishing is on the park's west side, where rivers tend to clear quickest from winter snowmelt. Fishermen flock to the **Firehole River** on opening day, a spectacular dry-fly stream weaving through some of the park's largest geyser basins; it's as tricky as it is beautiful, however, as the rainbow, brown, brook, and cutthroat trout in the river are used to the presence of anglers and wilier than most. By mid-July, the constant rush of thermal waters raise temperatures on the Firehole to 80 degrees in spots, limiting fishing until early September. To the north, the slender **Gibbon River** is also worth trying early in the season, and best fished along its wider stretches south of Norris. Formed by the confluence of the Gibbon and the Firehole, the celebrated **Madison River** flows west from Madison Junction in wide curves along the road to West Yellowstone before cutting north to Hebgen Lake. Amongst other things, the Madison is renowned for large brown trout, most often caught early in June or, better yet, September and October when surrounded by bright fall foliage

The star of the central and northern reaches of the park is the **Yellowstone River**, so complex and varied that entire books have been written on fishing this single river alone. To protect what is the finest cutthroat fishery in the country, fishing is not allowed on the river north of Yellowstone Lake until July 15, and several stretches are closed permanently (including LeHardys Rapids

Fly-fishing gear and guides

The following outfitters run **guided trips** on the rivers within Yellowstone, Grand Teton, and the surrounding national forests, and lessons can be arranged through most as well. The going rate for a full day with one or two people is around $400, including gear (if needed) and a packed lunch. All of the outfitters listed also run well-stocked **shops**, filled with the expected array of rods, lines, and leaders, along with cases of hand-tied flies, guidebooks, and maps (often free) to top fishing spots. The general stores within both parks stock a limited selection of flies and supplies as well, but you're better off stopping at one of the following dedicated fishing shops.

Cody

North Fork Anglers 1107 Sheridan Ave, ⓣ307/527-7274, ⓦwww.northforkanglers.com. Cody's best fishing shop, fully stocked and with reasonably priced guided trips to the North or South Fork of the Shoshone, the Clark's Fork of the Yellowstone, or into Yellowstone its elf. The "Cowboys and Cutthroats" trip heads down the Thorofare Trail on horseback for a week of backcountry camping and fishing.

Gardiner

Park's Fly Shop 2nd Street between Stone and Main, ⓣ406/848-7314, ⓦwww.parksflyshop.com. In business since in 1953, this excellent outfitter runs float trips on the Yellowstone River north of the park boundary, along with a variety of wading trips that include backcountry jaunts to "secret" tributaries within the park itself. They also hand out a free fishing map detailing Yellowstone National Park and the Gallatin and Missouri rivers.

Grand Teton

Will Dornan's Snake River Angler Dornan's in Moose, ⓣ307/733-3699 or 1-800/998-7688, ⓦwww.snakeriverangler.com. At the very least, anglers should stop in to pick up the *Jackson Hole Moosepaper* ($1 donation), filled with hatch charts and regional river maps. Located steps from the Snake River and stocked with dozens of

and Chittenden Bridge downstream to Silver Chord Falls). The longest undammed river in the lower 48, the Yellowstone boasts an estimated 200 miles of tricky trout water, with prime fishing inside the park found on the stretch of water north from Fishing Bridge to Mud Volcano, as well as throughout much of the Black Canyon of the Yellowstone (see H34, p.152). Outside the park, numerous access points line the highway from Gardiner north to Livingston some fifty miles away.

To the west of the Yellowstone river, the **Gardner River** and its many tributaries (including Panther, Indian, and Obsidian Creeks) make for relatively easy fishing for non-native brook trout; the Gardner is the one river in the park where children eleven years old and younger may fish with worms as bait. And to the east of the Yellowstone River and accessible by the road between Tower and the Northeast Entrance, both the **Lamar River** and its tributary **Soda Butte Creek** begin attracting serious anglers in swarms by late-July. By mid-August, grasshoppers also begin swarming the meadows bordering these rivers, giving skilled feather-throwers the joy of catching cutthroats and rainbows on large terrestrial flies. Flowing into the Lamar to the north and another popular late-summer stream is **Slough Creek**, with easy access near its eponymous campground; the best fishing, however, requires at least a two-mile hike out, with conditions improving the further you're willing to travel (see H5, p.124).

As for **lake fishing**, the two most accessible are **Yellowstone Lake** and **Lewis Lake**, both home to boat launches (see "Rafting and boating" on p.165

useful fly varieties, guided trips here focus on the Snake, Green, and South Fork rivers, though trips to Lewis Lake and the Firehole River in Yellowstone are also offered.

Jackson

Jack Dennis' Outdoor Shop 50 E Broadway, ⓣ307/733-3270 or 1-800/570-3270, ⓦwww.jackdennis.com. The back of this large sporting goods shop on Town Square is where you'll find the fly-fishing gear. Along with flies and supplies, you can pick up the information-packed *Western Fishing Newsletter* for free. A long list of guided float and wading trips offered, along with lessons and seminars including a two-hour casting class ($100 for 2 people) on a private trout-stocked pond.

Westbank Anglers 3670 N. Moose-Wilson Rd, ⓣ307/733-6483 or 1-800/922-3474, ⓦwww.westbank.com. On the banks of the Snake River three miles south of Teton Village, this outfitter organizes trips to trout hotspots around the world. Locally they focus on the Snake, Green and New Fork rivers, but run guided trips into Yellowstone as well. The onsite retail shop has a fine selection.

West Yellowstone

Blue Ribbon Flies 305 Canyon St, ⓣ406/646-7642, ⓦwww.blueribbonflies.com. Best priced guided trips in town, with a solid reputation to match. A wide variety of guided trips offered, including day-trips wading in Yellowstone, floats down the Madison, Hebgen Lake fishing and longer road trips hitting rivers throughout the region.

Bud Lilly's Trout Shop 39 Madison Ave, ⓣ406/646-7801 or 1-800/854-9559, ⓦwww.budlilys.com. A well stocked shop with guided trips into Yellowstone, along the nearby Madison, and on the Henry's Fork across the border in Idaho: trips on the latter two can be waded or floated in drift boats.

Jacklin's Flyshop 105 Yellowstone Ave, ⓣ406/646-7336, ⓦwww.jacklinsflyshop.com. A massive selection of flies, along with a crew of guides to help you pick out the current best. Rivers fished include the Madison, Henry's Fork, and all of Yellowstone's top streams.

for rental information). Shore fishing from Yellowstone Lake can be decent at times, but to hunt down the largest lake and cutthroat trout you'll want to fish by boat; the best time to fish the lake are the weeks directly after the June 15 opening. Historically fishless, Lewis Lake to the south now supports populations of brook, brown, cutthroat, and lake trout, and both spin- and fly-fishermen can have luck casting from the shore soon after the ice leaves in mid-June and in October when brown trout start spawning; throughout the rest of summer, the fishing is best by boat. Connected to Lewis Lake by a three-mile channel, **Shoshone Lake** has the same populations of fish and fishing schedule, though it sees far fewer anglers as they must hike or paddle out to fish. Other worthwhile backcountry lakes include: **Grebe Lake** and **Wolf Lake**, the headwaters of the Gibbon River and home to large populations of catch-and-release arctic grayling as well as rainbow tour; **Trout Lake**, a mile hike north of the Northeast Entrance Road and open July 15 has great cutthroat and rainbow fishing; and **Heart Lake**, accessed via a longer hike (see H37, p.155) and likewise opening July 15, a wonderfully isolated spot to reel in lake and cutthroat trout.

Within Grand Teton

Whether on a lake or river, to fish in Grand Teton a **Wyoming fishing license** is required; for non-residents of the state, these cost $11 (day) or $76 (year). In the park, licenses can be purchased at Will Dornan's Snake River Angler (see box, p.162), as well as the Signal Mountain Lodge, Colter Bay Village marina

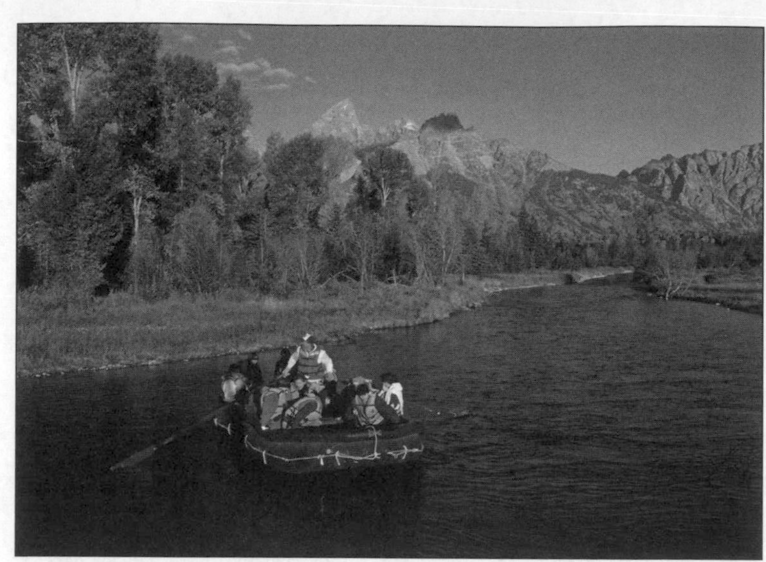

△ Floating down the Snake River

and store, and Flagg Ranch Lodge. You are responsible for following all regulations, including closures and catch limits, so read the pamphlet that comes with each license carefully.

The pride of fly-fishing in Grand Teton is the scenic **Snake River**, teeming with native cutthroat trout. Unlike Yellowstone's streams, the Snake is fishable via drift boat, letting anglers cover more water in a few hours than could possibly be fished in several days of wading and walking along the banks. Unless you have your own boat, however, you'll likely have to hire a guide to float down the river, a relatively expensive proposition (see box, pp.162–163). Some of the best spots from which to cast from the banks or in which to wade include the boat launch areas around Schwabacher's Landing and Deadman's Bar, along with the parking area at the end of bumpy RKO Road south of Signal Mountain (see p.106). Only artificial flies and lures can be used on the Snake and most of its tributaries from the Jackson Lake Dam south to Wilson Bridge outside of the park. The river is open to fishing year-round, though cutthroat caught Nov–March must be released. Runoff clouds up conditions throughout May and June, with the best fishing occurring mid-July to mid-Oct. Other popular trout rivers either in or just outside of Grand Teton include: the **Gros Ventre River**, particularly above and below Lower Slide Lake; **Flat Creek**, to the south within the National Elk Refuge; the **South Fork**, south of Jackson; and the **Buffalo Fork**, east of Moran Junction in the Bridger-Teton National Forest.

Anglers also flock to Grand Teton's lakes in great numbers, using both fly and spin rods. Most of the lakes are free of ice by early June, though all save **Jackson Lake** remain open to fishing year-round. Fishing on Jackson Lake is prohibited only throughout October, in order to protect spawning Mackinaw lake trout, and throughout most of the summer the best fishing is by boat, trolling deep down for the largest fish. Unlike Yellowstone Lake, lake trout are welcome in the lake and need not be killed upon capture. **Phelps**, **Taggart**, and **Bradley**

lakes all host healthy populations of cutthroat and lake trout, though **Jenny Lake** and **Leigh Lake** draw more fishermen as they're much more accessible to those in float tubes and canoes.

Boating

From kayaking along the shoreline in Yellowstone Lake's isolated lower "fingers" to buzzing about Jackson Lake on a pair of water skis, **boaters** have several renowned lakes on which to play within Yellowstone and Grand Teton. The Snake River is the sole major river with boat access, but add the seemingly endless supply of rivers and lakes in the neighboring national forests, and it's no surprise that the greater Yellowstone ecosystem is celebrated for its boating. For the thrills of a **whitewater rafting** trip, you'll have to head out of the parks; there are quality stretches on the North Fork of the Shoshone River outside of Cody, the Yellowstone River north of Gardiner, and the Snake River south of Jackson, but the region's best whitewater is on the Gallatin River in Big Sky (see p.236). If interested in a guided canoe or kayak trip in the parks, see the "Activity-based tours" listed on p.204.

A **permit** is required for all vessels – including float tubes – in the parks. In Yellowstone, these can be obtained at most of the entrance stations, as well as the Grant Village Backcountry Office and Bridge Bay Ranger Station. In Grand Teton they can be purchased at any of the marinas, as well as the Moose Visitor Center. Fees for non-motorized vessels are $5 (week) or $10 (annual), with motorized permits double the cost. Permits purchased in Yellowstone are honored in Grand Teton, and vice versa.

Within Yellowstone

In the early days of tourism, Yellowstone visitors could escape the dusty confines of their stagecoach to cross **Yellowstone Lake** on the steamboat *Zillah*, plunking down $2.50 to arrive at the *Lake Hotel* in style. Nowadays, boating in the park is much more of a do-it-yourself affair, with only the **Bridge Bay Marina** at the northern end of Yellowstone Lake offering rentals and dockage (mid-June to mid-Aug 8am–8pm, mid-Aug to mid Sept 8am–5pm; ⓣ307/344-7311). Typically covered in ice patches through May, the massive lake is no place for beginners; unless you're confident in your boating skills, do not head out without a guide and always stay close to shore when paddling as conditions can change almost instantaneously. Capsizing in the freezing waters can be lethal. **Rental** options at Bridge Bay Marina include rowboats ($10 hour, $43 day) and slightly larger outboard motorboats ($45 hour), along with 22ft ($140 two hours) and 34ft ($180 two hours) powerboats. The latter two can also be chartered for private four-hour **tours**, sightseeing or fishing, starting at $315. It's also possible to arrange drop-offs for backcountry exploring via kayak or canoe through the marina by calling ahead (ⓣ307/242-3876), and there's another less popular boat launch (no dock) onto the lake at Grant Village. There are more than three dozen boat accessible **backcountry campsites** edging the lake, allowing for overnight to week-long paddle tours; advanced reservations for these sites are recommended, and booking procedures are the same as with backcountry hiking sites (see p.148).

To the south towards Grand Teton is roadside **Lewis Lake**, third largest lake in the park and the only other one with a boat launch; canoes, kayaks and motorboats are all allowed. From the north end of Lewis Lake, it's possible to paddle upstream on the **Lewis Channel** to **Shoshone Lake**, the largest backcountry lake in the contiguous United States. This is the only stream in the park open to kayaks and canoes, and while the first two miles are easy, the final mile is shallow and rocky, and requires getting into the cold waters to drag your vessel upstream (waders and river-shoes highly recommended). The effort is well worth it, as padding the shorelines of Shoshone Lake and spending a night or more at one of twenty backcountry sites around the lake is an experience not soon forgotten. Due in part to the short season – the lake doesn't become ice-free until mid-June – the sites here are extremely popular, making advanced reservations essential. As with Yellowstone Lake, conditions on Shoshone Lake can change rapidly; only experience paddlers should visit without a guide.

Boats are prohibited on all other rivers in the park, including the entirety of the Yellowstone until it flows north out of the park at Gardiner.

Within Grand Teton

Much more so than Yellowstone, boating is high on **Grant Teton**'s list of popular activities. For starters, non-motorized float trips *are* allowed on the **Snake River**. These popular half-day excursions are a relaxing way to view the landscape, meandering past elk and moose and beneath soaring eagles, with the Teton Range towering splendidly to the west. Two of the best **operators** are Barker-Ewing (Ⓣ1-800/365-1800, Ⓦwww.barkerewingscenic.com; $50), rafting ten miles from Deadman's Bar south to Moose, and Snake River Anglers (Ⓣ1-888/998-7768, Ⓦwww.snakeriverangler.com; $50), floating twelve miles from Moose to Wilson Bridge outside of the park. If without a guide, a **permit** is required (same fees as Yellowstone); these are sold at the visitors centers in Moose, Colter Bay and Flagg Ranch, and should only be purchased by experienced rafters and kayakers as the Snake River is a deceptively difficult waterway to navigate.

Boats are banned from all other rivers within Grand Teton, but they are allowed on ten of the park's largest lakes, a luxury that tourists and locals take full advantage of. Motorized boats (no jet-skis) are permitted only on **Jackson Lake** and **Jenny Lake**, with engines limited to 10-horsepower on the latter, while canoes, kayaks and float-tubes are also allowed on Phelps, Emma Matilda, Two Ocean, Taggart, Bradley, Bearpaw, Leigh, and String lakes. For one of the best paddles in the park, put-in at String Lake and paddle north onto spectacular Leigh Lake; a portage is required between the two, and there are several backcountry campsites around Leigh Lake for overnight stays.

For those without a boat in tow, there's a good amount of tour and rental choices. Most popular are the **ferry rides** across Jenny Lake to the Cascade Canyon Trailhead (May 15–30 & Sept 16–30 daily 10am–4pm, June to Sept 15 daily 8am–6pm; Ⓣ307/734-922; $7.50 round-trip, $5 one-way); longer scenic cruises around the lake are also offered for $12, while canoes/kayaks ($12) and small motor-boats ($25) can be rented by the hour. Two marinas on busy Jackson Lake offer tours and rentals, with similar rates for canoes, kayaks and small motorboats. The **Signal Mountain Lodge Marina** (mid-May to mid-Sept hours vary; Ⓣ307/543-2831) also rents out faster runabouts ($50 per hour), large pontoons ($65), and deck cruisers ($75) with room for ten passengers. Guides sailboat tours are offered as well, starting from $65. To the north of the lodge, the **Colter Bay Village Marina** (June–August daily 8am–7pm; Ⓣ307/734-922) runs narrated hour-long tours via motorboat for $18, with more breakfast ($30) and dinner ($52) trips also available. Also north, **Leeks Marina** (mid-May to mid-September, earlier in dry years) has a boat launch and docks, but no rental options. At Dornan's in Moose, Adventure Sports (Ⓣ307/733-3307) rents out canoes and kayaks for $40 per day, including all necessary equipment to load atop your car.

Swimming

Swimming in the parks is a matter of thinking before you leap. Whether in a lake or river, pond or creek, the majority of water in the region too **cold** for a comfortable swim in all but the hottest of temperatures. And in some cases, conditions stretch beyond uncomfortable into dangerous; averaging a frigid 45 degrees, survival time for swimming in **Yellowstone Lake** is estimated to be only twenty minutes. Swift and filled with underwater hazards, the region's rivers are equally treacherous and unforgiving; **drowning** is the second leading cause of accidental death in the parks after car accidents.

That said, a swimsuit should still be packed alongside your thermal underwear. If you don't mind squishing into a murky bottom, many of Yellowstone's smaller backcountry lakes and creeks are suitable for a quick mid-hike dip come July and August, and if up for a splurge, the *Mammoth Hot Springs Hotel* has cabins with their own private hot tubs. Best of all, there are two superb natural swimming areas. Both are called the **Boiling River**, with swimming taking place in rivers warmed by the onrush of nearby thermal waters. The northernmost is within the **Gardner River** (see p.50), accessed via a short path from the parking area two miles north of Mammoth on the way to Gardiner. To the south and equally popular is the swimming area in the **Firehole River**, with limited parking along Firehole Canyon Drive (see p.69). Bathing suits are required and there are no lifeguards at either location. Both **close** at dusk and throughout early summer until the rivers have calmed from snowmelt highs suitably, and only the Gardner River stays open through winter for those brave enough to bathe in the arctic air.

To the south within the John D. Rockefeller, Jr. Parkway are the similar, though less frequently used bathing areas at **Polecat and Huckleberry Hot Springs** near Flagg Ranch (see p.114). In **Grand Teton**, swimming is allowed in all of the park's lakes, though their icy-cold temperatures will scare most bathers away. **String**, **Leigh** and **Jenny lakes** all have sandy beach areas, however, with shallower waters that go from cold to pleasantly cool later in summer. The *Jackson Lake Lodge* has a **pool** open to hotel guests and those staying within Colter Bay Village, and younger kids will have fun splashing around **Kelly Warm Spring** of the Gros Ventre Road to the southeast (see p.98). Swimming in the **Snake River** is dangerous and not recommended.

Soaking directly within a hot spring – know as "hotpotting" – is both illegal and foolhardy. Several unfortunate bathers, including park employees supposedly in the know, have died after slipping into the wrong spring. To soak safely, head to the swimming pools at **Chico Hot Springs** (see p.244), 45 minutes north of Gardiner, or the more rustic **Granite Hot Springs** (ⓣ307/739-5400, ⓦwww.granitehotsprings.net; $6), an equal distance south of Jackson on Hwy-191.

Bicycling

Bicyclists may have been here first – Yellowstone's first bike tourists date back to 1883 – but the car has long been king of the road, and on the whole the main highways within Yellowstone and Grand Teton make for poor **bicycling**. They're narrow, paved shoulders are inconsistent, traffic is constantly zipping past (including lane-hogging RVs), and drivers are often distracted, spending their time searching for wildlife instead of focusing on the road ahead. All in all, highway riding in the high season is a recipe for disaster, though plenty of long-haul bicyclists manage to avoid the hazards on tours each year. But for the average day-tripping bicyclist, there's a solid selection of minor highways and old service roads open to bikes in both parks. It's certainly most economical to bring your own bike along if possible, but **rentals** are available in most of the gateway towns, as well as the bike shop in Yellowstone's *Old Faithful Snow Lodge* and the sporting goods store at Dornan's in Grand Teton. Unless specified, riding on hiking trails is strictly forbidden in the parks.

Within Yellowstone

The best time to ride the roads in Yellowstone is from late March until late April, when several long sections of the park's **highways** have been cleared of snow but still remain closed to automobile traffic. Unless here specifically to cycle however, it's unlikely you'll be visiting in early spring as the park's roads aren't the only things closed; its hotels, restaurants, and majority of other amenities remain shuttered. If set on a long road ride within the park in the summer, the best portions of **highway** to tackle are the stretch from Mammoth east to Tower and onwards to Cooke City, one of the straightest sections with fair visibility throughout, and the highway from West Yellowstone to Grant Village via Old Faithful, notable for paved shoulders and good road conditions; both stretches are 47 miles long.

Off the main highways, more than a dozen unpaved side roads a mile or longer make for excellent mountain biking. A couple of these – namely the **Old Gardiner Road** (5 miles one-way; see p.50) and **Blacktail Plateau Drive** (7 miles one-way; see p.52) – are open to cars as well, while the remainder are open to bikers and hikers only. Two such hiking/biking paths – the service road up **Mount Washburn** (5 miles round-trip; H7) and **Natural Bridge Road** (3 miles round-trip; H16) – are covered in detail in Chapter 4: Day hikes.

The toughest of all the bike-accessible dirt roads is the six-mile **Bunsen Peak Loop Road**, starting south of the Golden Gate and leading east and then north around its eponymous peak to a trailhead south of the Mammoth Hot Spring Corrals; at close to halfway point, you can lock the bike up for the steep climb down to Osprey Falls (H3) to complete the finest hike/bike combination in the park. The **Fountain Freight Road** (5 miles one-way) heading from the end of Fountain Flats Drive south to the Fairy Falls Trailhead is another great bike with access to hiking trails; along with paths to Sentinel Meadows (H13) and Fairy Falls (H14), the old service road passes alongside the Midway Geyser Basin. South of here, starting in front of the *Old Faithful Inn* and heading 1.5 miles north to Morning Glory Pool, is perhaps the most popular bike route, a **paved sidewalk** within the Upper Geyser Basin leading past several of the park's most popular geysers, including Castle Geyser, Grotto Geyser, and Riverside Geyser. Lastly and well worth the trip out is the partially paved **Lone Star Geyser Road** (2 miles one-way), starting 3.5 miles southeast of Old Faithful; traveling beside the beautiful Firehole River, this trek is best timed to witness one Lone Star Geyer's dramatic eruptions (see H36 for details).

For more information, stop into the recently opened **bike shop** (Ⓣ307/545-4825) in the Old Faithful Snow Lodge. A godsend for bikers, the staff can help out with repairs and rents out mountain bikes; $35 gets you a bike, helmet, and lock for a 24-hr period, with hourly and half-day rates also available. Children's bikes, trailers, and trunk racks are also rented.

Within Grand Teton

Within Grand Teton, bikes are only allowed on the same roads that cars may travel. This isn't actually that big of a drawback, as there are several quiet, long and scenic roads that bikers flock to. Traffic on the major thoroughfare, **Hwy-191**, is heavy and fast, making for uncomfortable road riding during the high season. Slower and with better shoulders, twenty-mile long **Teton Park Road** is better for a road ride, particularly its southern half, with the bonus of side-trips up **Signal Mountain Road** and along the **Jenny Lake Scenic Drive**. Best of all is the **Gros Ventre Road**, leading east from the Gros Ventre Junction across the sagebrush plains of Antelope Flats in the park's southeastern corner; the mainly local traffic is sparse and used to sharing the road with bikers, and itineraries over 50 miles in length can be cobbled together, leading past abundant wildlife and sites like Kelly, the Teton Science School, and the Gros Ventre Slide within the Bridger Teton National Forest. A few miles past the slide area, the road turns to dirt, giving mountain bikers fifteen more potholed and scenic miles to explore. Other worthwhile mountain-biking roads include: **Shadow Mountain Road**, weaving up into the national forest north of Antelope Flats; **Grassy Lake Road**, a nearly 50-mile long rough stretch cutting between Grand Teton and Yellowstone; and the central **RKO/River Road** following the western bank of the Snake River from Signal Mountain south to Cottonwood Creek just north of Taggart Lake, a fifteen mile stretch of 4WD road that you'll often have to share with only grazing elk and bison.

For more **information** and **rentals**, stop by Adventure Sports (Ⓣ307/733-3307) within the Dornan's complex in Moose, who rent both road and mountain bikes for $25 per day, including helmet. More rental options, as well as a wealth of mountain biking trails, await in and around **Jackson** due south of the park (see p.219).

Horseback riding

In tune with the region's cowboy and ranching traditions, "stock" animals – mainly **horses**, but also mules and even llamas – are permitted on the majority of trails in Yellowstone and Grand Teton. As these large animals can't help but damage paths, overnight stock use is banned until trails are dry enough to absorb the animals' weight, typically the end of June. Should you want to take anything from a long day-trip or to a weeklong backcountry adventure, numerous operators are licensed to do so, including some working dude ranches in or bordering Grand Teton. Those bringing their own horses should check the park websites, where details on everything from grazing requirements to backcountry stock camps are listed. Most visitors seem content to saddle up on shorter nose-to-tail style **horseback rides** leaving from the concessionaire-run stables within both parks. At all of these, riders must be at least eight years old and 4ft tall, and there's a weigh limit of 250lb.

Within Yellowstone

One-hour ($33) and two-hour ($53) long **trail rides** depart from three corrals within Yellowstone, each managed by Xanterra (Ⓣ307/344-7311). The busiest corral (open early June to mid-Sept) is next to *Roosevelt Lodge*, from where trips lead north across the rolling sagebrush hills of the Northern Range. Other options from Roosevelt include five daily stagecoach rides ($10) and an Old West Cookout each afternoon, with rates starting at $61 per adult including horse and steak dinner. The corral at Canyon (open mid-June to early Sept) offers rides through pretty meadows and alongside Cascade Creek, while the Mammoth Hot Springs Corral (open mid-May to mid-Sept) opens earliest but rides cover the least inspiring terrain. For an **overnight pack trip**, West Yellowstone's Yellowstone Wilderness (Ⓣ406/223-3300, Ⓦwww.yellowstone.ws) and Gardiner's

North Fork Creek (Ⓣ406/848-7859, Ⓦwww.northforkcreekoutfitters.com) are two reputable outfitters. For an example of rates, Yellowstone Wilderness charges $1050 per person for a three-day trip alongside the Yellowstone River, and $2400 for a six-day, 80-mile trip one-way along the remote Thorofare Trail and back west via Heart Lake.

Within Grand Teton

The **Grand Teton Lodge Company** operates corrals (June–Aug; Ⓣ307/543-3100) at both Jackson Lake Lodge and Colter Bay Village. There's not much difference between the two, with simple hour ($30) and two-hour ($42) trail rides leaving from both; breakfast and dinner trips, either by wagon or horseback, are also offered and advance reservations are required.

If an afternoon of riding is not nearly enough, there are several working **dude ranches** in and just outside of the park. Two of the finest are the **Triangle X Ranch** (Ⓣ307/733-2183, Ⓦwww.trianglex.com), located across the highway from Cunningham Cabin, and the **Gros Ventre River Ranch** (Ⓣ307/733-4138, Ⓦwww.grosventreriverranch.com), just outside of the park's southeast boundary by Slide Lake. Both ranches offer all-inclusive weeklong stays, including meals and horseback riding, starting at around $1500 per person. You may be able to negotiate a shorter stay early or late in the season, and pack trips can also be arranged.

Rock-climbing and scrambling

While opportunities for climbing in Yellowstone are very limited, Grand Teton is a premier destination for **climbing** enthusiasts and the sight of the **Tetons** is enough to get many non-climbers thinking about roping up and having a go as well. As the youngest range in the Rockies, the jagged Tetons are laced with routes, from fun scrambles to challenging climbs suited for only expert climbers. Snow and ice climbs can be had, but the majority of routes are on hard granite. This trustworthy surface is one of the Teton's finest attributes, as is accessibility – though you'll still need to lug your gear on longish warm-up hikes to reach the start of most climbs.

Within Yellowstone

Older and rounded over by millions of years of erosion, the mountains within **Yellowstone** are not known for climbing. Most of the tallest peaks – including Mount Washburn (H8), Avalanche Peak (H19), and Mount Sheridan (H37) – can be hiked up with little or no scrambling involved, and climbing is prohibited within the crumbly confines of the Grand Canyon of the Yellowstone. The **Absaroka Range** attracts a handful of backcountry alpinists each year, particularly around **Eagle Peak** (at 11,358ft, it's the tallest in the park) in the park's isolated southeast corner, but these routes take several days of hiking to reach. The only accessible area to play around within is the **Hoodoos**, a field of boulders a short drive uphill from Mammoth en route to Norris. A couple of turnouts here access the rocks, some close to 20ft tall, providing a few hours worth of scrambling fun.

Within Grand Teton

Climbers tackle the peaks within **Grand Teton** year-round, but the most popular period is from early July through mid-September, when much of the high-altitude snow has melted. The obvious goal for many is the summit of

Grand Teton – at 13,770ft, it's the second-highest mountain in Wyoming and one with an interesting climbing history (see box, p.108). There are numerous established routes leading up the "Grand," all of them technical and requiring the appropriate equipment. Even inexperienced climbers, however, can summit the majestic peak on a three- or four-day introductory **climbing course** provided they pass each day's requirements. Two excellent mountain guide services work the park. Closest is **Exum Mountain Guides** (Ⓣ307/733-2297, Ⓦwww.exumguides.com), with a summer office located steps away from the Jenny Lake boat dock across Cottonwood Creek within the park. The company's namesake, Glen Exum (1911–2000), pioneered the difficult **Exum Ridge** up the southwest side of Grand Teton in 1931; he was only 18 at the time, and climbed the peak in football cleats without the use of ropes. In Jackson, **Jackson Hole Mountain Guides** (Ⓣ307/733-4979, Ⓦwww.jhmg.com) are similarly reputable. Both services offer a variety rock-climbing courses along with guided climbs cresting all the major summits; winter trips, including backcountry skiing and snowboarding, are also available. The most popular basic climbing courses run over three days (four if a course in snow climbing is required) and culminate in an ascent of the Grand Teton ($850–1100); those with climbing experience can join a two-day expedition ($550). Both services have base camps beneath Grand Teton at around 11,000ft.

Beside Grand Teton, other popular climbs in the range include: **Middle Teton**, featuring a half-dozen routes of varying difficulty including a non-technical route to the top with a fair amount of scrambling; **Cascade and Death canyons**, both lined with a variety of challenging wall climbs; and **Mount Owen**, the toughest of the tallest peaks to conquer. A tall lump of rock across the Snake River, **Blacktail Butte** is another very popular climbing spot; a parking lot just north of Moose Junction on Hwy-191 gives immediate access to a near vertical sport climb up a limestone face.

For detailed route information, the best overall book is *A Climber's Guide to the Teton Range* by Leigh Ortenburger and Reynold Jackson. **Permits** are not required for mountaineering, but climbers planning on camping out must obtain backcountry camping permits (see p.145 for details.) From June through September, these free **permits** can be collected from the **Jenny Lake Ranger Station** (May–Sept; hours vary; Ⓣ307/739-3343) near the Jenny Lake Visitor Center; headquarters for the park's climbing rangers, this should in any case be your first stop for information and advice on routes and conditions (note that snow may persist until Aug on some passes). The rest of the year, permits are available at the Moose Visitor Center.

A final valuable source for not only information but also accommodation and possibly climbing partners is the **Climber's Ranch** (Ⓣ307/733-7271, Ⓦwww.americanalpineclub.org), a cluster of shared cabins off of Teton Park Road a couple miles south of Jenny Lake. Run by the American Alpine Club, the bunk accommodations are rough (everything, including bedding, must be brought along), but the nightly rate ($10; climbers only) leaves little room for complaints. In the park, Moosely Seconds (Ⓣ307/739-1801) within the Dornan's complex sells and **rents** climbing shoes, ice axes, crampons and other climbing gear.

7 Winter activities

Blanketed in snow between November and April, **Yellowstone** takes on a whole new appearance in **winter**: a silent and strange world of white where waterfalls freeze in mid-plunge, geysers blast towering plumes of steam and water into the chilly air, and buffalo, beards matted with ice, stand around in frost-coated huddles. Elk, coyotes, bighorn sheep, and, most popularly, wolves likewise tough it out in the park, and can be spotted relentlessly searching for enough sustenance to power them through the season. Indeed, aside from hibernating bears, humans are the one summertime fixture whose presence decreases most dramatically. On average, 150,000 visitors enter Yellowstone in winter, only a sliver of the park's three million annual guests.

There are two major explanations for this huge drop off. First is that by early November, all but two of Yellowstone's five entrance gates are **closed** to car traffic, with only the North Entrance at Gardiner and Cooke City's isolated Northeast Entrance – accessible only from Gardiner throughout winter in any case – remaining open. All the other entrances (except for tiny Bechler) remain open to over-snow traffic, namely **snowmobiles** and **snowcoaches**, or human-powered cross-country skis and snowshoes. The second reason for limited visitors is, simply enough, the **weather**. In a region where summer snowstorms aren't all that uncommon, winter is long and unforgiving. Lower in altitude, the area around Mammoth tends to be less snowy than the rest of the park, attracting elk and other creatures to the easier to reach grasses. Deep snows four feet or higher are typical in other areas, and throughout the park sub-freezing temperatures are the norm.

All that said, with some solid pre-planning and the right cold-weather gear, winter in Yellowstone makes for a magical encounter, and one that's markedly different than summer. **Wildlife spotting** opportunities are superb, and the list of viewable attractions is a long one. **Mammoth Hot Springs** and the **Lamar Valley** are both reachable by car along the open northern road, while over-the-snow shuttles can pass by many of the sights on the Upper Loop road, including steaming **Roaring Mountain**, and all the sights on the nearly hundred-mile long Lower Loop, such as the **Grand Canyon**, **Old Faithful**, and **Midway and West Thumb geyser basins**. Plus, unlike the busy summer season, you'll share these sights with only a handful of other visitors, allowing for plenty of time to loiter and soak in the snowy views.

To the south, **Grand Teton** deals with many of the same issues as Yellowstone. Visitor numbers are similarly reduced, as are facilities; only the Moose Visitor Center remains open, with all other park-run operations shut for the season. However, the park's main artery – Hwy-191 – remains open, negating the need for snowcoach transportation and allowing for easy access to dozens

Winter road closures

The most important change to account for during the winter months are **road closures**. In **Yellowstone**, the vast majority of roads remain unplowed, with only the road from Gardiner to Cooke City via Mammoth Hot Springs kept open year-round to automobile traffic. All other roads close in early November and remain closed through late April or early May. Apart from the portion of the Northern Loop connecting Tower Junction to Canyon, the roads closed to car traffic remain open during the day to over-snow vehicles only (snowcoach and snowmobile). Obviously, these closures greatly limit travel options throughout the area. For example, instead of taking around one-and-a-half hours to drive 55 miles from Gardiner to West Yellowstone through Yellowstone as you can in summer, come winter you need to drive north from Gardiner to Livingston, then west to Bozeman and then back south to West Yellowstone, more than tripling your time and distance. Similarly, the only way to see most of the park – including Old Faithful and Canyon – is by booking a guided tour, either snowcoach or snowmobile.

To the south, Hwy-191 cutting north/south through **Grand Teton National Park** remains open from Jackson all the way to Flagg Ranch throughout the winter, though ice and wind-blown snow often coats the road. Several of the park's secondary roads, namely most of Teton Park Road, the Moose-Wilson Road, and Antelope Flats Road, are closed to automobile traffic. Outside of the parks, some lesser state highways close during heavy snowfall, but for the most part highways and passes remain open in all but blizzard conditions. The one notable exception is Hwy-212 east of Cooke City, including the Beartooth Highway, which closes in late Fall and doesn't reopen until mid-May. This closure essentially means Cooke City is the end of the road for half of the year, barring access to Yellowstone from Billings or Cody to the east. Keep in mind that the roads that do remain open and plowed both inside and outside the parks are often snow-covered and icy, and most are not maintained at night; see p.25-26 for **winter driving tips**, along with regional **road hotline** numbers useful for the latest latest road conditions.

of cross-country and snowshoe trailheads, along with roadside **views** of the park's mighty range. What Grand Teton lacks in terms of teeming wildlife and bizarre thermal features, it makes up for with stunning mountain vistas. Save for a summer sunset, the Tetons never look better than on a crisp snowy day, when the brilliant blue winter sky contrasts sharply with the pure-white frosted peaks.

Of course, winter activities in the region aren't limited to the parks. Along with more obscure cold-weather pursuits such as dog sledding or winter fly-fishing, visitors flock to the region for its stupendous **downhill skiing and snowboarding** at resorts like Jackson Hole Mountain Resort, Grand Targhee, and Big Sky. See the outlying town chapters for in-depth reviews of these resorts, along with details on other winter activities.

Winter practicalities

Roads aren't the only things that shut down in the region in winter (see box, above). As early as the day after Labor Day, businesses in the parks' gateway towns begin closing, remaining shuttered for as long as eight months until summer arrives again. Within the parks, the majority of visitor centers, hotels, campgrounds, and restaurants start closing in late September, with most boarded up by the time the roads are gated off in early November. In Yellowstone, only the **Albright Visitor Center** in Mammoth Hot Springs (daily 9am–5pm; closed Thanksgiving; ⓣ307/344-2263) and **Old Faithful Visitor**

Center (daily 9am–5pm; ⓣ307/545-2750) remain open, while in Grand Teton only the **Moose Visitor Center** (daily 8am–5pm; ⓣ307/739-3399) keeps its door unlocked. All three continue to run a limited schedule of worthwhile ranger programs throughout the winter. The helpful visitors centers in both Jackson and West Yellowstone also remain open, the latter hosting a Yellowstone ranger's desk.

Jackson and West Yellowstone, due in large part to downhill skiing and snowmobiling respectively, are the busiest of the gateway towns in winter, and a large chunk of their **accommodation** options remain open. That's not the case in the parks, with the only options in Grand Teton being Dornan's *Spur Ranch* and the *Triangle X Ranch*. In Yellowstone, only the hotel and campground at Mammoth Springs and Old Faithful's *Snow Lodge* remain open. See Chapter 8 for reviews of all these overnight options. Places to **eat** are equally limited, with three choices inside Yellowstone: the relatively expensive dining rooms (reservations required) at the *Mammoth Springs Hotel* and *Snow Lodge*, along with the latter's *Geyser Grill* snack bar. The general store in Mammoth Springs sells snacks and drinks and is by and large open daily 9am–6pm, though it may be closed on Sundays, holidays, and during particularly slow times; you're best off stocking up on supplies before arriving. Same goes for Grand Teton, where only Dornan's *Pizza Pasta Company* stays open for limited hours in winter (Mon–Fri 11.30am–3pm, Sat–Sun 11.30am–5pm; ⓣ307/733-2415). For full reviews, see Chapter 9 "Eating and drinking".

Winter wildlife watching

Winter wildlife watching in the parks is a unique experience, made all the more enriching by the lack of summer crowds. Visitors, however, should take into account that those animals who haven't migrated or hibernated are locked in a continuous struggle to take in more energy than they expend to stay alive in the tough, often arctic conditions. Take extra caution to not spook or stress animals by keeping your distance – no photo is worth wasting an animal's precious energy reserve.

Bison, often rimed with a coat of frost or a blanket of freshly fallen snow, are one of the stars of the winter season. Constantly on the move in search of food, herds are sometimes spotted traveling single file through chest-deep snow to conserve energy. With their strong neck muscles as the engine, bison use their massive foreheads as snow shovels, clearing a way back-and-forth to the greenery buried underneath. As with bison, **elk** scratch out a perilous living among whatever vegetation they can reach, constantly scraping away at the snow with their front hooves. While the biggest grouping of elk in the region can be seen in the National Elk Refuge due north of Jackson (see p.215), Yellowstone's Northern Range is home to a huge, if more dispersed, herd, and upwards of 15,000 elk winter in the park in total. Though spotted virtually everywhere, both elk and bison tend to gather at warm thermal and riverside locations, where the ground's heat melts away the snow and superb photo-ops await, plumes of steams framing the massive frosted animals. **Moose**, whose long legs have adapted to walk through high snow, aren't all that prevalent in Yellowstone; however, they're commonly spotted both in Grand Teton – look around the Buffalo Fork Meadows south of Moran Junction – and in surrounding areas, from the Gallatin's riverbanks in Big Sky to the ski slopes of Jackson Hole

Mountain Resort. Other larger mammals commonly spotted come winter include **bighorn sheep**, visible in Gardner Canyon north of Mammoth and along Hwy-191 entering Big Sky, and the ubiquitous **coyote**, sporting a puffed up winter coat making them look brawnier than their summer selves.

Of the large predators, **grizzlies** and **black bears** are smart enough to curl up and wait out the winter months by hibernating. Though uncommon, bears do awaken on occasion for a wander; in Yellowstone, they have been spotted out of their dens every month save for January. Interestingly, females give birth to cubs (typically two) in their den in a semiconscious state between mid-January to early February, but return to sleep for two months as their cubs nurse and sleep. Meanwhile, their competition – **wolves** and **mountain lions** – really come into their own. Though mountain lion sightings are exceedingly rare year-round, your best chance of spotting a wolf is in winter when the packs hunt and feed on elk – upwards of 90 percent of their winter diet – and launch into their February mating season; listen closely around this time for the shortened howl of a male wolf wooing a rival pack's female for a secret rendezvous. Highway closures throughout the majority of Yellowstone aren't much of a hindrance for wolf spotting, as the road from Mammoth to Cooke City cuts through the territories of at least six packs, a few of which move here come winter due to the Northern Range's shallower snow and wintering elk herd. As in summer, wolf sightings are most common at dawn or dusk, when they're most active. To increase your chances of tracking a pack, consider one of the Yellowstone Institute's winter **wolf-watching trips**, which are among the most popular activities offered by the organization (see p.203 and *The wolves of Yellowstone* color section).

Ospreys, sandhill cranes and peregrine falcons all soar away to warmer temperatures come autumn, but **bald eagles** – easy to spot perched in the clumps of leafless, cottonwood trees lining riverbanks – **trumpeter swans**, **American dippers**, and dozens of other attention-grabbing birds stick around through winter. Perhaps most visible are **ravens**, opportunistic scavengers who have learnt not only to follow hunting wolves – thirty or more hungry ravens accompany most wolf kills – but also stakeout parking lots and other areas humans gather. Remarkably, ravens have taught themselves to unzip backpacks, and many a snowmobiler or winter camper has returned from a short hike to find his gear ransacked and the best bits of food stolen by a raven.

Snowcoach tours

Along with snowmobiles, the only other motorized vehicles permitted on unplowed roads within Yellowstone are **snowcoaches**. The original snowcoaches, Canadian Bombardier-built machines popular in their homeland where plowed roads were less common, were allowed into the park in 1955. A few of these dark-red or banana-yellow Bombardiers, looking like the love child of a tank and a school bus, still rumble over the roads in Yellowstone, but nowadays most of the coaches are small buses, vans, or SUVs that have been converted by removing the tires and adding large skis to the front and treads to the back. As comfortable as a normal bus ride, including heat (something snowmobiles obviously can't provide), these modern coaches are used for both day-tours as well as general transportation into and through the park. Shuttles depart daily from Mammoth, West Yellowstone, and Flagg Ranch on the southern border,

Warming huts

Basically heated pit stops for skiers, snowmobilers, and snowcoach passengers, Yellowstone operates seven roadside **warming huts** throughout the park. While most are little more than an outhouse and fireplace, the warming hut at Madison also functions as snack bar, with warm coffee and hot chocolate available.

with most stopping at Old Faithful; confirm before booking that your trip will be on a modern coach, as the older models are cramped and rumble loud enough to require earplugs.

7

For those staying at Mammoth/Gardiner or looking for **transportation** into or through Yellowstone, the park's own **Xanterra** is the best option (Ⓣ307/344-7311, Ⓦwww.travelyellowstone.com). Costing between $50–60 per person, Xanterra runs daily one-way trips to Old Faithful from Mammoth (8am), West Yellowstone (12.30pm), and Flagg Ranch (1pm), along with onwards journeys from Old Faithful (most of which require an overnight stay). Xanterra also offers there-and-back **tours** to the Grand Canyon ($115) from Mammoth and Old Faithful, and similar trips to Old Faithful ($102) from Mammoth and West Yellowstone. In any case, all of Xanterra's regularly scheduled trips are considered tours as well, though just how much information you get depends on that day's driver and the patience of your fellow passengers; stops are made for wildlife spotting, as well as for quick walks around the likes of Fountain Paint Pots.

Since they're not also being used to transport employee and skiers/snowshoers set on reaching a trailhead, a **dedicated tour** can be a better choice for those just hoping to get a day-long look at Yellowstone in winter. There's more time spent at the sights along the way and guides, who rely on tips and good word of mouth for business, are typically more helpful and informative. Most of these tours depart from West Yellowstone, with average rates hovering around $100 per person for a round-trip to Old Faithful and $10 more for the same to Canyon. Top **operators** in West Yellowstone include Backcountry Adventures (Ⓣ406/646-9317 or 1-800/924-7669, Ⓦwww.backcountry-adventures.com), Buffalo Bus Touring Co (Ⓣ1-800/436-7669, Ⓦwww.yellowstonevacations.com), and Three Bear Lodge (Ⓣ1-800/646-7353, Ⓦwww.threebearlodge.com). If visiting via the more isolated east gate, try High Country Adventures (Ⓣ307/587-7669, Ⓦwww.yellowstoneadventuretours.com), who leave from the Wapiti Valley west of Cody.

Winter sports

A major element to enjoying **winter sports** in Yellowstone and Grand Teton is pre-planning. Unlike summer, when you can quickly stuff a daypack with necessities before lacing up and hiking a trail, most snowy sports in the parks are gear intensive and often require a reservation, guide, or shuttle trip. The most popular activities are **cross-country skiing**, **snowshoeing**, and **snowmobiling**, all of which require warm winter gear along with equipment readily available for rent in the region. We've broken down each of these sports in detail on the following pages. Other less popular activities in winter include **ice-skating** – rinks and skates are available to guests at both the *Mammoth Hot*

Springs Hotel and Old Faithful's *Snow Lodge* – and **ice-climbing** up frozen waterfalls in Grand Teton's backcountry; check with Exum Mountain Guides (Ⓦwww.exumguides.com) for details on the latter. In Yellowstone, the **fishing** season ends the first Sunday in November and doesn't start again until Memorial Day weekend. Fishing in Grand Teton, though, is allowed year-round on portions of the Snake River north of Moran and south of Moose (catch-and-release from Nov–March), while all the park's lakes, including Jackson Lake, are open to ice-fishing throughout winter. For more information on fishing, see Chapter 6.

Snowmobiling

There's no more contentious leisure activity in the region than **snowmobiling**. Since being allowed into the park in the late 1960s – the machines are forbidden in most national parks, including Glacier in northern Montana – winter in Yellowstone was defined in large part by the loud rumblings and gasoline-soaked fumes of snowmobiles, with as many as seventy thousand sleds entering the park each winter by the mid-1990s. Though most visitors obeyed traffic laws and stayed on designated roadways, tales of rowdy riders were legion, ranging from foolhardy "sledheads" zipping along at twice the maximum 45mph speed limit to groups heading off-road to buzz by bison and other wild game. To many, conditions were spiraling out of control: naturalists argued that the pollution and noise caused by the machines was dangerously stressing wildlife; skiers and snowshoers were frustrated by the lack of solitude and quiet; and many rangers were tiring of looking after out of control groups.

A winter-use plan issued in 2000 proposed to **ban snowmobiles** completely, an idea that was embraced by many – including the Clinton administration and the vast majority of US citizens polled on the issue – and the era of motorized sleds in Yellowstone seemed sure to end. However, both lawsuits and a change of administrations helped revoke the outright ban, much to the pleasure of outlying towns like West Yellowstone – self described "Snowmobile Capital of the World" – that rely greatly on the trade. At the time of writing, an uneasy truce has settled around the snowmobiling controversy, thanks in part to strict new rules. All snowmobiles are required to use the best available technology (currently meaning cleaner **four-stroke engines**), and the **maximum number** of riders allowed in the park per day is limited to 720 – a total that is rarely met in any case. Most controversially, groups must also be led by a professional **guide**, who's job is to ensure everyone stays single-file on the road, keeps their distance from animals, and generally behaves.

While ardent snowmobile proponents and opponents both feel their rights have been run roughshod over, the current comprise appears to be working. While you may not be able to ride off alone into the sunset, beer bottle in hand, you can still have plenty of good times riding atop nearly 200 miles of road within Yellowstone – and love them or hate them, one thing that's hard to deny is that riding a snowmobile is fun. As the official park concessionaire, Xanterra (Ⓣ307/344.7311, Ⓦwww.travelyellowstone.com) is the only option for a guided **snowmobile tour** starting from inside Yellowstone. A full day guided tour taking in either Old Faithful or Canyon costs $210 per snowmobile (1 or 2 riders), including helmet rental; a full clothing package with gloves, snowmobile suit, and boots costs an additional $25. Outside the park, most tours start from West Yellowstone and are markedly cheaper, ranging between $120–160 for day trips to Old Faithful or Canyon. Reputable tour operators include Backcountry Adventures (Ⓣ406/646-9317 or 1-800/924-7669, Ⓦwww.backcountry-adventures.com), Three Bear

Lodge (Ⓣ1-800/646-7353, Ⓦwww.threebearlodge.com), and Two Top Snowmobile (Ⓣ1-800/522-7802, Ⓦwww.twotopsnowmobile.com).

Regulations within Grand Teton are similar to Yellowstone in that four-stroke engines are also mandatory and numbers are limited (140 sleds per day), however guides are not required. This is partly due to the fact that only one trail is open to snowmobiles in the park, the **Continental Divide Snowmobile Trail** (CDST; info on Ⓣ307/739-3614). A favorite of riders across the country, the CDST stretches more than 600 miles from Lander, Wyoming, through Yellowstone to West Yellowstone; within Grand Teton, the trails enter via the Moran Entrance Station from the east over Togwotee Pass. From Moran, the trail follows Hwy-89 past Colter Bay to Flagg Ranch, close to 30 miles in total. From Flagg Ranch, groups have the option of either entering Yellowstone on a guided trip or cutting west instead on **Grassy Lake Road** (detailed on p.114), open to sledders all the way to Ashton, Idaho. Riders in Grand Teton are also allowed to cut off the CDST onto frozen Jackson Lake, but only to access areas for ice-fishing. Located directly on the CDST just east of the park, *Grand Teton Park RV Resort* (Ⓣ307/733-1980 or 1-800/563-6469, Ⓦwww.yellowstonerv.com) offers both non-guided snowmobile packages starting at $90 for a half-day, including helmet and suit, and tours from $220 per person.

Outside of the parks lies well over 500 more miles of groomed snowmobile terrain, mainly within the neighboring national forests where regulations are far less strenuous. West Yellowstone and Cooke City are the two most snowmobile-friendly towns, and further details can be found in their respective chapters.

Cross-country skiing and snowshoeing

Snowcoach and snowmobile tours allow visitors to view the area's winter wonderland from the road, but the only way to fully immerse yourself in the winter landscape is on a pair of **cross-country (Nordic) skis** or **snowshoes**. Huffing along with only the sound of your breath and the squeaking snow beneath you through a sparkling, snowy paradise dotted with panoramic views, steamy thermal features, and abundant wildlife is an experience few visitors experience but none ever forget. The good news is that neither sport requires a great deal of experience provided you're in decent shape; if you can walk, you can snowshoe with today's high-tech models, and cross-country skiing is nowhere near as difficult to pick up as downhill (Alpine) skiing. The serious news is that you must be properly prepared before heading out. Winter in the Rockies is unforgiving, and the odds of someone finding you trailside should an emergency occur are remote. Before heading out, check with a ranger or front desk for the latest weather report and leave an itinerary, wear several adjustable layers of waterproof clothing along with sunscreen and glasses/goggles, bring extra clothes and food, and always travel in a group. While free basic **maps** to winter trails are available at ranger stations and visitors centers, those heading beyond viewable distance of the road should also take along a compass and a detailed topographic map, as detailed on p.116 in Chapter 4 "Day hikes".

Off-road trails are not groomed in either park, though more often than not a path will have already been blazed ahead of you. Trails are typically flagged with orange tree markers and are easy to follow, but check with a ranger or local ski shop employee for tips for the easiest paths to follow if you're worried about losing your way. **Etiquette** requires that downhill skiers get the right of way, and when snowshoeing be sure to step beside ski tracks and never on them.

Within Yellowstone

While pretty much every path within Yellowstone is open for exploration to expert sliders and winter hikers, there are three main options for diving into the park's backcountry on established winter trails. Easiest is the series of trails located off the sole plowed, Gardiner-to-Cooke City road, meaning enthusiasts can drive to the trailheads themselves. A trio of free, basic maps (Mammoth, Tower, Northeast) covering this stretch is available at visitor centers and the Bear Den ski shops (see p.181). Some of the more popular trails hereabouts include the mainly flat 3.5mile one-way **Barronette Trail**, following the old

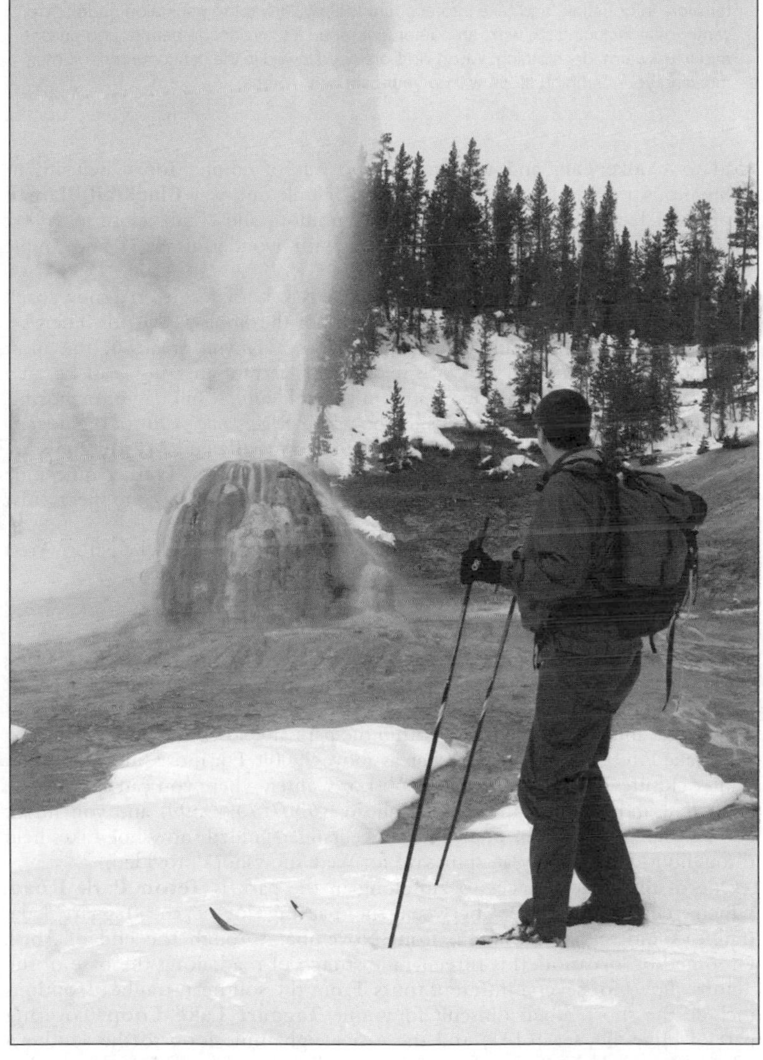

△ Skier at Lone Star Geyser

Winter camping

The only designated campground within both parks that remains open throughout the year is at Mammoth Hot Springs. **Backcountry camping** is allowed, however, with regulations being essentially the same as for summer. Backcountry permits are required, and can be picked up at the Mammoth, Old Faithful and Moose visitors centers. As in summer, it is essential to be prepared for all conditions, keeping in mind that temperatures of -30°F at night are routine. Frostbite and hypothermia are obvious **dangers**, as are avalanches, snow-covered thermal features, stream and lake crossings, and even bears (you must still hang your food throughout winter). See the backcountry hiking rules and guidelines and advice at the start of Chapter 5 for more information, and take into account that you'll want to pack along additional winter gear including ski wax, an equipment repair kit, avalanche beeper and probe, and extra warm, dry clothing. Wood-fires are not allowed in the backcountry in winter, meaning your camping stove will be your sole heat source.

road to Cooke City and weaving in and out of conifer forest beneath its eponymous peak, and the more difficult eight-mile one-way **Blacktail Plateau Trail**, which starts a short drive east of Mammoth and climbs close to 1000ft over the first six miles, rewarding skiers with wonderful views and ample wildlife spotting.

The second main option within Yellowstone is to book a ride on a snowcoach and be dropped off by a trailhead along one of the unplowed roads. There's a cluster of worthwhile trails located around the Canyon area, but the most popular option is the trail network in the Old Faithful area, not least because instead of trying to backcountry camp in the cold after a full day of exploring, skiers and hikers can bed down inside the warm *Snow Lodge*. Out of the dozen-plus trails around Old Faithful, trips out to **Fairy Falls** and **Mystic Falls** are among of the most popular, as is the **Lone Star Geyser Trail**, a nine-mile round-trip to the geyser (which erupts every three hours) along the spectacular Firehole River.

The final network of trails within Yellowstone are those reached from West Yellowstone, detailed on p.230.

Within Grand Teton

As Grand Teton's main roadway is plowed all the way from Jackson to Flagg Ranch, there are dozens of places to set off from for a memorable day of snowshoeing or Nordic skiing. Note, however, that for the protection of both people and animals, several zones within the park are closed in winter, including the Snake River floodplain and all areas above 9900ft. For more information on winter closures, stop in at the Moose Visitor Center, where you can also get the latest trail and weather updates; call ahead (☎307/739-3399) and you might also be able to sign up for one of their free, ranger-guided snowshoe hikes held throughout winter (daily at 2pm, save for Wed; snowshoes provided).

One of the flattest places to zip along in the park is **Teton Park Road**, which remains unplowed between the parking lot at the Taggart Lake trailhead and Signal Mountain from November through the end of April. Groomed on occasion, this fifteen-mile stretch of road along the base of the Tetons allows for several different tours. From the southern trailhead, options include the short, albeit difficult four-mile **Taggart Lake Loop** (covering part of Hike H31, see p.131) and the easier eight-mile loop to the southern edge of **Jenny Lake**. From the northern trailhead at Signal Mountain Lodge, you can tramp along the shores of **Jackson Lake** or test your stamina by huffing up **Signal Mountain Road**, a twelve-mile round-trip gaining close to 700ft elevation en route.

To the north of here, **Colter Bay** is open to easy exploration aside or on frozen Jackson Lake and past Swan Lake and Heron Pond, while even further north, at the edge of Yellowstone, some of the area's best, most secluded trails head out from **Flagg Ranch**. Along with the trails exploring the Snake River valley, you can also head out from Flagg Ranch on the easy 2.5-mile **Polecat Creek Loop**, which passes by natural hot springs pools perfect for a lunchtime soak. Towards the southern end of Grand Teton, the best trails are along the **Moose-Wilson Road**. Just north of Teton Village (home to it's own Nordic ski track; see p.222), the road closes for winter, giving access to a couple of flat, snowy miles along pretty Lake Creek. From the northern parking area on the Moose-Wilson Road, hardy skiers and hikers can huff up to the Phelps Lake Overlook (described on p.94), a five-mile round-trip that gains close to 600ft.

Rentals and tours

While you'll want to pack winter attire for Nordic skiing and snowshoeing, lugging gear along is not a necessity as **rental equipment** is readily available. In Yellowstone, the *Mammoth Hot Springs Hotel* and *Snow Lodge* each host a Bear Den Ski Shop (Ⓣ7307/344-7311), where gear can be rented by the half- and full-day. Rates are very affordable, with snowshoes running less than $15 per day, and skis/boots/pole packages for under $20. Both shops also offer ski repair and waxing services, custom tours services, and **lessons**; expect to pay around $25 for a two-hour group lesson. In Grand Teton, the sole rental stop is the Trading Post (Ⓣ307/733-2415) at Dornan's near the Moose Visitor Center; the shop is usually open daily 8am–6pm, but hours can be sporadic so call ahead.

As for **tours**, Xanterra runs a limited selection of cross-country ski and snowshoe trips in Yellowstone ranging from $40 for an afternoon trip from Old Faithful to Fairy Falls to their $115 full-day Grand Canyon Ski Tour starting from either Mammoth or Old Faithful. Most of the snowcoach companies listed on p.176 also offer snowshoe/ski tour extensions to their trips into Yellowstone. Within Grand Teton, several companies run cross-country and snowshoe tours, including Hole Hiking Experience (Ⓣ1-866/733-4453, Ⓦwww.holehike.com), who offer both half- ($70) and full-day ($100) naturalist led tours. Specialists in backcountry skiing and snowboarding trips, Rendezvous Ski Tours (Ⓣ307/353-2900 or 1-877/754-4887, Ⓦwww.skithetetons.com) leads both day ($225) and customizable overnight tours.

Details on additional rental and tour services in the gateway towns are listed in their respective chapters.

you can tramp along the shores of Jackson Lake, or test your stamina by hiking up Signal Mountain Road, a twelve-mile round trip climbing [illegible] to [illegible] elevation (moderate).

In the north of the park, Colter Bay [illegible] Swan Lake and Heron Pond [illegible] north at the edge of Yellowstone, some of the area's best [illegible] from Flagg Ranch [illegible] they [illegible] Two Ocean Lake [illegible] Grand Teton [illegible] along the Moose–Wilson Road [illegible] Teton Village [illegible]

[illegible] and [illegible] the Moose [illegible] the [illegible]

Bicycles and skiers

While you'll want to pack a mountain bike for [illegible] rental equipment [illegible] in Yellowstone [illegible] and Snake [illegible] Grand Teton [illegible] Teton Village [illegible] Alpine [illegible] many [illegible] Jackson [illegible] [illegible] companies [illegible]

[illegible]

Listings

Listings

8

Accommodation

If you're looking to stay in either park with a roof overhead, **accommodation** will be your trip's biggest expense. It can also be the biggest hassle if you don't plan ahead, as overnight options are limited and demand is high. While good for the concessionaires that manage Yellowstone's and most of Grand Teton's lodging, the blend of limited supply and high demand does not serve visitors very well, and for the most part you'll have to pay more for less, with plain motel-style rooms going for mid-range hotel room prices. Cabins are common as well, but while some look like the classic log structure from the outside, don't expect to find a wood-burning stove surrounded by cozy, hand-carved furniture on the inside – again, think "motel room" and you probably won't be let down. With high rates of staff turnover from summer to summer, service can also be spotty, and in-room amenities are rather basic – phones are rare, while TVs, radios, and bathrooms stocked with fine toiletries and jetted tubs are non-existent.

All that said, **staying in the parks** still makes sense. Rooms may not be the most memorable, but the lodges themselves and the surrounding views often are, and being able to take a post-dinner hike on a nearby trail to spot wildlife at dusk or enjoy a natural feature in solitude easily covers the extra money spent. The convenience of being near the action – and avoiding the wasted time driving back-and-forth from the gateway towns – is hard to beat, and after a long day spent exploring all you'll really want from your room is a place to sleep anyway. All of the lodging options within both parks are listed in this chapter, and deciding which **area** to stay in depends mostly on your itinerary. Given Yellowstone's size, it makes sense to stay in two or three different locations if you're planning to tour more than one area of the park – for example, a couple of nights in the Gardiner/Mammoth area and a few additional evenings around Old Faithful or Yellowstone Lake. In smaller Grand Teton, however, you should be fine with a single base – including Jackson, if you'd rather a town environment and are willing to drive for it – from where you can head out each morning to a new destination.

Pitching a tent in the great outdoors is easily the top accommodation bargain in the region, and choosing to camp in or outside the parks is a no-brainer. **Campgrounds** in both parks are reasonably priced ($12–17; $5 for hiker/biker sites), and while perhaps not always the quietest or most bucolic of places, they are nonetheless convenient and well run. Fireside ranger programs are held in many of the campgrounds, and star natural attractions and good hiking trails are rarely far away. Best of all, with most sites operating under a first-come, first-serve basis, you won't need to plan months ahead – provided you arrive early in the morning and not in the middle of a busy holiday period, you should be able to find a site. During the busiest times, check in at an entrance station or visitor center; rangers will have the latest details on site availability and can help point out the campgrounds you should try for first. The alternative to staying at the established campgrounds is to camp in the **backcountry** for free, though you'll need a permit for this – see Chapter 5 for more details. Bear in mind that rough camping by the roadside or in your car/RV in a parking lot is not permitted, and rangers and police officers will not hesitate in ticketing and evicting violators.

Most of the lodges and campgrounds in both parks are closed **during winter**; see Chapter 7 for details.

Yellowstone

All **accommodation** within Yellowstone is run by **Xanterra** (ⓣ307/344-7311, ⓦwww.travelyellowstone.com), who manage facilities in more than a dozen other national and state parks. **Reservations** – available by phone and online – are strongly recommended from June through September, and are essential over public holiday weekends. Before booking, be aware that some basic creature comforts are not available; save for a few high-end suites, there are no TVs in the rooms or cabins – a fact desk-clerks must patiently explain to incredulous guests on a daily basis – and radios, air-conditioning and Internet connections are all also absent. Should these conveniences be essential, you'll need to stay outside of the park. All rooms within Yellowstone are non-smoking as well. Overall, room **rates** are reasonable with some of the simplest cabins available for as little as $60 per night, and several of the historic lodges – especially the *Old Faithful Inn* and *Lake Yellowstone Hotel*, with basic rooms starting at $90 – are worth a tour even if not spending the night.

Xanterra also manages five of Yellowstone's twelve **campgrounds**. Reservations at these five – *Bridge Bay*, *Canyon*, *Grant Village*, *Madison* and the RV-only *Fishing Bridge* – should be made at least two months beforehand by calling ⓣ307/344-7311 or 1-866/439-7375 (same day call ⓣ307/344-7901); online reservations are not accepted. The remaining seven campgrounds, operated by the National Park Service, are available on a first-come, first-served basis; plan on arriving early in the day to get a site during June–August, as most fill by 11am. Camping stays are limited to fourteen days total between June 15–September 15, and 30 days the rest of the year. All campgrounds have toilet facilities (flush unless otherwise noted), but there are **showers** only at *Canyon, Fishing Bridge*, and *Grant Village* ($3.50; soap and towel rental extra). RV sites are available at all of the campgrounds, but only *Fishing Bridge* has hook-ups and the use of generators is banned at the following: *Indian Creek*, *Lewis Lake, Pebble Creek*, *Slough Creek*, and *Tower Falls*. A limited number of $5 hiker/biker sites are available at all campgrounds for those arriving under their own steam.

Hotels and cabins

Canyon Lodge and Cabins Open June to mid-Sept. As with the nearby campground, this accommodation's best selling point is its location, towards the center of the park and only a half-mile from the Grand Canyon of the Yellowstone. Starting as a tent camp in 1883, the area has always been one of the most popular bases for visitors, and it's a shame that the latest configuration of rooms and cabins – there have been many over the years – can't compete with the *Lake Yellowstone Hotel* or *Old Faithful Inn* for beauty or atmosphere. Tucked behind the long and low-slung *Canyon Lodge* (home to the area's restaurant, lounge, deli, and cafeteria) are several hundred cabins dating from the 1950s and 1960s, all en-suite. Most affordable are the bare-bones "Pioneer" cabins, a relative bargain at $61 per night; larger and slightly better decorated cabins range $85–130. The spruce rooms ($150) in the two hotel-lodge buildings nearby, built in the 1990s, are far more appealing, and each has its own bathroom, comfortable beds, and coffee-maker.

Grant Village Open late-May to Sept. This development – the southernmost in the park – has borne plenty of criticism for its lack of style, or empathy with its surroundings. Built in the 1980s, the architecture is reminiscent of the countless suburban condominium complexes that sprouted up across the country at the same time, with 300 small motel-style rooms ($130) divided evenly amongst six two-storey buildings. There's plenty to see and do in the direct area as rooms are only a stone's throw from Yellowstone Lake's southwest shore, but this uninspired option should be considered a last-choice alternative.

Lake Lodge Cabins Open early June to Sept. Just along the lakeshore from the *Lake Yellowstone Hotel* are 186 very well-priced cabins all with their own bath (none have actual lakeside locations), lined up behind the grand log-built *Lake Yellowstone Lodge*, a 1920s facility featuring a cafeteria, small bar, gift shop, guest laundry, and two huge roaring fires; the lake-facing deck is a serene place to curl up with a book. There's a stark trade-off in your choice of cabins, as those handiest to the lodge are shadeless, while those back towards the forest (sections H and J) are larger and enjoy more peaceful surrounds; the cheapest cabins are basic with one double bed ($70), while others have two doubles and can accommodate four people ($130).

Lake Yellowstone Hotel and Cabins Open mid-May to early Oct. Located on the northwestern shores of the lake, with parts dating as far back as 1889, the *Lake Yellowstone Hotel* is the oldest standing building in the park. It's a grand, buttercup-yellow colonial-style building reminiscent of an overgrown Southern plantation mansion; rocking back-and-forth on a wicker chair looking across the water is an unforgettable way to relax after a long day of driving or hiking. Rooms are on the small side but comfortable and decked out in cheery colors and the showers are hot with strong water pressure. Prices range from $140 a night for rooms in the newer, less atmospheric annex to $220 for an original room

△ *Lake Yellowstone Hotel.*

with lake view; two-room suites are offered at $500 per night. The entire hotel is bright and airy inside, and the "Sun Room," which looks directly over the lake, is one of the best places in Yellowstone for an evening drink. On the opposite side from the lake are 100-odd cabins ($110) that are basically shadeless boxes, though each has its own bathroom plus two double beds and are only steps from the hotel's common areas.

Mammoth Hot Springs Hotel & Cabins May to mid-Oct & mid-Dec to early March. Located at the north end of the park, this is the third hotel to be built on this patch of ground west of Mammoth's historic fort area, beginning with the quickly constructed *National Hotel* in 1883. Built in the 1930s, the exterior of the current wooden structure is sprucer than the rather dull and Spartan rooms inside. The nearly 100 cabins out back were also begun in the 1930s, and are likewise undistinguished. Rates are quite reasonable, however, with cheapest of the rooms ($85) and cabins ($75) having shared bath. Prices for a room or cabin with its own bathroom cost $25 more per night. Other options include a pair of larger suites with queen beds, sitting room and cable TV ($350), and a handful of cabins with a fenced in private hot tub out front ($180). While the main building boasts a cozy lobby and attached Map Room – well worth a look for the 18ft wide country map made from fifteen different types of wood – many people actually prefer to stay in one of the cabins for a little extra privacy; a number of elk often snooze the afternoon away on the grassy areas out front. Along with the *Old Faithful Snow Lodge*, this is the only other hotel in the park open in winter.

Old Faithful Inn Open May to mid-Oct. Spending at least one night in the Old Faithful area is really a must, ideally in a rustic room (some have own bath) at the amazing 1904 *Old Faithful Inn* (see p.75). Nearly all of the rooms have been remodeled in recent years, those without a bathroom starting as low as $90 per night; the cheapest en-suite rooms costing an additional $25. Premium rooms and suites, complete with two queen beds and a sitting room, range from $200–400. If possible, request a room in the classic "Old House" – the original building – as they are the most atmospheric. Regardless of where you end up, this is the most popular accommodation in the park and you'll need to book a couple of months in advance for any room during June–August.

Old Faithful Lodge Cabins Open May to mid-Sept. Built during the 1920s, the log-and-stone *Old Faithful Lodge* (see p.75) is the closest building to Old Faithful in the Upper Geyser Basin. There are no rooms in the lodge building itself, but there are over 100 cabins lined up behind it with some of the cheapest rates in the park. The "budget cabins" ($66) are similar to a low-end motel unit, though bathrooms are shared and showers are located a walk away in the lodge building's public restroom. The higher end, en-suite cabins ($100) are tad bit more polished, but have thin walls and can be noisy.

Old Faithful Snow Lodge and Cabins Open May to mid-Oct & mid-Dec to early March. Along with *Mammoth Hot Springs Hotel*, the *Snow Lodge* provides the only accommodation open in the winter. Opened in 1998, the lodge is by far the most modern in the park, as easily evidenced by a quick walk through its attractive interior. Designed to fill a pressing need for good winter accommodation around Old Faithful, there's not a lot of wasted space or soaring ceilings that would cost a small fortune to keep heated. The result is an exceedingly cosy space, with a charmingly small lobby with fireplace, comfortable seating areas, and a great bar and dining room. Rooms inside the lodge ($185) feature plenty of light-colored woods and contemporary bathrooms, while there are two varieties of en-suite cabins on offer: the cheaper duplex Frontier Cabins ($90) dating back several decades, and the less than ten-year-old Western Cabins ($130), which are quieter and have larger windows.

Roosevelt Lodge Cabins Open mid-June to early-Sept. Located a short drive from the Lamar Valley, the area around *Roosevelt Lodge* was supposedly Theodore Roosevelt's favorite in the park, and the pleasing ranch-like main building named for him blends in well, featuring unfinished log columns, an attractive restaurant and bar, two log-fires and rocking chairs on the outside deck. The latter overlooks rows of 82 rustic cabins, whose isolated location in the north of the park near the Lamar Valley

△ *Roosevelt Lodge*

and away from the most popular places to stay accounts for much of their appeal. The most basic cabins ($65) are little more than wooden shelters with two beds and a wood-stove, sharing communal bathroom facilities; en-suite cabins feature motel-like accommodation ($100).

Campgrounds

Bridge Bay 3 miles south of Lake Village; 7800ft. Open late May to mid-Sept. 432 sites; $17. Xanterra. The park's largest campground, located in an open area with very little shade; the further back you go towards the forest, the more shade there is and you may even find a site high enough for a lake view in one of two tent-only loops. Handy to the lake's main marina, it's an ideal spot for anglers and boating enthusiasts. Nearest pay showers and coin laundry are four miles away at *Fishing Bridge RV Park*.

Canyon Beside Canyon Village; 8000ft. Open June to mid-Sept. 272 sites; $17. Xanterra. One of the largest campground in the park, with the most tent-only sites, largely because it's densely forested and thus not well-suited to RVs. Nearly all of the sites are smaller and closer to other tents than elsewhere in the park, but the location and nearby amenities are hard to beat. Not far from the most photographed view in the park, at the south end of the Grand Canyon of the Yellowstone, and within walking distance of restaurants, stores, pay showers, and coin laundry.

Fishing Bridge RV Park Fishing Bridge; 7800ft. Open mid-May to Sept. 344 sites; $34. Xanterra. This campground is for RVs only, due to frequent bear activity in the area; reservations essential as spots fill up quickly upon opening and stay filled throughout summer. Full electrical hook-up available, pay showers, coin laundry, gas, and store. No maximum stay limit.

Grant Village; 7800ft Open mid-June to Sept. 425 sites; $17. Xanterra. A huge campground spread across a dozen loops, but in contrast to rooms at the lodge building, the sites here are very appealing, tree-shaded and close to the lakeshore. Restaurants, gas, store, pay showers, and coin laundry all nearby.

Indian Creek 8 miles south of Mammoth Junction on the north loop; 7300ft. Open mid-June to mid-Sept. 75 sites; $12. One of the park's most quiet and rustic campgrounds, with sites dotted around two loops in a lightly-wooded forest. Good fishing nearby in the Gardner, Panther, and Obsidian rivers. Vault toilets. First-come, first-served.

Lewis Lake 10 miles from the southern park entrance beside the lake; 7800ft. Open mid-June to early Nov. 85 sites; $12. The park's southernmost campground features plenty of quiet and shade, with the bonus of easy access to Lewis Lake. Vault toilets. Spread over four loops, including one particularly appealing "walk-in" tent only loop. First-come, first-served.

Madison Beside Madison Junction on the south loop; 6800ft. Open May–Oct. 277 sites; $17. Xanterra. Situated near the junction of the Madison and Firehole rivers, this pleasant campground is popular with anglers, with paths leading down to the Madison behind the campground. The tent-only Loop H is closest to the water. No showers or laundry, but West Yellowstone is only a half-hour drive away.

Mammoth At the bottom of the windy road below Mammoth Hot Springs; 6200ft. Open year-round. 85 sites; $14. This dry and dusty sagebrush plot sits right beside the road, making it the least desirable campground in terms of setting in the park. Still, Mammoth's amenities are only a half-mile walk away and the campground sports new and very clean toilets. Plus the chance of waking up to elk nibbling on brush by your tent is always high. The only campground open in winter. First-come, first-served.

Norris Just north of Norris Junction on the north loop; 7500ft. Open mid-May to Sept. 116 sites; $14. Pleasant forested sites dispersed across three loops elevated above the Gibbon River. Best is Loop A, with several sites within steps of the burbling brook. Trails lead to Norris Geyser Basin under a mile away. First-come, first-served.

Pebble Creek 9 miles west of the Northeast Entrance; 6900ft. Open June–Sept. 32 sites; $12. Creekside but still near the road, at the eastern end of the Lamar Valley. Popular spot for fishermen towards the second half of summer (Soda Butte Creek) and hikers heading into the backcountry, as a selection of fine trails is accessible from here. Vault toilets. First-come, first-served.

Slough Creek Turnoff is 5 miles east of Tower on main road through the Lamar Valley; 6250ft. Open late May to Oct. 29 sites; $12. Located 2.5 miles down a dirt road, this is one of the most popular

Saddle up

Provided you're happy to spend good portions of your day on horseback, staying at a **dude ranch** is the closest city slickers can get to living the life of cowboy short of signing on for a job. The Yellowstone region is liberally dotted with these establishments, known also as guest ranches, where you can experience everything from the full-on cowboy lifestyle of rising at dawn, mucking out the stables, and tending to the cattle to a more luxury approach involving horseback riding, fly-fishing, and fancy breakfasts that just happens to be centered on a ranch. Prices vary enormously depending on the level of luxury – cheaper options in basic, rustic cabins with no-frills communal meals start at around $150 per day including horses and meals, while ranches providing more opulent accommodation will set you back considerably more. Packages are typically organized by the week, though shorter options are sometimes available. A handy resource for planning a stay is the **Dude Ranchers Association**'s website (Ⓦwww.duderanch.org), where you can find additional information and local choices.

There are no actual dude ranches within **Yellowstone**, but drive out of the park in any direction and you'll quickly cross paths with arched gateways and dirt roads leading down to stables and a main house. A good area to look first is the real-life cowboy country of the **Wapiti Valley**, east of Yellowstone en route to Cody. Guest ranches here include the *Crossed Sabres Ranch* (Ⓣ307/587-3750, Ⓦwww.crossedsabres.com), where a trip to the Cody rodeo and a rafting trip is included in the weekly program. The area around **Big Sky** north of West Yellowstone is also home to several fine options, including the *320 Ranch* (Ⓣ406/995-4282, Ⓦwww.320ranch.com), where short stays along the Gallatin River are readily accepted. As for **Grand Teton**, several dude ranches reside within or on the park's borders, notably the *Triangle X Ranch* (Ⓣ307/733-2183, Ⓦwww.trianglex.com), situated south of Cunningham Cabin and run by the same family for four generations. *Triangle X* operates throughout the year, mixing in activities such as rafting trips and snowmobile rides with daily horseback tours depending on the season. Bordering the park's east side by the **Gros Ventre Slide**, the 160-acre *Gros Ventre River Ranch* (Ⓣ307/733-4138, Ⓦwww.grosventreriverranch.com) is a more upscale enterprise, with swanky log cabins, gourmet grub, and plenty of fine trout water nearby.

campgrounds in Yellowstone for fly-fishermen, who flock here beginning in July and fill the place throughout August and September. Ideal location beside Slough Creek, with handy access to some great backcountry hikes. Vault toilets. First-come, first-served.

Tower Fall Across the road from Tower Falls near Tower-Roosevelt Junction; 6600ft. Open mid-May to Sept. 32 sites; $12. Located up a steep and curvy half-mile road, this is a poor spot for RVs, with no room for anything over thirty feet. Tent campers, however, are close to wildlife viewing spots in the Lamar Valley, with "civilization," in the form of *Roosevelt Lodge* and its amenities, being three miles away. Vault toilets. First-come, first-served.

Grand Teton

The official concessionaire for **accommodation** within Grand Teton is the Grand Teton Lodge Company (Ⓣ307/543-3100 or 1-800/628-9988, Ⓦwww.gtlc.com). Started by the Rockefeller family more than 50 years ago, the company runs the facilities at *Colter Bay Village*, *Jackson Lake Lodge*, and *Jenny Lake Lodge*. Unlike Yellowstone, however, there's no monopoly on accommodation in the park as there are a handful of private in-holdings with overnight options, including *Signal Mountain Lodge*, *Dornan's*, *Moultan Ranch Cabins*, and

Flagg Ranch (actually just outside the park's boundaries). **Reservations** are advised for all properties, and ideally should be made at least three months in advance for July and August stays.

The park's five summer-only **campgrounds** all work on a first-come, first-served basis; sites cost $15 per night ($7.50 for Golden Age/Golden Access passholders). The *Signal Mountain* and *Lizard Creek* campground are managed by Signal Mountain Lodge (Ⓣ307/543-2831 or 1-800/672-6012), while the remaining three are run by the Grand Teton Lodge Company (Ⓣ307/543-3100 or 1-800/628-9988). Most fill every day in July and August, so plan in advance; *Jenny Lake* is the most popular and often fills by 8am. Visitor centers and entrance stations can advise on availability (Ⓣ307/739-3603 recorded information for campers). The only campground with shower facilities ($3) is *Colter Bay*, and the maximum stay at all campgrounds is fourteen nights, except for *Jenny Lake* (seven nights). In addition, *Flagg Ranch* north of the park has a campground, and there are also basic sites in the surrounding National Forests; Grassy Lake Road west of Flagg Ranch and Gros Ventre Road east of the Gros Ventre Slide are two of the closest places to look. **RVs** are allowed at all campgrounds save for *Jenny Lake*, though full hook-ups are only available at the trailer villages within Colter Bay and Flagg Ranch, and both *Signal Mountain* and *Lizard Creek* have a 30ft limit.

Cabins and lodges

Colter Bay Village Cabins and Tent Village Grand Teton Lodge Company. Cabins open late May to late Sept; tent cabins June–Aug. On the rustic side but nonetheless a very reasonably priced place to spend the night in the heart of the park. Along with a separate campground and RV park, the largest of Grand Teton's villages hosts 166 cabins along with dozens of canvas-roofed "tent cabins." The actual cabins, laid out suburban-style along several narrow roads, are rather dark and dowdy and come in several variations: basic one-room units with shared bathroom ($40), one room cabin-splits with private bathroom ($80–115), and two-room cabins with connecting bathroom ($125–150). None have kitchen facilities, phone, or TV, and the walls are very thin, meaning unless you rent out the entire cabin – most cabins are split into two units – you'll hear your neighbor's every move. A cheaper alternative is to stay in one of the basic log and-canvas tent cabins; each has four bunk beds, a wood-burning stove and outdoor barbecue grill and picnic table (no bed-linen supplied). Tent cabins cost $40 for two people, $5 extra for each additional person. Guest amenities include Internet on a shared computer at the check-in office, along with access to the pool at *Jackson Lake Lodge*.

Dornan's Ⓣ307/733-2522, Ⓦwww.dornans.com. Open all year. This private ten-acre in-holding in the tiny hamlet of Moose by the park's south entrance, with breathtaking views of the main Teton peaks, has been owned and operated by the same family since its early days as a homestead. Along with a grocery, restaurant, wine shop, and outdoor stores, Dornan's offer year-round lodging in the *Spur Ranch Log Cabins*. The dozen one- and two-room cabins by the Snake River come decked out with attractive lodgepole-pine furniture and fully-equipped kitchen, along with a private bathroom; the two-bedroom cabins can accommodate up to six people. Built in the early 1990s, the cabins are clean and popular, and you'll need to book far ahead to secure one in high season. One-bedroom cabins $165 summer, $135 winter; two-bedroom $230 summer, $175 winter.

Flagg Ranch Resort Ⓣ307/543-2861 or 1-800/443-2311, Ⓦwww.flaggranch.com. Open mid-May to mid-Oct. Nestled in light pine forest at the northern edge of Grand Teton, this resort doesn't have the mountain views enjoyed by the lodges to the south, but it occupies an ideal location for access to both national parks (or a nice stopover in between), and offers a full range of services. Accommodation is in well-appointed cabins ($170), each with a king bed or two queens, coffee-maker, and clean bathroom with full-size tub. The main log-built lodge building also has a restaurant and bar.

Jackson Lake Lodge Grand Teton Lodge Company. Open late May to early Oct.

△ *Jackson Lake Lodge*

Designed by Gilbert Stanley Underwood of Yosemite's *Ahwahnee Hotel* fame and completed in 1955, this lodge, just north of Jackson Lake Junction, enjoys a peerless view of the Tetons from above the marshy expanse of Willow Flats and is worth visiting even if not spending the night. Those that do stay pay a premium for the setting, with the least expensive of the lodge's 37 motel-style rooms starting at $160, while those with mountain views start at $260. The rooms are on the plain side (no TV, no radio), but decently sized with two comfortable double beds plus private bath; a handful of more impressive suites are offered at closer to $500 per night. In front of the lodge on both sides of the swimming pool sits an array of beige-and-green cinder-block cabins split into 350 "cottage rooms" – these no-frills units are similarly split between non-view ($180) and mountain view ($260), and are also comfortable enough though again you'll pay extra for the location. As with the cabins at Colter Bay, the walls are thin, so bring earplugs. Wireless Internet access is available in the lodge's second floor lobby.

Jenny Lake Lodge Grand Teton Lodge Company. Open June to early Oct. This is the park's premium lodging and dining property, boasting outstanding service to go along with 37 luxury log cabins – each with its own bathroom, a huge pine bed, and patio with rocking chairs. While the quiet setting isn't as grand as *Jackson Lake Lodge*'s bluff, the string of cabins and main building are only a quarter-mile from the north shore of its namesake lake, within easy walking/riding distance to several worthwhile trails. The exorbitant rates – the cheapest options starts at over $400 per night with a high-end of $725 – are tempered by the fact that breakfast and dinner are included, along with horseback rides and free use of the lodge's bicycles. Reservations for this high-end property are made on a separate line (ⓣ307/733-4647).

Moulton Ranch Cabins Mormon Row ⓣ307/733-3749, ⓦwww.moultonranchcabins.com. Open June–Sept. Only steps away from the oft-photographed barns on Mormon Row (and still owned by a descendant of original barn builders), this is one of the few privately owned parcels of land remaining in the area. While the owners decamp for Idaho Falls in the winter, throughout summer they live in the main building and manage five attractive and clean cabins around it, a few recently built while the other two date back upwards of 100 years (one's the original homestead and the other cabin was formerly used for storing grain). The smallest cottage fits two snugly and rents for $75 per night, while the largest sleep up to six and goes for $185.

Signal Mountain Lodge and Cabins ⓣ307/543-2831, ⓦwww.signalmountainlodge.com. Set on the southeast shore of Jackson Lake, this lodge offers a wide array of accommodation choices, all only steps from the water – all are also on the dated side, though the reasonable rates make up for it for the most part. Least desirable are the bland motel-style units ($150), each with two doubles or a king bed, bathroom, microwave and fridge. A better bet are the array of one- and two-room log cabins ($110–160), more airy than those at Colter Bay and sleeping up to six people. Best of all are the two-room "lakefront retreats" ($225), the only units actually looking out over the lake with small kitchens and decks with jaw-dropping views. Open mid-May to mid-Oct.

Campgrounds

Colter Bay Colter Bay Village; 6800ft. 350 sites; $15, RVs $30–44. Open mid-May to late-Sept. Large and utilitarian, this isn't the park's prettiest campground. The heavily wooded sites, though, are fortunately divided into separate tent and RV zones, and the wealth of facilities available at Colter Bay Village include stores, a marina, restaurants, horse corral, and a network of worthwhile trails. Fills by noon in summer, with limited $5 hiker/biker sites available.

Flagg Ranch John D. Rockefeller, Jr. Parkway; 6900ft. 175 sites; tents $20 for two adults, $5 per additional adult, RVs $45. Open June–Sept. Most popular with RV-driving visitors, with 100 of the sites here reserved for trailers. The wooded campground is close to some good fly-fishing on the Snake River, though most tent campers will want to stay here only if the *Lizard Greek* campground in Grand Teton to the south or *Lewis Lake* in Yellowstone to the north are fully booked. Facilities include 24hr showers, laundry, full hook-ups, and a nearby grocery and restaurant. Reservations can be made in advance on ⓣ1-800/443-2311

Gros Ventre Between Gros Ventre Junction and Kelly; 6600ft. 360 sites; $15; Open May to mid-Oct. The largest campground in Grand Teton spreads out along eight separate loops alongside the cottonwood-lined banks of the Gros Ventre River in the Park's southeast corner, less than ten miles from Jackson. One of the loops – some 50 sites – is tent-only, and generators are barred from the ground's southern half. Still the large sites in this dry, sagebrush-covered area are ideal for big RVs, a fact that keeps many campers away. Located further from the park's main attractions, it's always the last to fill (if it does at all). There's a campfire ranger program in the onsite amphitheater, and good mountain biking nearby.

Jenny Lake South Jenny Lake; 6800ft. 51 sites; $15; Open mid-May to mid-Sept. Laid out in a sparingly wooded area close to Jenny Lake, these are the most coveted campsites in Grand Teton, and you'll need to plan ahead to stake out a tent-only site; in mid-season, don't even bother arriving on a Saturday morning as all the picturesque sites will be taken. Very popular because of the absence of RVs and proximity to some of the most popular hiking trails in the park. A limited amount of $5 hiker/biker sites are also available, and vehicle length is limited to 14ft.

Lizard Creek North end of Jackson Lake; 6850ft. 60 sites; $15; Open early June to early Sept. Located a small peninsula at the north end of Jackson Lake, this campground feels mightily forlorn by the end of the summer, when the lake here abouts has drained. Before then, however, the two loops – one for tents, one for RVs (30ft vehicle max) – buzz with visitors enjoying this relatively secluded spot's superbly shaded sites and great views down the lake. Fills by 2pm in summer.

Signal Mountain Signal Mountain Lodge; 6800ft. 81 sites; $15; Open mid-May to mid-Oct. A fantastic lakeside location and there's a fair amount of pine tree shade to boot. You'll need to arrive early – or wake and move spots early on your second day – to nab one of the small sites with lake views. Facilities at the nearby lodge include gas, groceries, bar, and restaurants, and it's as short walk to the beach and marina. Fills by 10am in summer, and vehicles are limited to 30ft.

9

Eating and drinking

Few visitors return from a Yellowstone and Grand Teton vacation bragging about all the amazing meals they've eaten inside the parks. The town of Jackson hosts a line-up of **cuisines** both gourmet and eclectic, but the rest of the region, gateway towns and the parks themselves, lean on a menu heavy on broiled steaks, pan-fried trout, grilled burgers, and wilting salads, all served with the ubiquitous side of greasy french fries. There are a handful of notable restaurants within both parks featuring high-end food with prices to match, and while the ambience in these is typically superb, overall quality can be spotty, particularly early in the summer season when newly imported staff members are busy learning on the job. Diner-style platters and fast-food meals can be found at most major intersections, and are generally fairly priced. No trip to the parks is complete without sampling a locally made huckleberry sundae or milkshake – available at one of the many **ice cream** stands typically found in general stores and major lodges buildings.

If cooking tent-side it pays to load up on supplies before heading into the parks. The **supermarkets** in the gateway towns stock all but the most exotic ingredients, while the general stores in both parks are strong on snacks and beverages, including beer and liquor, but less reliable for fresh meats and produce. For a **picnic** lunch, there are several delis and snack bars with take-out food within both Yellowstone and Grand Teton, and packed lunches – including a sandwich, fruit, chips and beverage – can be ordered the night before from most establishments.

Yellowstone

Entirely run by concessionaires, Yellowstone's snack bars and restaurants aren't cheap, but considering the fact they have a monopoly they're not hideously expensive either. Besides the do-it-yourself approach, there are three options for eating in the park: diner-style meals inside one of the **general stores**; basic grub at one of the self-serve park **cafeterias** or **cafes**; or a full-blown meal at one of the lodge **restaurants**. The sit-down restaurants share many of the same items – including similar breakfasts, vegetarian dishes, and drink/dessert menus – but to keep things varied each maintains their own list of house specialties. There's not a lot of price difference among the restaurants, where you can expect to pay $15–25 per entrée; however the dining rooms inside the *Old Faithful Inn* and *Lake Yellowstone Hotel* are the clear standouts for food and ambience, while the barbecue grub at *Roosevelt Lodge* is a family favorite. Note that **dinner reservations** are essential during summer at the *Old Faithful Inn*, *Lake Yellowstone Hotel*, and *Grant Village*. The restaurants are open for lunch and breakfast too; they usually offer a small breakfast buffet including fresh fruit, cereals, pastries, and standard cooked breakfast items, all for around $10.

Hours vary at the dozen or so **Yellowstone General Stores** (Ⓦwww.yellowstonegeneralstores.com) located at busy points throughout the park, though most stay open 7.30am–9.30pm throughout June–August; only the Mammoth store is open for limited hours in winter. Only a sliver of the stores are given over to actual groceries; souvenirs of all shapes and sizes, along with books and limited outdoor goods take up most of the space. They're certainly handy for quick purchases of canned goods, fresh bread, snacks, milk, beer and booze, but campers should ideally stock up on groceries in one of the gateway towns before arriving. Several of the stores also have a **soda fountain**, small old-school diners slinging burgers and fries along with ice cream cones and shakes to rows of customers on stools; these friendly spots are terrific places to strike up a conversation with both park employees and fellow visitors.

Unlike Grand Teton, there are no real standout spots to linger over a **drink** while enjoying the view; if hoping for just that, you're best off lugging along a bottle of wine and plastic cups on a short hike for an alfresco nightcap. The best places for an indoor drink are the bars at *Old Faithful Inn, Old Faithful Snowlodge* or *Lake Yellowstone Hotel*'s colonial-style "Sun Room"; the bar at *Canyon Lodge* is relaxed but has very little charm.

Canyon

Save for the soda fountain inside the large General Store across the parking lot, all of the dining options within the Canyon area are located in a row within the long and low-slung Canyon Lodge.

Canyon Cafeteria At one end of the Canyon Lodge is a workaday cafeteria, serving three meals a day from 6am–9.30pm; dinner items include bison sausage ($12), roast turkey ($10), and prime rib ($13–16).

Canyon Lodge Dining Room Housed on the opposite end of the Canyon Lodge from the cafeteria is the Canyon Lodge Dining Room and its bar/lounge, sporting funky late-1950s chandeliers and open fireplace straight from a Space-Age bachelor pad. Relaxed and low key, the dining room does not take reservations for any of the three daily meals, and the dinner menu features the likes of pecan shrimp ($17), pork chops ($16), and spinach ravioli ($14), with a trip to the large salad bar $4 extra. The lunch menu includes over a dozen different types of well-prepared burgers – the Thanksgiving Burger, for example, is a turkey patty topped with stuffing and a cranberry mayo ($9) – while breakfast features an all-you-can-eat buffet for $10.

Picnic Stop Next door to the cafeteria, this handy deli features pre-made sandwiches and salads that can be eaten inside at one of just a few tables or, better yet, taken to-go to be enjoyed halfway through a hike. If stopping in, buy your drinks at the General Store nearby, as beverage are marked up to restaurant prices. Daily 11am–9.30pm.

Grant Village

As with its accommodation scene, it's difficult to get excited about **Grant Village**'s utilitarian eating options. Even the General Store is a letdown, with an unexciting fast-food restaurant instead of a soda fountain located within, though at least ice cream and milkshakes can still be ordered.

Grant Village Dining Room Grant Village's biggest dining hall is housed in its own shake-shingled building at the lake end of a large parking lot. The dinner special is trout sautéed in lemon butter ($19), with meatier options including prime rib ($21) and osso buco ($22). Lunch and breakfast both feature an all-you-can-eat buffet, along with expected menu items like omelettes and burgers. Dinner reservations are required (Ⓣ307/344-7311).

Lake House Located waterside, this informal eatery is open for breakfast (7.30–10.30am) and dinner (5–9pm) only. Mornings see a breakfast buffet, while dinner is centered on pizzas and pastas. Windows looking out onto the lake at least offer up nice view, while there's a paved waterside path nearby good for post-meal ambles.

Lake Village and around

Lake Village is the hub of dining activity on Yellowstone Lake's northern shores; Fishing Bridge has a fine Soda Fountain, but there are no sit-down options at Bridge Bay.

Fishing Bridge General Store The sole sit-down option by the Fishing Bridge intersection a couple miles east of the *Lake Yellowstone Hotel* area is the Soda Fountain inside the Yellowstone General Store. It's arguably the best such "fountain" in the park thanks to its warm ambience, tucked into a cozy spot at the back of the store. A great place to stop for a cinnamon roll, coffee, and chat early in the morning.

Lake Deli Tucked into a small side room on the *Lake Yellowstone Hotel*'s ground floor, this basic café serves eight simple sandwiches ($5–7), including the likes of tuna salad, pastrami and Swiss, and a vegetarian option. Soups include a decent chili, while snacks like cookies, muffins, and yogurt with granola are also available. Bottled beers and espresso drinks, too.

Lake Yellowstone Hotel Dining Room This restaurant has plenty to brag about; along with the best dining views in the park, the *Lake Yellowstone Hotel Dining Room* also has great service and an adventurous menu. Served in a large and airy colonnaded hall, prices are fair, with dishes like rack of lamb ($28) and elk medallions and lobster tail ($36) being amongst the most popular dishes. Another favorite is the seafood *cioppino* ($21), a tomato-broth stew with shrimp, crab, mussels, and salmon. The lunch menu holds onto some of these gourmet flourishes, including a duck breast salad ($14) or Cuban chicken sandwich ($9) to go with less noteworthy burgers. Breakfast includes the expected buffet ($11), though it's a slightly larger spread than at other spots in the park. Dinner reservations required (ⓣ307/344-7311).

Lake Lodge Cafeteria Inside the attractive, overgrown log cabin known as the *Lake Lodge* down the road from the *Lake Yellowstone Hotel* is one of the park's three casual cafeterias; hit-or-miss mains here include chicken and trout, both fried and around $9 a plate including sides.

Mammoth

Housed in a separate building across the street from the *Mammoth Hotel* are both of the area's eating options, the *Terrace Grill* and the *Mammoth Dining Room*. The Mammoth General Store, one further building over, is good for a coffee or ice cream cone, but there's no soda fountain inside and full meals are not available.

Terrace Grill Despite the somewhat fancy name, this is a basic and rather dingy fast-food spot. Breakfast sandwiches served early in the day, with burgers, chicken sandwiches, and french fries later on for lunch and dinner. Closed in winter.

Mammoth Dining Room Just like the hotel next door, this rather pricey dining room is casual and on the plain side. Views out onto the old fort's parade grounds are nice, and the American dinner menu is above average, including a few vegetarian friendly mains along with Creole shrimp ($20), broiled steak ($20), and several house-smoked meats including a creamy linguini with smoked chicken ($17). As at other dining rooms in the park, consider saving room for the Yellowstone Sundae, made with delicious huckleberry ice cream dropped onto a piece of crumb cake. The lounge area inside sometimes has a TV on, and is one of the few spots in the park to catch a big game. The lunch menu includes a bagel topped with smoked trout ($10), while breakfast offers both an all-you-can-eat buffet ($10) as well as a la carte items. Dinner reservations for the dining room required only in winter (ⓣ307/344-7311).

Old Faithful

Dining options within Old Faithful are divided up evenly between the three largest buildings within view of the famed geyser – the *Old Faithful Inn*, the *Old Faithful Lodge*, and the *Old Faithful Snow Lodge*. The latter is the newest of the bunch, open throughout winter and featuring the park's hippest bar.

Old Faithful Inn Having a leisurely dinner in the park's most memorable dining room (provided you made a reservation) surrounded by the inn's distinctive burled wood columns is well worth the gamble of eating here, where food and service varies unpredictably from outstanding to mediocre. A massive stone fireplace and antique painting of the nearby geysers add to the historic flair. Recommended entrees include the pricey elk medallions ($31) and the Idaho trout in tomatoes and capers ($19); there's also a nightly dinner buffet ($26) that includes roast bison, shrimp, soup, and salads. Buffets are offered at lunch ($12; trout and bbq chicken) and breakfast ($10; park standard) as well, though you're better off ordering from the menu at both meals. Dinner reservations required, ☎307/344-7311. The nearby *Bear Paw Snack Shop* serves deli sandwiches and salads for lunch and dinner.

Old Faithful Lodge Closest to world's most famous geyser itself, dining choices within the *Old Faithful Lodge* are basic. Largest is the cafeteria, a simple and straightforward affair open 11.30am–9pm daily for lunch and dinner; specialties include bison meatloaf ($9) and fried trout ($9). Easily the best facet of the cafeteria, the attached covered deck is lined with rocking chairs looking directly out onto Old Faithful only a hundred yards away. Breakfast in the lodge is taken care of by the *Bake Shop*, an open counter open 7am–10pm that features massive cinnamon rolls ($3) and muffins ($2) with breakfast burritos and egg bagels ($4–6). Lunch and dinner snack choices, also available to go, include deli sandwiches and fried chicken.

Old Faithful Snow Lodge Located in the most modern of Yellowstone's many lodges, it comes as no surprise that the Snow Lodge's *Obsidian Dining Room* features the park's most contemporary dining experience. Unlike other park choices, both the menu and ambience feel more like city dining than a rustic retreat, and what the space lacks in views or historical significance it makes up for with attentive service. Top evening specialties include shrimp étouffée ($20) and a black-pepper NY strip steak ($30), with a smoked-gouda tuna melt ($8) and salmon b.l.t. ($11) being the best bets on the lunch menu. Breakfast is similar to other park restaurants, including an all-you-can-eat buffet ($10). First-come first-served, with dinner reservations accepted only in winter (☎307/344-7311). The attached *Firehole Lounge* is Yellowstone's swankiest bar, with several wines by the glass along with top-shelf whiskies and a few microbrews on tap. At the lodge's opposite end, the bright *Geyser Grill* is a tidy fast food café that fills up fast after each Old Faithful eruption with customers wolfing down burgers and chicken sandwiches. There's also a small espresso bar in the hotel lobby.

Tower/Roosevelt

The choices for eating around *Roosevelt Lodge* are Yellowstone's most distinctive, with a cowboy theme that kids in particular happily latch onto. The lodge has a Wild West-style menu heavy on bbq. South at Tower Falls, the only food option is the small general store; along with a small grocery, the tiny snack bar inside serves only hot dogs, bratwurst, nachos, and ice cream, to be eaten outside on a row of covered picnic tables.

Old West Cookout While there's certainly a whiff of Disney-like orchestration to them, the cookouts organized by the Roosevelt Corrals make for an undeniably fun evening of food and entertainment. Depending on whether you want an hour ride beforehand, horses and covered wagons depart at either 3.30pm or 4.30pm from the corrals, and lead to an outdoor cookout spot where hungry "dudes" are fed steak, beans, apple pie, and coffee (starting from

▽ Old West Cookout

Best bets: eating and drinking

Best cheap eats

Yellowstone Fishing Bridge General Store. See p.196.
Grand Teton *Pizza & Pasta Company* (Dornan's). See p.200.
Cody *La Comida*. See p.258.
Cooke City *Buns n Beds Deli*. See p.247.
Gardiner *Helen's Corral Drive-Inn*. See p.242.
Jackson *Billy's*. See p.216.
West Yellowstone *Running Bear Pancake House*. See p.229.

Best splurge dining

Yellowstone *Old Faithful Inn*. See p.196.
Grand Teton *Jenny Lake Lodge*. See p.200.
Cody *Irma's*. See p.257.
Cooke City *Beartooth Bistro*. See p.247.
Gardiner *Antler Pub and Grill*. See p.246.
Jackson *Old Yellowstone Garage & Rendezvous Bistro*. See p.216.
West Yellowstone *Bullwinkles*. See p.228.

Best bars

Yellowstone Fishing Bridge General Store, *Firehole Lounge*, *Old Faithful Snow Lodge*. See p.197.
Grand Teton *Blue Heron Lounge* (*Jackson Lake Lodge*). See p.199.
Cody *Silver Dollar Bar*. See p.258.
Cooke City *Beartooth Bistro*. See p.247.
Gardiner *K-Bar*. See p.242.
Jackson *Snake River Brewing Co*. See p.218.
West Yellowstone *The Wolf Pack*. See p.229.

$61 per adult). Fireside sing-alongs make up the entertainment. Reservations required, often weeks in advance, on ⓣ307/344-7311.

Roosevelt Lodge Dinging Room Taking up most of the small and rustic *Roosevelt Lodge* building is this relaxed dining room with around two-dozen plain tables lined up between raw, wooden columns. The menu here is big on sweet barbecued meats, with dinner prices ranging from $17 for bbq chicken or beef brisket to $22 for a massive portion of baby back ribs, all served with delicious, sugary baked beans. A few fish and pasta dishes are also on offer, along with Mexican-inspired appetizers like quesadillas ($7) and a black bean tostada ($12). Mains during lunch are burgers and bbq sandwiches ($7–10), while breakfast is the expected mix of pancakes ($6) and omelettes ($8), along with *huevos rancheros* ($7) and a vegan breakfast burrito made with tofu ($7). No reservations accepted.

Grand Teton

As with its accommodation, restaurants in **Grand Teton** are split between official concessionaire-run establishments and privately operated ones. Given this competition the restaurants on the whole are better than Yellowstone's but still a little pricey, with the gourmet option at *Jenny Lake Lodge* being both the best and most expensive. Taking top honors for an evening drink with **mountain views** is the back deck at *Jackson Lake Lodge*, although the views from Dornan's *Pizza & Pasta Company* and the lakeside deck at *Signal Mountain Lodge* are also outstanding. If staying in Grand Teton for more than a couple of nights, consider driving into nearby **Jackson**, home to the region's finest array of restaurants and bars (see Chapter 11 for reviews). Campers cooking out will likewise want to stop in Jackson to stock up on groceries at one of the large in-town supermarkets; the half-dozen **markets** dotted throughout the park are fine for picking up an item or two, but you'll pay a small fortune to buy a few day's worth of supplies. The one exception is the impressive wine shop at Dornan's, stocked with thousands of reasonably priced varieties from around the world.

Colter Bay and north

Located side-by-side, the two eateries within Colter Bay Village are Grand Teton's least inspiring choices, both for their setting and the cuisine. To the north, the sole dining choice before reaching Flagg Ranch is a pizza joint at Leeks Marina.

Café Court Pizza & Deli Colter Bay Village. The cheaper of the two options in Colter Bay Village is the circular *Cafe Court Pizza & Deli*, where young staffers sling out burgers ($6) and chilli or beef stew ($5), along with bottles of beer; the bland pizzas ($8) are best left untouched.

Chuckwagon Colter Bay Village. The *Chuck wagon* is an acceptable option for a moderately priced breakfast (6:30–11am) or lunch (11.30am–1.30pm). At dinner (5.30–9pm), stick to the standards including fried chicken ($17) or rainbow trout ($15) and skip the global cuisine tour featuring Swedish meatballs ($13), Hunan pork loin ($15), and eggplant parmesan ($11).

Leeks Marina Pizzeria The pizzeria here is run by the same team who operate *Headwall's Pizza* located at the top of Jackson Hole Mountain Resort's gondola. The thick, chewy pies are above average and a fair value, making for a filling pre or post cruise snack. Open daily 11am–10pm as long as the marina stays open (typically late May to early Sept).

Flagg Ranch

While not likely a destination in on its own, Flagg Ranch makes a convenient pit-stop for hungry drivers between Yellowstone and Grand Teton.

Bear's Den Flagg Ranch Resort ⓣ1-800/443-2311. Inside the resort's main lodge building, this smart and cozy restaurant dishes out classic mountain cuisine, including steaks ($20), sauteed trout ($16), and meatloaf ($15), alongside a limited wine list. There's a full breakfast menu too, and sandwiches, burgers, and salads for lunch ($7–9). The fireplace at the attached *Burnt Bear* bar is the perfect place for a post-dinner whisky.

Jackson Lake Lodge

The *Jackson Lake Lodge* houses two worthwhile restaurants and a bar with unparalleled views, all located off the second floor's large common area.

Blue Heron Lounge The park's prime spot for an evening drink, where you can recline in comfortable chairs on the back deck with a potent Moran Sunset cocktail or huckleberry margarita (both $6) and watch the ever-changing blues, grays, purples, and warm pinks glow off of Mount Moran.

Mural Room Serving meals throughout the day, the *Mural Room* is aptly named for its Old West painting on one side and huge picture-window looking straight at the Tetons on the opposite. The menu is an expensive and for the most part delicious array of meat and seafood dishes (entrees $20–32), including coffee-bean roasted lamb, pan seared sea scallops, and buffalo steaks. Cheaper lunch items include sandwiches and salads, and there is a superb breakfast buffet daily featuring piping-hot Belgian waffles. Reservations advised on ⓣ307/543-2811.

Pioneer Grill This buzzing eatery (daily 6.30am–10pm) is a classic counter-and-stools diner, with inexpensive food (burgers, veggie wraps and such $6–8) along with a few higher end items like pan-fried trout ($14) and St Louis ribs ($17). There's no view, but you can order a takeout meal to eat on nearby Lunch Tree Hill.

▽ *Jackson Lake Lodge* Pioneer Grill

Moose

The busy junction around Moose may act as park headquarters, but all the dining options here are located across the Snake River in the privately owned Dornan's complex. Along with the choices below, the grocery at Dornan's has a deli, good for packaged sandwiches to take along when hiking, biking, or rafting nearby.

Dornan's Chuckwagon A summer-only, all-you-can eat outdoor restaurant serving sourdough pancakes for breakfast ($9), burgers and bbq sandwiches at lunch ($12), and heaping platters of ribs, bbq chicken, steak and trout for dinner ($14–18). The prices and riverside picnic tables are great and guests are welcome to bring a bottle from the wine shop as well, but the food is hit-and-miss.

Pizza & Pasta Company Next door to Dornan's superb Wine Shoppe, the cheery *Pizza Pasta Company* (daily 11am–7pm; limited hours off-season; ⓣ307/733-2514) serves up delicious individual pizzas ($11–13), along with basic pastas, meatball subs, and salads. There's a full bar (with a TV) inside, though the deck in the shadow of the Tetons is where most visitors head; a pizza chased down with a bottle of wine from next door is a local post hike tradition well worth emulating.

Teton Park Road

Surprisingly, there are no dining options around buzzing south Jenny Lake save for snacks and coffee at the small Jenny Lake Store. The sole options found along the twenty-mile Teton Park Road are to the north, either at the swanky *Jenny Lake Lodge* or north again at the more down to earth *Signal Mountain Lodge*.

Jenny Lake Lodge This is the park's finest dining choice, with a rotating fixed-price menu for breakfast and dinner, plus an a la carte menu at lunch (dinners range $40–75 per person, not including drinks). In the evenings, you can expect superb gourmet dishes such as soy glazed New York strip and porcini-dusted leg of duck to anchor the five-course meal. The service is always impeccable, and the wine-list suitably impressive. Jackets "preferred" reservations required for breakfast and dinner, advised for lunch (ⓣ307/733-4647). Request a window side table if available.

Signal Mountain Lodge ⓣ307/543-2831. A bit on the musty side, the dinner-only *Peaks Restaurant* offers roasted elk medallions, Thai chicken, and king salmon (entrees $20–33); the food is a bit fancy and none-too-cheap, but the mountain views across the lake should ease the pain when the bill arrives. Next door, the *Trapper Grill* has a tasty breakfast (7–11am), with buffalo sausage, fresh trout, and a range of omelettes, all in the $6–8 range; lunch and dinner (11am–10pm) is the standard range of burgers, salads, and so on ($6–8). The lodge's one-room *Deadman's Bar* is open noon to midnight and has one of the park's few TVs, but the lakeside deck is far better entertainment on a summer's day.

10

Park programs and tours

Considering the wealth of must-see sights and tantalizing outdoor activities within the parks, it's easy to overlook the **ranger programs** on offer. Don't, as attending even the shortest program can add great overall insight, plus the opportunity to grill Yellowstone and Grand Teton's finest for insider know-how. Easiest to attend are the lectures and walks organized by the main visitor centers, which are on the short side but still packed with useful tidbits on all manner of subjects. Similarly, the **fireside chats** held throughout the summer at nearly all of the campgrounds are worth hitting up, both for the congenial atmosphere – don't be surprised if an older ranger wills everyone into a sing-along session – and the informative lectures. Free and fun, these programs require no reservations and you can just show up and take part.

If looking to delve deeper into a particular topic or activity, you'll need to do some advance planning. With topics ranging from ancient supervolcanoes to re-introduced wolves, it comes as no surprise that several outfits concentrate on comprehensive **interpretive tours and courses**. Leading the charge is the phenomenal **Yellowstone Association**, offering more than 400 field seminars and guided trips per year; attending any one of them is the highpoint of a Yellowstone trip for many a visitor. Along with letting you hobnob with like-minded visitors, guides are exceedingly knowledgeable and plugged into the local network, where news such as recent wolf or grizzly sightings travels fast. Quality gear is supplied as well, giving access to items such as expensive spotting scopes. Several companies in the area also offer **general tours** of both parks. As most of them attempt to cover too much territory in too short of time, they're only advisable for visitors without their own transportation.

Ranger programs and evening entertainment

Along with the **ranger programs** listed below, the main visitor centers in both parks offer a worthwhile selection of lectures, films, and short ranger walks each day. These include programs such as tours around Old Faithful's Geyser Hill, a ten-minute lecture at Canyon's Artist Point, and a wildflower walk along the floor of Jackson Hole. We've listed some of the best examples throughout the park tour chapters. Most programs run from early summer through Labor Day, with a limited selection starting up again for the winter

△ Ranger-lead tour at Upper Geyser Basin

season; check the park newspapers handed out upon arrival for the latest updates. The fireside chats provide most of the **evening entertainment**, though the hotels occasionally run slide shows or hire a piano player for the night and the various bars throughout both parks are pleasant stops for chatting over a nightcap.

Fireside chats Ranger-hosted fireside chats are a great way to end a day of exploration and are held in amphitheatres and firecircles conveniently located within walking distance of most campgrounds throughout Yellowstone and Grand Teton. The hour-long discussions/slideshows cover all manner of subjects, from geological history to wildflower spotting, with the weekly schedule clearly posted within each campground. Most of the chats kick off around 9–9:30pm, save for the more family-oriented discussions at Norris in Yellowstone and Lizard Creek in Grand Teton, which start at 7.30pm. Bring a flashlight for the walk back, and warm clothing – the fires are typically small and used more for atmosphere, not as a heat source.

Junior Ranger Program Provided you'll be in Yellowstone at least a couple of days, all kids ages 5–12 should enroll in the Junior Ranger Program. For $3, each child receives a twelve-page activity booklet, including a wildlife spotting checklist and a list of objectives with goals like hiking a trail and attending a ranger program. The program is headquartered at the Madison Information Station, though kids can sign up at most of the visitor centers and ranger stations. Upon completing the booklet, participants are then "sworn in" by a ranger in a quick and fun ceremony, and receive one of three patches depending on age and season. Grand Teton runs a similar program called "Young Nauralist" out of the Colter Bay and Moose visitor centers ($1).

Ranger Adventure Hikes From mid-June to late-Aug, rangers in Yellowstone lead at least one hike each day. Unlike many other park-run interpretive programs, there is a fee for the guided excursions ($15 adults, $5 for ages 7–15, free 6 and under). They're well worth the price, as they go far beyond the average boardwalk tour both in distance and depth of discussion, travelling 4–8 miles into the backcountry with rangers stopping often to point out interesting features and to answer questions. Examples include the steep trail up Avalanche Peak (H8), the Beaver Ponds Loop from Mammoth (H1), and a six-mile trek into the Hayden Valley. Most hikes start 8am, but tickets must be purchased a day ahead at the Albright, Old Faithful, Grant, Fishing Bridge, or Canyon visitor centers.

Interpretive tours and courses

More than just general tours sticking to the highways and boardwalks within the parks, these companies and nonprofits specialize in in-depth **interpretive tours and courses**, often zeroing in on a particular animal, historical subject, or geological oddity. Scores of outfitters

The Yellowstone Association

The **Yellowstone Association** (Ⓣ307/344-2294, Ⓦwww.yellowstoneassociation.org) is an invaluable resource for all visitors, from first-timers to lifelong Yellowstone devotees. The nonprofit organization operates in partnership with the National Park Service, with all net proceeds funneled directly into the park. Since its inception in 1933, it has funded millions of dollars worth of projects, including most recently a significant portion of costs for the new Canyon Visitors Center. Even if not signing up for a class, consider becoming a member either online or at any of the nine association-run bookstores scattered across the park; tax-deductible **membership** rates start at only $30, and with the park service struggling through years of budget cuts, the money will certainly be well spent. Membership benefits include the informative *Yellowstone Discovery* quarterly publication, fifteen-percent off on the items sold in the bookstores and online, and discounts on courses and off-season accommodation.

For three decades, the association's **Institute** has offered courses on Yellowstone's natural and cultural history. Headquartered at the Buffalo Ranch in the Lamar Valley, classes typically run from one to four days in length, and are led by a cast of experts spanning from local biologists, naturalists, and professors to recognized authors and artists. Along with the popular field seminars on wolf-watching and wildlife photography, an extensive selection of more esoteric courses covering the likes of bats, wilderness essay-writing, and even Yellowstone's "ghost hotels" are offered. Also available are a selection of four-day trips into the backcountry, hiking alongside in-the-know locals such as park historian and waterfall expert Lee Whittlesey, and "Personal Ed-Ventures," private interpretive tours of the park starting at $400 per day for up to seven guests.

Check the association website for a complete course listing. A real bargain, rates average $80–100 per day, with discounts for members. For overnight courses, two different sleeping options exist: you can stay either the rustic three-person cabins at the Buffalo Ranch ($25 per night; shared kitchen), or arrange your own accommodation in the hotels and campgrounds within and around the park.

throughout the region lay claim to leading expert-run excursions within Yellowstone or Grand Teton, and undoubtedly many of them do. The following, however, all come highly recommended and can be relied on for an enjoyable day or longer spent exploring and learning.

A Naturalist's World (Ⓣ406/848-9458, Ⓦwww.tracknature.com). Based in Gardiner, A Naturalist's World focuses on the art of animal tracking. Co-owner James Halfpenny has written several books on the subject (as well as the superb *Yellowstone Wolves in the Wild*; see p.289), and is regarded as one of the country's pre-eminent trackers. Halfpenny leads most of the classes, including several winter courses when animal tracks in the snow are far easier to follow. Prices average $250 for a two-day course, though more expensive, all-inclusive trips as far away as the Arctic Circle to study polar bears are also offered. Halfpenny also teaches classes, including popular wolf-watching programs, through the Yellowstone Institute.

Teton Science School (Ⓣ307/733-1313, Ⓦwww.tetonscience.org). Split between a wooded main campus east of Moose Junction by Grand Teton's eastern border and a new set of buildings two miles from Jackson, the Teton Science School features courses ranging from multi-day seminars similar to those at the Yellowstone Institute to year-long graduate programs. Founded in 1967, the school is particularly strong on youth and family programs, including summer camp stays for tweens and teenagers. Run through the school and most popular with the average visitor, Wildlife Expeditions (Ⓣ1-888/945-3567, Ⓦwww.wildlifeexpeditions.org) run biologist-led half-day ($115) and full-day tours ($250–300) within Grand Teton and Yellowstone.

Multi-day tours themed around the likes of winter wolf-watching and the fall mating season are also offered, along with combination trips taking in a float trip or fly-fishing along with a driving tour.

Yellowstone Safari Co. (ⓣ1-866/586-1155, ⓦwww.yellowstonesafari.com). Started by Bozeman-based naturalist and historian Ken Sinay, the upbeat private tours offered by the Yellowstone Safari Co. aren't particularly cheap, but each can be custom-made to suit your group's purposes. A full-day interpretive tour of Yellowstone starts at $550 for two, with rates rising $100 with each additional guest. Half-day to multi-day safaris of the park are offered, as are snowshoe tours in winter and overnight backcountry hiking tours through the Black Canyon of the Yellowstone and along the Bechler River in summer. North of the park, Sinay, a Lewis and Clark buff, also runs a full-day float on the headwaters of the Missouri River, including plenty of entertaining stories and stops at expedition campsites.

Activity-based tours

While the interpretive tour companies listed above can also organize **backcountry hiking** trips, we've included a couple of additional hiking outfitters below, along with companies dedicated to boating and biking. Contact details for **fly-fishing outfitters** for day-trips or longer excursions can be found in the box on p.162. For more information on the two exceptional **climbing schools** in Grand Teton see p.171.

Big Wild Adventures (ⓣ406/848-7000, ⓦwww.bigwildadventures.com). Based north of Gardiner in Emigrant, Montana, Big Wild runs half-a-dozen hiking trips deep into Yellowstone's backcountry from mid-June to mid-September, along with additional trips into the wilds around the Absaroka Range to the northeast. Prices for a week average $1700 per person, including food, all gear, guides, and transportation to the trailheads and back. If bringing your own hiking equipment, shave $200 off the price.

The Hole Hiking Experience (ⓣ1-866/733-4453, ⓦwww.holehike.com). Well-run guided hiking trips into the Teton Range. Along with several different day-trips, their overnight backpacking ventures include an easy two-night naturalist-led tour of Horseshoe Canyon ($600) and a moderate four-night tour of the isolated Jedediah Smith Wilderness to the west of Grand Teton ($1000).

O.A.R.S. (ⓣ1-800/346-6277, ⓦwww.oars.com). Starting off as a raft-running outfit in the Grand Canyon, O.A.R.S. now organizes trips across the country and beyond. Guided Wyoming excursions include a half-day kayak trip past geysers lining Yellowstone Lake's West Thumb ($80), a two-day tour in Grand Teton including a guided day-hike along with Snake River float-trip and kayaking on Jackson Lake ($400), and a five-day multi-sport trip in both parks combining the two with additional kayaking ($1100).

Snake River Kayak (ⓣ307/733-9999, ⓦwww.snakeriverkayak.com). The best local kayaking guide service has a long list of paddle tours in the area, including several Yellowstone Lake tours ranging from day paddles to a six-day adventure. A two-night camping trip along the shores of Shoshone Lake via Lewis Lake is also offered several times through July and August, as are fishing trips via kayak and canoe. A good place to look for courses on river kayaking as well.

Teton Mountain Bike Tours (ⓣ1-800/733-0788, ⓦwww.tetonmtbike.com). Jackson-based company running bike tours up to five days in length in the parks and the surrounding national forests, where trail riding is allowed. Example trips include an easy eight-mile peddle across Antelope Flats ($55), a twelve-mile dirt road ride alongside the Snake River, and a 15-mile tour in the Old Faithful area ($125); rates include bikes and transportation to and from Jackson. The five-day regional tour, including B&B accommodation and a whitewater rafting trip, costs $1900 per person.

General park tours

As most visitors explore the parks with their own transportation, there's not an overwhelming need for **general park tours** in the summer. The excursions offered by the following companies are mostly hurried loops throughout a section of Yellowstone or Grand Teton, with quick stops at the major attractions and a boardwalk stroll or two. Though you get to see a lot in a short time, there's little time for exploration or investigation, and they're best left for those without transportation or with little time to spend in the area. For tours starting outside of either park, you'll need to tack on the national park entrance fee to the overall price if you haven't purchased a pass. For winter tours, see Chapter 7.

Buffalo Bus Tours 415 Yellowstone Ave, West Yellowstone (Ⓣ1-800/426-7669, Ⓦwww.yellowstonevacations.com). One of the best of several companies offers tours out of West Yellowstone. Tours of one loop run $50; both loops $95. Trips start at 8.15am, with free motel and campground pick-ups.

Gray Line Jackson (Ⓣ307/733-4325 or 1-800/443-6133, Ⓦwww.graylinejh.com). Picking up from all accommodation within Jackson and Teton Village ($10 extra), Gray Line runs full-day narrated bus tours of Yellowstone's lower loop ($95) and Grand Teton ($80).

Grand Teton Lodge Company (Ⓣ307/543-2811 or 1-800/628-9988, Ⓦwww.gtlc.com). Grand Teton's main concessionaire offers half-day narrated bus tours of both Grand Teton ($34) and Yellowstone ($55), along with a combined two-day tour of both Parks ($72). There's also a shorter Wildlife Photo Tour ($18), with plenty of stops for snapping images.

Xanterra (Ⓣ307/344-7311, Ⓦwww.travelyellowstone.com). Yellowstone's top concessionaire runs several day-tours, most departing from the *Mammoth Hotel*, *Lake Hotel,* or *Old Faithful Inn*. The overly ambitious "Yellowstone in a Day" outing ($60) starts at Gardiner/Mammoth and takes eleven hours to complete both loops, while the more relaxed "Circle of Fire" tour travels only the lower loop in around 9 hours. Other tours include a three-hour morning "Photo Safari" ($55), and a two-hour sunset drive around Yellowstone Lake in a historic 1937 touring bus ($26). Three times a week, Xanterra also runs a trip down into Grand Teton ($54). On most of the tours, children under twelve can tag along for free.

Out of the Parks

Out of the Parks

11

Jackson and around

Named in 1829 for renowned trapper and mountain man Davey Jackson, **JACKSON HOLE** is a broad river basin, hemmed in by the Gros Ventre mountains to the east, the Snake Range to the west, and the Tetons to the north; it measures 48 miles north-to-south and varies between five and ten miles across. In the nineteenth century, "Hole" was a noun often employed to describe high mountain valleys, and indeed the Rockies were once peppered with "Holes." Tucked in at the south end of Jackson Hole is the town of **JACKSON**. To describe Jackson as an anachronism in the cowboy state of Wyoming is to put the situation mildly: art galleries, fine restaurants, flashy boutiques, and gift stores dominate retail spaces here, and it's fair to say that not everyone who visits is terribly enamored of the moneyed-vacation culture upon which the town thrives. Happily, however, much of the laidback neighborhood surrounding the tiny downtown still consists largely of simple cottages, betraying little evidence of the vast fortunes tied up in local real estate.

Clogged with visitors throughout summer, Jackson sits just east of the Snake River, only five miles south of the entrance to Grand Teton National Park and 57 miles south of Yellowstone's southern entrance. Winter, while more sedate, still draws crowds, mainly here to ski and snowboard. Jackson's in-town ski hill is **Snow King**; the more famous **Jackson Hole Mountain Resort** is twenty minutes' drive northwest of town, and **Teton Village** is the cluster of accommodation and services based at the bottom of the slopes. Bordering Grand Teton National Park, the resort's runs are rugged enough to attract the occasional foraging moose, but skiers should save their wildlife spotting for the lifts; they'll have plenty of other obstacles – namely boulders, bumps, and steep bowls – to worry about while skiing. A third ski area, easy-going **Grand Targhee**, can be visited from Jackson too, about an hour's drive away near the Idaho border.

There's no question the area has gone up-market in the last decade, and spearheading this evolution from Wild West to Mild West has been a slate of openings by several **high-end hotels**, none bigger than Teton Village's slopeside *Four Seasons*. In Jackson itself, some 35 galleries line the downtown streets, and the range of eating and nightlife options are easily the region's best (and most expensive). Unlike similar Western glamor destinations like Aspen, Colorado, however, millionaires here dress and act like regular folk, and in the main live in relative seclusion on ranches several miles from the town itself. There's no mistaking the pulling power of this area for the rich and famous, as evidenced by the daily line-up of private Lear jets on the airport runway, but an atmosphere of jeans and fleece jackets still rules the day, for now at least.

Arrival, information, and getting around

Jackson's charming **airport** is actually within Grand Teton National Park, eight miles to the north; it's linked to town by AllTrans **shuttle service** (Ⓣ307/733-3135 or 1-800/443-6133; $15 one-way to Jackson, $22 to Teton Village), while the regular **taxi** fare is around $26 into town, $46 to Teton Village. The excellent **Jackson Hole and Greater Yellowstone Visitor Center**, 532 N Cache St (daily: May–Sept 8am–7pm; rest of year 9am–5pm; Ⓣ307/733-3316, Ⓦwww.jacksonholechamber.com), has an ATM, restrooms, a good bookstore, and tons of information on the area. Indeed, it's a sight unto itself, with beautiful stuffed animal displays and a daily slate of free talks. Nearby, the **Bridger-Teton National Forest Headquarters**, 340 N Cache St (Mon–Fri 8am–4.30pm; Ⓣ307/739-5500), has details of hiking and camping in the Gros Ventre mountains to the east.

Transport around Jackson Hole is provided by START buses (Ⓣ307/733-4521, Ⓦwww.startbus.com), which run three color-coded routes, from roughly 6.30am to 10pm daily. It's a good idea to grab a timetable on board or from the information center as service frequency varies seasonally; rides within the town of Jackson are free, while trips to Teton Village are $3 one-way.

Accommodation

Jackson's **accommodation** scene is split in two, with one chunk located in town and the other huddled around the ski slopes in Teton Village to the north. During the busy summer season, there are few bargains to be had in the town proper, while the odd deal can be found at one of the mainly high-end options by the slopes. Conversely, once skiers and boarders start arriving, slope-side rooms are at a premium, while in-town rates drop by up to thirty percent, meaning a basic motel room can be exceptional value come winter. If here to **ski or snowboard**, it's easy enough to stay somewhere in town and commute to Jackson Hole Mountain Resort, twenty-minutes' drive away, though many find the convenience of sliding straight to the lifts worth the extra price.

Town Square Inns (Ⓣ1-800/483-8667, Ⓦwww.townsquareinns.com), manages over four hundred rooms in three **mid-range motel properties** in downtown Jackson (*Antler Inn*, *49er Inn & Suites*, and *Elk Country Inn*), and is worth a try if you can't get a room at any of the places listed below. Jackson Hole Resort Lodging (Ⓣ307/733-3990 or 1-800/443-8613, Ⓦwww.jhresortlodging.com) manages a full range of accommodation around Teton Village, from basic motel rooms to **condos**, townhouses, and four-bedroom lodges.

There's **hostel** accommodation both in Jackson and by the ski slopes at Teton Village, but only one **camping** option in Jackson itself. Alternatives for campers include Grand Teton's *Gros Ventre Campground* (see p.193); the pricey *Teton Village KOA*; or several USFS campgrounds perched by the Snake River between Hoback Junction and Alpine, including *Cabin Creek* (19 miles south of Jackson; $12), *Elbow* (22 miles south; $15), *East Table Creek* (24 miles south; $15), and *Station Creek* (25 miles south; $15).

Jackson

Hotels, motels, and inns

49er Inn 330 W Pearl St Ⓣ307/733-7550, Ⓦwww.townsquareinns.com. This downtown motel is nothing fancy, but the rooms, decorated in a combination of rustic Western decor and standard motel fittings, are much larger than average. Extras include two very large hot tubs and a skimpy continental breakfast. A

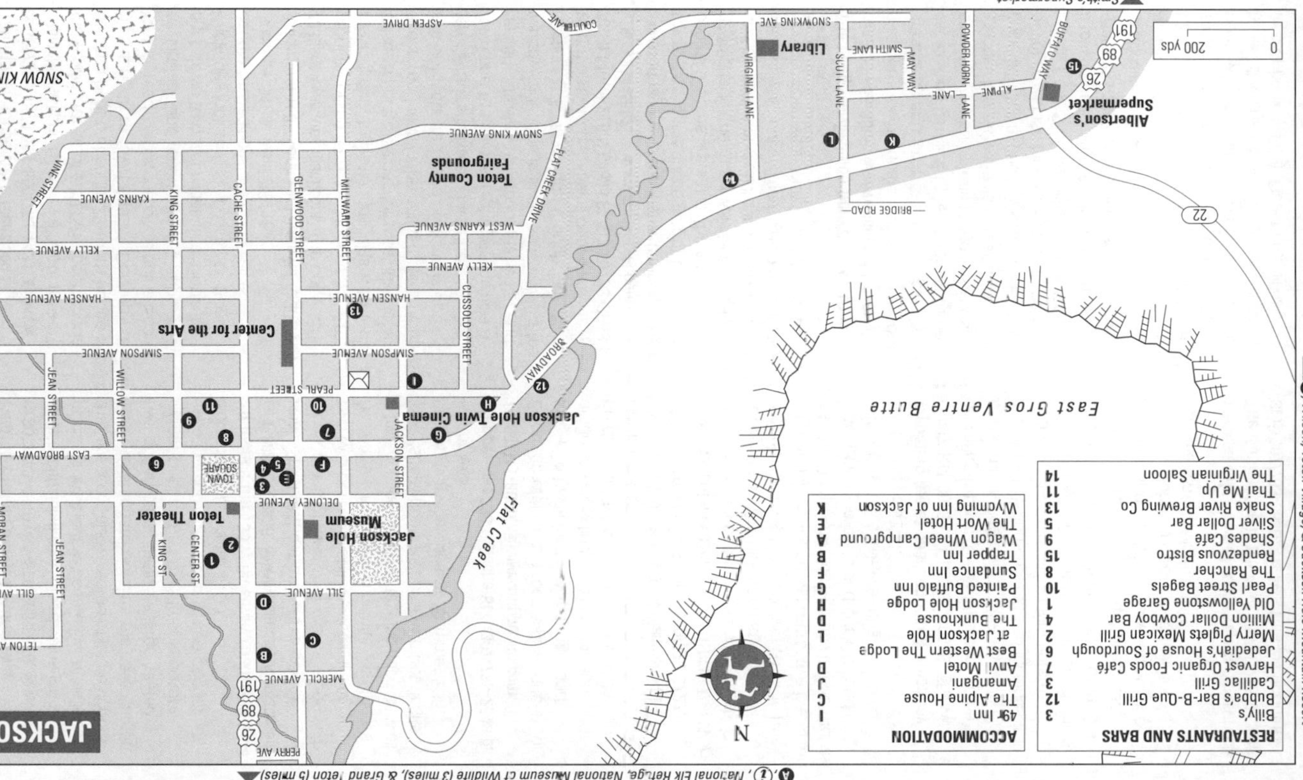
JACKSON
RESTAURANTS AND BARS
Billy's 3
Bubba's Bar-B-Que Grill 12
Cadillac Grill 3
Harvest Organic Foods Café 7
Jedediah's House of Sourdough 6
Merry Piglets Mexican Grill 2
Million Dollar Cowboy Bar 4
Old Yellowstone Garage 1
Pearl Street Bagels 10
The Rancher 8
Rendezvous Bistro 15
Shades Café 9
Silver Dollar Bar 5
Snake River Brewing Co 13
Thai Me Up 11
The Virginian Saloon 14
ACCOMMODATION
49'r Inn I
The Alpine House C
Amangani J
Anvil Motel D
Best Western The Lodge at Jackson Hole L
The Bunkhouse D
Jackson Hole Lodge H
Painted Buffalo Inn G
Sundance Inn F
Trapper Inn B
Wagon Wheel Campground A
The Wort Hotel E
Wyoming Inn of Jackson K
A, i, National Elk Refuge, National Museum of Wildlife (3 miles), & Grand Teton (5 miles)
J, Wilson, Teton Village, & Jackson Hole Mountain Resort
Smith's Supermarket
East Gros Ventre Butte
Flat Creek
Jackson Hole Museum
Teton Theater
Town Square
Jackson Hole Twin Cinema
Center for the Arts
Teton County Fairgrounds
Library
Albertson's Supermarket
Snow King
Perry Ave
Mercill Avenue
Gill Avenue
Deloney Avenue
Jackson Street
Pearl Street
Simpson Avenue
Hansen Avenue
Kelly Avenue
West Karns Avenue
Karns Avenue
Clissold Street
Millward Street
Glenwood Street
Cache Street
King Street
King St
Center St
Vine Street
Snow King Avenue
Aspen Drive
Coulter Ave
Flat Creek Drive
Broadway
East Broadway
Willow Street
Jean Street
Moran Street
Teton Avenue
Gros Ventre Street
Virginia Lane
Scott Lane
Smith Lane
May Way
Powder Horn Lane
Alpine Lane
Buffalo Way
Snowking Ave
Bridge Road
N
0 200 yds

few two-room suites are available for larger groups. Summer $95, winter $75.

The Alpine House 285 N Glenwood St ⓣ307/739-1570 or 1-800/753-1421, ⓦwww.alpinehouse.com. Billed as a "Country Inn", the *Alpine House* offers B&B accommodation in a bright, cheerful 22-room house two blocks north of Town Square. Decked out in light-colored timber, the place has a Scandinavian feel, and rooms are well-appointed, right down to guest robes and slippers. Packages including ski passes or cross-country expeditions are good value. Summer $160, winter $115.

Amangani 1535 North East Butte Rd ⓣ307/734-7333, ⓦwww.amangani.com. The only US property of the renowned Indonesian Aman resort group, the *Amangani* vies with Teton Village's *Four Seasons* for most luxurious accommodation in the entire region. Housed in a gorgeous redwood and sandstone temple-like structure on a butte between town and the slopes, highlights include a heated cliffside pool, spa treatments, and window-side tubs in every suite. With rates *starting* at $700 a night, though, only those with money to burn need consider.

Anvil Motel 215 N Cache St ⓣ307/733-3668 or 1-800/234-4507, ⓦwww.anvilmotel.com. Situated at one of the busier intersections in town, it's not the quietest spot but is very central. Rooms are small, the interiors are in good shape (the motel was built in 1991), and the fridge and microwave in each room are a useful bonus. There's also an outdoor hot tub, open year-round. Summer $90, winter $60.

The Lodge at Jackson Hole 80 Scott Lane ⓣ1-800-458-3866, ⓦwww.lodgeatjh.com. A mile from Town Square, this pleasant hotel attracts an equal mix of business clients and vacationing families. Spread across three attractive log-and-stone lodge buildings, touches like elk-antler lamps add life to the good sized chain-hotel rooms. Free large buffet breakfast, laundry, workout room and indoor pool. Summer $200, winter $150.

Jackson Hole Lodge 420 W Broadway ⓣ307/733-2992 or 1-800/604-9404, ⓦwww.jacksonholelodge.com. A range of units is available at this motel-lodge, located near the town center. The standard rooms are small with either one or two queen-size beds, while the studio and condo units all have full kitchen facilities and can sleep up to six people ($250). Guest amenities include heated indoor pool, two hot tubs, and a sauna. Summer $175, winter $140.

Painted Buffalo Inn 400 W Broadway ⓣ307/733-4340 or 1-800/288-3866, ⓦwww.paintedbuffaloinn.com. Good value inn a few blocks from the town center, with facilities that are a cut above some of its neighbors. The 140 standard hotel rooms have one or two queen beds, there's a large heated indoor pool and an on-site coffeeshop serving sandwiches and baked goods. Summer $38, winter $100.

Sundance Inn 135 W Broadway ⓣ307/733-3444 or 1-888/478-6326, ⓦwww.sundanceinnjackson.com. Small, basic motel with a central location and ground-floor rooms, along with two two-bedroom suites upstairs. The owners are friendly and helpful, and there's a free continental breakfast included as well as a "social hour" (5–6pm) with hot drinks and homemade cookies. Summer $95, winter $75.

Trapper Inn 235 N Cache St ⓣ307/733-2648 or 1-800/341-8000, ⓦwww.trapperinn.com. Central motel whose rooms have queen- or king-size beds (some with fridge) and amenities including small indoor and outdoor hot tubs and a guest laundry. Summer $130, winter $120.

The Wort Hotel 50 N Glenwood St ⓣ307/733-2190 or 1-800/322-2727, ⓦwww.worthotel.com. Built in 1941, *The Wort* is the most venerable high-end property in town, combining old-world style with modern facilities that include two large hot tubs, a grill-bistro, and an attractive bar (see p.218). Rooms are furnished with enormous lodgepole pine beds and big TVs, and bathrooms have full-size tubs. Summer $300, winter $270.

Wyoming Inn of Jackson 930 W Broadway ⓣ307/734-0035 or 1-800/844-0035, ⓦwww.wyoming-inn.com. One of the best in the upper mid-range market, the *Wyoming Inn* is completely nonsmoking and includes free continental breakfast, laundry, Internet access, and complimentary airport shuttles. There are coffee-makers in each of the 73 guest rooms, and suites all have a gas fireplace and hot tub; a huge log fireplace gives the lobby a cozy lodge feel, too. Summer $160, winter $140.

Hostels and campgrounds

The Bunkhouse In the Anvil Motel, 215 N Cache St ⓣ307/733-3668. There's little joy about this windowless bunker; kitchen facilities amount to a lone microwave oven and two fridges, there's no cooktop and no utensils and the 22 beds are clustered haphazardly into one big dorm space. On the upside, the lounge/TV area is spacious, bathroom facilities are clean and well-maintained and there's a guest laundry. The rate is the same year-round, making it poor value in winter when there are plenty of cheap motel rooms to be had. $22.

Wagon Wheel Campground 525 N Cache St, behind the Wagon Wheel Village **ⓣ307/733-4588.** This is about the only spot to pitch a tent in Jackson itself – beside Flat Creek and a ten-minute walk north of the town square. Basic toilet and shower facilities and not much shade. $16.

Teton Village and around

Hotels, motels, and inns

The Alpenhof Lodge ⓣ307/733-3242 or 1-800/732-3244, ⓦwww.alpenhoflodge.com. Classic Tyrolean lodge which offers 42 handsomely appointed guest rooms, some with fireplaces and balconies. Extras include a heated outdoor pool and hot tub, sauna, ski shop, and laundry. There's a casual bistro as well as the *Alpenhof Dining Room*. Summer $150, winter $170.

Best Western The Inn at Jackson Hole ⓣ307/733-2311 or 1-800/842-7666, ⓦwww.innatjh.com. Standard chain hotel accommodation, offering 83 mid-size rooms with either one queen bed or two doubles, along with a few lofts. Amenities include heated outdoor pool and hot tubs, laundry, and on-site tuning shop and the village's popular sushi restaurant. Summer $175, winter $250.

Four Seasons ⓣ1-888/402-7888, ⓦwww.fourseasons.com. The largest and newest slopeside structure is worth a peek even if not a guest, if just to check out the rough-hewn stones and native artifacts in the main lounge. Elegant suites come with marble bathroom counters and leather couches, while the heated outdoor pool, massive fitness center and spa, and full ski concierge services are all to be expected for nightly rates starting in the $500 range.

Snake River Lodge and Spa ⓣ307/732-6000, ⓦwww.snakeriverlodge.com. The attractive lobby, decorated with antler chandeliers, deep leather couches, and river rock fireplace, sets the tone for this ski-in/ski-out lodge, only a short step down the luxury ladder from the *Four Seasons* next door. Accommodation includes deluxe queen- or king-bed rooms and even more luxurious

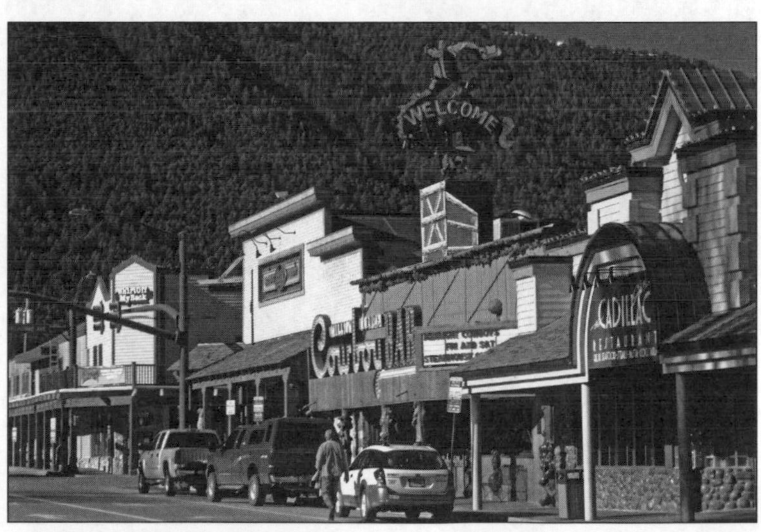

△ Downtown Jackson

one- to three-bedroom suites, all loaded with extras like goose-down comforters, cotton robes, and granite countertops. Guests get access to massive onsite spa and the indoor/outdoor pool and hot tubs within. Rates include breakfast. Summer $275, winter $325.

Hostels and campgrounds

Hostel X ⓣ**307/733-3415,** ⓦ**www.hostelx.com.** Excellent slopeside hostel accommodation, with a lounge with fireplace, TV and game room, ski lockers and tuning room, microwave oven (no kitchen), coin-operated laundry, and a ping-pong and pool table. Each private room, either a king-bed or four twin beds, is rented as a unit, and sometimes requires a five-night minimum stay. All rooms have private bathrooms. Year-round rates: double room $55, four-bed room $68.

Teton Village KOA ⓣ**307/733-5354 or 1-800/562-9043.** Halfway between Jackson and Teton Village, this campground offers some decent shady sites, all the usual facilities plus a games room, but it's not budget camping by any means. Tent sites $30, RVs $40.

The Town and around

The main street running east–west through **Jackson** is bustling Broadway, while Cache Street is the north–south divide; most of the bars, restaurants and services are within four blocks of the junction of these two streets. The **center of town** is marked by an attractive tree-shaded square featuring an arch of tangled elk antlers at each corner; on summer evenings, an amateurish **shoot-out** is staged here (daily 6.15pm; free). For a couple of blocks on all sides of the square, Old West-style boardwalks line streets filled with low-slung wooden buildings housing galleries, eateries, outfitters, and tourist traps like Ripley's Believe It or Not.

Twenty minutes drive to the northwest, there's not a great deal to actually see within the hodgepodge cluster of Western lodges and alpine chalets that make up **Teton Village**, though there's plenty to do outdoor-wise in any season, along with several fine places to eat. This is also the way to enter Grand Teton

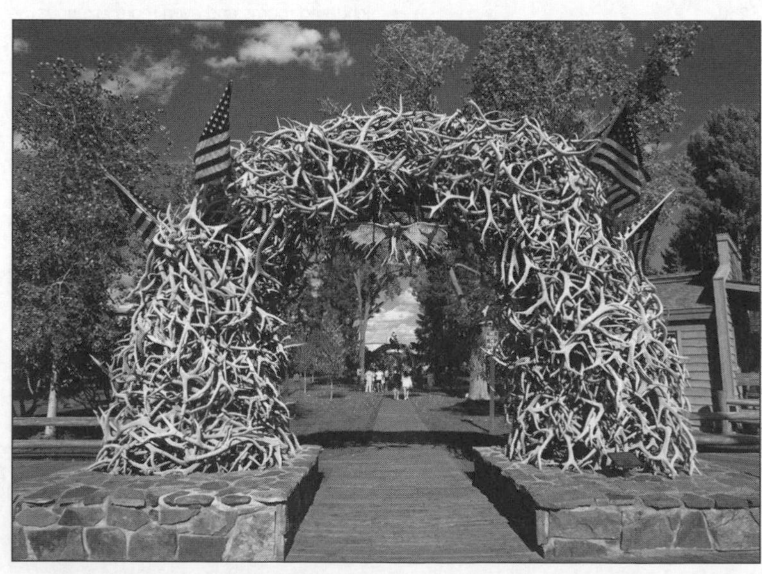

△ Jackson's Town Square

National Park via the Granite Canyon Entrance Station, described in detail on p.93. The tiny hamlet of **Wilson**, five miles west of Jackson, is of little interest apart from a notable bar and an excellent restaurant.

Jackson Hole Museum

The obligatory Old West exhibit space in town is the **Jackson Hole Museum** (June to early Sept Mon–Sat 9.30am–6pm, Sun 10am–5pm; closed rest of year; $3). Located a short walk from the town square at 105 N Glenwood St and topped by a hokey covered wagon, it's no high-end historical venue. The artifacts inside the two-room museum, however, are still diverting enough to warrant a half-hour visit. The collection kicks off with items associated with the local Tukudeka, or Sheepeaters, tribe including over a dozen samples of the type of beads used in trades with them. Colorful and modern looking, the prized beads, known as "foo-faw" by natives, came from glassworks in Italy, France, Czechoslovakia, and even China. The era of the Mountain Man is similarly represented, with plenty of gear and traps carried by the beaver hunters on display, along with looks at homesteading and early tourism. The collection ends with a nod to locally filmed movies, such as John Wayne's first starring role in 1930s *The Big Trail* and the famed Western *Shane*.

The National Museum of Wildlife Art and National Elk Refuge

Less than three miles north of town is the hillside **National Museum of Wildlife Art** (daily 9am–5pm, with limited Sunday hours in winter; ⓣ307/733-5771, ⓦwww.wildlifeart.org; $8), an impressive global collection that trails only Cody's Buffalo Bill Historical Center for best museum in the region. Opened in 1994, the sandstone fortress exhibits a winning mix of more expected classic landscape works alongside bright, modern concoctions like John Nieto's day-glo portraits of a coyote, buffalo, and wolf. The German-born Carl Rungius (1869–1959) is given the most space, with dozens of paintings ranging from his melodramatic early works to the more vivid paintings of wildlife featuring abstract backgrounds that he moved onto later in life. Of equal note is the recreated studio of local painter John Clymer (1907–1989), packed with marvellous Western ephemera. Look out as well for the permanent collection documenting the travails of the American bison, anchored by Robert Bateman's stupendous "Chief," depicting a life-size bull ready to stampede through a foggy canvas.

Elk are obviously the lead attraction across the highway from the museum at the **National Elk Refuge** (ⓣ307/733-9212). Established in 1912, the refuge protects nearly 25,000 acres of prime winter habitat, used by upwards of 7500 elk that begin migrating here in November. The animals have literally had to be kept alive through the winter months ever since the town's expansion left them cut off from vital winter feeding-areas. Today, forage vegetation is seeded and cultivated on the refuge, and during the harshest months up to thirty tons of alfalfa pellets are fed to the animals each day. From mid-December until early April you can take an hour-long **sleigh ride** ($15) onto the refuge to watch and photograph them up close; the tours start from the Jackson Hole and Greater Yellowstone Visitor Center (see p.210).

Alongside elk, the refuge host creatures large and small, ranging from moose, bighorn sheep, and coyote to nearly 175 species of birds, including the trumpeter swans living on the marshes surrounding **Flat Creek** just north of Jackson's visitor center. Also attracted to Flat Creek are fly-fishermen throughout the August–October season. For more on local trout, stop by the **National Fish Hatchery** (free), located just off the main highway at the northern end of the refuge. Around half-a-million cutthroat are raised here yearly, and it's possible to watch them being spawned one by one throughout April–June. There's also a free stocked pond on-site that's great for kids, with a catch limit of one trout per day.

Eating

Jackson's **restaurants** more or less divide between good-value family favorites and high-end eateries, with not too much in between. Most establishments are located within easy walking distance of Town Square and, regardless of price, have a generally laid-back vibe. As winter is the off-season in town, a good percentage of restaurants close early in the colder months and are open for breakfast and lunch only.

Teton Village's **slopeside dining** breaks down in a similar manner. Along with the pricier options reviewed below, there's a decent range of smaller cafés – like *Bridger Bagels* in the Bridger Center and the *Village Café and Bar* in the Village Center – that offer affordable breakfasts and lunches. Though future plans call for more restaurants on the slopes themselves, the current situation is a bit dire; the best option – a café atop the gondola – is notable mainly for the view.

Jackson

Billy's 55 N Cache St ⓣ307/733-3279. Attached to the much smarter *Cadillac Grill* (see below), this is a cheery place to sit on a barstool and tuck in to an enormous cheeseburger ($6 including fries) in a 1950s diner ambience. Daily for lunch and dinner.

Bubba's Bar-B-Que Grill 515 W Broadway ⓣ307/733-2288. Located a long walk (or short drive) west of town square, this is the best place in town to fill up on barbecued babyback ribs, sandwiches, burgers, and steaks, all at great value. It's also a favorite locals' breakfast venue, so expect at least half an hour wait for a table on weekend mornings. A huge omelette with grits, biscuits, and coffee is around $5. Daily 7am–9pm.

Cadillac Grill 55 N Cache St ⓣ307/733-3279. Fancy Art Deco restaurant on the main square, offering the same huge burgers as *Billy's* but also buffalo, wild boar, caribou, antelope, and seafood entrees for $12–20. A two-for-one happy hour special (5–7pm) in the jazz bar helps pass the wait. Reservations recommended. Daily 11.30am–2pm & 5.30–10pm.

Harvest Organic Foods Café 130 W Broadway ⓣ307/733-5418. Health food store with a veggie counter in back. Menu items include garden burgers, tofu dishes, baked goods, gourmet sandwiches, and thick fruit smoothies. Eat in the small dining area or order to go. Mon–Sat 7am–7.30pm, Sun 8.30am–4.30pm.

Jedediah's House of Sourdough 135 E Broadway ⓣ307/733-5671. A block east of Town Square, the casual and inexpensive *Jedediah's*, famed for their fluffy sourdough pancakes, also serves massive egg platters as well as filling sandwiches at lunch. Daily 7am–2pm.

Merry Piglets Mexican Grill 160 N Cache ⓣ307/733-2966. Reliable and inexpensive Tex-Mex entrees ($9–12) go nicely with the restaurant's margaritas, which you can get by the "half-yard." Daily for lunch and dinner; takeaway also available.

Old Yellowstone Garage 175 Center St ⓣ307/734-6161. One of Jackson's finest restaurants, offering flawless service and a (brief) northern Italian-themed menu that changes daily. Items often include rare elk tenderloin and roasted sweet pepper risotto (entrees $20–38), accompanied by a choice wine list. On Sunday night the menu is ditched altogether in favor of an all-you-can-eat pizza extravaganza ($15). Daily dinner only.

Pearl Street Bagels 145 W Pearl Ave. Very popular for fresh and tasty bagels, from tomato-herb to cinnamon-raisin, plus the finest cappuccinos in town. There's an outpost in tiny Wilson as well. Free wireless Internet. Daily 6am–6pm.

Rendezvous Bistro 380 S Broadway ⓣ307/739-1100. Well-priced bistro on the outskirts of town (south of Albertson's) that locals try to keep secret. Starters include a crispy frog legs and mussels, along with fresh oysters. Mains range from simple steak frites to lamb chops and ahi tuna, all of which are recommended. A good selection of bottled wine under $30 adds to the attraction. Daily 5.30–10pm, closed Sun in winter.

Shades Café 82 S King St ⓣ307/733-2015. Unpretentious and affordable café that's a good choice when the lines for *Pearl Street Bagel* around the corner are out the door. Along with pastries, breakfasts selections include an egg scramble for $3, while later in the day the likes of veggie burritos ($6) are served, eaten either at one of tiny tables inside or on the larger, shady deck to the side.

Thai Me Up 75 E Pearl St ⓣ307/733-0005. Standards like Pad Thai alongside lots of seafood and vegetarian variations (entrees $12–16) keep Jackson's best Thai restaurant busy. The food is fresh and well-presented and the service pretty quick too. Takeaway and delivery also available. Daily from 6pm.

Teton Village and around

Alpenhof Dining Room and Bistro Alpenhof Lodge ⓣ307/733-3462. Fine dining restaurant with an extensive wine list and a menu specializing in fondue along with Western exotica such as venison and continental standards like foie gras and duck confit (entrees $25–35). Meals at the lodge's bistro are more moderately priced ($10–15), and a large log fire lends a warm and cheerful ambience. Reservations advised.

Game Fish Snake River Lodge ⓣ307/732-6040. Pricey, but the eclectic Southwestern combinations – elk quesadillas, grilled trout with roast corn cakes, crispy rabbit with a cranberry compote – ensure a memorable dinner. Expect to pay around $70 for two, including drinks.

Masa Sushi Best Western The Lodge at Jackson Hole ⓣ307/733-2311. Standard sushi and sashimi menu in this cozy upstairs nook, a nice change from buffalo burgers. Prices are reasonable (two-piece sushi orders $3–4), and reservations are essential year-round. Closed Mon.

Nora's Fish Creek Inn 5600 W Hwy-22, in the nearby hamlet of Wilson ⓣ307/733-8288. Popular locals' spot for a huge, leisurely breakfast of pancakes or omelettes. Lunch and dinner menu features tasty prime rib, salmon, and trout along with homemade desserts, at moderate prices. Reservations advised especially on weekends.

Nightlife and entertainment

The year-round tourist trade has made Jackson's nightlife scene the liveliest in Wyoming, but you need to know what's happening on which night as people tend to pack in to one or two places and abandon the rest. Check the free *Jackson Hole Daily* for details on bands and special happy hour sessions. Up in Teton Village, the raucous *Mangy Moose* fills quickly once the lifts shut down, while the classier **bars** in the *Snake River* and *Alpenhof* lodges pull in those looking to sip wine rather than guzzle beer. The *Peak Bar* in the *Four Seasons* combines a bit of both, with free pool and shuffleboard.

Beyond pints and pool cues, Jackson has several central **cinemas**, including the single-screen Teton Theater (ⓣ307/733-4939) off Town Square and the Jackson Hole Twin Cinema (same phone), across from the post office on Pearl Street. More cultured activities include the long list of programs such as dance and theater at the new **Center for the Arts**, 240 S. Glenwood (ⓣ307/734-8956, ⓦwww.jhcenterforthearts.org), as well as Teton Village's annual **Grand Teton Music Festival** (ⓦwww.gtmf.org), a summer-long series of classical music concerts.

Jackson

Million Dollar Cowboy Bar 25 N Cache Drive ⓣ307/733-2207. Cheesy it may be, but everyone who visits Jackson ducks in at least once to this hugely touristy Western-themed watering hole, to sit on one of the saddles at the bar, get out on the dance-floor, or even indulge in a little drunken karaoke. There are also four pool tables. Cover most nights $5. Daily noon until late.

The Rancher 20 E Broadway. There's nothing remotely stylish about this upstairs pool hall on Town Square, but it's the drinking venue of choice for a mostly younger crowd who lounge around the eight full-size tables downing $6 pitchers of Bud. Happy hour 4–7pm. Daily until late.

Silver Dollar Bar ***Wort Hotel*****, 50 N Glenwood St.** This is the closest thing to an upscale bar in town, but it's still pretty relaxed and casual; hosts mellow country bands, singers, and piano players of variable quality. The silver dollars embedded in the bar-top number 2032. No cover charge.

Snake River Brewing Co 265 South Millward ⓣ307/739-2337. Highly recommended brewpub located several blocks southeast of Town Square and thus frequented mainly by locals. The pastas and wood-fired pizzas ($9–12) are well worth trying, but it's the award-winning and constantly rotating beer ($3.50 a pint) selection that packs 'em in. The afternoon happy hour – $2.50 pints and delicious jumbo pretzels for a buck – is an especially joyous occasion. No smoking. Daily noon–midnight.

The Virginian Saloon ***Virginia Lodge*****, 750 W Broadway.** Just your basic watering hole, but a good place to retire to for happy hour (4–7pm) and watch a game on the big-screen TV. Daily from noon until 11pm or midnight.

Teton Village and around

The Mangy Moose ⓣ307/733-9779. The *Moose*, liberally strewn with Western bric-a-brac, is Jackson Hole's legendary ski-bum hangout, famed for its apres-ski sessions that segue into rowdy evenings of live rock or reggae. The bustling upstairs dining room does decent burgers, chicken, and pasta, best chased down with a locally brewed Moose Juice Stout; *The Rocky Mountain Oyster* downstairs dishes up a pretty ordinary $7 skiers' breakfast buffet. Cover charge for live bands $5–20. Daily from 11am until late.

Stagecoach Bar 5755 W Hwy-22, in the nearby hamlet of Wilson ⓣ307/733-4407. Worth the drive for its renowned Thursday "disco night" – for which you're encouraged to dress up – as well as Sunday's crowded "Church" sessions, an extremely popular open-mic affair. Pool tables, darts, and a jukebox provide the entertainment on other nights.

Summer activities

More so than in winter, when local ski resorts buzz with life, **summer activities** in Jackson revolve around the options found within Grand Teton and, to a lesser extent, Yellowstone further to the north. There's still, however, plenty of choice outside the activities listed in chapters 4, 5, and 6.

Rafting

Dozens of Jackson companies offer **float trips** on the Snake River, and there's no doubt that coasting along while gazing up at the magnificent Tetons is the town's quintessential summer experience. We've listed the best companies for relaxing floats trips within Grand Teton National Park on p.166. South of town, thrill-seekers might opt for **whitewater rafting** trips can done on the Snake River, where, after leaving Jackson Hole, the Snake River Canyon constricts the waterway, producing mostly Class III rapids. You can expect to get drenched in cold water throughout the summer, though runs are most thrilling (and coldest) mid-May through June. Reliable operators include Dave Hansen Whitewater, 515 N Cache St (ⓣ307/733-6295 or 1-800/732-6295, ⓦwww.davehansenwhitewater.com), and Mad River, 1255 South Hwy-89 (ⓣ307/733-6203 or 1-800/458-7238, ⓦwww.mad-river.com). Expect to pay around $45 for a half-day run, including transportation and waterproof outerwear. An alternative to getting onto the river is in a **kayak** or **canoe**: Snake River Kayak & Canoe School (ⓣ307/733-9999, ⓦwww.snakeriverkayak.com) offers instruction (from around $130), river trips (from around $45), and all manner of rentals.

Fishing

The Snake River and its cousins boast plenty of superb spots to try your hand at **fly-fishing** outside of the parks (details *in* the parks are listed on pp.160–165). Meandering through the National Elk Refuge north of town, **Flat Creek** – Wyoming's sole fly-only river – opens to fishermen for three months starting in August. It's a tricky river, requiring quiet stalking from the banks and a good selection of dry flies, but its location and beauty are hard to beat. Other worthy waterways include the stretch of the **Gros Ventre River** below Slide Lake to the north (see p.98), and the **Hoback River** through its eponymous canyon to the south.

As with the streams and lakes within Grand Teton National Park (but not Yellowstone), a **Wyoming fishing license** is required. On the town square, Jack Dennis' Outdoor Shop, 50 E Broadway (Ⓣ307/733-3270 or 1-800/570-3270, Ⓦwww.jackdennis.com), sells licenses along with a good selection of gear, and is a good first stop for information, including the handy *Western Fishing Newsletter* (free). They also run one of the best guide services in town, with float and wading trips starting at $180 for two. Westbank Anglers (Ⓣ307/733-6483 or 1-800/922-3474, Ⓦwww.westbank.com) near Teton Village runs another highly recommended guide service with similar rates, while the Orvis shop at 485 W. Broadway (Ⓣ307-733-5407) is home to Jackson's largest selection of fly-fishing equipment.

Mountain biking

As **mountain biking** within the parks is forbidden on most trails, dedicated riders must stick closer to Jackson for fat-tire excitement. Fortunately, there's a wealth of choice, starting with the trails at Jackson Hole Mountain Resort, where riders can use the Teewinot Lift ($15) to access seven miles of trails of various abilities. Most locals, however, choose to ride the slopes closer to town at Snow King, part of a free extensive trail network known as the "Backyard Trails." At the base of Snow King, the **Cache Creek Trailhead** is one of the finest places to start pedalling from, with access to the twenty-plus mile Cache-Creek to Game-Creek loop. Riders can also hop onto the eight-mile Tiny Hagen/Putt-Putt Loop from here, featuring thrilling single-track biking.

The above only scratches the surfaces for off-trail riding. For more information and/or **bike rental** ($25–40 per day), call in at either Teton Cycle Works, 175 N Glenwood St (Ⓣ307/733-4386, Ⓦwww.tetoncycleworks.com), or Hoback Sports, 520 W Broadway (Ⓣ307/733-5335, Ⓦwww.hobacksports.com); the latter also runs guided **bike tours** in the Jackson Hole area for $45–60 including equipment, and sells the useful *Jackson Hole Ride Guide* ($4), a map of local bike trails. For tours ranging 1–5 days, check with Teton Mountain Bike tours (Ⓣ307/733-0712 or 1-800/733-0788, Ⓦwww.tetonmtbike.com).

Horseback riding

Those who fancy riding **horses** can go for a traditional nose-to-tail trail ride from Teton Village into Grand Teton National Park with Scott's Jackson Hole Horseback Rides (Ⓣ307/733-6992; half-day $50, full-day $80). More customized rides are available with Mill Iron Ranch, ten miles south of Jackson near Hoback Junction (Ⓣ307/733-6390 or 1-800/808-6390, Ⓦwww.millironranch.net), who run 2, 4 and 8 hour day-trips. Longer itineraries can include a cowboy cookout and even fly-fishing, and cost $80–120 for a full day.

Winter activities

With the region's best range of snowy activities, Jackson makes a prime winter destination, whether or not you chose to head north into the national parks. **Snowshoeing**, **Nordic skiing**, and **snowmobiling** each bring in a small share of visitors, but downhill skiing and snowboarding are the biggest draw. There could hardly be more contrast between the **three ski resorts**: **Jackson Hole Mountain Resort** is the premiere mountain with a huge vertical drop and terrain best suited to upper intermediate-to-expert downhillers, while **Grand Targhee**, on the west side of the Tetons has minimal development and mind-boggling snow statistics. The third choice is smaller, family-friendly **Snow King**, best for night-skiing options and early season openings.

To **rent** equipment in Teton Village, head for the Bridger Center in Teton Village; skiers can choose from K2, Rossignol, Salomon, and Atomic packages ($25–30) at JH Sports (Ⓣ307/739-2690), while the Hole in the Wall Snowboard Shop (Ⓣ307/739-2689) offers demo packages with the latest Burton and Salomon boards ($35). In Jackson, Hoback Sports, 40 S Milward (Ⓣ307/733-5335, Ⓦwww.hobacksports), carries a full range of quality skis and boards.

Jackson Hole Mountain Resort

Famed as a premier destination for the true skiing or boarding connoisseur, **Jackson Hole Mountain Resort** (Ⓣ307/733-2292 or 1-888/333-7766, Ⓦwww.jacksonhole.com) truly earns the accolades. This *is* a special mountain,

Jackson Hole's backcountry

Few places, if any, in North America reward **backcountry skiers and snowboarders** as much as Jackson Hole. The backcountry **gates** at Jackson Hole Mountain Resort access merely a portion of the explorable off-piste areas in the Brider-Teton National Forest and Grand Teton National Park, but it's a wonderland of natural bowls, chutes, and thigh-burning runs up to 4000ft in length, if also extremely dangerous. Not a single inch is patrolled and deadly avalanches are far too common. If you do not have a partner and the appropriate safety equipment and experience, don't even think about heading out here.

The most popular entry gate, atop Rendezvous Bowl, leads into Cody Bowl and Rock Springs Bowl, from where it's possible to ride back into the lower Hobacks. Hooking up with one of the resort's ski school backcountry **guides** (Ⓣ307/739-2663 or 1-800/450-0477) is highly recommended. A full-day tour for a group of up to five runs around $450, while a half-day for a similarly sized group costs $250–350. For more backcountry experience, the ski school's three-day backcountry **camp** ($500), run twice a year and covering safety equipment and etiquette along with plenty of off-piste exploring, is likewise worth investigating.

The resort's ski school also offers guided trips into nearby **Teton Pass** (8429ft), a favorite local backcountry entry point. Accessed via a parking lot on Hwy-22 just west of Wilson, bootpack trails lead into a mountain playground of powder-packed bowls than can often be skied as late as June. Jackson Hole Mountain Guides (Ⓣ307/733-4979 or 1-800/239-7642, Ⓦwww.jhmg.com) offer tours here. A final option is **heli-skiing** with High Mountain Heli-Ski Village (Ⓣ307/733-3274, Ⓕ307/733-3529, Ⓦwww.heliskijackson.com), into the Snake River, Hoback, Teton and Gros Ventre mountain ranges. A day typically consists of six long, heart-pumping runs (10,000–15,000 vertical). However you choose to head out-of-bounds, check **current conditions** on Ⓣ307/733-2664 or Ⓦwww.untracked.com/forecast.

arguably the best in the country for confident intermediates and advanced skiers and boarders to challenge themselves on run after run. Fifty percent of the terrain is rated expert-only, and it boasts a huge vertical drop of 4139ft; many a slider has stepped up to the slopes cocky and over-confident only to be left quickly humbled. Respect both the slopes and your abilities, though, and you'll have a field day on the potent mixture of terrain, from silky groomers and deep powderfields to precipitous bowls and unpatrolled backcountry – just don't expect to wake up feeling pain-free the next morning.

The 2500 acres of skiable terrain divides into three areas; starting from right to left on the trail map there's **Apres Vous Mountain**, the **Casper Bowl** area, and the much-vaunted **Rendezvous Mountain**, each progressively more difficult. Fans of the resort were gutted when it was announced that the 2005–2006 season would be the last for resort's iconic **aerial tram,** a 63-passenger air-bus that zipped to the spectacular, wind-blown summit of Rendezvous Mountain (10,450ft) in ten minutes. At the time of writing, a new plan to replace the tram with an even larger, faster one had been announced, with a hoped completion date of 2008. Whether by tram or a temporary double chair – requiring several other uphill lifts to reach – access to the peak is still guaranteed, below which a free-riding nirvana awaits, including the heralded **Hobacks**, where nothing is off limits and some 2000 vertical feet of powder fields await. The speediest way up the mountain is now the eight-person **Bridger Gondola**, dropping off below **Casper Bowl**, home to some of the finest intermediate terrain at the resort, including long, groomed runs like Easy Docs It and the Moran Woods, a superb spot to test out your tree riding skills. It takes two quads to ride to the peak of the mountain's final chunk, Apres Vous Mountain (8481ft), one reason why this portion of Jackson Hole is relatively under-skied. That makes it a good bet on busy days – especially **Saratoga Bowl**, which hides powder stashes after the rest of the mountain is ridden out. Beyond the resort's five boundary gates lies some of finest accessible **backcountry** skiing and riding on earth; see the box on p.220 for more.

At $70, **lift tickets** at Jackson Hole are not cheap, and savings through multiday packages are minimal – the only way you can really save are the ski-and-stay packages offered by Jackson Hole Central Reservations (Ⓣ1-800/443-6931). Jackson Hole's respected **ski school**, founded by Olympic gold-medal skier Pepi Stiegler, offers up a wider range of programs than the average resort. Though not a recommended mountain for beginners, the school does offer the typical first-timer courses ($70) and a comprehensive kids' program. Beyond the basics, the school runs plenty of **clinics** for intermediate and advanced riders looking to ratchet their skills up a notch.

Grand Targhee

Dominated by the bulky, jagged peak of Grand Teton towering up 13,800ft in the background, **Grand Targhee** (Ⓣ307/353-2300 or 1-800/827-4433, Ⓦwww.grandtarghee.com) on the Wyoming/Idaho border is far less daunting than its rugged neighbor Jackson Hole under an hour's drive away. A quick peek at the trail map reveals an abundance of wide-open blues spilling down the mountain's 2000 acres, along with a substantial green web of runs by the base. Some terrain is suitable for advanced riders only, but this is not a mountain for adrenaline-crazed kamikazes looking to break the sound barrier. Plain and simple, the thrills here are all about blasting through powder, an arcing spray of snow behind you and large swathes of untouched terrain ahead.

Indeed, snow is the resort's strongest attribute. In an average year over forty feet of **fresh powder** falls, while in an amazing season sixty feet come down. Even with these impressive figures, the slopes remain secluded, as the only other group besides locals and the powder-hound contingency that seems to have already caught on are families, who take advantage of the affordable prices, quality ski school, and kids-ski-free programs. It's not all good news at Grand Targhee, however. When storms get hung up on the surrounding peaks, they also wreak havoc on visibility, and it's possible to vacation in "Grand Foghee," as locals sometimes call it, for several days and never see the towering Tetons above. Off-slope activities are minimal, the nightlife scene is meager, and nearby **Driggs**, Targhee's closest town base, twelve miles away across the border in Idaho, has few options.

All things considered, it's not surprising then that many visitors base themselves in Jackson and drive over Teton Pass to visit. Should you not have a car (or would rather leave the perilous mountain driving to an expert) a daily round-trip **shuttle bus service** from Jackson and Teton Village to the resort is run by Targhee Express, leaving at 7–8am and returning at 4.15pm; reservations are required by 9pm the night before (ⓣ307/734-9754; $20, or pay $60 with lift ticket). Grand Targhee's **lift tickets** run around $50 for an all-day pass, while kids' and seniors' tickets are closer to $30.

Snow King

Sloping above Jackson's small downtown, Wyoming's **Snow King** (ⓣ307/733-5200 or 1-800/522-5464, ⓦwww.snowking.com) would look like little more than a pocket-sized playground if placed next to nearby Jackson Hole. There's a bit more to this 400-acre ski area than meets the eye though, and it has successfully carved its own happy niche. Locals appreciate the mountain (Wyoming's first, opened in 1939) for the fact that lifts, thanks to solid snowmaking, typically begin running a couple weeks before Jackson Hole's, allowing atrophied early-season muscles time to warm up on runs dropping up to 1500 vertical feet. The ski area is also a more comfortable proving ground for beginners than its larger neighbor, and Snow King also runs the sole **night skiing** program in the area, with a pair of lifts staying open until 8pm, Tuesday through Saturdays, perfect for those hoping to pack the maximum amount of skiing into the minimum amount of time.

Cross-country skiing and snowmobiling

The Jackson Hole Nordic Center (daily 8.30am–4.30pm; ⓣ307/739-2629) in Teton Village has several looping **cross-country ski** trails of variable ability adding up to 17km in total. Trail fees are $8, rental packages range $18–22, and lessons are available. Far more impressive are the half- and full-day tours that the Nordic Center runs into Grand Teton National Park. Full-day tours run $160 for the first person, $40 per additional person, including lunch.

Skirmishes over recent legislation and environmental impact studies mean **snowmobiling** opportunities have been somewhat limited, but if you're interested in the sport, you're not likely to find a more exhilarating locale. Tours run by local outfitters include rides past buffalo and elk to Old Faithful in Yellowstone (around $200 per driver, $80 for passenger); trips over Togwotee Pass (around $150 per driver, $75 for passenger), featuring great views and large meadows; and a Granite Hot Springs excursion that travels through Granite Canyon to 110-degree springs, where you can take a dip in a snow-rimmed pool before tucking into lunch (around $150 per driver, $75 for passenger).

Companies to check with include Jackson Hole Mountain Tours (Ⓣ307/733-6850 or 1-800/633-1733, Ⓦwww.jacksonholesnowmobile.com) and High Country Tours (Ⓣ307/733-5017 or 1-800/524-0130).

Listings

Avalanche hotline Ⓣ 307/733-2664.

Banks Foreign exchange and 24-hour ATM access are available at Jackson State Bank, corner of Center St and Deloney Ave. Other ATMs include Bank of Jackson Hole, corner of Cache St and Broadway, and Community First, corner of Glenwood St and Pearl Ave.

Car rental Alamo Ⓣ307/733-0671, Avis Ⓣ307/ 733-3422, and Hertz Ⓣ307/733-2272 are based at the airport; in town you'll find Budget Ⓣ307/733-2206, Eagle Ⓣ307/739-9999, National Ⓣ307/733-0735, and Thrifty Ⓣ307/739-9300.

Hospital St John's, 625 E Broadway Ⓣ307/733-3636, has 24-hour emergency care.

Internet Teton County Library (see below) has a row of 15 min access terminals that are free of charge and in high demand; Albertson's supermarket also has free WiFi access in a reading area towards front of store.

Laundry Soap Opera, 835 W Broadway (daily 7am–10pm; Ⓣ307/733-5584).

Library Teton County Library, 125 Virginian Lane (Mon–Thurs 10am–9pm, Fri 10am–5.30pm, Sat 10am–5pm, Sun 1–5pm; Ⓣ307/733-2164).

Pharmacy Inside Albertson's supermarket (see below).

Post office Jackson: 220 W Pearl Ave Ⓣ307/733-3650 (Mon–Fri 7.30am–5.30pm); Teton Village: Ⓣ307/733-3575 (Mon–Fri 9.30am–4pm).

Supermarket Albertson's, at the junction of Broadway and Hwy-22 (daily 6am–midnight; pharmacy hours Mon–Fri 9am–9pm, Sat 9am–7pm, Sun 10am–4pm).

Taxis All-Star Ⓣ307/733-2888; AllTrans Ⓣ307/ 733-3135.

12

West Yellowstone and Big Sky

Snug up against Yellowstone's western border, **WEST YELLOWSTONE** is a busy, commercialized grid where family restaurants and motels, souvenir shops and outfitters elbow each other for your business. Unlike Gardiner and Cooke City, Montana's other gateway towns which retain a frontier atmosphere, West Yellowstone's main drags have a tourist trap vibe and the town's overarching calling is plain: provide comfort and entertainment to park visitors. In summer the town overflows with tourists, bikers on Harleys, even hot rod conventions, and in winter it becomes a haven for snowmobilers.

Tourism has been West Yellowstone's main economic engine from its founding, when the first stagecoaches made the arduous journey from Monida, Montana, through the area to the nascent national park in 1881. In 1907, the town (then called Riverside) became an official park entrance, and the following year the Union Pacific's Oregon Shortline Railroad arrived, shuttling tourists in on the *Yellowstone Special*. That same year the town was renamed Yellowstone (it only became West Yellowstone in 1920 to avoid confusion with the park). Tourists were provided for by *Murray's Yellowstone Hotel* (now the *Madison Hotel*) and a general store operated by Sam and Ida Eagle that continues to trade under their surname. With the development of the highway from Bozeman, more tourists began to arrive by car, and the train service was discontinued in 1960. Today the depot is a museum dedicated to regional history.

While the railroad spurred on West Yellowstone's rise, **BIG SKY** an hour's drive north can thank air travel for its present-day boom. The resort area has always been able to boast world-class **downhill skiing** and **whitewater rafting**, but a real estate explosion fuelled in part by regular flights into nearby Bozeman has seen Big Sky transform itself in the last decade from sleepy Rockies hideaway to Jackson Hole's northern cousin.

West Yellowstone

Although "**West**," common shorthand in the region, is not a particularly peaceful place, it's an undeniably handy stopover to stock up on supplies, grab

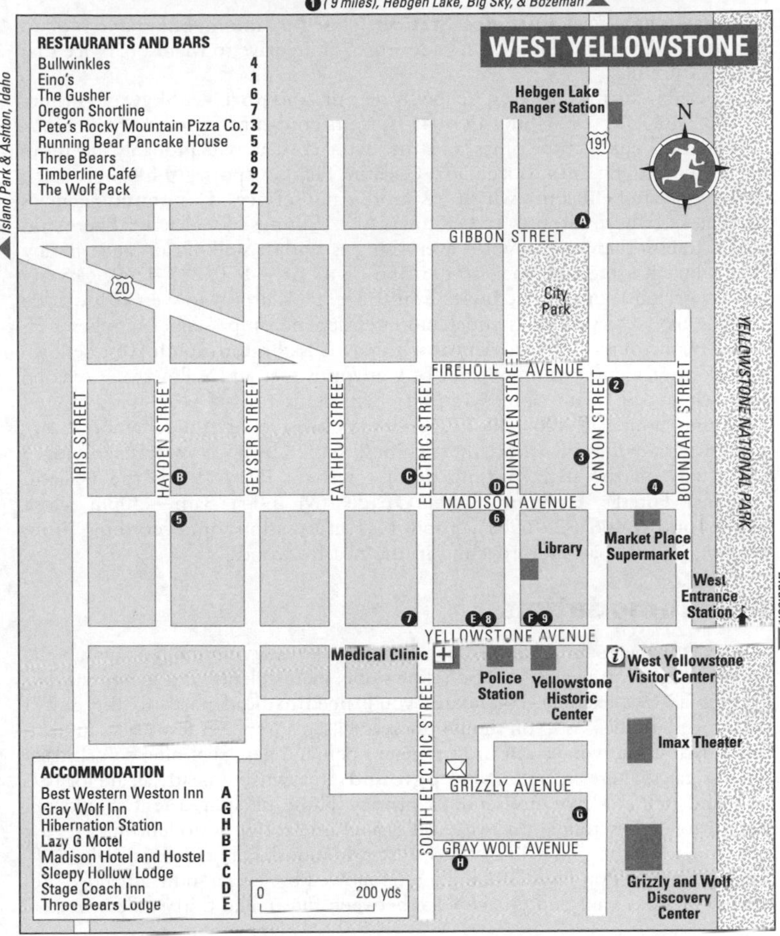

a quick meal, and perhaps spend a few nights. There are few of points of real interest around town, but the area's menu of outdoor activities in Yellowstone and the surrounding Gallatin National Forest is superb.

Arrival and information

West Yellowstone is ninety miles south of **Bozeman** on Hwy-191, and the picturesque drive takes just over two hours under normal conditions; the turnoff leading up Lone Mountain in **Big Sky** marks the halfway point. Cutting diagonally out of town, Hwy-20 heads west into Idaho over Targhee Pass (7072ft) before turning south through Island Park en route to Ashton 50 miles away and Yellowstone's Bechler Ranger Station 20 mile further on. West Yellowstone's town grid is easy to negotiate; Hwy-191 forms the main drag of Canyon Street, which intersects with Yellowstone Avenue leading a block east to Yellowstone's **West Entrance Station** (closed to automobile traffic Nov to mid-April). From the entrance, it's a fourteen-mile drive to Madison, twice that to Old Faithful.

It's possible to fly into West Yellowstone's tiny **airport** via Skywest Airlines (ⓣ406/646-7351 or 1-800/453-9417) from mid-June through September. Considering connection times and the extra cost, it will probably be more convenient to fly into Bozeman's Gallatin Field Airport (ⓣ406/388-8321, ⓦwww.gallatinfield.com), which has more daily services. **Car rental** agencies have desks at both airports and in town (see "Listings" for details). There's no public transportation in town – everything is within walking distance in any case – but Karst Stage, Inc. (ⓣ406/556-3540 or 1-800/287-4759, ⓦwww.karststage.com) runs shuttle **buses** from Bozeman's airport to West Yellowstone and Big Sky; reservations essential and rates depend on passenger numbers.

The main source for **information** in town is the top-notch West Yellowstone Visitor Center at the corner of Canyon Street and Yellowstone Avenue (May–Sept daily 8am–6pm; Mon–Fri 8am–5pm rest of year, with limited weekend hours; ⓣ406/646-7701, ⓦwww.westyellowstonechamber.com); along with town information, there's a desk staffed by a Yellowstone employee for details on the park. Just north of town on Hwy-191 is the Gallatin National Forest's **Hebgen Lake Office** (Mon–Fri 8am–4.30pm, close noon–1pm; ⓣ406/823-6961), good for information on everything from camping to off-road motorcycling in the nearby woods.

Accommodation

Located on the main drag, the *Ho-Hum Motel*'s name succinctly sums up the **accommodation** picture in West Yellowstone: there's plenty of places to stay, but nothing all that exciting. For luxury you'll need to head north to Big Sky. If planning a summer visit, you should reserve well in advance. A few places in town shut down in the winter, but most remain open and generally offer substantially reduced rates. There are several **campgrounds** in town, but nearly all are for RVs only and lack shade or any sense of privacy. Those pitching a tent should opt instead for Yellowstone's *Madison Campground* (see p.189) fourteen miles to the east or one of the sites within the Gallatin National Forest; *Baker's Hole* ($14), three miles north on Hwy-191 is closest, followed by several more attractive sites around Hebgen Lake and Quake Lake between fifteen and thirty miles away.

Best Western Weston Inn 103 Gibbon St ⓣ406/646-0000 or 1-800/528-1234. One of three *Best Western* hotels in town. The standard motel rooms could use an update, but are clean and quiet nonetheless and reasonably priced at $115–130 a night. Amenities include in-room Internet, free continental breakfast, outdoor pool, and hot tub.

Gray Wolf Inn 250 S Canyon St ⓣ406/646-0000 or 1-800/852-8602, ⓦwww.graywolf-inn.com. A large, relatively new motel on the southern half of town with spacious, comfortable rooms, free continental breakfast, plus a laundry, sauna, small indoor pool and hot tub. Open year-round, with summer rates starting at $90 for a basic room with double beds and rising to $250 for a three-room suite.

Hibernation Station 212 Gray Wolf Ave ⓣ1-800/580-3557, ⓦwww.hibernationstation.com. Located on the southern edge of town, this is easily the most eclectic accommodation option in West. Shoehorned into a couple of sculpture-rich acres are nearly fifty cabins, each individually decorated with themes ranging from the Wild West to a suite known as "The Wizard" after the Gandalf-like carving in king-size bed's frame. Prices range from a basic cabin with queen bed for $110 to a two-bedroom family unit with three queen beds for $280.

Lazy G Motel 123 Hayden St ⓣ406/646-7586. Basic wood-panelled motel rooms with some of the best rates in town ($50–60). For $15 more, you can get a simple kitchenette. Open in winter, with snowmobile rentals on-site.

Madison Hotel and Hostel 139 Yellowstone Ave ⓣ406/746-7745 or 1-800/838-7745, ⓦwww.wyellowstone.com/madisonhotel. A fair choice for budget-minded visitors travelling solo, this is one of the few hostels in the region. The attractive log-hewn building dates back to 1912 and has rooms with bunks for up to four people ($26 each). Room rates in the motel in a separate building stretch from $55 for the most basic room to $115 for a "deluxe" with two queen beds. Internet access in the lobby. Open late May to early Oct.

Sleepy Hollow Lodge 124 Electric St ⓣ406/646-7707, ⓦwww.sleepyhollowlodge.com. A dozen attractive log cabins with fully equipped kitchens and a basic continental breakfast, plus a fly-tying bench and guide service for anglers. Good value at $80–100 per night, but note that there are no in-room phones (phone available in office).

Stage Coach Inn 209 Madison Ave ⓣ406/646-7381 or 1-800/842-2882, ⓦwww.yellowstoneinn.com. One of the town's oldest and most historic buildings, this block-long inn features straightforward hotel rooms ($90–120), a smart lobby and reading area, two indoor hot tubs, small laundry, and a friendly attached saloon (poker played nightly). Open year-round and there are some great off-season deals.

Three Bears Lodge 217 Yellowstone Ave ⓣ406/646-7353 or 1-800/646-7353, ⓦwww.three-bear-lodge.com. Spread across a series of buildings, this motel houses 75 good-sized rooms averaging $115 in summer, with the two-bedroom family units (sleeping six) $100 more. On-site amenities include Internet, outdoor pool, indoor hot tub, cinema, and a friendly diner. Open year-round, with some of town's best snowmobile packages.

The Town and around

West Yellowstone is small enough to wander around quite easily, although peak-season crowds lead to a certain amount of ducking and weaving on the streets. Along with a flood of trinket and t-shirt shops, the town's biggest visitor draw is the **Grizzly and Wolf Discovery Center**, 201 S Canyon St (daily 8.30am–dusk; $10; ⓦwww.grizzlydiscoveryctr.org). It's the one place around Yellowstone where you're guaranteed to see grizzly bears. The center houses "problem" grizzlies and non-native Kodiak bears that had either become addicted to raiding garbage cans or were orphaned at a young age and thus could no longer live safely in the wild. Though it's rather sad seeing these animals hemmed in by fences, proponents of the center rightfully argue that the only other option is to have them put down. You can get up to within a few feet of the bears, and inside there's some very good interpretive displays, including several stuffed grizzly and black bears and shocking photos of illegally gotten bear gallbladders, sold for upwards of $20,000 in Asia for their alleged medicinal wonders. Opposite the bears' pen there is another smaller enclosure home to a gray wolf pack born in captivity, though their inclusion feels rather tacked on; there's almost no interpretive wolf information displayed inside.

The **Yellowstone IMAX Theater** (daily May–Sept 9am–9pm; Oct–April 1–9pm; $8; ⓣ1-888/854-5862) next door has regular showings of *Yellowstone* – a feature that ineffectively attempts to stuff the park's geological and human history into forty minutes – all projected on to a six-storey screen. Around the corner on Yellowstone Avenue, the **Yellowstone Historic Center** (mid-May to early-Oct daily 9am–9pm; $6) is more worthwhile, housed in the 1908 Union Pacific Depot. The building itself is perhaps the main attraction, beautifully renovated including the original ticket window. Exhibits focus on the early years of tourism in the park, including a day-by-day description of the Grand Tour visitors once took via stagecoach, though there are also side rooms covering the Yellowstone fires of 1988 and the major earthquake that struck north of here in 1957 (see Quake Lake below). Perhaps most popular is the stuffed bear known as Snaggletooth, a 1000-pound grizzly who famously roamed around town with a crooked grin in the 1960s before being illegally shot. Though not part of the museum, take a moment to admire the equally attractive buildings to the west that were also part of the depot during its heyday and designed by eminent national park architect Gilbert Stanley Underwood.

Hebgen and Quake Lakes

It's a delightful eight-mile drive north on Hwy-191 between thickly timbered hillsides to the turnoff on Hwy-287 at **Hebgen Lake**. A hangout for fishermen, boaters and even wind-surfers, the idyllic lake is circled by aspen groves, a particularly beautiful photo spot come fall. To the west is six-mile long **Quake Lake**, and a cursory glance at the dead trees poking above the surface of it indicates that it's no ordinary lake. Indeed, there wasn't even a lake here until August 17, 1959, when an **earthquake** measuring 7.1 on the Richter Scale released a vast slide of rock, damming the Madison River Canyon. Twenty-eight people camping in the area were killed, and Hebgen Lake's north shore dropped by eighteen feet causing a tidal wave to race down the lake and sweep over Hebgen Dam, which miraculously held under the pressure. The incident is remembered at the **Earthquake Lake Visitor Center** on Hwy-287 at the west end of Quake Lake around 25 miles from West Yellowstone (June–Aug daily 8.30am–6pm; ⓣ406/682-7620; $3), from where there's a good view of the scene and an interpretive trail.

Eating and drinking

When it comes to **food** and **drink**, West Yellowstone doesn't do fancy very well. However, if in the market for a heaping plate of huckleberry pancakes to start of the day or an affordable and filling dinner for the entire family to end it, you've come to the right place. There are several bars dotted about, but the most popular evening entertainment come summer is a town stroll, rapidly melting ice-cream cone in hand. Come winter, sled-heads bar-crawl via snowmobile, buzzing from place to place before getting too buzzed to continue. Along with the IMAX theater, the *Three Bear Lodge*'s **cinema** (ⓣ406/646-7777) plays the latest Hollywood hits, and the Playmill Theatre on Madison Avenue (ⓣ406/646-7757) has been putting on a nightly stage performance throughout summer for forty years.

Bullwinkles 19 Madison Ave ⓣ406/646-7974. Named after the huge bull-moose head hanging above the dining room, this relaxed restaurant and bar is the town's best. The expansive menu includes pub grub (the $7 burgers are huge), pastas ($16), and selection of steaks and chops. Best of all are the pan-fried fish – both the rainbow trout ($17) and walleye ($19) are highly recommended – and a welcome range of meal-sized salads.

Eino's Tavern 8955 Gallatin Road ⓣ406/646-9344. A one-of-a-kind rustic roadhouse nine miles north of town just past the Hwy-287 turnoff at Hebgen Lake. A favorite of fishermen and snowmobilers, the decor consists of hundreds of signed dollar bills taped virtually everywhere, and the beer is cold and free-flowing. As for food, you grill it yourself in a mottled open kitchen; burgers $5 per pound, steaks $15 and up, and you know whom to blame if your meal is burnt.

The Gusher 40 Dunraven St ⓣ406/646-9050. One of the top spots in town for quick, cheap eats. Friendly counter service to go with a solid range of pizzas, sandwiches, burgers, and even vegetarian dishes, plus free delivery.

Oregon Shortline In the *West Yellowstone Conference Hotel*, 315 Yellowstone Ave

☎406/646-7365. Upmarket dining with a local touch – bison meatloaf and mountain trout are on the menu, which will set you back $15–22. Check out the perfectly preserved 1903 rail car next to the restaurant before you dine.

Pete's Rocky Mountain Pizza Co. 104 Canyon St ☎406/646-7820. Busy family restaurant with a varied menu of pastas – you can order the spaghetti with either meatballs ($10) or hot Italian elk sausage ($11) – plus build-your-own pizzas.

Running Bear Pancake House 538 Madison Ave ☎406/646-7703. The first place to come for a filling, affordable breakfast. The friendly servers' most popular order is the plate-sized pancakes served with huckleberry syrup, though the omelettes and biscuits and gravy are tasty as well. Lunch options include fish 'n' chips, sandwiches and a few Mexican dishes like burritos and quesadillas. Open daily 7am–2pm.

Three Bears Restaurant 215 Yellowstone Ave ☎406/646-7811. Popular restaurant with a cozy log interior and interesting old black-and-white photos and artifacts around the walls. Good range of American cuisine – save room for the Apple Brown Betty a la Mode dessert – and dinner shouldn't cost more than $20. Open for breakfast (from 6.30am) as well.

Timberline Café 135 Yellowstone Ave ☎406/646-9349. Next door to the *Madison Hotel*, this diner serves filling platters of grub from 6am–10pm throughout the summer. In the morning, $7 will get you eggs, sausage, a stack of pancakes and coffee, with omelettes running a dollar more. Lunches are closer to $10, while dinner menu entrees – including standards like country-fried steak and breaded shrimp – average $15. Their homemade pies are well worth calling in for alone.

The Wolf Pack 139 N. Canyon St ☎406/646-7225. West Yellowstone's own brewing company, with a good range of traditionally brewed beers heavy on hoppy flavors. Limited menu as well, but the beer is the main draw.

Outdoor activities

Despite the obvious attractions of the national park, you may want to get out and play outside of its boundaries, not least because there are **fewer restrictions** here on what you can do – mountain bikers and snowmobilers, for instance, will find more trails open to them, and anglers are faced with fewer fishing regulations. The following information details only outdoor activities found outside of Yellowstone and Grand Teton, though most of the outfitters listed have permits to run trips into the parks; for specific details inside the parks, see Chapters 6 and 8 (including winter **snowcoach tours** into the park). For information on the excellent **whitewater rafting** and **downhill skiing** options in Big Sky to the north, see the end of this chapter.

Fishing

The area around West Yellowstone is excellent **fishing** territory. The Madison is within easy reach, with especially good fishing in autumn – at this time large brown trout and rainbows travel into the river from Hebgen Lake for spawning. Huge trophy-sized brownies also lurk in several nearby beaver ponds, for which you'll need a guide or willing local to lead you to. And a short drive west into Idaho on Hwy-20 is the community of **Island Lake**, a paradise for fly-fisherman strung out along the Henry's Fork of the Snake River, regarded as one of the finest dry fly streams in the US. There are numerous fishing outfitters in West Yellowstone, with the three best for information, gear, and guide services being Bud Lilly's Trout Shop, 39 Madison Ave (☎406/646-7801 or 1-800/854-9559, Ⓦwww.budlillys.com), Blue Ribbon Flies, 305 Canyon St (☎406/646-7642, Ⓦwww.blueribbonflies.com), and Jacklin's Flyshop, 105 Yellowstone Ave (☎406/646-7336, Ⓦwww.jacklinsflyshop.com).

Horseback riding

There are good routes for **horseback riding** about ten miles north of town at Whit's Lake Road trailhead on US-287, and also two miles further on at Red Canyon Road, which opens up to great views of the mountains of the Madison Range. Local outfitters include Yellowstone Wilderness Outfitters (Ⓣ406/223-3300, Ⓦwww.yellowstone.ws), along with Diamond P Ranch, 2865 Targhee Pass Hwy (Ⓣ406/646-7246), and Parade Rest Guest Ranch, ten miles west of town at 7979 Grayling Creek (Ⓣ406/646-7217, Ⓦwww.paraderestranch.com). Look at spending around $75 for a four-hour trail ride and $150 per night for accommodation packages.

Mountain biking

Mountain bikers will find some good trails on old logging roads and technical single-track close to West Yellowstone. The eighteen-mile **Rendezvous Trail System** starts from Geyser Street on the south side of town and is especially popular with its mix of rolling terrain and steeper ascents and descents. More details, including trail maps, are available from Free Heel & Wheel, 40 Yellowstone Ave (Ⓣ406/646-7744), and Yellowstone Bicycles, 132 Madison Ave (Ⓣ406/646-7815), who also rent bikes for around $30 per day.

Snowmobiling

The clearest sign of West Yellowstone's dedication to **snowmobiles** is that come winter, the town's main streets are left unplowed so that sleds can zip around in peace (albeit a smelly and noisy peace). The community, which relies heavily on snowmobiling, has taken an economic hit in recent years due to restrictions within Yellowstone (for more information, see p.177). A good percentage of hotels, motels, and restaurants still stay open throughout winter to serve sledders, and you won't win many sled-banning arguments in town (in fact, you're best off not tabling the discussion if that's your belief).

There is no shortage of riding possibilities around town. Along with the necessary **guided tours** into Yellowstone, there are hundreds of miles of **trails** leading from town into Montana, Idaho, and Wyoming, varying from steep expert trails such as the ten-mile Lionhead Loop to Two Top, the first designated snowmobile trail in the US. The trail takes around three hours to complete, although additional loops can shorten or lengthen the ride. The trail begins just west of town and climbs up past several "play areas" to the Continental Divide from where there are magnificent views.

There are almost as many snowmobile **rental outfits** around West Yellowstone as there are miles of trails; among these are Backcountry Adventures (Ⓣ406/646-9317 or 1-800/924-7669, Ⓦwww.backcountry-adventures.com) and Two Top Rentals (Ⓣ406/646-7802 or 1-800/522-7802, Ⓦwww.twotopsnowmobile.com); the *Three Bear Lodge* (see "Accommodation", has the town's best selection of overnight package deals. Daily rates in town start at around $100 per day for basic sleds up to $175 for 700-horsepower monsters; the more environmentally friendly four-stroke engines are not required outside of the park, though conservation-minded visitors should forego a bit of speed and opt for one of them.

Cross-country skiing

As evidenced by the fact the US Ski and Biathlon Team uses the town as a training camp, West Yellowstone boasts excellent **cross-country skiing** trails. The **Rendezvous Trail System** (Ⓦwww.rendezvousskitrails.com) is the big attraction, with over 35 kilometers of groomed trails that start on the south side of town on Geyser Street. Day passes costs $5 and can be purchased at Free Heel and Wheel (see "Mountain biking") or Bud Lily's Trout Shop (see "Fishing", p.229); both shops also rents out skis and snowshoes for around $15 per day. Either store, along with town's main visitor center, should stock a free handout with details on trails into Yellowstone accessed directly from town and via Hwy-191 to the north. From Boundary Street, the **Riverside Trail** ranges up to four miles in length, covering a series of loops along the pretty Madison River. North along Hwy-191, over a half-dozen more trailheads access the park, including long trails along **Specimen Creek** and up **Bighorn Pass**.

Listings

Airlines Skywest is the only commercial airline with flights into West Yellowstone Airport. The following airlines fly into Bozeman's Gallatin Field Airport: Big Sky Airlines, Delta, Horizon, Northwest, and United. See p.22 for contact details.

Car rental West Yellowstone's airport hosts Avis and Budget desks (May–Oct only); in town options are Budget (ⓣ406/646-7735 or 1-800/231-5991, ⓦwww.budget-yellowstone.com) and Big Sky Car Rental (ⓣ406/646-9564 or 1-800/426-7669, ⓦwww.yellowstonevacations.com). Companies at Bozeman's airport include Alamo, Budget, Enterprise, Hertz, and National. See p.27 for contact details.

Hospital The Clinic at West Yellowstone, 236 Yellowstone Ave (ⓣ406/646-0200).

Internet Several shops in town offer access, including Send It Home, 27 Madison Ave (Mon–Fri 9am–9pm, Sun 9am–7pm; $5 half-hour).

Laundry There are several laundromats in town, including Swan Cleaners, 510 Madison Ave, and one attached to the Econ-Mart at 307 Firehole Ave.

Library Dunraven Street between Madison and Yellowstone avenues (Tues and Thurs 10am–6pm, Wed 10am–8pm, Fri 10am–5pm, Sat 10am–3pm; closed Sun and Mon).

Police Emergencies ⓣ911; the local station is at 124 Yellowstone Ave (ⓣ406/646-7600).

Post office 209 Grizzly Ave (24hr lobby; desk open Mon–Fr 8.30am–5pm).

Supermarket Market Place Supermarket, 22 Madison Ave (daily 7am–10pm).

Big Sky and the Gallatin Valley

North of West Yellowstone, an hour's drive on Hwy-191 leads to **BIG SKY**. Centered around towering **Lone Mountain** in the winter and the fast-moving **Gallatin River** in the summer, the resort area is blessed with an outstanding selection of outdoor activities, along with some of Montana's best upmarket restaurants and lodges. There are still places to camp or bed down on the cheap, but as the Sotheby's real-estate signs dotting the landscape attest, Big Sky now competes with Jackson, Wyoming, in attracting the moneyed elite. Unlike Jackson, however, there's no town center to speak of, and even with a new slopeside base village being built, the area's Achilles' heel remains a serious lack of things to see or do once you've had your fill of strenuous activities and gourmet cuisine.

Fortunately, much of the area's development boom has been clustered around the bases of the two ski resorts or hidden off the road in small subdivisions, and the drive north from West Yellowstone is defined by its scenic splendor. The first half of the drive on Hwy-191 weaves in and out of Yellowstone (the sole highway in the park with a speed limit of 55mph), past deep-green forested hills and the occasional patch of burnt woods. As with any highway in the region, be alert for animal crossings; over the past decade, several wolves have been hit

△ Lone Mountain

and killed along this stretch. Cross-country skiing and hiking **trailheads** line the route, with the most popular – Gneiss Creek, Bighorn Pass and Specimen Creek – leading east into the Gallatin Range in Yellowstone's little-visited northwest corner.

Between the latter two trailheads, Hwy-191 passes by the Gallatin River's source, from where the natural beauty only increases. Following the clear waters as they flow out of the park and north past Big Sky and onwards to **Bozeman**, the roadway is framed on either side by steep crags and forested hillsides rising to the Gallatin Range to the east and the Madison Range to the west. The twisty highway was constructed in 1911, and ever since has been a major artery for travelers to Yellowstone, who can get their first eyeful of the region's **wildlife** en route as moose are frequently photographed munching on riverside willows and bighorn sheep spotted grazing roadside. Also commonly seen are the fishermen and rafters that flock to the river. One sight you certainly won't miss is the magnificent Lone Mountain, an 11,166ft pyramid of snow and rock that dominates the western skyline, attracting adventure-minded skiers and snowboarders looking to test their mettle on the connected runs at **Big Sky Resort** and smaller **Moonlight Basin**.

Orientation and information

Bozeman is 45 miles to the north of Big Sky, and you won't get lost traveling south through the scenic Gallatin Valley en route as the only major road is Hwy-191, with just the occasional turnoff into the mountains either side. The one turnoff you won't want to miss is Hwy-64 (Big Sky Spur Road) leading west up to Big Sky Resort, located approximately 50 miles from both West Yellowstone and Bozeman. At the turnoff, look for the unostentatious **Soldier's Chapel**, a small log building commemorating Montana soldiers who died in World War II; step inside to see the window behind the altar that perfectly frames Lone Mountain's peak. Karst Stage, Inc. (Ⓣ406/556-3540 or 1-800/287-4759, Ⓦwww.karststage.com) runs shuttle **buses** from Bozeman's airport Big Sky; reservations essential and rates depend on passenger numbers.

On the eight-mile drive up to Big Sky Resort's **Mountain Village**, you'll pass the small settlements of **Meadow Village**, a couple of miles after the turnoff, and **West Fork Meadows**, about four miles further up the road. Both have been built to cater to the tourist trade and part-time residents, and have regular **shuttle services** to and from the ski slopes. For more information on the area, check in with the Big Sky **chamber of commerce** (Ⓣ406/995-3000 or 1-800/943-4111, Ⓦwww.bigskychamber.com), or look out the free *Big Sky Weekly* newspaper.

Accommodation

Where you choose **to stay** depends largely on the season. In winter, try to get accommodation in Mountain Village if you can afford it as it saves the drive up to the ski hill, a hassle after heavy snow. Slopeside accommodation is run by Big Sky Resort (Ⓣ1-800/548-4486, Ⓦwww.bigskyresort.com), including a wide array of popular condominiums. In summer, options lower down are better for their proximity to the river and hiking trails within the Gallatin Valley. If roughing it, there are several of **campgrounds** ($11) in the surrounding Gallatin National Forest. The USFS also manages a sprinkling of **backcountry cabins** ($20–30) equipped with wood stoves and cots or bunk beds; some cabins you can drive to, others require a hike. For more information, contact the Bozeman District Office (Ⓣ406/522-2520, Ⓦwww.fs.fed.us/r1/gallatin/).

Mountain Village

Huntley Lodge Big Sky Resort. The resort's original and most affordable hotel received a facelift several years back, sprucing up the still rather drab rooms a notch. The facilities, though, are excellent, and include a swimming pool, hot tubs, workout room, and the popular *Chet's Bar and Grill*. Rates include an incredible buffet breakfast, and ski-and-stay packages help cut the cost. Doubles $175.

Shoshone Condominium Hotel Big Sky Resort. Ski-in, ski-out suites with private bedrooms, full kitchens, gas fireplaces, and balconies, plus access to *Huntley Lodge*'s health club, sauna, steam room, and lap pool. In summer a four-person condo can be had for little more than $225 per night; in winter, expect to pay $100 more at least.

Summit at Big Sky Big Sky Resort. Opened in 2000 and the most modern of Big Sky Resort's accommodations, the ten-storey *Summit* features large, elegant rooms, most with good mountain views along with wet bars, small kitchens, fireplaces, and large tubs. There is also a workout room and an onsite spa. Hotel rooms start at around $200, with condo-accommodations kicking off at $350 and reaching over $2000 per night.

Off-mountain

Best Western Bucks T-4 Lodge Hwy-191, less than a mile south of the Big Sky turnoff Ⓣ406/995-4111 or 1-800/822-4484, Ⓦwww.buckst4.com. *Bucks*, a former hunting lodge, exudes far more personality than most *Best Westerns*. Though rooms are standard – comfortable queen beds, TV, coffeemaker, free wireless Internet – the common areas are anything but, including a pleasant lobby with fireplace, large country hall hosting the occasional concert and a highly recommended restaurant (see p.237).

Rates include a buffet breakfast. Doubles average $120 a night.

Comfort Inn Hwy-191, less than a mile south of the Big Sky turnoff ⓣ406/995-2333 or 1-800/228-5150, ⓦwww.comfortinnbigsky.com. A relatively new addition, this chain motel has added a much-needed dose of affordable accommodation in Big Sky. There are over sixty rooms in total; facilities include an indoor pool (with long water slide) and laundry. A standard double with two queen beds averages $85, and several larger family suites ($100–150) are available. Continental breakfast included.

The Corral Motel Hwy-191, five miles south of Big Sky turnoff ⓣ406/995-4249, ⓦwww.corralbar.com. This small motel, attached to the valley's most popular roadhouse), is most popular with snowmobile enthusiasts in winter, though a shuttle is available for the longish drive to Big Sky's slopes. Come summer, it's well located for rafting and horseback riding, and the clean if plain rooms all include queen beds, cable TV and access to a large hot tub. A double room averages $60, while the available quad room is a deal at $80.

Rainbow Ranch Lodge Hwy-191, five miles south of Big Sky turnoff ⓣ406/995-4132 or 1-800/937-4132, ⓦwww.rainbowranch.com. Relaxed, luxury accommodation only a few steps from the Gallatin River. Accommodations are mixed between individually decorated rooms – including new larger suites with a fireplace overlooking a stocked trout pond – and deluxe cabins. There's an outdoor hot tub, Western lounge featuring a roaring fireplace and overstuffed leather couches, and a very fine restaurant and wine cellar. Rates in summer start at close to $300 per night.

Big Sky Resort

Rugged and crowd-free, the best single word to describe **Big Sky Resort** is massive. Indeed, now that the resort has teamed up with neighbor and one-time bitter rival Moonlight Basin (see p.235) to offer access to both trail networks, the combined 5300 acres of terrain makes this the largest ski area in the country. The brainchild of American newscaster Chet Huntley, who, with other major investors bought a huge chunk of Lone Mountain in 1969, current owners Boyne Developments have massive designs of their own; a decade-long plan to build a pedestrian village similar to those at Whistler in British Columbia and Keystone in Colorado has begun, though for now nature still holds the upper hand at the wild ski hill where moose and bear sightings are not unheard of.

The resort's terrain spreads across three mountains (Lone Mountain 11,166ft, Andesite Mountain 8800ft, and Flat Iron Mountain 8092ft), with 3600 acres open to **skiing and snowboarding** and the third longest **vertical drop** (4350ft) on the continent (only Whistler and Snowmass, Colorado, have bigger drops). Lines at the fourteen lifts are virtually unheard of, and the only place you'll wait is for a ride up the thrilling fifteen-passenger Lone Mountain Tram, topping out at to the summit of Lone Mountain and coming within an arm's breadth of the mountain's vertiginous crags. The **annual snowfall** is a mighty 400 inches, and the resort can open as early as October (weekends only), though the official season lasts from mid-November to mid-April.

Beginners may feel a little left out here; green runs make up only fifteen percent of the mountain, while twice that are rated intermediate blues and the rest are designated blacks. Intermediates will love cruisers such as Bighorn on Andesite Mountain for its reasonably challenging pitch and wide-open curves. Advanced skiers have a huge range of options, from the bumps of Snake Pit and Mad Wolf on Andesite to the big bowl beneath Turkey Traverse or the double-blacks beneath the aptly named Challenger Lift on Lone Peak. Experts will want to take on the challenge of the fantastically steep double-black runs high up Lone Peak, including perhaps **Big Couloir** and even nastier **Little Couloir**, 45-degree slopes that requires you to have a partner and avalanche rescue gear. Freestyle riders will want to head over to Andesite Mountain, where there's a **terrain park** and **half-pipe**, though the natural gully on the front face of Lone Peak is a blast as well.

Cross country skiers will find 80 kilometers of top-notch trails at Lone Mountain Ranch (Ⓣ406/995-4644, Ⓦwww.lmranch.com), a couple of miles down the spur road from Mountain Village (passes $12; rentals $17). **Summers** around the resort are laid-back to the point of boredom, with most business coming in from corporate conventions. There's decent hiking around Lone Mountain, and lift-accessed **mountain biking** is also available (daily 9.30am–4.30pm June–Oct; starts at $35, including rental), but there's more to do and see down in the valley.

Big Sky Resort practicalities

With so much terrain, it takes several days at Big Sky (Ⓣ1-800/548-4487, Ⓦwww.bigskyresort.com) to cover everything. It makes little sense therefore to splurge on the combined Big Sky/Moonlight **Lone Peak Pass** ($78), an option better left for expert locals and their season passes. **Lift tickets** for just Big Sky start at $65 per day, with slight discounts on multiday purchases. Facilities include *The Dugout* on Andesite Mountain, which does good barbecues, and several restaurants and ski and board rental shops in the Mountain Village – expect to pay around $30 a day for skis or board rental. If you're staying down below, there's a free **shuttle** bus between the villages from 7am–11pm.

Moonlight Basin Resort

Sharing Lone Mountain to the north of Big Sky Resort, **Moonlight Basin** (Ⓣ1-877-822-0430, Ⓦwww.moonlightbasin.com) opened its ski area in 2003, the final piece to a real estate development over a decade in the making. Already at odds with their larger neighbor, within a year the two sides were battling out in court, allegations of trespassing and even errant avalanche explosions being lobbed back and forth. The fight wasn't helping either side win positive publicity or, more importantly, real estate sales, and the resorts reconciled and announced a partnership in 2005. While great for media hype, for most skiers the interconnected trails means nothing more than a more expense lift ticket option, and the average visitor should only head to Moonlight's **1900 acres** of terrain open to skiing after they've tested out Big Sky's offerings. **Lift tickets** at the smaller resort start at $47, and access a quirky network of trails that are flat at the bottom and scarily steep at the top, with not a great deal in between. The one group who has gained most from the combined pass are adrenalin-junky skiers and boarders, who can now ride up Big Sky's Challenger lift to quickly access the double-black diamonds of Moonlight's **Headwater Chutes**. Likewise, Moonlight's daring **North Summit Snowfield** can only be accessed via Big Sky; both zones are seriously experts-only, and should only be attempted with a knowledgeable local in tow.

The Gallatin Valley

Despite the fact that Hwy-191 follows nearly every twist and turn of the **GALLATIN VALLEY** and its eponymous river, this detracts very little from the beauty of one of Montana's finest fly-fishing regions and the filming location for much of *A River Runs Through It*. But keep your eyes glued to the road when driving as this is reputedly one of the most accident-prone stretches of highway in the state.

In summer, **whitewater rafting** is the biggest draw, and enthusiasts will find plenty of challenges on the river here – stretches such as the "Mad Mile" on its upper reaches have plenty of Class IV–V rapids. Be prepared to get soaked and freeze a bit; outfitters supply wetsuits, but the water is still frigid year-round. One of the best local guides is Geyser Whitewater Expeditions, located due south of the Big Sky turnoff (Ⓣ406/995-4989 or 1-800/914-9031, Ⓦwww.raftmontana.com), with half-day trips ($46) ranging from a scenic float to a thrilling run through the rapids, along with a strenuous full-day voyage that combines both with a deli lunch ($82).

Anglers can pretty much pull off the road anywhere to access quality fishing, and while boat fishing is prohibited on the Gallatin, there's no closed fishing season; drive past in winter and you'll spot dedicated anglers clearing ice from their lines as they stand waist deep in the river. Some of the best access points include the *Greek Creek* and *Red Cliff* campgrounds (both off Hwy-191 in the Gallatin Canyon), but first-timers should consider a guide as the river is fast and lined with deep holes. One of the best local outfitters is Gallatin River Guides (Ⓣ406/995-2290, Ⓦwww.montanaflyfishing.com), with a well-stocked shop on Hwy-191 a half-mile south of the Big Sky Resort intersection.

With spectacular mountains either side of the valley and 25 peaks over 10,000ft in the Gallatin Range alone, this is not an area short of great **hiking** and **climbing** opportunities. One of the most popular spots to trek in is the **Lee Metcalf Wilderness Area**, which runs west of the valley along much of the Madison Range. Within the wilderness area, the **Spanish Peaks** are laced with some unforgettable hiking trails, although their height means the upper reaches are still covered in snow until July. Both Big Sky's chamber and the Gallatin National Forest's Bozeman District Office (Ⓣ406/522-2520, Ⓦwww.fs.fed.us/r1/gallatin/) can supply trail guides. If you'd rather ride than walk into the wilds, several ranches in the area offer one-hour ($30–35) to week-long trips on **horseback**; one of the longest established is the *320 Guest Ranch* (Ⓣ406/995-4283 or 1-800/243-0320, Ⓦwww.320ranch.com), found a dozen miles south of the Big Sky turnoff.

Eating and drinking

One thing you won't go short on around Big Sky is good food – there's a wide selection of memorable dining spots both on the mountain, in the villages below, and strung out along the Gallatin Valley, from high-end, sophisticated **restaurants** to true-grit Western **bars**. A few of the slopeside bars and restaurants stay open year-round, but be warned that in summer things are rather dead; even in winter, things are on the mellow side, and skiers requiring a more rowdy scene should consider Jackson Hole instead.

Mountain Village

Bambu Arrowhead Mall Ⓣ406/995-4933. Pan-Asia bistro with a menu touching on all the hits, from sushi to pad thai (mains $8–20). Best for its late night scene, when an international crew of seasonal employees hit the dance floor.

Chet's Bar & Grill Ⓣ406/995-5784. Located in *Huntley Lodge* and generally busy immediately after the lifts close thanks to a happy hour that includes nightly entertainment. If you stay around after happy hour try the smoked pheasant quesadilla appetizer, or the char-grilled buffalo strip steak main. Appetizers average $10, entrees $15 up.

Mountain Top Pizza Mountain Mall ☎406/995-4646. Decent pizzas and salads served from lunchtime onwards. Expect to pay around $14 for a large with a few toppings; free delivery.

M.R. Hummers Mountain Mall ☎406/995-4343. One of the most popular apres-ski spots in the village, with good baby back ribs to go with your beer, and filling sandwiches for around $10.

Off-mountain

Allgood's Westfork Meadows ☎406/995-2750. Attracting a younger crowd, this bar and grill specializes in barbecued ribs and chicken ($12–14) and is also open for breakfasts (omelettes $6–8). The lively bar has a pool table, darts, and poker.

Blue Moon Bakery Westfork Meadows ☎406/995-2305. Good coffee and freshly baked bagels and pastries make this a great breakfast stop on the way up Lone Mountain. During the lunch and dinner hours, the menu expands to include pizzas, pastas, salads, and sandwiches.

Bucks T-4 Hwy-191, less than a mile south of Big Sky turnoff ☎406/995-4111. Probably the only *Best Western* restaurant featured in *Gourmet* and *Wine Spectator* magazines, *Bucks* specializes in imaginatively prepared exotic and local game. Standout entrees include the grilled venison drizzled in port-wine butter and the bacon-wrapped pheasant breast. Mains run from $25 to $40, and reservations are essential.

The Corral Hwy-191, five miles south of Big Sky turnoff ☎406/995-4249. Open for breakfast from 7am, but it's the buffalo burgers ($9), prime rib ($20–30), and local rainbow trout ($19) for lunch and dinner that make *The Corral* worth a visit. It's also *the* place to come in the valley for a brew in a genuine Western roadhouse atmosphere; the attached motel is handy if you've had one too many.

Rainbow Ranch Lodge Hwy-191, five miles south of Big Sky turnoff ☎406/995-4132. Expensive, but mains like a gorgonzola-crusted buffalo rib-eye ($35) and fine starters like a goat cheese ravioli with arugula pesto ($8) make dinner here well worth the splurge. Ask to see the Bacchus Room, an extraordinary 10,000-bottle wine cellar with a private dining table.

13

Gardiner and the Paradise Valley

The only Yellowstone access point open to cars year-round, the dusty Montana town of **GARDINER** is only five miles north of park headquarters at Mammoth. Strung above the Yellowstone River in desert-like surroundings, the town's more often than not the hottest and driest spot in and around the park, averaging a paltry ten inches of rain a year. What Gardiner lacks in precipitation it makes up for in hospitality; compared to the other gateway towns, it's not as isolated as Cooke City, as far off as Cody, or as over-commercialized as West Yellowstone. And as for comparing the easy-going place to the region's most famous town to the south, a popular local t-shirt states the case best – "Gardiner: It Ain't No Jackson Hole."

Though named after the fur trapper Johnson Gardner (see box, below), the town, like so many in the West, owes its existence to miners and then the railroad. The Northern Pacific's spur line from Livingston fifty-miles to the north didn't actually terminate in Gardiner until 1902, but for decades passengers – making up the first major wave of Yellowstone tourists – were shuttled here on stagecoaches

There's no "I" in Gardner: Gardner vs. Gardiner

After tumbling down Osprey Falls, the **Gardner River** flows north alongside the North Entrance Road and then spills into the Yellowstone River just east of **Gardiner**, the town. Driving alongside the river, many first-time visitors understandably think they've uncovered a misspelled sign or map, and in a way they have, although the typo dates back well over a century. A tough character who allegedly scalped his fair share of Indians and met his doom in a similar manner, fur-trapper **Johnson Gardner** trudged through the area's dry valleys in the 1830s, and in the same way Davey Jackson earned lasting fame with Jackson's Hole to the south, the headwaters of the local river soon became known as Gardner's Hole. The name stuck until the Washburn Expedition rolled through in 1870. Famed teller of tales **Jim Bridger** (see box, p.64) was working in the area, and when asked for the name of the river, it's believed his thick Virginia accent added an "i" sound between the two syllables. "Gard-i-ner" was thus born on the expedition's maps, and the name stuck until new map projects in the 1940s changed the river's name back to its proper spelling. By that time the town had long been settled, however, and its name remained unchanged.

from the Cinnabar terminus in the **Paradise Valley**, twenty miles north. Gardiner still retains a faint whiff of the frontier about it, and there's a laidback quality to the town's relationship with world famous Yellowstone and the tourists it brings in; many of the region's biologists and naturalists live here, and the **Yellowstone Heritage and Research Center** opened next door to the town's school in 2005.

North of Gardiner, the scenic Paradise Valley is well worth a visit, even if it's only to enjoy the roadside views. Active pursuits in the valley center mainly around the Yellowstone River, with the firm favorite being a **whitewater rafting** trip through narrow Yankee Jim Canyon. Kayakers and fly-fishers also flock to the river, but for the most relaxing of all water-based recreations head for the mineral baths at **Chico Hot Springs**, a 45-minute drive north of town.

Arrival and information

The closet major **airport** to Gardiner is in Bozeman, 75 miles away. Karst Stage, Inc. (ⓣ406/556-3540 or 1-800/287-4759, ⓦwww.karststage.com) runs shuttle **buses** from the airport to Gardiner, along with Chico Hot Springs and Mammoth; reservations are essential and rates depend on passenger numbers. You'll find tourist **information** at the Gardiner Chamber of Commerce on Park Street (late-May to early Sept Mon–Fri 8am–8pm, 10am–6pm Sat & Sun; rest of year Mon–Fri 10am–3pm; ⓣ406/848-7971, ⓦwww.gardinerchamber.com); for outdoor recreation information outside of Yellowstone contact the USFS Gallatin National Forest Gardiner Ranger Station, 805 Scott Street (Mon–Fri 8am–5pm; ⓣ406/848-7375). The **post office** is on Scott Street, and **Internet access** is available for fifteen cents per minute from *Racoons* on Park Street. If you're around in mid-June you may catch the small-scale **Gardiner Rodeo**, while late-September's **Brew Festival** features breweries from Montana, Wyoming, and Idaho sharing samples of their tipple in Arch Park.

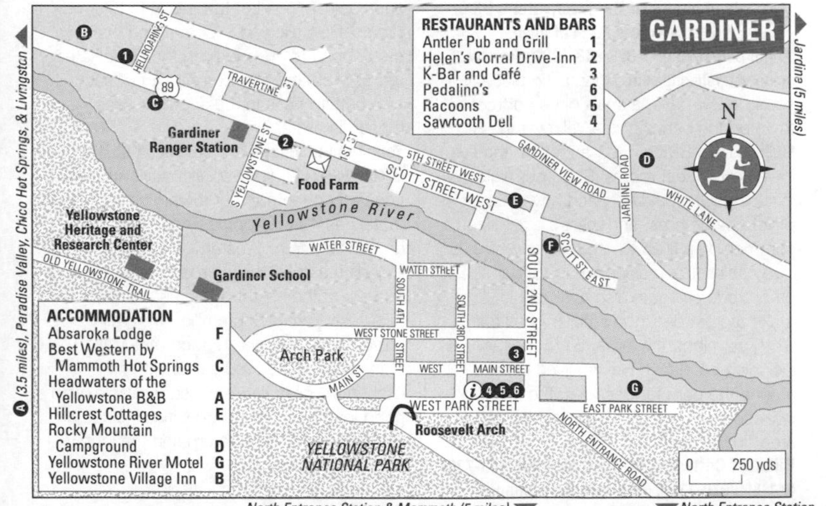

Accommodation

Gardiner has a fair selection of mid-range **accommodation**, but it can be booked up in summer, so it pays to make reservations. Scott Street (Hwy-89) is the main strip for chain motels such as a *Comfort Inn* and *Super 8*, but even their prices are not especially cheap ($80–100 per night in July and August). If **camping**, Mammoth's campground is only four miles away, and there are also several USFS **campgrounds** in the area. Closest is the *Eagle Creek Campground* (16 sites; $7), two miles north of Gardiner on a steep dirt road en route to Jardine; the nearest site on Hwy-89 north of town via the Paradise Valley is the *Canyon Campground* (16 sites; $7), seventeen miles away. Both sites are very basic and open all year.

Absaroka Lodge **310 Scott St ⓣ406/848-7414 or 1-800/755-7414, ⓦwww.yellowstonemotel.com.** Great location on the north side of Yellowstone Bridge, and all of the pleasant if plain rooms at this motel have small TVs and decks overlooking the river. Open year-round, double rooms with two queen beds are $95 mid-June through late Sept, $10 more for a kitchen suite. Off-season rates dip to as low as $45 a night.

Best Western by Mammoth Hot Springs **Scott Street ⓣ406/848-7311 or 1-800/828-9080, ⓦwww.bestwestern.com/mammothhotsprings.** One of the more upmarket options, on the western edge of town, this chain hotel offers spacious rooms, a large indoor pool, hot tub, sauna, and Internet, plus restaurant, lounge, and casino. Rates vary throughout the year, with a standard room costing $135 in the heart of summer and dipping to $60 in the off-season. Family-suites with kitchen sleeping up to six also available.

Headwaters of the Yellowstone B&B **Hwy-89, 3.5 miles north of town ⓣ406/848-7073 or 1-888/848-7220, ⓦwww.headwatersbandb.com.** A fantastic place to spend a few days, a short drive north of town on the banks of the Yellowstone River. Built to be a B&B on a 3-acre plot, the five lower-level guest rooms ($120 per night, including full breakfast) each have their own private bathrooms, and there's a fair sized common area filled with books and local art. Two cabins – one sleeping up to four, the other up to six – are also available and make a great deal: the smaller goes for $145 per night, the larger $175, neither including breakfast. Having lived in and around the park for decades, the friendly innkeepers will gladly help in setting up an area itinerary.

Hillcrest Cottages **200 Scott St ⓣ406/848-7353 or 1-800/970-7353, ⓦwww.hillcrescottages.** Within walking distance of Park Street, the collection of seventeen cottages available here, from tiny one-room units to two-bedrooms sleeping up to eight, make up one of Gardiner's most affordable options. Though basic and dated, most of the cottages come with kitchenettes, and with rates starting at $65 ($135 for the biggest unit) there's little reason to complain.

Rocky Mountain Campground **Jardine Road ⓣ406/848-7251.** One of two campgrounds catering mainly to RVs in town. The 55 RV spots cost $43 per night July and August, $28 at other times. There's a few grassy tent sites available, along with a store, laundry, showers, and wireless Internet access. Fine views of the river below, with trail access for the fishing set.

Yellowstone River Motel **14 Park St ⓣ406/848-7303 or 1-888/797-4837, ⓦwww.yellowstonerivermotel.com.** Clean if a bit musty motel accommodation with phones and cable TV in all of the nearly forty small rooms. Pets allowed in some, and there's a pretty bbq area overlooking the river. Rates run $75–85 throughout the heart of summer, with better prices in the shoulder seasons. Closed in winter.

Yellowstone Village Inn **1102 Scott St ⓣ406/848-7417, ⓦwww.yellowstonevinn.com.** Located on the edge of town, this high-end motel has 43 tidy rooms, most themed around wildlife or Western Americana, including a John Wayne room. Doubles cost $85–95 at the height of the season from mid-June to mid-September, with rates halved from October through mid-May. Three carpeted condo suites with full kitchen sleeping 4–6 are also available, with good long-stay deals. Amenities include an indoor pool, wireless Internet in the lobby, and onsite laundry.

The Town

Supporting a population of just under one thousand, Gardiner is split in two by the **Yellowstone River**. There's no real town center, and the north side is dominated by a strip of motels, restaurants, and tourist facilities along Hwy-89 – known as **Scott Street** as it runs through town parallel to the river, and then 2nd Street once it turns south and crosses the Yellowstone Bridge to the south side of town. This southern side is older and more attractive, with elk and deer seen grazing in local gardens bordering parklands. The main thoroughfare here, **Park Street**, makes for a short but enjoyable stroll, lined as it is with ice cream shops, saloons, and the town's visitor center. At street's end looms the **Roosevelt Arch**, marking the entrance to the park and dedicated in 1903 by President Teddy Roosevelt in front of several thousand people at the tail end of his two-week trip into the Yellowstone. Bearing the inscription "For the benefit and enjoyment of the people," the stone structure was designed by the park's head engineer Hiram Chittenden to erase visitors' "very unfavorable" first impression of the arid north entrance area, and it remains a popular photo-stop today.

A short dive past the arch and built a century later is the **Yellowstone Heritage and Research Center** (Ⓣ307/344-2664, Ⓦwww.nps.gov/yell/technical/museum; Mon–Fri 8am–5pm), housing more than 5 million items in its various collections, making it the second largest such archive in the Park Service behind New Jersey's Thomas Edison National Historic Site. Opened in 2005, artifacts inside the attractive facility include several of painter Thomas Moran's original field sketches from the Hayden Survey of 1872, journals and notes dating from early explorers and army officials up to last year's ranger logbooks, thousands of pieces of antique furniture and souveniers, and even the skulls of the original 14 wolves reintroduced in 1995. It's a remarkable collection – much of it moved from the leaky basement in Mammoth's Albright Visitor Center – that is unfortunately mainly open only to biologists, geologists, writers, and other accredited researchers. The center, however, does offer limited but very worthwhile hour-long **tours** of the collection to the general public (late May to early Sept Tues & Thurs; free); reservations several days in advance are required. The onsite **library** (Tues–Fri) is open to all during business hours.

Eating and drinking

In keeping with the town's stripped-down take on tourism, there's not a whole lot of variety to Gardiner's collection of **restaurants** and **bars**. While hungry diners can easily fill up on burgers and pizzas, there's little else on offer. Bar goers will have no trouble finding a place to down a drink, as several saloons line Park and Main streets; when there's a big game on, you'll be able to catch it at any of them, though take extra caution if driving back into the park afterwards as the winding road to Mammoth is dark and elk-crossings are frequent. As for **supermarkets**, head for the Northern Entrance Food Farm at 701 Scott Street (Mon–Sat 7am–9pm, Sun 8am–8pm).

Antler Pub and Grill 107 Hellsroaring St Ⓣ406/848-7536. Located inside the lobby of the *Comfort Inn*, this green-carpeted restaurant with bar upstairs certainly won't be winning any design awards. The food, however, is some of the best in town, with a menu created by the cook at the town's now-defunct *Park City Grill*. Mains include the likes of pepper steak ($21), filet mignon ($25), and several pasta dishes including the Crazy Pasta, a surprisingly good blend of penne, Italian sausage, chicken, red peppers, and more.

Helen's Corral Drive-Inn south side of Scott Street, half mile west of 2nd St bridge ⓣ406/848-7627. This unassuming burger shack with covered picnic tables out front makes for the perfect reward after a long hike or overnight stays in the backcountry. Things are certainly greasy, but the legendary burgers ($5–8) are huge, juicy, and delicious, and the thick milkshakes are impossible to pass up. For a little less grease, opt for a buffalo burger.

K-Bar and Café 202 Main St ⓣ406/848-9995. Basic watering-hole with a bar, slot machines, and pool table upfront, and plain tables in the back. One of their large, run of the mill pizzas costs $14, while a filling calzone goes for $6. No salads served, but there are several varieties of beer on tap.

Pedalino's 204 Park St ⓣ406/848-9950. Formerly the *Park City Grill*, this is one of the town's newest and most upmarket restaurants. Within walking distance of the Roosevelt Arch, the mainly Italian menu includes an array of pastas from around $15 a plate, with steaks costing $10 more. Expect to pay $60 for two, more if you splurge on a bottle of wine from the short list.

Racoons 210 Park St ⓣ406/848-2240. The place to come for a midday break or dessert, featuring heaping ice cream cones and thick milkshakes to go with a variety of espresso-drinks. Internet access also available on a series of computers for 15-cents a minute.

Sawtooth Deli 220 Park St ⓣ406/848-7600. A friendly deli featuring good-sized hot and cold sandwiches ($7) and salads, plus vegetarian specials, and there's a covered outdoor patio for dining and a nightly barbecue pit. Open June–Sept 8am–9pm, with limited hours in shoulder seasons; closed winter.

Outdoor activities

As float trips on the Yellowstone River are banned within the park, Gardiner has become a popular base for **whitewater rafting** trips north of the boundary line. While the rapids are not as ferocious as those on the Gallatin River in Big Sky (see p.236), there are still some rollicking Class III rapids to negotiate, and leaving from Gardiner to float north through the Paradise Valley on the wide river, past clusters of speedy pronghorn and graceful grazing elk, is wonderful way to spend a summer day. The longest-established outfitter in town is the Yellowstone Raft Company (ⓣ1-800/858-7781, ⓦwww.yellowstoneraft.com), with half-day trips costing $33 and full-day $72; also recommended is Montana Whitewater (ⓣ1-800/799-4465, ⓦwww.montanawhitewater.com), with similar trips and rates. Both rent **kayaks** as well. **Anglers** should call in at Park's Fly Shop, 2nd Street between Stone and Main (ⓣ406/848-7314, ⓦwww.parksflyshop.com), for a free fishing map of Yellowstone National Park and the Gallatin and Missouri rivers. In business for over fifty years, the splendid shop stocks both fly tackle and spinning gear, and runs guided trips at $350 for a full day with two anglers. Come winter, the store is also the best place for **cross-country ski** rentals ($13 per day, third day free) and information on the park's Nordic trails. Good **horseback** riding trips into Yellowstone and the Absaroka-Beartooth Wilderness are offered by North Fork Creek Outfitters (ⓣ406/848-7859, ⓦwww.northforkcreekoutfitters.com); they also run **hunting** trips in the Fall, mainly for elk and mule deer, though a limited amount of tags for bear, moose, bighorn sheep, and even mountain lions are made available each year. Wolf permits have not yet been offered, though the trigger-fingers of some less conservation-minded local hunting guides are itching at the prospect.

The Paradise Valley

North of Gardiner, Hwy-89 leads into the **Paradise Valley**, weaving between the **Absaroka Mountains** and the **Gallatin Range** on its way to Livingston just over fifty miles away. This was the first access route to Yellowstone and is still one of the most popular, though activities in the valley itself are increasingly causing folks to stick around for a day or two instead of zipping straight through. The Yellowstone River flowing along the valley floor is the longest undammed river in the lower 48, running some 680 miles east to join the Missouri in North Dakota. Its route here is paralleled by Hwy-89, along with the less traveled East River Road (Hwy-540) in the valley's northern half, a considerably narrower drive that gives you a better feel for the valley and landscape.

Between Gardiner and Livingston there are few settlements of any real size, and much of the land is taken up by large ranches – some of them the second homes of Hollywood stars – as well as the compound of the **Church Universal and Triumphant**, whose retired leader Elizabeth Clare Prophet unsuccessfully predicted Armageddon several times throughout the 1980s and '90s, leading members to build massive bomb-shelters within the complex. The once icy relationship between Yellowstone and the church has thawed in recent years due to large land donations and an overall mellowing out of the church. One can only guess, however, what these new age churchgoers think of **Devil's Slide**, the first sight of note heading north out of Gardiner. A pullout five miles from town gives the best view onto this geological oddity, a long red gash cutting down the face of Cinnabar Mountain, caused by the oxidation of iron in the rock-face. Also nearby, look out for the steam rising from **LaDuke Hot Springs** spilling into the river. If you haven't spotted a bighorn sheep yet, take your time here as well; a series of turnouts access some of the best viewing areas in the entire region.

Continuing north, Hwy-89 passes several access points for fishing and floating on the Yellowstone, before diving into **Yankee Jim Canyon**, named after Jim George, who dynamited a toll road to Yellowstone through here in the 1870s; the railroads soon followed, buying out his right-of-way and laying

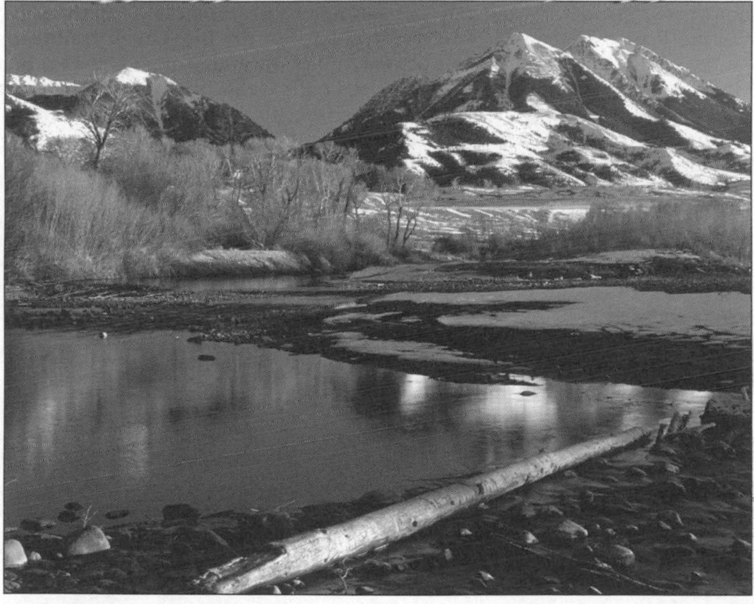

△ Absaroka mountains

down tracks to Gardiner. There's an easy interpretive trail on the river's western banks exploring the history of transportation through the narrow canyon, along with the Gallatin National Forest's *Canyon Campground* (18 site; $12). Cruising into the scenic heart of the Paradise Valley, the highway passes by the last turnoff of note before Livingston, a side road some thirty miles from Gardiner heading to **Chico Hot Springs** (Ⓣ406/333-4933 or 1-800/468-9232, Ⓦwww.chicohotsprings.com). The low-key resort has been pulling people in to soak in its naturally fed swimming pools for over a century (daily 6am–midnight; $6.50 non-guests); the attendant main lodge is suitably decked out in antiques and has three floors of small, but atmospheric rooms. Several other more-expensive accommodation options – including fully equipped cabins and even houses – are on offer, as is the valley's finest **restaurant**, featuring delicious stuffed pork chops ($24) and a renowned beef Wellington for two ($50). The poolside **bar**, a classic honky-tonk, is well worth a visit.

Outdoor activities

Often dry and dusty due to drought conditions, the Paradise Valley offers up plenty of worthwhile **outdoor activities**. The Yellowstone River here is yet another prime local fly-fishing area, usually at its best from July to September. It's also popular with rafters; any of Gardiner's outfitters can help get you out on the water.

As for hiking, one of the best overnight options leads up to the foothills of the somewhat forbidding **Mount Cowen**, at 11,206ft the highest point in the Absarokas. It's a tough eighteen-mile round-trip that starts easily enough on Trail 51 before turning north on to Upper Sage Creek Trail to climb relentlessly for over 3000ft to Elbow Lake; there are backcountry campsites at the lake. To get to the trailhead turn east onto Mill Creek Road (Forest Road 486) off Hwy-89 about thirty miles north of Gardiner; after eleven miles turn northeast onto Forest Road 3280 and drive a final mile to the trailhead. To explore the Gallatin Range on the valley's west side, check out the **Big Creek trailhead**, on the west side of Hwy-89 about twenty miles north of Gardiner and up Big Creek Road, where there is access to several trails leading up to alpine lakes and high mountain country. Though no trails are specifically marked for **mountain biking**, any route outside the Absaroka-Beartooth Wilderness is open to bikers, and there's a good network of logging and forest service roads in both ranges. For advice on the best riding, stop by the *Sawtooth Deli* in Gardiner, which also rents mountain bikes for $20 a day.

Whether hiking or biking, it pays to be aware that you're in prime **rattlesnake** country; when it's hot, these snakes lurk under bushes and wood debris, and when cooler they sun themselves on hiking paths and on top of rocks. Watch where you step and you should be able to avoid any encounters.

14

Cooke City and around

Hugging the northeast corner of Yellowstone, **COOKE CITY** (7651ft) is the park's least visited gateway, a one-street town that can almost entirely be taken in with a single glance. Surrounded by dense wilderness, the low-key town is accessible year round from the west, as the road through Yellowstone from Gardiner is kept plowed all winter. However, the spectacular **Beartooth Highway** (Hwy-212) to the east is impassable from mid-October to late May, meaning that for much of the year the isolated outpost, home to around only 100 year-round residents, is literally the end of the road. Between Cooke City and the park entrance four miles away sits even tinier **Silver Gate**, whose full-time population come winter dips into the single digits.

Montana's Cooke City got its start around 1870, when a group of trappers found gold in the gravel of **Soda Butte Creek**. They were quickly chased out by Crow Indians, but as news about the discovery leaked out, the natives were inevitably pushed out in exchange for smelters and saloons. In 1882, Cooke City, formerly known as both Galena and Shoofly, was named after a Pacific Railroad contractor promoting the development of the railroad. The railroad never came, hamstringing the hamlet's fortunes that fluctuated with the luck of local mines. Known as the **New World Mining District**, the area was mined extensively for gold, silver, lead, zinc, and copper until the 1950s, when the costs of isolation and heavy winters helped to shutter the mines. Historic ruins now dot the forested hills throughout the area, visited by a mishmash of hikers and off-road vehicles in summer, and cross-country skiers and snowmobilers in winter.

Arrival and information

Located 55 miles from Gardiner, Montana, to the west and eighty miles from Cody, Wyoming, to the south, the national park landscape to Cooke City's west is complemented by the rugged Absaroka-Beartooth Wilderness surrounding the town. The sole road, Hwy-212, is known as **Main Street** as it cuts through town, ending just to the east once snowfall closes the road. Once the highway shuts, dedicated **winter visitors** coming from the east can park near the junction of Hwy-212 and Hwy-296 (Chief Joseph Scenic Byway; see p.260) thirteen miles east and then snowmobile in. Whether or not this is an option, those driving

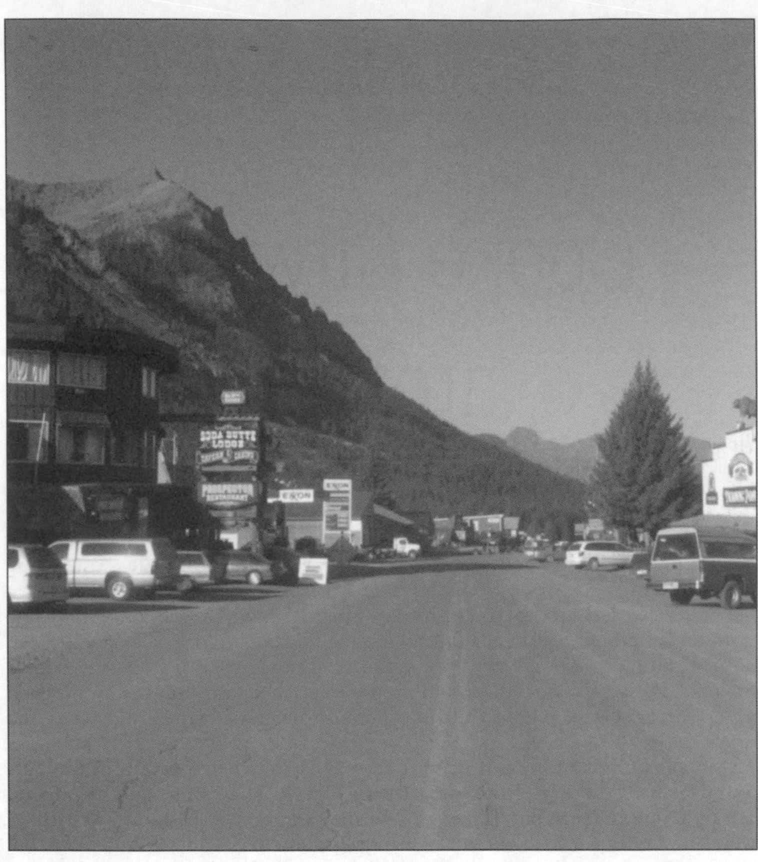

△ Main Stree, Cooke City

hereabouts in spring or fall should check with Montana's road report (Ⓣ1-800/226-7623) for the latest conditions. Housed in a tiny hut toward the bottom end of town is the simple **Cooke City Chamber**, 205 Main Street (late May to mid-September daily 11am–6pm, closed rest of year; Ⓣ406/838-2495, Ⓦwww.cookecitychamber.org), best visited for the backcountry maps on hand.

Accommodation

There's only around a dozen **accommodation** options to choose from in and around Cooke City, split between motel rooms on Main Street and cabin-rentals in the outlying areas, making reservations essential during busy periods. There's no luxury options to speak of, but prices are very reasonable across the board, with little fluctuation between the summer and winter seasons. If pitching a tent, a handful of no-frills Gallatin National Forest **campgrounds** ($10) line Hwy-212 just east of town, while the closest to the west is Yellowstone's *Pebble Creek Campground*, Nine miles from the Northeast Entrance Station.

Alpine Motel **105 Main St ⓣ406/838-2262, ⓦwww.ccalpinemotel.com.** A range of 25 basic but tidy motel rooms for rent, from $62 for a single to $77 for a double with two queen beds. Two two-bedroom suites, sleeping up to five each and with tiny kitchen areas, are also available. Guest laundry on site.

Big Moose Resort **715 Hwy-212 ⓣ406/838-2393, ⓦwww.bigmooseresort.com.** The six modern cabins at this highway-side "resort" three miles east of town, ranging $65–85 per night, are a superb deal. All have plenty of space along with satellite TV, clean bathrooms, and Internet access, and three boast full eat-in kitchens. The highway is not plowed, meaning during the snowy months the *Big Moose* can only be accessed via snowmobile.

Elkhorn Lodge **103 Main St ⓣ406/838-2332, ⓦwww.beartooths.com/elkhorn.** Two cabins ($75) and six motels rooms ($65) are available at this centrally located lodge, all with full bath, TV, mini-fridges, microwaves, and coffeemakers. Rooms as decorated plainly, but are uniformly clean.

Super 8 Motel **303 Main St ⓣ406/838-2070 or 1-877/338-2070.** The newest addition to Cooke City's plain row of Main Street accommodations, featuring chain-style motel rooms ($65) with large TVs, queen beds, and Internet access.

Eating and drinking

Eating out in and around Cooke City is a straightforward affair. Choices are limited to the **restaurants** strung along Main Street, plus a couple of seasonal eateries in Silver Gate down the road. As for **nightlife**, there are several bars along the main drag that fill with bikers in the summer and hard-partying snowmobilers come winter; best of the bunch are the *Miner's Saloon*, 108 Main Street, and the tavern within the *Soda Butte Lodge* a short stumble away. Limited **supplies** can be found at the atmospheric Cooke City General Story (daily 8am–7pm) on Main Street, open since 1866, but it's best to stock up on groceries before arriving.

Beartooth Bakery **309 Main St ⓣ406/838-2040.** One of the newest Main Street additions, perfect for a coffee and take-away muffin or cinnamon roll to kick start the day. Internet access also available.

Beartooth Bistro **214 Main St ⓣ406/838-2160.** Formerly the much loved *Joan and Bill's* café, this is one of the larger restaurants in town, good for a basic fireside breakfast omelette ($6–8) or a simple lunch. Dinner is a more elaborate affair, though a bit pricey, with the likes of rack of lamb ($24) or fried scallops ($16) served in a simple setting.

Beartooth Café **209 Main St ⓣ406/838-2475.** The best and most original dining option in town, this café buzzes with conversation both inside and on the patio, thanks no doubt to the menu of 100-plus beers. Competing with the suds are tasty dishes like hickory smoked trout ($18) and the garlic heavy Funk Burger ($8).

Buns n Beds Deli **201 Main St ⓣ406/838-2030.** The choice for filling sandwiches ($6–8), eaten either in the basic dining area or taken away for a trailside meal. Daily bbq specials as well. The "beds" in the name are three basic cabins (no phone, no TV) out back, typically rented by the week or longer.

Log Cabin Café **Silver Gate ⓣ406/838-2367.** Attractive log-cabin café that's been serving meals throughout summer in tiny Silver Gate since 1937. The hand-painted trout on the windows advertise the menu's star ingredient, though steaks and hickory smoked bbq meats are also available.

Outdoor activities

A fair percentage of Cooke City visitors are here not to visit Yellowstone, but instead to play around in the surrounding national forests, where less stringent regulations are in effect. If gassing up is a prerequisite for your outdoor fun,

The Absaroka-Beartooth Wilderness

The brooding mass of the Absaroka Range, and to the east the smaller but more rugged alpine landscape of the Beartooth Range make up the nearly 100,000-acre **Absaroka-Beartooth Wilderness**. Lying across the Montana/Wyoming border, much of the wilderness area can be viewed on the spectacular 10,000ft-high **Beartooth Highway** east out of Cooke City, one of the most scenic drives in the country. This alone is reason enough to visit the region, but mountaineers and hikers will also be drawn by Montana's highest mountain, rugged **Granite Peak** (12,799ft), which rises above a series of wind-scoured tundra plateaus and alpine meadows incised by steep canyons.

More secluded than Yellowstone, there's a solid network of trails here that lead up through silent timbered mountainsides and alpine meadows that erupt with bright wildflowers during the brief six-week July and August growing season. Above the treeline, it's a harsh but beautiful high-alpine landscape that can see snow at any time of year. If you only have time for a day-hike, try the flat six-mile round trip to **Rock Island Lake**. At 8000ft, this is a great introduction to the area and there are several other fine trails from the lake if you decide to stay out in the wilds a little longer. The trailhead is reached from US-212 ten miles east of Cooke City, where you turn north onto Forest Road 306 for about one mile to Trail 3. Follow Trail 3 past Kersey Lake to Trail 566, which takes you to the convoluted shoreline of Rock Island Lake beneath craggy mountaintops.

For maps and more **information** on trails within the wilderness area – including a trio of isolated glaciers imbedded with millions of frozen grasshoppers – call in at the Cooke City Bike Shack (see below) or the Beartooth Ranger Station, three miles south of Red Lodge on US-212 (Mon–Fri 8am–4.30pm; ⓣ406/446-2103).

there are plenty of options. A Mecca for east coast "slednecks" from December through May, when **snowmobiles** easily outnumber cars on Main Street, there are more than 60 miles of superb groomed trails accessing thousands of acres of backcountry terrain in the Gallatin National Forest just outside of town. Unlike Yellowstone, guides are not required, nor are the slower but more eco-friendly four-stroke engines. Snowmobiles, however, are not allowed in any part of the nearby Abasaroka-Beartooth Wilderness. Rentals are available from both Cooke City Exxon (ⓣ406/838-2244, ⓦwww.cookecityexxon.com) and Cooke City Motorsports (ⓣ406/838-2231, ⓦwww.cookecitymotorsports.com); expect to pay $125–225 per day, depending on the quality of the sled. In summer, 4WD jeeps and ATVs take over, with miles of bumpy forest roads to explore.

You can pick up limited **supplies** within town for backpacking and fishing in Yellowstone or the Abasroka-Beartooth Wilderness (see box, above), but you're best off bringing all that you can with you. **Information**, however, is plentiful at the Cooke City Bike Shack (ⓣ406/838-2412, ⓦwww.cookecitybikeshack.com). Along with espresso drinks and bike repair (though no bike rentals), the store is a one-stop shop for details on regional activities from owner Bill Blackford, who also rents a backcountry yurt ($90 per night for up to six) and runs affordable **backcountry skiing** tours on Mount Abundance within the Gallatin National Forest; in recent years, he's led pro riders and video crews in search of the area's plentiful powder. Fishermen and hunters can stop in at Beartooth Plateau Outfitters, 302 Main Street (ⓣ406/838-2328, ⓦwww.beartoothoutfitters.com), who run a variety of horseback pack trips both into Yellowstone and the Absaroka-Beartooth Wilderness; they also have a small selection of fly-fishing gear onsite.

Cooke City to Red Lodge: the Beartooth Scenic Highway

Constructed in the 1930s, the snaking 65-mile **Beartooth Scenic Highway** (Hwy-212) takes two-hours to connect Cooke City to the one-time coal mining town of Red Lodge. Other roads in the Rockies may be higher, but none gives quite such a top-of-the-world feeling as this succession of tight switchbacks, steep grades, and overwhelming overlooks. Even in summer, the springy tundra turf of the 10,940ft Beartooth Pass is covered with snow that (due to algae) turns pink when crushed. All around are gem-like tarns, deeply gouged granite walls, stretches of scree, and huge blocks of roadside ice. Pull-outs along the way allow you to view the sights without the risk of driving off the road, and there are a number of trailheads along the way to explore the area on foot (see the Absaroka-Beartooth Wilderness box, p.248). One longer turn-off that shouldn't be missed on a clear day is the **Clay Butte lookout**, eight miles east of the junction with the Chief Joseph Scenic Byway (Hwy-296). Here, a rough dirt road winds several miles, past a trailhead accessing Granite Lake, to a concrete lookout tower affording stunning panoramic views.

The highway is only **open** late May through October, and early in the season you can also access thousands of acres of "corn snow" from the road for some fun backcountry skiing. In the spring of 2005, a large stretch of the highway on the north side of the Beartooths was closed after being wiped out by a series of mudslides, but a $20 million reconstruction project has since reopened the entire stretch.

Cody and around

The eastern gateway to Yellowstone, Wyoming's **CODY** sits alongside the North Fork of the Shoshone River some 52 miles east of the park. Mountain man John Colter stumbled through the Shoshone Canyon here in the early 1800s, dubbing the area – and not Yellowstone itself, as many histories inaccurately claim – **Colter's Hell** for its now-inactive geysers and sulphur-rich airs. While the sickly smell of sulphur still occasionally wafts through town, Cody owes its existence not to Colter, but to the sponsorship of an even more famed Western hero. The town was the brainchild of investors, who in 1896 persuaded **William "Buffalo Bill" Cody** to get involved in their development company knowing his approval would attract homesteaders and visitors alike. Being at the western end of the dry Bighorn Basin, it was always clear that Cody would need a significant irrigation source if the town was to grow into a center of agriculture and a gateway for Yellowstone tourism. Bill Cody was probably the only person who could have drawn the support and funding for the dam and reservoir that today bear his name, so the town, whose population is closing on 9000, really does owe its existence to the man.

During summer, tourism is big business, but underneath all the Buffalo Bill-linked attractions and paraphernalia, Cody manages to retain the feel of a rural Western settlement. There's still plenty more pick-up trucks than Subaru wagons cruising the streets of the "rodeo capital of the world," and the town is more relaxed and low-key than Jackson – which is about the same distance away from Yellowstone. The priority for the vast majority of visitors to Cody is a visit to the **Buffalo Bill Historical Center**, before hightailing it across the Wapiti Valley to Yellowstone.

Arrival, orientation, and information

Cody sits at the junction of I-20, US-14A and Hwy-120. **Yellowstone Regional Airport** (ⓣ307/587-5096, ⓦwww.flyyra.com), which receives daily flights throughout the year from Denver (United Express/Skywest) and Salt Lake City (Delta/Skywest), is located 1.5 miles east of downtown, just off I-20. **Orientation** is easy enough as most of what is of interest is strung along two main sections of I-20: Sheridan Avenue takes in the ten blocks that make up the downtown precinct, while Yellowstone Avenue, stretching west towards the national park, has a handful of motels and campgrounds as well as the rodeo grounds and the town's secondary attractions. From June through mid-September, the COLT **public bus service** picks up at thirty spots throughout town (daily 9am–6pm; ⓣ307/527-7043; $1). A map of the bus route can be picked up at the town's helpful **visitor center**, 836 Sheridan Ave (June–Sept Mon–Fri 8am–6pm, Sat 9am–6pm, Sun 10am–3pm; rest of year Mon–Fri

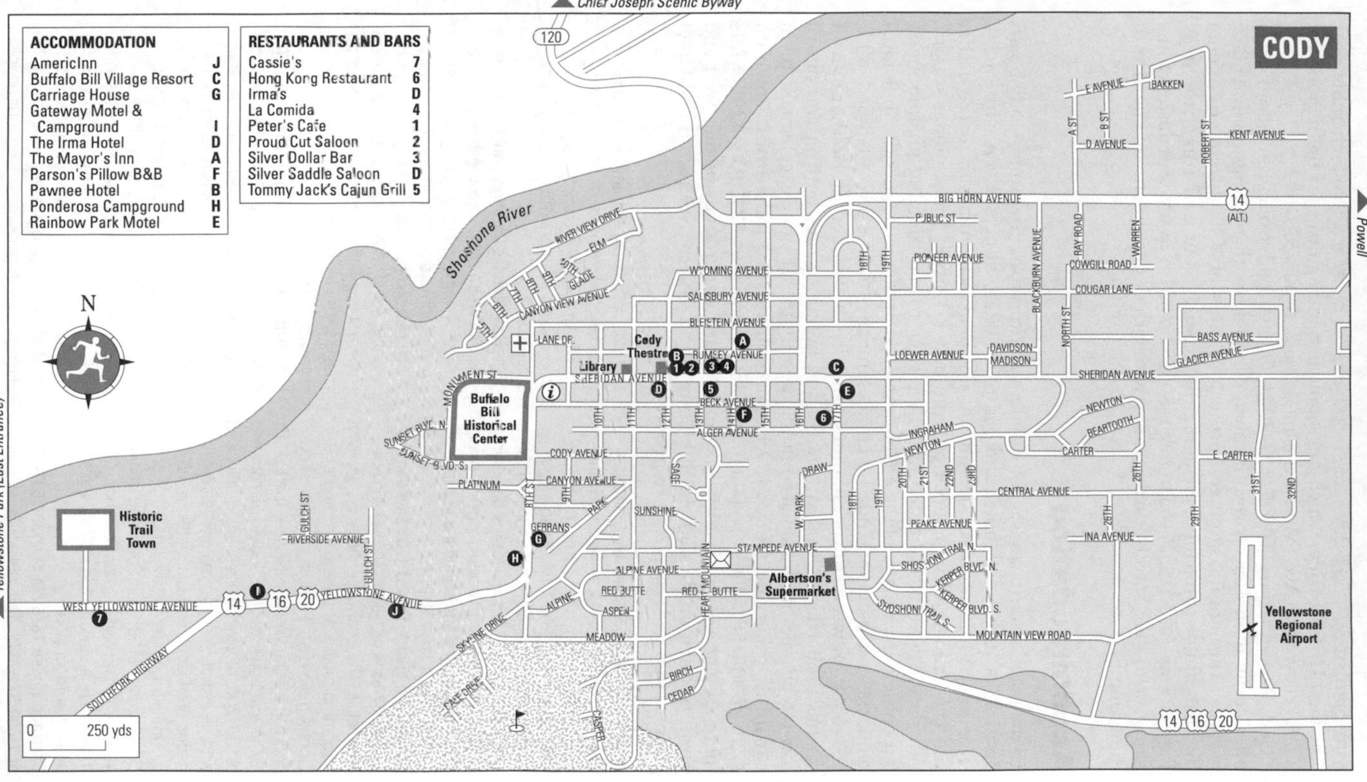
CODY
ACCOMMODATION
AmericInn J
Buffalo Bill Village Resort C
Carriage House G
Gateway Motel & Campground I
The Irma Hotel D
The Mayor's Inn A
Parson's Pillow B&B F
Pawnee Hotel B
Ponderosa Campground H
Rainbow Park Motel E
RESTAURANTS AND BARS
Cassie's 7
Hong Kong Restaurant 6
Irma's D
La Comida 4
Peter's Cafe 1
Proud Cut Saloon 2
Silver Dollar Bar 3
Silver Saddle Saloon D
Tommy Jack's Cajun Grill 5
Chief Joseph Scenic Byway
Powell
Yellowstone Park (East Entrance)
Shoshone River
Buffalo Bill Historical Center
Historic Trail Town
Cody Theatre
Library
Albertson's Supermarket
Yellowstone Regional Airport
N
0 250 yds
SHERIDAN AVENUE
BIG HORN AVENUE
WEST YELLOWSTONE AVENUE
YELLOWSTONE AVENUE
SOUTHFORK HIGHWAY
MOUNTAIN VIEW ROAD
STAMPEDE AVENUE
CENTRAL AVENUE

8am–5pm; ⓣ307/587-2297 or 1-800/393-2639, ⓦwww.codychamber.org). The local **USFS office**, which can supply free hiking maps for the region, is at 203A Yellowstone Ave (Mon–Fri 8am–4.30pm; ⓣ307/527-6921).

Cody Trolley Tours (ⓣ307/527-7043, ⓦwww.codytrolleytours.com; $15) offer corny hour-long **tours** of town, complete with running commentary, everyday throughout summer. Further off, tours of Yellowstone are offered by a handful of companies, including the expensive but well-run Grub Steak Expeditions (ⓣ307/527-6316 or 1-800/527-6316. ⓦwww.grubsteaktours.com), who take mostly small groups with prices dependent on the size of the group.

Accommodation

As the main eastern gateway for driving vacations to Yellowstone, Cody boasts upwards of fifty motel, hotel, and bed & breakfast choices. Even with such a large selection, **accommodation** fills up quickly in summer, so the earlier you can call ahead for reservations, the better. During the shoulder seasons, you should have little trouble finding a place to stay arriving unannounced, but come winter many of the establishments shut down. Besides the individual properties listed below, Cody Lodging Company (ⓣ307/587-8048 or 1-800/587-6560, ⓦwww.codyguesthouses.com) has a number of B&B rooms at various properties, as well as cottages and homes to rent both in and out of town. Cody has no hostel accommodation, but does offer excellent in-town **camping**; otherwise, Cody's *KOA* campground is 2.5 miles east of town on I-20 (ⓣ307/587-2369 or 1-800/562-8507; tent sites $21, RVs $29), while there are cheaper, more rustic national forest campgrounds further west and north of town on the Buffalo Bill Cody Scenic Byway (see p.259) and Chief Joseph Highway (see p.260) respectively.

AmericInn 508 Yellowstone Ave ⓣ307/587-7716 or 1-800/634-3444, ⓦwww.americinn.com. One of Cody's newer accommodations, opened in 2000, this three-star chain property is a clear cut above most of the other mid-range places. Rooms have king beds and large TVs; facilities include pool and hot tub, and the continental breakfast is free. Rates start at $125.

Buffalo Bill Village Resort 1701 Sheridan Ave ⓣ307/587-5544 or 1-800/527-5544, ⓦwww.blairhotels. The anchor property on a row of accommodations at the eastern end of Cody's main drag. Fronted by a gift-shop sporting a false Western facade, the *Buffalo Bill Village* consists of 83 individual cabins ($100–200) of various sizes, all en-suite and with pleasantly tacky rodeo or Western decor. Next door, and run by the same group, is a both a *Holiday Inn* ($125) and a *Comfort Inn* ($100), each boasting chain-style furnishing and wireless Internet. All three share access to the *Holiday Inn*'s heated outdoor pool.

Carriage House 1816 8th St ⓣ307/587-3818 or 1-800/531-2572. This collection of cute c 1920 cabins constitutes one of the more charming inexpensive options in town. Some of the bathrooms have tubs; all the cabins are nonsmoking. Rates start at $65.

Gateway Motel & Campground 203 Yellowstone Ave ⓣ307/587-2561, ⓦwww.gatewaycamp.com. The tiny, rustic cabins ($65 nightly) here on the western edge of town are pretty bare but each has a gas stove (no fridge or cooking utensils), so if you're equipped to self-cater, it may suit just fine. There are also a half-dozen basic motel rooms along with grassy tent sites for $20.

The Irma Hotel 1192 Sheridan Ave ⓣ307/587-4221 or 1-800/745-4762, ⓦwww.irmahotel.com. The hotel built and named for Buffalo Bill's daughter in 1902 remains a downtown landmark. A wing was added during the 1980s, and you should specify that you don't want to stay there (though these rooms are cheaper; $75–100); rooms in the original building ($115–140) boast classic corner sinks, chunky antique wardrobes, and some stylish old radiators and light fittings. The larger suites sleep four people.

△ *The Irma Hotel*

Non-smokers beware that the hotel's public areas are typically smoky.

The Mayor's Inn 1413 Rumsey Ave ⓣ 307/587-8004 or 1-888/217-3001, ⓦ www.mayorsinn.com. Dating to 1909, *The Mayor's Inn* was moved here piece-by-piece from its original Sheridan Ave location in the mid-1990s, and lovingly restored as a B&B. Furnishings include pieces salvaged from houses around Cody, as well as from the *Irma Hotel*. The five rooms have luxury touches like fluffy robes and bubble-jet tubs in each bathroom. Rates ($105–205) often negotiable for stays of three nights or more.

Parson's Pillow B&B 1202 14th St ⓣ 307/587-2382 or 1-800/377-2348, ⓦ www.parsonspillow.com. Built in 1902, this quaint little B&B was originally a Methodist-Episcopal church and the current owners replaced the missing bell tower and steeple in 1996. The five guest-rooms ($100) each feature their own distinct bathroom touches including an antique clawfoot tub or an oak-framed "prairie tub."

Pawnee Hotel 1032 12th St ⓣ 307/587-2239. This two-story c 1900 hotel has 22 somewhat dark and gloomy rooms, but the downtown location is great. All rooms are non-smoking and have more personality than a bland highway motel. The best rooms feature full-size clawfoot bathtubs. Rates start at $70.

Ponderosa Campground 1815 Yellowstone Ave ⓣ 307/587-9203, ⓦ www.codyponderosa.com. The best camping in Cody, friendly and well run, with exceptionally clean shower and toilet facilities. There's also a general store, laundry, and games room. Options include a basic tent site ($20), a tepee (sleeping mat and bag required; $30), or camper-cabin ($45); go for a site in the "rustic tenting" area, which is below the main campground and right beside the Shoshone River. Open May to mid-Oct.

Rainbow Park Motel 1136 17th St ⓣ 307/587-6251 or 1-800/710-6930, ⓦ www.rainbowparkmotel.com. A basic motor court featuring 40 rooms with the bonus of a grassy area in the center of the parking lot; rooms are not flashy but perfectly clean and feature cable TV, a/c, and a guest laundry. Rooms from $55.

The Town and around

Cody's main thoroughfare, **Sheridan Avenue**, is wide enough for a couple of wagon teams at least, but really there's little else to evoke the feel of the Old West. Even the historic **Irma Hotel** fails to inspire as part of the streetscape, despite its Buffalo Bill lineage. Native American arts, crafts, and jewelry feature heavily among the stores along the main drag, and there's a huge shop which sells every conceivable variation on the cowboy hat – although in presentation and price, it's clearly aimed at cowboys from LA and London, rather than northwest Wyoming.

The hokey **gunfight**, a staple of Western towns like Cody, is quite a production with up to twelve participants shooting off their mouths and guns to entertain the crowds; it kicks off in front of the *Irma Hotel* at 6pm Monday to Saturday throughout summer. The town's biggest annual festival is the **Cody Stampede**, held on the weekend of July 4 (ⓣ307/587-5155 or 1-800/207-0744), which features parades, street performances, fireworks, and of course, a huge rodeo. Smaller though still popular, Cody's **night rodeo** (June–Aug nightly 8.30pm; ⓣ307/587-5155 or 1-800/207-0744; $10–12), takes place at the western edge of town at 421 W Yellowstone Ave.

Buffalo Bill Historical Center

The nation's most comprehensive collection of Western Americana, Cody's phenomenal **Buffalo Bill Historical Center** at 720 Sheridan Ave, comprises five distinct museums (June to mid-Sept daily 7am–8pm; mid-Sept to Oct daily 8am–5pm; Nov–March Tues–Sat 10am–3pm; April daily 10am–5pm; May daily 8am–8pm; ⓣ307/587-4771, ⓦwww.bbhc.org; $15, students $10, youth (5–12) $6); keep your ticket for a free return visit the following day, as there's a lot to get through.

Artifacts from William Cody's various careers, such as guns, gifts from European heads of state, billboards, clothes, and dime novels, help the **Buffalo Bill Museum** to chronicle the years of the Pony Express, Civil War, Indian Wars, and Wild West shows. Among the highlights are the nine-passenger Deadwood stagecoach ridden in the Wild West Show, and the remains of Cody's celebrated Springfield rifle, the Lucrezia Borgia, used to hunt down countless buffalo and named after the Italian countess whose name was synonymous with death. It's interesting, too, to see the contrast between some of the photos of Buffalo Bill on display; in one he looks like an overdressed and overweight dandy, while in another he's in classic mounted pose, cutting a dash with a leather gauntlet in hand, experience and gravitas etched into his weathered face.

The lives of western Native Americans are celebrated in the atmospheric **Plains Indian Museum**, the center's most affecting museum. Many of the ceremonial garments are in stunning condition; one prize exhibit is a shirt – made from deer-hide and brightly decorated with horse and human hair, glass beads, porcupine quills, and more – that belonged to Red Cloud, a Lakota Sioux chief who visited Washington several times during the 1870s to petition for peace on behalf of his people. As marvellous is the circle of six buffalo-horn bonnets, worn to capture the sacred power of the buffalo before big hunts. The collection is given a tragic note by the display of Ghost Dance shirts. In the late 1880s, the religious revelation of the Paiute prophet Wovoka swept the western tribes. He declared that ritual purification through song and dance would hasten the day when all whites would be buried by a heaven-sent fall of soil, and their dead warriors, along with huge herds of buffalo, would return to the Plains. The US Army condemned Ghost Dances as unacceptable shows of resistance, and mobilized troops to disrupt ceremonies.

Next door, in the **Whitney Gallery of Western Art**, the contrasting styles of Frederic Remington and Charles M. Russell command the most attention. The propagandist Remington, whose studio is also on display, dwells on conflict, depicting the Indian as a savage in the path of progress, while Russell's work shows a consistent respect for native life. Amongst scores of painting with titles like *Last of Their Race* and *Last of the Buffalo* by other painters, look out for Edgar Paxson's *Custer's Last Stand* (1899), an epic painting displayed alongside a diagram pointing out all the major players within the battle scene; Custer stands, gutshot and near death, in the middle of the melee.

Buffalo Bill

One of the most famous Americans of his era, **William Frederick Cody** was born on February 26, 1846. Within fifty years of his modest start in a small Iowa farmhouse, upwards of 500 pulp-novels starring **"Buffalo Bill"** had been published and his Wild West Show had circled the globe. Cody's much-mythologized exploits began at an early age, soon after his father – a anti-slavery free-soiler who had recently moved his family to Kansas – was stabbed to death after making his views known to an angry, pro-slavery mob. After his father's death, Cody, the eldest living son at only 11 years old, took work on a wagon train to support the family. To escape from an ambush on one early outing, Cody reputedly shot a man for the first time, earning him fame as the "Boy Indian Slayer"; four years later, he became the youngest rider on the **Pony Express**, averaging a blazing 15mph on his leg of the legendary mail route.

The day after his mother's funeral, Cody, still under-age at 17, signed on to fight for the Union Army in the **Civil War**. His wartime heroics during this time (whether real or trumped-up) are relatively under-reported, but after this stint fighting for the Union, Cody found work – and a lifelong nickname – supplying buffalo meat to workers laying down tracks for the Kansas Pacific railroad. Under contract to kill a dozen buffalo per day for $500 a month, Cody claimed to have killed over 4200 in just eighteen months, before rejoining the army in 1868 as its chief scout. In the next decade, when the **Plains Indian Wars** were at their peak, he earned a Congressional Medal of Honor and a remarkable record of never losing any troops in ambushes. Among battles in which he took part was the 1877 encounter with Sioux forces when he killed – and some legends claim scalped – Chief Yellow Hand. During this time, Cody also was introduced to author **Ned Buntline**, who cemented Cody's fame back East with a series of exaggerated accounts of Cody's adventures in scores of "dime novels," starting with *Buffalo Bill, King of the Border Men* (1869).

As the Indian Wars calmed, Cody took to guiding Yankee and European gentry on buffalo hunts, including the likes of grand dukes and famed generals Sherman and Custer. The theatrical productions he laid on for his rich guests developed into the world-famous **Wild West Show**. First staged in 1883, these spectacular carnivals usually consisted of a re-enactment of an Indian battle such as Custer's Last Stand, featuring Sioux (including **Sitting Bull** for a short time) who had been present at Little Bighorn, stagecoach attacks, trick riders, buffalo, clowns, and a shooting and riding exhibition by the man himself. Later shows expanded to include a "Congress of Rough Riders of the World," complete with Arab horsemen, Russian Cossacks, Cuban rebels, and the sharp-shooting **Annie Oakley**. The show spent ten of its thirty years in Europe, where, dressed in the finest silks and sporting a well-groomed goatee, Cody stayed in the grandest hotels and dined with heads of state. Ever the showman, in Italy Cody hoped to hold his show in Rome's crumbling Coliseum, but found it too dilapidated to suit his purposes. And in England, Queen Victoria was so enthusiastic in her admiration that rumors circulated of an affair between them.

In his latter years, a mellowing Cody played down his past activities, to the point of urging the government to respect all Native American treaties and put an end to the wanton slaughter of buffalo and game. Cody also spent more time living on a ranch near to his adopted home town of **Cody, Wyoming**, describing the Big Horn Basin to the east as "one of nature's masterpieces" and "the Mecca of all appreciative humanity." Although the Wild West Show was reckoned to have brought in as much as one million dollars per year, his many investments failed badly, and, on January 10, 1915, a penniless 69-year-old Buffalo Bill died at his sister's home in Denver. His grave can be found atop Lookout Mountain, outside Golden, Colorado.

For something altogether different, head for the center's newest addition, the **Draper Museum of Natural History**. Opened in 2002, the circular gallery is lined with interactive exhibits and beautifully laid-out taxidermy displays, all working to highlight the geology, wildlife, and human presence in the Greater Yellowstone region. As part of the museum's "participatory experience" approach, classes are frequently offered, and visitors are invited to share their own views. One recent display on whether wolves should remain around Yellowstone featured handwritten responses such as "Wolves – government sponsored terrorists" and "Save the elk, moose, and buffalo babies – shoot the wolves" – opinions shared by many in this rancher-friendly corner of Wyoming.

A quick tour of the center's final gallery, the **Cody Firearms Museum**, is worthwhile for a look at some of the superbly crafted rifles, pistols, and revolvers dating back to the 1500s – particularly those made through the course of the nineteenth century, when manufacturers strove to outdo each other with their designs. There are more than 6000 pieces in all, including European rifles and pistols and the largest collection of US firearms in the world.

Historic Trail Town

Although it's a pretty random collection of old log cabins, firearms, wagons, and other relics salvaged from all over the region, **Historic Trail Town**, 1831 DeMaris Drive (mid-May to mid-Sept daily 8am–8pm; $8, children 6–12 $2),

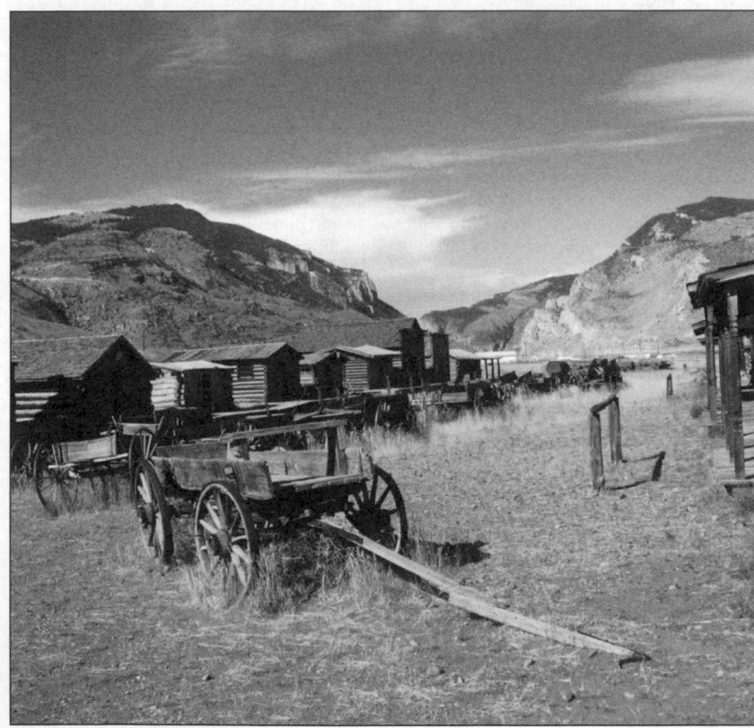

△ Historic Trail Town

makes for a handy one-stop viewing of frontier culture. The 25 buildings date between 1879 and 1901, and include a re-created general store, schoolhouse, trapper's cabin, and blacksmith's shop. Photographs in the buffalo hunter's cabin give some idea of the scale of the infamous buffalo slaughter, with piles of hides depicted, as well as some of the hapless beasts being skinned. In Curley's Cabin there are some surprisingly good pictures of Curley, the Crow Indian scout and acolyte of Custer's who survived the battle of Little Bighorn. And in the cabin hideout of the famed Hole in the Wall Gang, where the Sundance Kid and other outlaws bedded down, more photos await, including a gruesome shot of three unnamed outlaws being hanged near Laramie in the late 1800s.

At the western end of Old Trail Town you'll find a memorial to the mountain men of the fur-trapping era, and a number of gravesites of various trappers and buffalo hunters. Among them is the grave of the infamous John (Jeremiah) "Liver Eating" Johnston, who some claim earned his nickname by killing, scalping, and then eating the livers of Crow Indians who had killed his wife.

Buffalo Bill State Park

The **Buffalo Bill State Park**, four miles west of Cody along I-20, sits prettily in the midst of Absaroka Range, but most of the action takes place on the boomerang-shaped, man-made lake at its center. The obvious first stop – and the only one needed for those not fishing or camping – is the free **visitor center** for the Buffalo Bill Dam and Reservoir (May–Sept Mon–Sat 8am–6pm; ⓣ307/527-6076). Exhibits inside detail the dam's construction, which spanned from 1904 to 1909, and how on completion it was the highest in the world at 325 feet. Additions in 1993 raised the height to 353 feet, and its worth a quick stop mainly for the stomach-churning view straight down the front of the narrow dam and into Shoshone Canyon. Besides providing water for the residents of Cody and other towns in the Bighorn Basin, the reservoir is popular for fishing and boating. Two state park **campgrounds**, North Shore Bay and North Fork, cost $9 per night for a bare and windswept site (the reservoir is ideal for windsurfing and kite-surfing; day-use costs $5).

Eating and drinking

For a town that sees over one million visitors pass through each summer, Cody is hardly over-endowed with interesting **restaurants**. A good steak is easy to find, but the options beyond that are fairly limited. At least most of the best establishments are located on or just off Sheridan Avenue, meaning you can take in most menus on a lazy stroll. The major fast-food chains are represented just off the main drag, and those heading on to Yellowstone should definitely stock up at the large Albertson's supermarket (see Listings p.259). Cody's **pubs** are pretty basic watering holes, although having a beer at *Irma's* famous bar is a requisite for any visitor. During summer a variety of bands do come through town, but entertainment is otherwise limited to a little boot-scooting or a game of pool.

Restaurants

Hong Kong Restaurant 1201 17th St ⓣ307/527-6420. You get the usual Americanized Chinese selections here, but they're all pretty tasty and good value too (entrees $8–13). Daily for lunch and dinner plus brunch (a dim sum of sorts) on Sundays.

Irma's In the *Irma Hotel* ⓣ307/587-4221. A good spot for a slab of prime rib for dinner, and the breakfast and lunch buffets are great for filling up on a range of dishes (both $8); the selection is expanded for Sunday brunch ($10) to include roasts, hot veggies, plus plenty of salads and desserts. Take heed, though, that the dining area and the bar are often smoky.

La Comida **1385 Sheridan Ave ⓣ307/587-9556.** If you're in Cody for only one night, consider eating out on *La Comida*'s attractive patio. These affordable Mexican standards are augmented by light selections such as *pechuga* salad (bites of chicken in cream and green chilis over leafy greens), and the white-chocolate almond cheesecake ($4) is a winner too. Entrees $7–12. Daily for lunch and dinner.

Peter's Cafe Bakery **1219 Sheridan Ave.** A bright, cheerful place for a full breakfast or simpler selection of bagels and muffins to go with a range of coffees. Come lunchtime, deli sandwiches of titanic proportions crowd the menu. Take-out available. Mon–Sat 6.45am–8pm.

Proud Cut Saloon **1227 Sheridan Ave ⓣ307/587-7343.** Self-described "Cowboy Cuisine" is dished out at this local favorite, including a big lunchtime garlic burger ($8) and even bigger dinnertime steaks ($14–24), but the service is disorganized and slow. Daily for lunch and dinner.

Tommy Jack's Cajun Grill **1134 13th St ⓣ307/587-4917.** One of Cody's more upmarket choices, combining Cajun cuisine with blues music in a smooth bistro setting. Gumbo and catfish are the menu's top picks, while the bar cranks out a steady stream of assorted martinis. Expect to pay $25 per person, including a drink and tip.

Bars and pubs

Cassie's **214 Yellowstone Ave ⓣ307/527-5500.** You may need a cowboy hat to feel comfortable at *Cassie's*, but for a Wyoming cultural experience this is a good bet. Entertainment at this 1920s roadhouse ranges from line-dancing classes to country and country-rock bands, and there are pool tables too. You can settle in for a full evening here including dinner, but the meaty menu, while pretty good, is surprisingly expensive (entrees $14–30). There are regular weekday lunch specials too.

Silver Dollar Bar **1313 Sheridan Ave ⓣ307/587-3554.** This should be the first place you check for live music – mostly rock, and definitely for those who would not be seen dead in *Cassie's*. Otherwise it's the scene of lively drinking, pool-playing, and Cody's best burger, gloriously greasy and served in a basket with onion rings for $6 either at the bar or on the large street-side patio.

Silver Saddle Saloon **In the *Irma Hotel*, 1192 Sheridan Ave.** The *Irma's* most famous feature is its gorgeous imported European cherrywood bar, which at $100,000 reputedly cost twenty grand more than the hotel itself. Happy hour (5–7pm) pulls in a fair mix of locals and tourists.

Outdoor activities

Along with trout fishing and wind-surfing at the Buffalo Bill Reservoir, your best bet for most outdoor pursuits in the region are found on your own en route to Yellowstone, whether in the Wapiti Valley to the east or north off the Chief Joseph Scenic Byway, both covered later in this chapter. There are, however, several outfitters and tour companies in town should you be in need, most likely for a whitewater expedition close to town. Thanks to the dam's water control, there's consistent **rafting** (Class II–IV; half-day around $50) throughout the summer on the North Fork of the Shoshone River west of town, and also gentler sightseeing **float trips** (2–3hr, around $25); wildlife including elk and bighorn sheep can often be seen from the river. Try Core Mountain Sports, 1019 15th St (ⓣ307/527-7354), or Wyoming River Trips, 233 Yellowstone Ave (ⓣ307/587-6661 or 1-800/586-6661). **Fishing** enthusiasts can get great advice and licenses from the centrally located North Fork Anglers, 1107 Sheridan Ave (ⓣ307/527-7274, ⓦwww.northforkanglers.com), who boast a superbly stocked fly shop and also run guided trips on the North or South Fork of the Shoshone, the Clark's Fork of the Yellowstone to the north, or into Yellowstone itself ($300–430 per day). Lastly, those searching for advice on local **mountain biking** trails should check in with Absaroka Bicycles (Mon–Sat 10am–6pm; ☎307/527-5566), located in the K-Mart plaza on 17th south of downtown.

Listings

Airlines Sky West/Delta ☎307/587-9740 or 1-800/221-1212; United Express ☎307/587-9740 or 1-800/864-8331.
Banks Community First, Sheridan Ave and 11th St and Shoshone First, Sheridan and 14th, have 24hr ATMs.
Car rental Budget ☎307/587-6066, Hertz ☎307/587-2914, and Thrifty ☎307/587-8855 have depots at the airport.
Hospital West Park Hospital, 707 Sheridan Ave ☎307/527-7501, has 24hr emergency care.
Internet Free access is available both at the library (see below) and the town's visitor center (see p.250); WiFi access is available for $8 per day in the area surrounding the visitor center.
Laundry Cody Laundromat, 1728 Beck Ave (☎307/587-8500; open 24hr).
Library Park County Library, 1057 Sheridan Ave (Mon & Thurs 9am—8pm, Tues, Wed, & Fri 9am–5.30pm, Sat 9am–4pm).
Police 1131 11th St ☎307/527-8700; emergencies ☎911.
Post office 1301 Stampede Ave (Mon–Fri 8am–5.30pm, Sat 9am–noon).
Supermarket Albertson's, 1825 17th St (daily 5am–midnight; pharmacy hours Mon–Fri 9am–8pm, Sat 9am–6pm, Sun 10am–4pm).

Cody to Yellowstone: the Wapiti Valley

The hour-long drive west from Cody to Yellowstone is a superb preparation for the splendors of the park itself, worthy of a half-day of explorations – or more – should time permit. The first half of the drive begins by skirting the Buffalo Bill Dam and Reservoir, then runs alongside Shoshone River into the open **Wapiti Valley**, the heart of Wyoming's "beef country" and home to a handful of dude ranches and horsepacking outfitters. At the halfway point, I-20 enters the Shoshone National Forest on the **Buffalo Bill Cody Scenic Byway**. A busy two-lane affair that runs into the park alongside the North Fork of the Shoshone, the byway is lined by fantastical rock formations, known as "hoodoos," that'll have you thinking you stumbled upon the set of a psychedelic Spaghetti Western. The crenulated buttes and sandcastle bluffs are made from breccia, a mixture of rock and ash deposited by volcanic eruptions 50 million years ago and eroded ever since, and are unlike anything you'll see in either nearby national park. Be sure to stop at the pullout 28 miles west of Cody (25 miles from Yellowstone) to marvel at perhaps the most extraordinary of the rock formations, known as the "**Holy City**" – its silhouette supposedly mirroring that of the city of Jerusalem.

There's more to appreciate beyond geological formations, and passengers should scan the landscape to spot the likes of bighorn sheep, pronghorn, and mule deer; there is also a fair amount of grizzly activity on the south side of the highway. The river here is also **prime fly-fishing territory**, with a wealth of access spots, and a half-dozen **trailheads** for both hiking and cross-country skiing lead into the volcanic landscape of the North Absaroka and Washakie wildernesses to the north and south respectively; note that mountain biking is not allowed. For more information, pull into the historic **Wapiti Ranger Station** (Memorial day to Labor Day daily 9am–4pm; ☎307/578-1200), located two miles west of the "Holy City," where you can gather maps and the like on the country's first national forest, designated as such in 1891.

Practicalities

Other than during the busiest period (July & Aug), not many people stop overnight en route to the park, although there are some very pleasant places to do so; some of the **campgrounds** and **lodges** are within a few miles of the park's east entrance, and are worth considering as a base, especially if interested in fly-fishing and horseback riding. Only two miles east of the park boundary is *Pahaska Teepee* (Ⓣ307/527-7701, Ⓦwww.pahaska.com), Buffalo Bill's one-time hunting lodge – Pahaska, meaning "long hair," was Cody's Indian name. Along with a gift-shop and restaurant, *Pahaska Teepee* offers an array of attractive A-frame cabins ($100 per night and up), along with trail rides into the Shoshone National Forest. Similar accommodations and activities are available at the *Shoshone Lodge* one mile further east (Ⓣ307/587-4044, Ⓦwww.shoshonelodge.com), and the *Elephant Head Lodge*, another seven miles towards Cody (Ⓣ307/587-3980, Ⓦwww.elephantheadlodge.com). The eight appealing USFS campgrounds strung along the Buffalo Bill Scenic Byway have drinking water, vault toilets, fire rings, and essential bear-proof storage bins and are usually open May to early October. The three closest to Yellowstone are the RV-only *Three Mile* (3 miles; 33 sites), *Eagle Creek* (7 miles; 20 sites), and *Newton Creek* (14 miles; 31 sites); each costs $10 per night.

Cody to Cooke City: the Chief Joseph Scenic Byway

If you arrive in Cody from Yellowstone on the Buffalo Bill Scenic Byway, consider looping back into the park via Cooke City and the northeast entrance on the **Chief Joseph Scenic Byway**. Though not as immediately impressive as the drive through the surreal Wapiti Valley, the 1.5 hour-long journey through the Sunlight Basin and Clark's Fork Valley boasts dramatic vistas and plenty of opportunities for wildlife spotting and outdoor activities.

Start by heading north out of Cody on Hwy-120 as it cuts through lonely ranchlands. Local landmark **Heart Mountain** dominates the view to the northeast, long a geological puzzle as it is topped by a 300-million-year-old limestone cap, loaded with the fossils of invertebrate sea creatures, that's markedly older than the rock *beneath* it. After seventeen miles, the highway runs into Hwy-296, know as the Chief Joseph Scenic Byway and named after the chief of the Nez Percé tribe as the road follows the route of their historic flight (see box, opposite). The first eight miles of the 47-mile long course weaves past herds of grazing cattle on the private Two Dot Ranch before entering the Shoshone National Forest. For the next five miles, the road climbs ever higher, eventually cresting at **Dead Indian Summit** (8060ft). A turnoff here provides spectacular views of the Abasaroka and Beartooth mountains ahead, lined with some two-dozen peaks stretching over 12,000ft.

The highway then spaghettis steeply downward past *Dead Indian Campground* (12 sites; $10) and into the **Sunlight Basin**, named as such by nineteenth-century trappers because sunlight was the only thing that could get into this remote area come winter. Nowadays a gravel road cuts into the basin, leading to a rustic campground and a trailhead twelve miles west into the isolated wilderness area. Beyond the turnoff the Chief Joseph Scenic Byway crosses the **Sunlight Creek Bridge**, Wyoming's highest at over 300ft, spanning the deep and narrow Sunlight Creek Gorge. For a photo, walk down the short path east of the parking lot on the bridge's south side to take in the entire bridge and dizzying drop. Around fifteen-miles on, the highway passes over the Clark's

Retreat of the Nez Percé

By the time the first white settlers moved into the northwestern states in the nineteenth century, the **Nez Percé** had been living in what is now north central Idaho and adjacent Washington and Oregon for thousands of years. Their first contact with whites was when Lewis and Clark passed through the area in 1805. Relations with the expedition members and whites who followed were friendly, and remained this way for the next half-century. An 1855 treaty moved the peaceable tribe to the **Nez Percé Reservation**, a 5000-square-mile-area that reserved much of their traditional lands for exclusive use. However, after gold was discovered on the reservation, a new treaty was drawn up in 1863 that reduced the reservation to a tenth of its previous size.

The majority of the Nez Percé, under the leadership of **Chief Joseph**, refused to recognize the agreement. In 1877, after much vacillation, the government decided to enact its terms and gave the tribe only thirty days to leave. The Nez Percé asked for more time to get things in order, and the general in charge refused. This refusal led to skirmishes that caused the deaths of a handful of settlers – the first whites ever to be attacked by Nez Percé – and a large army was gathered to round them up. Chief Joseph then embarked upon the **Retreat of the Nez Percé**, a 1500-plus mile trek from Oregon through Yellowstone and Montana. Around 250 warriors (protecting twice as many women, children, and the elderly) outmaneuvered army columns many times their size, launching frequent guerrilla attacks in a series of daring escapes. After four months, the Nez Percé were cornered just thirty miles from the relative safety of the Canadian border. Chief Joseph then (reportedly) made his much-quoted speech of surrender:

"It is cold, and we have no blankets. The little children are freezing to death. Hear me, my chiefs! I am tired. My heart is sick and sad. From where the sun now stands I will fight no more for ever".

The campaign, which had been closely followed out East, created considerable sympathy for the plight of the Nez Percé. Despite this, and although promised that they would be returned to reservations in the northwest, the Nez Percé were soon taken to Fort Leavenworth, Kansas, then moved to Oklahoma. In 1885, the 268 members of the tribe who were still alive were allowed to return to the northwest.

Fork River – a legendary fly-fishing and kayaking river – and through tiny **Crandall**. Here you'll find the Painter Estate Outpost, with gas, a tiny market and RV park, and a café (*Clark's Fork and Spoon*; daily 8.30am–7.30pm) that's best for a $10 Sunday brunch buffet. Past Crandall, the dramatic Index and Pilot peaks come into view, and soon after the Scenic Byway ends at Hwy-212. East heads up the epic Beartooth Scenic Byway, while west leads to Cooke City, thirteen miles away: both are covered in detail in Chapter 14.

Contexts

Contexts

History

What follows is a condensed **history** of America's most hallowed national park, one that faced several precarious junctures throughout its story. Were it not for the efforts of many judicious and preservation-minded individuals – some of whom are spotlighted on the following pages – the mighty Yellowstone River would probably be dammed today and Old Faithful little more than a factory to convert steam into electricity. This account also touches on the greater Yellowstone region, but for a detailed look at the creation of **Grand Teton National Park**, see the box on p.92. Certainly the area's story starts well before recorded history, and we've covered the early **geology** under "Geology, flora, and fauna" from p.278.

Native history: Hunter-gatherers to the Sheepeaters

For a whole host of reasons, whites in the nineteenth and early twentieth centuries loudly claimed that **Indians** refused to inhabit or often even visit the Yellowstone region, frightened off like superstitious children by the gurgling mudpots and bellowing geysers. In fact, humans have been living in and traveling through the area for more than 11,000 years, arriving soon after the last wave of glaciers and ice sheets receded to the north. The first peoples to inhabit the region were **hunter-gatherers** subsisting on seeds, roots, and game, including Ice Age mammals like the giant bison and the mammoth. As these creatures gradually disappeared, the attention of hunters shifted to the smaller game familiar to park visitors today. Obsidian projectile points, grinding stones and tools have all been excavated by archeologists throughout the area, helping paint a picture of the lives of these early inhabitants. Moving **seasonally**, groups would arrive from the neighboring plains in spring, camping by lakes and streams to pick wild onion and balsamroot, and hunt the plentiful game. As summer arrived, the groups would split into smaller family parties to follow both the game and blooming plants such as biscuit-root and whitebark pine, moving up to the high-altitude tundra for several weeks. Along with the points from throwing spears known as an **atlatl**, large stone circles thought to hold some religious significance have been found at these sites high upon mountaintops. As the cold autumn winds blew in, the seasonal circle was completed, with the groups returning back to lower grounds.

For thousands of years, this system evolved only gradually, with technological advances including the introduction of the **bow and arrow** along with the development of bison **corrals** and **traps** for catching bighorn sheep. Native use and exploration of the area seems to have continually increased, but it takes until the 1400s before names can begin to be ascribed to any of the tribes. Ancestors of the **Shoshone**, **Bannock**, **Blackfeet**, **Nez Percé**, **Bannock**, and several other tribes all crisscrossed Yellowstone on numerous trails, with the Fishing Bridge area often used as a rendezvous site. Another major stopping point was **Obsidian Cliff** (see p.63), a vital source for obtaining the material used for spear and arrow tips. Generally speaking, the Shoshone and Bannock tribes spent the most time in and around Yellowstone, with Blackfeet territory to the north in modern day Montana and Nez Percé to the west in Idaho.

The arrival of the horse in the Rockies around 1700 helped create the last major shift before the coming of whites, with **Crow** peoples occupying the region to the east and northeast. One group who didn't take to the horse, however, were the **Sheepeaters** (also known as **Tukaduka**), a branch of the

Shoshone who were the primary occupiers of Yellowstone when the first whites arrived in the early 1800s. Moving seasonally, Sheepeaters spent summers hunting bighorn sheep high in the mountains (hence their name), though they also fished and tracked smaller mammals such as squirrels and porcupine. Come winter, they huddled in riverside camps, sometimes in **wikiups**, teepee-like shelters made by balancing hundreds of long branches. In the spirit of the era, Sheepeaters were typically disparaged by the whites they encountered as dirty and poor, but trapper Osborne Russell (see p.288) writes positively about meeting a family in his journals, noting they were "neatly clothed in dressed deer and sheepskins of the best quality and seemed to be perfectly happy," and he gladly traded for top-quality elk, deer, and sheep skins. Along with being expert tanners, Sheepeaters were skilled bow-makers, using material from a ram's horn to construct bows powerful enough to send an arrow completely through a bison.

Early exploration

The first non-native to explore Yellowstone was probably **John Colter**, who entered the region as a private with the **Lewis and Clark** expedition. The famed two-year, 8000-mile long expedition left from the then frontier town of St Louis in 1804, passing north of Yellowstone country on the Missouri River, en route to the Pacific Ocean. In no rush to return to civilization, Colter was given permission to leave the group on the expedition's return journey, joining up with two other fur trappers – Forest Hancock and Joseph Dixson – to hunt for riches along the Missouri River in August of 1806. Colter soon had a falling out with his temporary partners, and left to trap on his own. This launched the Kentucky native into years of adventure, including one of the West's great stories in which Colter, captured by a band of Blackfoot, was stripped naked and given a head-start before a band of braves set off in deadly pursuit. Running for his life, Colter eluded his attackers by hiding out in a freezing river and then escaped on a 300-mile march back to the nearest trading post, eating roots for survival.

Colter's other great journey took place in 1807, while working under the employment of **Manuel Lisa**, a Spaniard from New Orleans. Lisa ran the first organized crew of trappers in the area out of a fort by the confluence of the Yellowstone and Big Horn rivers, east of where Billings is today. Colter left the fort at the start of winter on what ended up becoming an epic **500-mile circuit** through portions of modern day Yellowstone and Grand Teton National Parks. Specifics are hazy, including even which direction, clockwise or counter-clockwise, Colter followed on the loop. But it has been established that Colter passed both Yellowstone and Jackson lakes, and stumbled across many of the area's bizarre thermal features. One steamy, sulfurous area – barely active today on the outskirts of Cody – became known as **Colter's Hell**, a designation later mistakenly applied to thermal basins within Yellowstone.

The **War of 1812** between the United States and Great Britain halted much of the US-led trapping in the region for years, giving Canadian and French fur trappers a near monopoly on the trade. In 1818, a group of trappers led by Canadian **Donald McKenzie** recorded spotting "boiling fountains," though not enough detail was given to locate exactly which geysers they may have come across. Both the war's end and published reports from the Lewis and Clark expedition helped to spark excitement about what the West had in store for courageous explorers. In the East, newspaper ads were placed to recruit trappers to fulfill, in part, the booming demand for the beaver pelts used to make hats that were all the rage on both sides of the Atlantic. By 1825, famous **Mountain Men** like tall-tale teller **Jim Bridger** (see box, p.64), the journal keeping **Osborne Russell** (see review, p.288) and **Davey Jackson**, namesake of Jackson Hole, began heeding the call, becoming part of the first wave of trappers to flock to the region.

The life of a fur trapper in the Rockies was far from easy, filled with cold nights, tyrannical deals with their companies, and many a tough slog through swamps in search for beaver. Most trappers worked alone or with a partner, disappearing into the mountains for the winter and spring months, when the beavers' fur was at its most thick and lush. They would emerge in the summer with as many as 150 pelts, bushy beards, and tall tales of survival against the odds. Some of these tales included details of the natural wonders within Yellowstone, helping confirm Colter's stories, which many had believed to be great exaggerations at best and mirage-like delusions at worst.

By 1840, due to **over-trapping** and the **decline in fashion** for hats made with beaver pelts, the heyday of fur trapping had run its course in the Northern Rockies. Those Mountain Men who stayed behind tried their luck at homesteading, became guides to rich tourists and the army, and organized businesses such as trading posts and ferry crossings. Still, for the next two decades, whites rarely visited the Yellowstone plateau, and a collection of Indian tribes continued to maintain the strongest grip on the land.

Official exploration

As with so many other areas in the rugged and unforgiving Rockies, it took the discovery of **gold** to motivate whites into moving in to scratch out a living in semi-permanent settlements. Gold strikes in Idaho in the early 1860s is what drew fortune-seekers into this portion of the Northern Rockies, and mining activity and exploration saw small parties of whites re-entering Yellowstone, ending what had been virtually the exclusive haunt of Indians since the end of the fur trade some two decades earlier. Quite a few parties marched through today's Yellowstone National Park in the mid-1860s, but as they were looking for riches, not the fame of exploration, they noted little – and found little gold as well. The arrival of miners and their ensuing arguments over jurisdiction did, however, lead to the carving out of the **Montana Territory** in 1864 and the **Wyoming Territory** in 1868, roughly along the same lines that border Yellowstone today.

While miners found only traces of gold, they did bring back fantastic tales describing the wonders of Yellowstone, adding more credence to the ever-expanding series of Mountain Man "myths" from the last sixty years. These stories, passed around at bars, meeting halls, and the streets of Montana's burgeoning mining towns helped kick-start a **series of planned outings** in the area that finally confirmed Yellowstone's awesome sights to the rest of the world.

The Cook-Folsom Expedition

First out of the gate was the **Cook-Folsom Expedition** in 1869, a three person party consisting of Charles Cook and David Folsom, two Quakers, and William Peterson, a former sailor, all of whom had spent several years mining in the Northern Rockies. Leaving in early September from Helena, Montana, the trio entered Yellowstone from the north, via Bozeman, with five horses and limited supplies. Encountering small parties of Sheepeaters along the way, they followed the Yellowstone River south, passing Tower Fall and camping at the

Grand Canyon in view of its falls. They got as far south as Yellowstone Lake's northern shores, where they gorged on trout and water fowl, before turning west to wander past Great Fountain Geyser, where it is claimed they all took off their hats and hollered with astonishment. Upon returning home on October 11, just over a month after leaving Helena, their stories quickly spread through town and eventually out East, where the *New York Tribune* and *Harper's* both refused to publish details as they felt the information too far-fetched and fantastic to be reliable.

The Washburn Expedition

Big city papers may not have trusted the Cook-Folsom stories, but Helena's citizens certainly began to, and in the following year a larger, better organized, and fully funded expedition set off. Known as the **Washburn Expedition**, the nineteen-man expedition was led by **Henry Dana Washburn**, surveyor general of Montana and formerly a Civil War officer and congressman. Known for his fairness, Washburn died soon after returning from the explorations due to frail health stemming in part from his practice of taking on extra guard and scout duties. Along with an escort of soldiers led by crack shot **Gustavus Doane** and a handful of helpers, the expedition included the likes of bank president and later governor of Montana Territory **Samuel Hauser**, a Yale lawyer and later state senator **Cornelius Hedges**, and **Nathaniel Pitt Langford**, soon to become the first superintendent of Yellowstone and the expedition's most successful diarist; see p.288 for a review of his journal.

The forty-day adventure left from Helena on August 22, 1870, following a similar route as the Cook-Folsom Party. The group spent the first few days feasting on venison, elk, and trout, before tackling, in order, **Tower Fall**, which they named, the Grand Canyon and Yellowstone Falls, and Yellowstone Lake. Instead of heading west at the northern edge of the lake, however, they continued south along its eastern edge and circled the massive body of water, mapping it out clearly for the first time. After that, they marched through exceedingly difficult country to reach the Upper Geyser Basin, marveling at the accuracy of **Old Faithful**, a name bestowed by Washburn himself. In regards to naming, the group agreed before setting out to not identify any features after themselves, but the promise of immortality must have been too great, as evidenced by other names left behind including **Mounts Washburn**, **Langford**, and **Doane**.

The group returned to Helena hungry and emaciated, but healthy nonetheless on September 22. There were no battles with natives or grizzly attacks to spice up their tales, and along with nearly starving to death towards the end of their trip the worst incident to befall the group happened to **Truman C. Everts**, the oldest of the band of explorers at 54, who got lost for 37 days in the wilds to the south of Yellowstone Lake before being found (see p.51). Along with leaving behind a string of names still used today, the group's most lasting contribution was helping boost the idea of creating a national park for the area, a thought Langford captured in his journal on their way home on September 20, 1870:

> **"I do not know of any portion of our country where a national park can be established furnishing to visitors more wonderful attractions than here. These wonders are so different from anything we have ever seen – they are so various, so extensive – that the feeling in my mind from the moment they began to appear until we left them has been one of intense surprise and of incredulity. Every day spent in surveying them has revealed to me some new beauty, and now that I have left them, I begin to feel a skepticism which clothes them in a memory clouded by doubt."**

The Hayden Survey

During the winter after their return, **Langford** of the Washburn Expedition gave a series of lectures on his experiences in the Yellowstone region. **Dr. Ferdinand V. Hayden**, head of the US Geological Survey of the Territories, was at one such lecture at Lincoln Hall in Washington DC, and soon afterwards Hayden asked Congress for funding for a larger expedition. Incidentally, Hayden had already come close to surveying Yellowstone's natural wonders years earlier in 1859 while working on a two-year exploration of the upper Missouri River. With Jim Bridger as his guide, Hayden's partly began heading south towards Yellowstone, but a blizzard blocked their path and they ended up turning back. The Civil War soon put on hold any further explorations by Hayden at that time, who rose to become the Union army's chief medical officer.

Congress approved some $40,000 for the expedition, and by July of 1871 an even larger group than the Washburn Expedition was ready to set off for additional mapping, surveying, and adventure. Close to three-dozen men signed on to take part in the Hayden Survey, the first government-sponsored survey of Yellowstone, including Hayden's right-hand man **James Stevenson**, topographer **Anton Schoenborn**, who took his own life soon after the expedition ended, and photographer **William Jackson**. The painter **Thomas Moran** was also added to the group at the request of the North Pacific Railroad, whose head **Jay Cooke** had already begun hatching plans for monopolizing railroad routes to a region that Americans would undoubtedly want to flock to. Jackson's black-and-white photographs and Moran's elegant landscapes both ended up being instrumental in convincing Congress to create the national park.

The large group departed from Fort Ellis in the Gallatin Valley in July of 1871, and quickly crossed paths with the **Barlow-Heap Expedition**, a smaller military team that was also visiting Yellowstone and with whom the Hayden Survey ended up often exploring in concert. The two groups followed a similar route from the two preview expeditions, including a stop at the Grand Canyon where Moran created the pencil and watercolor field sketches used to paint his famed seven-by-twelve feet **oil painting** of the canyon and falls upon returning home to his studio; look closely at the painting and you'll notice members of the survey team, including Hayden and the artist himself, in the foreground. The group also launched *Anna*, a 12ft canvas-side boat onto Yellowstone Lake, making it the first boat to cross its waters.

The Hayden Survey, which continued in 1872 as well, ended up creating the finest maps yet of the area and named more than one hundred features within Yellowstone. Names bestowed by the group include **Electric Peak**, named as such after a literally hair-raising storm suffered by Hayden and two other members of the party upon its summit, and several landmarks dedicated to members of the group including **Mount Stevenson** and **Stevenson Island**, both named after Hayden's trusty assistant, and **Mount Chittenden** after one of the group's topographers.

A park is born

Hayden's subsequent reports on his forays in the summer and fall of 1871 put to rest once and for all any doubts on the wonders of Yellowstone, and by December of the same year a draft bill for the creation of a national park was introduced into Congress. This wasn't the first time such an idea had been voted on; eight years earlier, then President Abraham Lincoln signed into the law the **Yosemite Grant** of 1864, setting aside California's Yosemite Valley and the great redwoods within the nearby Mariposa Grove as an area reserved for public use and recreation. Responsibility for the new park, however, was given to the state of California, making it a state park. While the congressional draft for the creation of Yellowstone National Park used much the same language as the Yosemite Grant, a major difference was the notion of federal control over Yellowstone, needed in part to avoid a battle between Montana and Wyoming, both of whom had a stake in the region.

Several interested parties helped push along the natural park idea, none more influential than the Northern Pacific Railroad's chief Jay Cooke, who longed to build tracks by and into the region that could shuttle tourists by the thousands. Cooke's influence in congress can hardly be understated, and thanks to his persistence, along with Moran's grand paintings and Jackson's awe-inspiring photos, the bill was signed into law on March 1, 1872 by President **Ulysses S. Grant**, creating the country's – and the world's – **first national park**. While capitalistic desires were the engine for the park's creation, high ideals still persevered, as noted by the bill's eloquent notion that Yellowstone was "dedicated and set apart as a public park or pleasuring-ground for the benefit and enjoyment of the people…"

Not all "the people," though, were pleased with the region's new designation. Editorials in Montana and Wyoming warned that keeping the area protected would shut out businesses and keep away the roads and railways needed for people to come visit, and for the first few years these skeptics were proved correct, as little was done to improve access to the park. The penny-pinching Congress had no plans for funding Yellowstone, and instead figured that once the Northern Pacific Railroad was extended into Montana, tourists would begin arriving and that would launch dozens of concessionaires from whom the government could charge rent and other fees. In short, the park would get money when it started earning money. However, the financial **Panic of 1873** threw these plans into disarray. The countrywide economic crisis was started by none other than Jay Cooke, who, upon finding his banking and railroad interests way over-extended, was forced to declare bankruptcy. It would take close to ten more years before the railroad reached Yellowstone.

The early years

As the man put in charge of the newly formed national park department, Secretary of the Interior **Columbus Delano** was responsible for picking the **first superintendent** to manage the nascent park. On May 10, 1872, he appointed **Nathaniel Langford** to the post, a position carrying few actual powers and no salary. Known thereafter as "National Park" Langford, the diarist's first order of business was to tag along on the Hayden Survey's second trip into the region in the summer of 1872, this one ever better funded than the survey a summer earlier.

The **Hayden Survey of 1872** split into two groups, a northern Division and a southern Division, and both headed into Yellowstone in early July, sticking it out through September and mapping some 9000 square miles of terrain. Langford joined the southern Division, led by Hayden's right-hand man James Stevenson, which hiked south through the park, past Shoshone Lake and Lewis Lake, and close by today's Southern Entrance. Continuing onwards, the party reached the Tetons, where Langford and Stevenson claim to have crested **Grand Teton** on July 24; for more on this controversial claim, see p.108. The southern Division continued to map the Teton Range until early August, after which they marched back to Yellowstone for a reunion with the Northern division at the Lower Geyser Basin.

Langford quickly left the survey behind to check on an unauthorized toll road being built to **Mammoth Hot Springs**, an area starting to attract invalids to bathe in the supposed therapeutic waters. These bathers were among the first Yellowstone **tourists**, though there was far from a flood of them. It's estimated that less than 300 visitors came in 1872, with no more than 500 annually all the way through 1877. Those few tourists who did visit, however, brought back stories of the park's **mismanagement** and neglect, including the wanton slaughter of game by professional hunters. Langford was relieved of his duties in 1877 after a new Secretary of Interior, **Carl Schurz**, received one too many letters detailing Langford's lack of action. To be fair, Langford had no funds and little power, but he was also far from proactive, visiting the park only two times as superintendent, and refusing virtually all requests from concessionaires to build or operate services in the park. Even more damning, it appears that Langford's loyalties weren't with "the people" but the Northern Pacific Railroad; he was waiting for the company to rise back up so he could assign plum concessions to them.

Superintendent Norris

With Langford let go, **Philetus W. Norris** was appointed the second Superintendent of Yellowstone on April 19, 1877. Quite the opposite from Langford, Norris, as described by Yellowstone historian Aubrey L. Haines, was a natural leader, kind, and sincere, whose "sense of stewardship had a biblical purity as evident to the mountaineer as it was to the savant." One of his first orders of business was to help lead the first of many military tours through the park, this one led by Civil War leader **General William Tecumseh Sherman**, who brought along a small band of soldiers on a sight-seeing expedition. Ironically, as Sherman left the park to the north, some 600 natives entered Yellowstone from the west via the Madison River Valley on the infamous **Retreat of the Nez Percé** (see box, p.261). Having been cheated out of their land yet again, Chief Joseph's tribe was on the run, hoping to reach safety in Canada. Within Yellowstone, scouting parties of Nez Percé braves ran into two separate groups of tourists, attacking them and stealing their supplies. For two weeks warfare ensued in the park before the tribe left and headed north on a path following today's Chief Joseph Highway.

In 1878, Congress finally approved minimal funding and a salary for superintendent position, meaning Norris, who often patrolled in full buckskin regalia, could start on much-needed **road-building** projects. Soon after receiving the $10,000 annual stipend, only a fraction of which went to his own salary, Norris commenced in building a rough road from Mammoth to the Firehole Basin, through the intersection that now bears his name. Road building and trail blazing are perhaps Norris' finest legacy, and during his four-year reign the park's totals increased from 32 miles of road to 150 miles, and from 108 miles of trails to over 200 miles. Norris was also the first to officially record the park's weather and geyser eruptions – noting correctly the link between earthquakes and eruption schedules – and also supplied a great deal of archeological and historical research, much sent straight to the Smithsonian Museum back East. He also hired **Harry Yount** to live in the Lamar Valley in an attempt to stop **poachers** from slaughtering game, one of the park's most pressing problems; Yount lasted less than a year in his lonely position, but is considered by many to be the first national park ranger.

Along with naming the likes of Rustic Falls, Monument Geyser Basin, and Excelsior Geyser, Norris also designated a handful of features after himself (Mount Norris, Norris Fork, Norris Geyser Basin, and Norris Pass), for which he was ridiculed in the local press. His allegedly egocentric naming system wasn't the only thing that got Norris in hot water, as he also found himself alienated from the powerful railroad interests that once again began plotting routes into the Yellowstone region. Embroiled in a political fight in which he was powerless and facing character assassination from pro-railroad interests in the press, Norris was pushed out in 1882.

Monopolies take hold

The new superintendent put in charge was the well-connected **Patrick Henry Conger**, whose brother was both a Michigan senator and, more importantly, a staunch supporter of the "iron horse." Petty and ineffectual, Conger lasted two years, and over the next four years two more leaders shuttled in and out. The most important event during this time had little to do with any of these superintendents, but instead foreshadowed the eventual influence of the Army within Yellowstone. In 1882, **General Phillip Sherman** of the US Army toured the park on a large junket including some 150 men and 300 horses. Soon after blazing the Sheridan Trail from Jackson Hole to the thumb of Yellowstone Lake, his party encountered a construction crew from the reformed Northern Pacific Railroad working beyond the park's northern boundary. From speaking to employees of the railroad, the general began to work out a better understanding of the so-called **Yellowstone Park Improvement Company**, who had recently worked out a deal with the Secretary of the Interior that ensured them a **monopoly** on future facilities and services, including accommodations, park guides and even horses within the park. Among other rights, the group of influential investors was also given permission to cut as much lumber as needed for fuel, and allowed to raise crops and raise cattle – all for a rental fee of no more than $2 per acre.

Sherman quickly made his views on the situation known, and his warnings helped create new legislations curtailing the power of the Yellowstone Park Improvement Company, limiting their monopoly to a ten-year lease and forbidding any further exclusive privileges from being granted by the Secretary of the Interior. While all the political wrangling was occurring, the company was furiously at work to make eviction impossible, and by 1883 they had opened a portion of the **National Hotel** at Mammoth. Torn down in 1935, the hastily erected building had room for upwards of 500 guests, who were often, much to their surprise, forced to share a room and even beds with unknown guests. In the same year, the Yellowstone Park Improvement Company also opened three expensive, poorly run tent-hotels at the Grand Canyon and the Norris and Upper Geyser basins.

The busiest year yet for Yellowstone, the Northern Pacific Railroad also completed their **branch line** connecting Livingston – a town whose population had exploded from less than 100 to more than 3000 in the past year – to **Cinnabar** in the Paradise Valley, twenty miles north of Gardiner. With a railroad connection finally completed, both the Northern Pacific Railroad and Yellowstone Improvement Company hosted **lavish tours** of the park and its new facilities late in the summer of 1883, bringing along such guests as ex President Ulysses Grant and numerous senators – so expensive, in fact, were the tours that the heads of both companies ended up getting fired, in part, for overspending. As if there weren't enough dignitaries stuffed into the park, **President Chester Arthur** visited with his own party for a tour during the same time. Yellowstone was now open for business, though who would control the trade was still being fiercely debated.

The Army arrives

Business may have been booming in Yellowstone by the mid-1880s, but so was poaching and squatting, and many of the park's finest features were in danger of being chipped away to nothing by souvenir-stealing vendors and visitors. Congress, tired of the inactive and ineffectual stewardship, refused to give any more money to park administrators, forcing the Secretary of the Interior to call on the War Department for assistance. The **Army** was given control of the park, and on August 13, 1886, **Captain Moses Harris** marched 50 men of Company M from Fort Custer in the Montana Territories to Mammoth. Upon arriving, Harris assumed the title of Park Superintendent, the first of twelve Army officers to run the park, and run it well, for the next thirty years.

The army had marched into a volatile situation; frontiersmen in the region had no regard for the park's toothless rules and regulations, and some citizens, upset with park administrators, had taken to setting fires to woods and grasslands within Yellowstone in fits of petty revenge. Led by Harris, the troops immediately set about enforcing a long list of park **regulations** including the cutting of green timber, banning the molestation of natural curiosities (particularly throwing items into springs and "soaping" geysers to force eruption), stopping the sale of liqor, and forbidding all hunting and allowing fishing with line and hook only. Preparing for the winter, Harris also set about beginning the construction of **Camp Sheridan** in Mammoth, erecting five buildings, including a large barracks. His timing couldn't have been better, as the Army's first winter in the park was a brutal one and a wake up call to many of his soldiers who had come from the milder southwest and Great Plains to the east.

Almost immediately, the troops reversed the park's steady decline into chaos, taking lead in everything from fire fighting to road building. The soldiers, stationed at various tourist hot spots such as Old Faithful throughout the summer, also kept an eye on tourists, making sure they obeyed the rules. Indeed, the soldiers were so dedicated to the laws that they even arrested and expelled executives from the Northern Pacific Railroad in the summer of 1888 after their guide, **E.C. Waters**, soaped Beehive Geyser to make it erupt. Waters, manager of the *National Hotel* at that time, took umbrage and would become a thorn in the side park administrators for years to come.

Ed Howell and the Lacey Act

The Army's status as the absolute administrator and law enforcement of Yellowstone continued to grow, with **Fort Yellowstone** replacing Camp Sheridan in 1891. What started off as a dozen buildings – including a prison and barracks for 60 men – would continue to expand to a complex of 37 structures by 1917. Over the same period, sixteen **Soldier Stations** were built throughout the park, allowing soldiers to patrol Yellowstone year-round from locations as isolated as Sylvan Pass to the east (1094) and Bechler (1911) to the southwest. However, as evidenced by the eviction of E.C. Waters for soaping Beehive Geyser, the Army remained hamstrung during their formative years in the park by one major issue: the ability to prosecute law breakers. The Army's sole penalty for everyone from the more innocuous souvenir taker to the careless campfire keeper to the dastardly and still hugely problematic poacher was expulsion from the park. While the Army had taken to confiscating the hunting gear and traps of poachers along with expulsion, it still took only days for illegal hunters to stock back up and return to their trade.

All of this changed, however, with the watershed arrest of Ed Howell in 1894. In the words of Yellowstone historian Aubrey L. Haines, "a scoundrel seldom accomplishes so much." A known poacher, Howell was tracked down and arrested in a daring capture by two soldiers on snowshoes in the Pelican Valley on March 13. Caught literally red-handed – the poacher was removing the heads of five slaughtered buffalo to sell to a taxidermist – Howell was being marched back to Fort Yellowstone when the soldiers happened to bump into a group of writers exploring the park for *Field and Stream* magazine. Writer **Emerson Hough** dashed off a story relating Howell's crime and capture, and quickly sent it back East. Upon learning of the weak punishment Howell was to receive, public anger boiled over, spurring Representative **John F. Lacey** of Iowa to introduce a bill into Congress that would finally dole out the appropriate powers to punish rule breakers. Known as the **Lacey Act**, the bill was quickly pushed through and signed into law on May 7, 1894, less than two months after Howell's arrest. The bill, which called for "… the preservation from injury or spoliation of all timber, mineral deposits, natural curiosities, or wonderful objects within [Yellowstone]; and for the protection of the animals and birds within the park, from capture or destruction…" gave the Army the power to fine, imprison and permanently banish rule breakers, and also helped kick start a wave of **wildlife preservation and protection** that continues today. Ironically, Howell himself was the first person arrested under the act later that summer when he returned to Yellowstone against the orders of the Army.

Representative Lacey, who would go on to support and help several more federal conversation bills of note, incidentally played a part in another notable happening within Yellowstone. A frequent visitor to the park, he was robbed at gunpoint during one of the Yellowstone's storied stagecoach robberies in 1887, undoubtedly spawning his interest in increasing law enforcement within the region.

△ Soldiers posing with poached bison heads

Trains, reigns, and automobiles

Right through the Army's time in power, tourism numbers in Yellowstone climbed at a steady clip, rising from an estimated 5000 visitors in 1886 to more than 35,000 by 1916. The catalyst for this steady increase was the **railroads**, which, along with building lines closer and closer to the park's entrances, continued to funnel money into concessionaires within the park, playing a shell game with their finances to play down any monopolistic appearances. To get an even stronger stranglehold within the park, the railroads lobbied fiercely throughout the late 1800s and early 1900s for the rights to lay tracks into and through Yellowstone. Railroad executives and government officials in their debt attempted to push numerous pro-railroad bills through Congress – one proposal even called for an electric railway, to be powered by the waterfalls on the Yellowstone River – though all were blocked by more forward-looking politicians.

By the early 1900s, tourists were being brought to the borders of Yellowstone by two main routes. Most popular was the **Northern Pacific**, whose mainline branched south at Livingston to connect with Cinnabar, until 1903 when the extension to **Gardiner** on the park boundary was completed. Less popular but still frequently used was the **Oregon Short Line Railroad** to **Monida**, Montana, located some seventy miles west of Yellowstone; this line was also extended, reaching **West Yellowstone** by 1908. The other rail options completed throughout Yellowstone's railroad era were the **Burlington Line** to Cody, completed in 1903; the **Chicago Northwestern** to Lander, Wyoming, finished in 1921; and lastly, the **Chicago, Milwaukee**, and **Saint Paul** to the Gallatin Gateway Inn, just south of Bozeman, completed in 1921.

As the railroad tracks never snaked their way through Yellowstone, visitors needed to be shuttled around the park – this was the job of the **stagecoach**. The stagecoach tours that departed from bordering train stations were far from cheap (most were run by the railroads themselves), making them the domain of middle and upper class visitors. Indeed, "sage brushers" – visitors who rolled through under their own steam, unable to afford the all-inclusive tours – were looked down upon and made to feel unwelcome. The dusty, bone-rattling horse-drawn tours were mostly taken in eleven-passenger "**Yellowstone Wagons**" that took five days to complete a grand loop of the park. Beginning in Mammoth or West Yellowstone, the tours worked their way clockwise, passing sights such as Obsidian Cliff and Roaring Mountain, past the Lower, Midway, and Upper Geyser Basins, and on to Old Faithful. From here, the tours would head east to Yellowstone Lake, then turn north to the Grand Canyon and eventually back to Mammoth. Overnight stops included accommodations that stand today – the **Lake Yellowstone Hotel**, built in 1891, and the **Old Faithful Inn**, started in 1903, for example – and some that don't, such as the **Canyon Hotel**, which featured a chained-up bear out back, and a collection of candy-stripped tent camps run by **William Wylie**, a former Bozeman school teacher and successful Yellowstone entrepreneur.

The stagecoach era came to an abrupt end with the introduction of the **automobile**. While cars had made the occasional foray into Yellowstone as early as 1902, they were banned for more than a decade due in part to their startling, often dangerous effect on horses. In the summer of 1915, however, they were officially permitted, provided they followed a series of regulations including a speed limit of 20mph (lowered to 12mph for uphill travel and 10mph downhill). Within a year, it was obvious that stagecoaches and cars could not coexist, and the car won out – buses and other motorized transport were brought in, while stagecoaches disappeared virtually overnight.

A new Service – and a new park

Along with killing off the stagecoach, the automobile played a role in ending the Army's reign in Yellowstone. Among other car-related tasks, the Army refused to take on the responsibility of checking in cars at all entrances, necessitating the hiring of four park rangers to man the gates. At the same time, the federal government was realizing that something needed to be done to better manage the growing number of independently run national parks and monuments across the country. On August 25, 1916, President Woodrow Wilson signed the **National Park Service Act**, creating an agency to "to conserve the scenery and the natural and historic objects and the wildlife therein" of more than a dozen national parks.

By 1918, **National Park Service Rangers** – including some soldiers formerly stationed at Mammoth – were officially in charge of Yellowstone. In a fortunate twist of fate, the new superintendent in charge was **Horace M. Albright**, who ran Yellowstone successfully before eventually taking over as head of the National Park Service. Along with expanding interpretive facilities, Albright's main mission was to make Yellowstone more suitable for the automobile, both for the benefit of tourists and of the park itself. He set out at once to improve the roads from one-lane stagecoach paths to two-lane highways, and also ordered the building of general stores, service stations, campgrounds and cabins. In the ten years that Albright led Yellowstone, numbers more than quadrupled from 62,000 visitors to 260,000. His most lasting legacy, however, is found due south with **Grand Teton National Park**, created in 1929 thanks in large part to the behind-the-scenes work of Albright (see the box on p.92 for more).

World War II to the new millennium

During **World War II**, budget cuts and the loss of employees to the war effort caused facilities in the park to slide into disrepair. This problem was compounded by a lack of incoming money due to limited visitor numbers, a direct effect of gasoline rationing and the fact that many families were reticent to vacation while the country was at war. As soon as the war ended, however, visitor numbers spiked – reaching the one million mark in Yellowstone for the first time in 1948 – but many of the facilities were still in desperate need of improvement. In 1955, the Park Service kicked off a program known as **Mission 66**, an intensive plan to modernize amenities by 1966. Among other projects completed was Canyon Village, built around a large parking lot and a clear indication that the car was indeed king for tourism.

Throughout the 1960s and 70s, attitudes on how to manage and experience Yellowstone continued to evolve, switching from a concept of the park as a vacationer's playground, to an awareness of its unique ecological habitats that needed to be protected and preserved. The active "management" – i.e. slaughter – of wildlife like elk and bison was halted after the publication of the **Leopold Report**, a watershed document influenced greatly by **Aldo Starker Leopold** (1887–1948), a biologist who advocated for natural regulation within national parks to let ecosystems find their natural balance. Other important environmental laws enacted in the era include The Clean Air and Clean Water Acts, along with the Endangered Species Act passed in 1973.

The most dramatic and newsworthy event in the region during the second half of the twentieth century were the **wildfires of 1988**. Described in the box on p.80, these fires ended up destroying close to 800,000 acres in Yellowstone alone. In the following few years, Yellowstone slowly woke from its fire-induced hangover to find that, contrary to some expert opinions, visitor numbers did not drop precipitously, and the landscape itself began to attract life again, becoming a visible living example of the positive effects of fire on forest systems. Before the century ended, another major newsworthy event occurred with the **reintroduction of wolves**, beginning in 1995. Though plenty controversial to this day, the successful addition of wolves back into the landscape – along with the halting of divisive plans for opening the **New World Mine** on Yellowstone's northeast border in 1996 – had Yellowstone entering the new millennium with an optimistic step.

Yellowstone today

With two or more sides to seemingly every issue being heatedly debated, it's easy to create a laundry list of **problems** facing Yellowstone and Grand Teton today. Staff budget cuts to the National Park Service under that Bush administration have begun seriously damaging both morale and the effectiveness of park rangers. Naturalists are up in arms at the idea of delisting both grizzlies and wolves from the roll call of endangered species, a near certainty at the time of writing. Diseases and invasive species are destroying native populations, from cutthroat trout to the whitebark pines that grizzlies rely on for much of their autumn diet. Issues over the management of bison and use of snowmobiles continue to cause deep divides locally and nationally. And the over-development of suburban tracts and large second-home mansions throughout the greater Yellowstone ecosystem is destroying a frightening amount of the hunting and migratory land of the region's fauna. And that, as any ranger will tell you, is only scratching the surface.

Still, with Yellowstone nearing its 135th birthday and Grand Teton closing in on 80, it's impossible to deny that the grand park experiment has been an amazing success. And it's equally difficult to feel that the parks won't continue to find compromises, sometimes brilliant and sometimes brittle, to their problems. What started out as experiment with the creation of Yellowstone National Park in 1872 has morphed into a global movement, leading citizens in nations across the world to realize the preciousness of the land and the importance of preserving it.

Geology, flora, and fauna

One of the major thrills of traveling through the Yellowstone region is the chance to see some of North America's most distinctive wildlife in its natural habitat; it should also go without saying that those habitats – vast meadows and sagebrush flats, hydrothermal wonderlands, and the surrounding mountain ranges – are among the most dramatic on the continent. The determining factors for the kinds of animals and birds you might encounter while exploring are altitude, terrain, and vegetation. All three are inextricably linked, with altitude and terrain determining what kinds of vegetation can grow in a given area; the region is thus made up of a number of distinct ecosystems, each one supporting particular types of animals and birds.

Geology

While nowadays bison, grizzly bears, wolves, cutthroat trout, and the rest of the region's incredible array of wildlife share the spotlight, both Yellowstone and Grand Teton were originally set aside as national parks for one reason: they're home to some of the most incredible **geological wonders** on the continent. What follows is an overview on how many of these wonders came about, but for more in-depth explanations, look for some of the books reviewed on pp.287–290. For a specific look at how the mighty **Tetons** came into existence, see the box on p.103.

At a glacial pace

The region's various mountain ranges – including the **Absaroka**, **Beartooth**, **Teton**, **Snake River**, and **Wind River** mountains – all are a part of the **Rocky Mountains**, which extends some two thousand miles from central New Mexico all the way up to northeastern British Columbia in Canada, effectively dividing North America in a manner not unlike that of the Mississippi River to the east; indeed the mountains delineate what is known as the **Continental Divide**, from which the pattern of water flow is dictated in North America. Rivers on the west of the divide drain into the Pacific Ocean, those on the east into the Atlantic or Arctic oceans.

The Rockies are relatively young mountains, formed mainly by the **Laramide Revolution**, a period of tectonic uplifts that took place in the late Cretaceous Period, around 65 million years ago, which was followed by volcanic activity and folding and faulting that continued into the early Tertiary Period. By contrast, the Blue Ridge Mountains in the eastern United States are thought to have formed some 200 million years ago, with the first great tectonic collision.

Much of the landscape on view today was sculpted, geologically speaking, a short time ago. As with the rest of the continent, the Yellowstone plateau has experienced several periods of intense **glaciation** over the last couple of million years. During these ice ages, most of the region was buried beneath massive migrating glaciers. These glaciers were formed when more snow fell throughout the year then melted. Once snow depths reached a certain level, their overall size and weight forced gravity into action, moving them as they crushed and picked up rocks along their routes. The two most recent glacier eras are the **Bull Lake Period**, which covered the region around 140,000 years ago, and the **Pinedale Period**, at its peak only 25,000 years ago. During both of these eras, giant rivers of ice inched their way across the land, grinding down mountains, carving out massive U-shape canyons, and leaving behind **terminal moraines** that turned into natural dams forming the likes of Jenny Lake. The size of these ice-sheets are mind-numbing; during the Pinedale Period, for example, Yellowstone Lake was covered in a 4000ft thick sea of ice, with only the tallest peaks of ranges like the Beartooths and the Tetons remaining above the ice – which is why today they still remain jagged, not worn smooth like shorter neighboring peaks. As temperatures warmed, the glaciers melted and retreated, dropping off random rocks in their wake – known as **erratics** – along with large chunks of ice that melted to form **kettle lakes**. Glacial activity continues to affect the landscape of the area's higher mountain ranges even today, as evidenced by the dozen glaciers, including **Teton Glacier** (the largest), still viewable high up the Tetons.

A hydrothermal wonderland

Along with ice, fire has played a vital role in Yellowstone's geological story. Beneath much of the park lies what is termed a **hotspot**, where molten rock from the Earth's mantle called **magma** rises to within three miles of the surface. Originally located to the west, this hotspot is now beneath Yellowstone as the continental plate on which the park sits has been drifting to the southwest over the past several million years. The volcanic activity of this hotspot across this same period has been epic, with several cataclysmic **ash-flow volcanic eruptions** occurring; these eruptions dwarf any in recorded history, with the biggest being 2500 times more powerful than Mount St Helen's significant 1980 eruption.

The largest, the **Huckleberry Ridge** eruption, occurred some 2 million years ago, spreading thick layers of ash as far as California and the Gulf of Mexico. A smaller, though still earth-shattering explosion, known as **Island Park** eruption, occurred 1.3 million years ago, followed by the larger **Lava Creek** eruption some 640,000 years ago. During this later eruption, a huge underground chamber disgorged 250 cubic miles of molten rock, and then promptly collapsed upon itself, creating the **Yellowstone Caldera**; its rim measures about 47 miles by 28 miles at its broadest. With these **supervolcano** eruptions occurring on average every 650,000 years, Yellowstone – geologically speaking – is due for another major eruption.

Also playing an important role in Yellowstone's ever-changing geology are **earthquakes**. An average of 2000 earthquakes are recorded yearly in the region, though they are only occasionally felt and are rarely disastrous; see **Quake Lake** (p.228) just outside of West Yellowstone for an example of one that was. Even those earthquakes that aren't felt, however, play an important role; their shakes and rattles ensure that the region's hydrothermal features remain active

Hot shots

You'll undoubtedly want to **photograph** a gushing geyser in its full splendor, but keep in mind you may only have one good chance so be at the ready. Position yourself upwind, otherwise you'll be photographing a big cloud of steam instead of the actual water spout, and always keep thermal spray off your camera lens as deposits within the mist can cause permanent damage.

by breaking any clogs formed by mineral deposits that would otherwise seal off and eventual shut down geysers and hot springs.

Hydrothermal features

Into the **Yellowstone Caldera** are crammed more than half the world's geysers, plus thousands of fumaroles jetting plumes of steam, mud pots gurgling with acid-dissolved muds and clays, and hot springs. Most of the park's hydrothermal features sit within the caldera – as does much of Yellowstone Lake – but there is plenty of peripheral volcanic activity as well, as evidenced by the Norris Geyser basin and Mammoth Hot Springs, both of which are outside the caldera boundary. For an in-depth look at the park's geysers, hot springs, and other assorted hydrothermal springs, see the "Hydrothermal Yellowstone" color insert.

Fauna

Yellowstone is home to 61 different **mammals**, a line-up that includes the most fascinating and charismatic megafauna on the continent: the grizzly bear, the North American bison, the moose, the mountain lion, and the gray wolf, to mention but a few. Inevitably, there's a mix of excitement and frustration that goes with spotting animals, because they don't show up on demand; in fact, the more intelligent and secretive of them make a point of avoiding human contact altogether. You can, however, reliably expect to see certain animals, especially bison and elk, and even to have quite close encounters with some of them.

If wildlife **viewing and photographing** is a priority, you should definitely bring along binoculars or a spotting scope, as well as a powerful zoom lens (200–300mm) for your camera.

Large mammals

The title of Yellowstone mascot goes to the **American bison**, the largest land mammal in North America. Known alternatively though incorrectly as buffalo, these magnificent creatures once roamed the Rockies and Great Plain in vast herds that could each total as many as five million animals. Their rapid destruction is a well-known story, and Yellowstone is the sole place in the lower 48 states to host a continuous bison population since the eve of their decimation. Though poaching saw their population dip to as low as two dozen by the early 1900s, the creation of the Buffalo Ranch in the Lamar Valley (see p.55) helped them survive and their presence in the parks is now strong, with bison easily spotted everywhere from the Gardiner area in northern Yellowstone to the southern reaches of Grand Teton. There are upwards of 5000 bison in the area, living in three major herds in Yellowstone; the Lamar Valley's Northern Herd, the Mary Mountain Herd in the Hayden and Firehole valleys, and the Pelican Valley Herd. Feeding on grasses and sedges, male bulls can weigh as much as 2000 pounds but still run at up to 30mph and jump heights taller than themselves. Save for the summer mating season, bulls spend most the year living alone, while cows and their reddish brown calves cluster in herds year-round. Both sexes sport horns, with those on males being wider at the base and slightly less curved.

One more of the larger animals you're virtually guaranteed to encounter is the **elk** (also called "wapiti" an appropriately descriptive Shawnee meaning

△ Two male elk interlock horns

"white-rumped deer"). Approximately 30,000 elk summer in Yellowstone (half that come winter), and the larger bulls – weighing up to 900 pounds and sporting huge antlers that alone can weigh as much as fifty pounds – are quite a sight. Save for the mating season, bulls generally live a solitary existence, while cows and calves herd together in groups; all spend most their time grazing on grasses and woody vegetation. The most dramatic time to observe elk is during the fall rut, which generally begins in September and may go on into early November. The bulls strut and display their necks and antlers to the cows, but the most extraordinary part of their display is an unearthly call to a potential mate called "bugling" – a bizarre ear-piercing squeal.

Another beautifully antlered ungulate is the **mule deer**. Roughly one-third the size of an elk – and only a quarter of the weight – the mule deer is further distinguished by the much lighter, almost tan coloring of its coat, an overly generous set of mule-like ears, and a short, black-tipped tail attached to its cream-colored rump. The male's antlers are quite delicate too, flowing with balance and symmetry. Around 2000 mule deer call Yellowstone home in the summer, though nearly all migrate out come winter. Similar in size but much scarcer are **white-tailed deer**. The few who summer in Yellowstone are most often spotted streamside in the park's northern reaches. Somewhat smaller than the mule deer is the **pronghorn**, a particularly prominent animal in Wyoming, occupying grassy flatlands and often seen grazing on sagebrush by roadsides and on ranch properties. Sometimes spotted in the Lamar Valley and the sagebrush flats of Jackson Hole, pronghorns have a pale reddish hide, large white rump and short horns that jut inwards; males are easily sorted by their pronged horns and patch of black the cheek. Capable of sprinting in quick spurts up to 70mph, they are North America's fastest land animal.

The largest member of the deer family is the **moose**. With the largest bulls reaching seven feet at the shoulder and weighing 1000 pounds, their bulbous heads topped by a broad spread of antlers, and with a pendulous dewlap slung beneath the chin, this marvelous animal, once encountered, is not easily forgotten. More so then any other deer, however, moose can be ornery, and you should always keep your distance. Their long gangly legs are built for wading, and moose generally browse the wetland grasses and aquatic plants found along rivers and in riparian meadows; amazingly, moose have been spotted diving down as deep as 20 feet to munch on aquatic planets. It is estimated that fewer then 500 moose live in Yellowstone, with the 1988 fires playing a strong role in their decreasing population due the loss of winter habitat. They're more commonly spotted in Grand Teton, especially in the Willow Flats area behind the *Jackson Lake Lodge*.

Equally photogenic are **bighorn sheep** – there is no more indelible image than a lone bighorn perched on a rocky ledge, lord of all he surveys. Both rams and ewes grow horns, although the two are easily distinguished as the ram has the classic "C"-shaped horns, while the ewe's grow as almost vertical spikes, up to eight inches long. Rams, which can weight as much as 300 pounds, put on an extraordinary display during the rutting season, roughly mid-November through December, when they square off and crack horns with a sickening impact to assert their authority and establish mating rights. Bighorns are the archetypal high-country dwellers, great at negotiating rocky ledges and dealing with cool temperatures, and mostly stick to the alpine reaches in Yellowstone including Mount Washburn and the Gardner Canyon.

Predators: bears, wolves, and mountain lions

Many visitors are hoping most of all to see predators such as the grizzly bear, mountain lion, and gray wolf. There are special rules of engagement that go with encountering these animals, particularly the at times fearsome **grizzly bear**. It's worth noting some of the differences in appearance between the grizzly and its slightly smaller cousin the **black bear** – also a resident in the area – to be able to distinguish between the two. They both come in similar shades of color, so that's of little help: the black bear can range from blond to cinnamon to brown to black, and grizzlies from cinnamon to a deep reddish brown. More useful are distinctions related to the animals' body shape: grizzlies have a fairly pronounced hump behind their necks, a feature the black bear lacks; also, a grizzly's hindquarters slope downwards, while a black bear's tailbone sits level with or just above the height of its shoulders. For advice on what to do in bear encounters, see the box on p.118.

Park officials estimate that some six hundred grizzly bears live within Yellowstone, most commonly spotted early in the morning or at dusk in the Hayden and Lamar valleys. Males can weight up to 700 pounds, and sprint as fast as 45mph. A similar number of black bears call the area home, with males weighing upwards of 300 pounds. Both mate mid-May to mid-July, though remarkably embryos don't begin to develop for four months, allowing females to store energy until entering hibernation in December; cubs are born during hibernation in January or February, and males take no part in raising them afterwards. Indeed, adult males have been known to kill cubs in order to mate again more quickly and eliminate future competition. Voracious eaters, grizzly and black bears treat the Yellowstone ecosystem like a vast, all-you-can-eat buffet, feasting on virtually anything. They hunt elk calves and spawning trout; dig out rodents from their underground homes; slurp down insects such as ants and moths; chow on plant life, ranging from roots and bulbs to berries and whitebark pinenuts, the latter of which they often steal from hording squirrels; and, lastly, they are talented scavengers, taking food from both humans and fellow predators like wolves, often stealing kills to quickly feast on twenty pounds of fresh meat. Their hunger reaches epic levels in fall before denning, when bears enter a state known as hyperphagia and eat furiously to pack on enough calories to sleep through winter.

The **gray wolf** is one of Yellowstone's greatest success stories, and simply hearing a howl is an unforgettable highlight for many visitors. Wolves were once the most abundant predator in North America, with at least five sub-species in existence and a population of up to two million spread coast to coast. They were hunted to extinction in the region by the mid 1900s, but beginning in 1994 31 gray wolves from western Canada were relocated here. Population totals in the region tend to swoop up and down dramatically due to disease and natural selection, but at the time of writing some 140 wolves roamed the region in approximately fourteen packs. See "The wolves of Yellowstone" color sections for more details on the park's successful wolf program, along with information on wolf behavior and wolf-watching.

Far more secretive – and as well potentially dangerous – is the **mountain lion**; also referred to as a puma or cougar, this sleek, muscular animal has perhaps the most accurate Latin name of all – *felis concolor*, or the one-colored cat. Mountain lion sightings are exceedingly rare in the region, and it's estimated that fewer than twenty live full time within Yellowstone, mainly in the park's northern expanses. Solitary hunters, mountain lions, which weigh between 100–165 pounds, mainly prey upon elk and mule deer, though they have been known to kill bighorn sheep, pronghorn, coyotes and even porcupine. After killing their prey with a quick bite to the neck or base of the skull and feasting, they cache their kill to eat from later – provided a bear doesn't find it first.

Smaller mammals

Affectionately known to some Native American peoples as the "singing trickster," the **coyote** is a highly adaptable and opportunistic predator fairly common in the region. Coyotes hunt small prey such as rodents and ground squirrels, but also hunt elk calves in spring and scavenge the carcasses of bigger animals such as elk, deer, and even bison when the opportunity arises. Sometimes confused with wolves from afar, coyotes are much smaller (weighing around thirty pounds, in comparison with 120 pounds for a gray wolf) and unlike wolves, they'll often appear by roadsides and in populated areas where a free meal might present itself. Along with ranchers, coyotes are probably the least enthusiastic local group when it comes to wolf restoration. Before wolves returned, their sole major predator was the mountain lion; now the coyotes find themselves several rungs lower on the food chain, and some biologists claim the coyote population has decreased by as much as half thanks to marauding wolf packs; other experts, however, believe their numbers haven't gone down nearly so much, but just that the flexible scavenger has adapted and now is better at hiding.

Tragically, the **beaver** has failed to be so malleable in the face of danger, and their story is one of the sorrier tales of human impact on wildlife. The pelt of nature's most energetic engineer was at one time so desired for making hats that the animal was very nearly wiped from the face of the earth. Weighing up to 60 pounds, the beaver, the largest rodent in North America, is entrusted with designing and building wetland habitat for countless plants and animals. Its dam-building creates ponds and marshy meadows which in turn support wetland grasses and trees such as willow and cottonwood, as well as waterfowl and grazing animals like moose, elk, and deer. It's thought that somewhere around seven hundred beavers live in Yellowstone, scattered in upwards of a hundred colonies; for visible evidence of their handiwork, visitors are best of looking for lodges in the Beaver Ponds area by Mammoth or in the isolated Bechler River region; in Grant Teton, the ponds in the Colter Bay area are active beaver grounds.

Among the long list of other smaller mammals within the region are the **red fox**, **squirrels** (unita ground, red, and golden manteled), **chipmunks**, **weasels**, **martens**, and **snowshoe hares**. You'll need a fair bit of luck to see a **lynx**, **bobcat**, **wolverine**, or **river otter**, though more common are the **pika**, a small but rotund rodent which announces its presence by squeaking loudly as it pops out from its rocky hideaway, and the **yellow-bellied marmot**, which closely resembles a groundhog. Marmots are inveterate sunbathers, and may be seen on exposed, sunny rock outcrops at lower mountain elevations and almost anywhere on the alpine tundra; called "whistle-pigs" by early homesteaders, marmots make a loud, whistle sound when distressed.

Birds

Well over 300 species of birds have been spotted in Yellowstone, and close to 150 of them are known to nest in the area. The leading lights for casual birders are the predators, including the **bald eagle**, **peregrine falcon**, and **osprey**, all three of which are typically spotted near water. Osprey prey almost exclusively on fish, while bald eagles also swoop down on unsuspecting water fowl; peregrine falcons feast on water fowl too, along with songbirds, which they snatch out of mid-air on high speed dives that can exceed 200mph. Osprey and falcons migrate south come fall, while bald eagles stick around year-round – look for them perched on cottonwood branches streamside. Other predators to watch out for include the **golden eagle**, **red-tailed hawk**, **cooper's hawk**, and **turkey vulture**.

Easier to spot and just as remarkable are the region's herons and waterfowl, including **American white pelicans**, which summer on Yellowstone Lake; surprisingly graceful, author Gary Ferguson sums them up in *Hawk's Rest* (see p.287) as "startling in their ability to seem both heavy and full of grace – size 16 ballerinas, on a planet with half the gravity of earth." Also large and white is the equally balletic **trumpeter swan**, a species that came perilously close to extinction in the early 1900s. Today several thousand winter in the region, though they're often confused with the **tundra swan** that only passes through the region (to make sure it's a trumpeter, look for pink streak along their black bill.) Other notable waters birds include the long-legged **great blue heron**, the greenish-black **double-crested cormorant**, the black and white **barrow's goldeneye**, and the rare but beautiful **harlequin duck**. Also found waterside are the playful **American dipper**, small gray birds that dive in and out of rivers in search of water bugs, and **sandhill cranes**, which nest in the region in summer.

Nearly a dozen species of owls are known to call the region home, including the **great horned owl** and the **great gray owl**, the later featuring a distinctive dish-shaped face. Any equal variety of woodpeckers can be spotted, such as the **three-toed woodpecker** and **black-backed woodpecker**, most often seen pecking for bugs on the remains of charred trees. Other popular terrestrial birds include the **Steller's Jay** and **Clark's Nutcracker**, both commonly found harassing picnickers for crumbs of food, and the oft-spotted **raven**, the air version of a coyote which deserves special mention for its trickster personality. As well as being a good way to spot wolves (see *The wolves of Yellowstone* color section), ravens are practised thieves, having learnt to unzip the backpacks of careless snowmobile riders come winter for a free snack.

Fish, amphibians, and reptiles

Fish are abundant in the region's numerous mountain lakes and rivers, and even if you've no interest in casting for them, you can't fail to miss seeing folks throwing a line in any available stream. You don't have to be an angler to enjoy watching fish, however, and when hiking take time to sit still streamside, watching trout face upstream in search of incoming snacks. Most celebrated is the native **cutthroat trout**, sporting a telltale red slash along its jaw, which is divided into three subspecies – the Yellowstone cutthroat, Snake River cutthroat, and the westslope cutthroat. All three are facing an uphill battle nowadays, and both whirling disease and **lake trout** have cut a swathe through their overall population (see the box, p.84). The two other native sports fish are the **artic grayling** and **mountain whitefish**, though most anglers are just as happy to reel in non-native **rainbow trout**, **brown trout**, and **brook trout**.

Sharing the water with these fish are four species of amphibians, namely the **boreal spotted** and **Columbia chorus frogs**, **boreal toad**, and the yellow-spotted **tiger salamander**. Found in many of Yellowstone's ponds and lake, the wide-headed tiger salamander grows up to 10 inches in length, coming out of hibernation in May or June. As for reptiles, there are a half-dozen species in Yellowstone, including the harmless **valley** and **wandering gartner snakes**, and the **bullsnake**, which grows up to six feet in length and is the largest reptile in the region. Bullsnakes are often confused with the **prairie rattlesnake**, as both coil up and produce a rattling noise when disturbed. Found sunning themselves on rocks and paths only in the drier, northern reaches of Yellowstone and not at all in Grand Teton, the prairie rattlesnake is the only dangerously venomous snake in the region; however, according to park sources, only two bites have been known to occur in Yellowstone's history, proving that these snakes are far more frightened of humans than we should be of them.

Ecosystems and flora

Stretching across portions of Idaho, Montana, and especially Wyoming, the greater Yellowstone ecosystem covers close to 30,000 square miles of terrain. Along with the rich variety of wildlife detailed above, some 1100 species of plants grow here, and the types of forests, plants, and flowers that you'll encounter depends mainly on the altitude you're at. As with the rest of the Rockies, the mountain environment here consists of three essential ecosystems: the **montane** (6000–9000 feet), **subalpine** (9000–11,500 feet), and **alpine** (above 11,500 feet).

Most prevalent is the montane, where you'll find immense forests of tall and straight **lodgepole pine**, by far the most common tree in the region; upwards of 80 percent of Yellowstone's forested area is made up of the amazing lodgepole (see p.79). Also found in this zone are forests of **Douglas fir**, picked out by its reddish-brown bark and cones with prominent three-pointed bracts sticking out, as well as strands of **aspen**, also known as quaking aspen for the way its leaves quiver in the wind. A part of the willow family, aspens grow in large colonies derived from a single seedling, which is why come fall entire patches turn gold together seemingly overnight. **Engelmann spruce** (grayish, scaly bark, and slender, cylindrical cones), **subalpine fir** (gray, smooth bark with larger, purplish cones), and **whitebark pine** (yellow-green needles in bundles of five with smallish, purple cones) take over above 9000 feet, where the temperatures get a bit cooler, and more open meadows begin to appear. The seeds and nuts from whitebark pine are a particularly important food source for everything from Clark's Nutcrackers to squirrels to grizzly bears, an alarming fact as a disease known as **white pine blister rust** has been devastating large forests of these trees across the Rockies.

Above the montane zone, the **alpine tundra** supports only slow-growing plants such as mosses, lichens, and a variety of delicate wildflowers, all of which can survive on the thinnest soil and air and with a minimal supply of water. Because they grow so slowly – the tiniest wildflower may take many years to reach maturity – any damage done to these plants impacts dramatically on the alpine ecosystem, so hikers have a special duty of care while exploring these areas.

Another important zone in the region is the **sagebrush valley**, which makes up much of Grant Teton's flatlands and is dominated by **big sagebrush**. Though the dry and dusty sagebrush flats seem devoid of life, in reality a wide variety of plant and animal life live here, ranging from a variety of tough grasses to pronghorn and sage grouse.

Wildflowers

Of all the different forms of flora in the region, **wildflowers** draw the most attention. While few hikers walk with checklists to mark off the different varieties of lichens or bushes they've encountered, many floral enthusiasts do just that, stooping low to photograph their favorite types. As soon as the snows begin to melt in April, wildflowers bloom, starting at the lowest altitudes and working their way up mountainsides as summer progresses. On the sagebrush plains, the yellow **arrowleaf balsamroot**, purple **low larkspur**, and **scarlet gilia** begin sprouting in late spring. By late June, the wildflower show is in full production, with the montane and subalpine zones staging the likes of yellow **monkeyflowers**, red **bitterroots,** pink **elephant's heads**, purple **harebells**, **larkspurs** and **fringed gentian**, **blue camas**, and white **yarrow** and **phlox**. Later in the season, high up in the alpine zones, the likes of skunk-scented purple **sky pilots** and blue **alpine forget-me-nots** show themselves off. There are several excellent books wildflowers that include color photos to help with identification; see "Books" on p.287 for some favorites.

Books

Many of the following **books** can be found in the visitor centers in and around Yellowstone and Grand Teton. If you're hoping to do some background reading before heading out, most can also be purchased through the "Park Store" on the Yellowstone Association's website (ⓦwww.yellowstoneassociation.org), or via major online booksellers such ⓦwww.amazon.com and ⓦwww.alibris.com. Particularly recommended books are marked with the 🏃 symbol.

Travel and impressions

Tim Cahill *Lost in My Own Backyard* (Random House). Montana native Tim Cahill takes readers along on an engaging, far-too-brief tour of his favorite Yellowstone hikes, including a trio of backcountry trails into the park's most isolated corners. Written in Cahill's characteristic style, combining historical and scientific tidbits with humorous and occasionally trenchant observations on the park and people within.

Gary Ferguson *Hawk's Rest* (National Geographic Adventure Press). Another full-summer account by Ferguson (see below), this one spent at the isolated Hawk's Rest patrol cabin just outside Yellowstone's southeastern corner within the Thorofare passage. Wolves and bears abound, but so does a not-so-peaceful mix of hippy hikers, trail crews, and ornery outfitters, the latter group drawing Ferguson's ire for their rough camping and illegal use of salt to bait elk for hunting.

Gary Ferguson *A Walk Down the Wild* (Harper Collins). Ferguson's account of summer spent completing a giant 500-mile loop hike from his home in southwestern Montana, south towards Jackson and back. Spending only around a third of the time actually with the boundaries of Yellowstone and Grand Teton, the tale highlights the importance of Greater Yellowstone ecosystem, and is most interesting for the author's take on the regenerating landscapes left by the major fires of 1988.

🏃 **Norman Maclean** *A River Runs Through It* (University of Chicago Press). While the movie adaptation of the book was filmed on the Gallatin River in Big Sky north of Yellowstone, the action within the novel takes place mainly around the Blackfoot River in western Montana far to the north. That said, Maclean's lyrical masterwork is still essential reading for anyone with an interest in fly-fishing or, broader yet, Rocky Mountain literature.

Paul Schullery *Mountain Time* (Roberts Rhinehart). A fine hiking companion, this memoir contains a series of essays on life in Yellowstone by a long-time park employee, from wry observations on tourists within to insights gained from days spent fishing and wildlife spotting alone in the park's more secret corners.

Paul Schullery (ed) *Old Yellowstone Days* (Colorado University). A collection of journal entries, stories, and essays on Yellowstone's early days by the likes of John Muir, Theodore Roosevelt, Owen Wister, and, most engagingly, Rudyard Kipling. Well worth searching out for in local used books stores.

Mark Spragg *Where Rivers Change Direction* (Riverhead Books). A raw memoir by novelist Mark Spragg, who grew up tending to both horses and dudes on the Crossed Sabers Ranch just east of Yellowstone en route to Cody. There's little about Yellowstone, but plenty of illuminating essays on everything from bear hunting with tourists to spending an isolated Wyoming winter caretaking for a rich couple's home. One of the finest, most candid looks at the tough life of a cowboy in rural Wyoming.

History and biography

Gary Ferguson *The Great Divide* (WW Norton). An elegant cultural history of the Rocky Mountains, covering the rise of the mountain men and tourism to the arrival of '60s counter-culture and modern times. While there's little specific information on the greater Yellowstone region, it's a concise study of America's evolving relationship with this grand range.

Aubrey L. Haines *The Yellowstone Story* (University of Colorado). Acknowledged as the definitive Yellowstone history, Haines' incredibly detailed chronicle is broken into two large volumes. The first details the park's history up into the arrival of the Army, while second volume – notable for an entertaining chapter on stagecoach tourism – stretches into the 1970s. Whether you'll want to wade through both volumes is debatable, but it's a one-of-a-kind reference.

Burton Harris *John Colter: His Years in the Rockies* (Bison Books). More information than most interested in Colter probably need, but nonetheless the trapper's best biography. Much of the book is dedicated to piecing together Colter's winter circuit of Yellowstone in 1807.

Nathaniel Pitt Langford *The Discovery of Yellowstone Park* (Bison Books). A journal chronicling the 1870 Washburn Expedition, by Nathaniel Pitt "National Park" Langford, who later became the first superintendent of Yellowstone. Petty at times – the immodest Langford cuts down fellow explorer Jake Smith at every opportunity – the entries detailing the forty days spent exploring the region nonetheless capture well the expedition's awe and disbelief upon crossing paths with the Grand Canyon, Yellowstone Lake, and Old Faithful.

Osborne Russell *Journal of a Trapper* (Stackpole Books). A superb first-person account chronicling the final years of the Mountain Men lifestyle. Russell spent years trapping beaver and hunting the likes of grizzly, buffalo and elk in and around the Yellowstone region, and his prosaic day-to-day travel accounts are enlivened by tales of hardship, fascinating run-ins with native tribes, and the author's own inspired reflections on the landscape around him.

Helen Cody Wetmore *Last of the Great Scouts* (Forge Books). A loving biography of William Cody, written by his younger sister, in which the heroic Buffalo Bill never loses a race nor misses a shot. Historically suspect it may be, but it's still a rollicking read of the multi-tasking showman's life. Includes an equally effusive short forward and epilogue by Western author Zane Grey.

Lee H. Whittlesey *Death and Yellowstone – Accidents and Foolhardiness in the First National Park* (Roberts Rinehart). An offbeat, gloomy inventory of deaths within Yellowstone, ranging from the expected – drowning, the number one cause of death outside of car crashes – to the more startling, including poisonous fumes, boiling hot springs, and, yes, the odd grizzly attack. A potent reminder that wilderness demands attention and respect, or else.

Landscapes: geology, flora, and fauna

Peter Alden (ed) *National Audubon Society Field Guide to the Rocky Mountain States (Knopf)*. Lavishly illustrated and extremely informative guide to the flora and fauna of the Rockies, covering everything from lichens and wildflowers, spiders and beetles, to feral horses and mule deer. There's also an appendix detailing parks and preserves, images of the constellations you can see at night, and sections on the topography and geology, ecology, and weather patterns of the region.

T. Scott Bryan *The Geysers of Yellowstone* (University Press of Colorado). Now in it's third edition, this is the quintessential guide for geyser gazers. Along with descriptions of the most popular geysers in the Upper Geyser Basin and the like, the guide covers backcountry basins around Heart Lake, Shoshone Geyser Basin, Seven Mile Hole, etc. Also includes and appendix listing all the world's known geyser basins.

Mary Ann Franke *To Save the Wild Bison* (University of Oklahoma Press). An up-to-date account of the bison's struggle in and around Yellowstone, from early days of poaching and the Lacy Act up to today's pressing brucellosis and migration issues. Often weighed down by an over abundance of facts and figures, Franke nonetheless does an admirable job critiquing current policies and suggesting possible compromises.

James Halfpenny *Yellowstone Wolves In the Wild* (Riverbend). A short but first-class overview of wolves in Yellowstone, both for the chapters on subjects ranging from hunting and reproduction to tips on wolf spotting, and for the dozens of eye-catching color photos throughout. The author has led wolf tours in Yellowstone for years, and is also known as one of the top animal trackers in the country.

Bernd Heinrich *Mind of the Raven* (Harper Perennial). An eye-opening, readable book that'll have you looking at ravens in a whole new light. From Yellowstone to the Artic to his home in Maine, famed biologist Heinrich gives plenty of insight onto his study of ravens, detailing everything from their relationship with wolves to how they care for their young.

Scott McMillion *Mark of the Grizzly* (Falcon). While grizzly attacks are fairly uncommon in the mountains, this book documents eighteen that took place between 1977 and 1997, several of them in and around Yellowstone. Well written and more intriguing than you might think.

John McPhee *Rising from the Plains* (Noonday). Those who can't tell their Pleistocene Age from their Miocene Age will still enjoy this landmark work. Following renowned Rocky mountain geologist and former Jackson resident David Love (1913–2002) across Wyoming, McPhee weaves their discussions on the region's incredible array of geology together with the fascinating history of Love's frontier family.

Paul Rubinstein, Lee H. Whittlesey, and Mike Stevens *The Guide to Yellowstone Waterfalls and Their Discovery* (Westcliffe). The name says it all. Covers nearly 300 waterfalls, including photos, details of their "discovery" and tips on how to reach them by car or by foot.

Jean L. Seavey *Wildflowers of the Yellowstone Area*. Available at park bookstores, this inexpensive and handy set of identification cards gives details on nearly a hundred different wildflowers known to bloom in Yellowstone.

Douglas W. Smith and Gary Ferguson *Decade of the Wolf* (Lyons Press). Told from the point of view of Douglas W. Smith, a leader on Yellowstone's wolf reintroduction program from the start, this book provides an insider's account of the successful return of wolves. Light on the bureaucratic battles that have tried to hamstring the plan, the book instead focuses on the responsibilities of local biologists and volunteers, along with the wolves themselves – including several outstanding "portrait" chapters on specific animals.

Robert Smith and Lee Siegel *Windows into the Earth: The Geologic Story of Yellowstone and Grand Teton National Park* (Oxford Press). As advertised by the title, this is an exposition on the weird and wonderful geology of the Greater Yellowstone region. Lucid and filled with incredible facts, the book includes wonderful color photos and ends with a handy tour of both parks.

Outdoor activities

Mark C. Marschall *Yellowstone Trails: A Hiking Guide* (Yellowstone Association). Once you've checked off all the hikes within this guide, pick up this excellent work by a former Yellowstone backcountry ranger. Now in its seventh edition, nearly one hundred hikes are detailed in clear and concise terms.

Craig Mathews and Clayton Molinero *The Yellowstone Fly-Fishing Guide* (Lyons Press). A comprehensive rundown of the park's many fishable streams, giving as much insight to small creeks as it does the Yellowstone River.

Leigh Ortenburger and Reynold Jackson *A Climber's Guide to the Teton Range* (Mountaineer Books). With well over one hundred routes detailed, including some ice-climbing routes, this is the definitive Teton climber's bible.

Richard Rossiter *Teton Classics: 50 Selected Climbs in Grand Teton National Park* (Falcon). This illustrated handbook features succinct descriptions of fifty fine climbing routes in the Tetons.

Small print and

Index

A Rough Guide to Rough Guides

Published in 1982, the first Rough Guide – to Greece – was a student scheme that became a publishing phenomenon. Mark Ellingham, a recent graduate of English from Bristol University, had been traveling in Greece the previous summer and couldn't find the right guidebook. With a small group of friends he wrote his own guide, combining a highly contemporary, journalistic style with a thoroughly practical approach to travelers' needs.

The immediate success of the book spawned a series that rapidly covered dozens of destinations. And, in addition to impecunious backpackers, Rough Guides soon acquired a much broader and older readership that relished the guides' wit and inquisitiveness as much as their enthusiastic, critical approach and value-for-money ethos.

These days, Rough Guides include recommendations from shoestring to luxury and cover more than 200 destinations around the globe, including almost every country in the Americas and Europe, more than half of Africa and most of Asia and Australasia. Our ever-growing team of authors and photographers is spread all over the world, particularly in Europe, the USA, and Australia.

In the early 1990s, Rough Guides branched out of travel, with the publication of Rough Guides to World Music, Classical Music, and the Internet. All three have become benchmark titles in their fields, spearheading the publication of a wide range of books under the Rough Guide name.

Including the travel series, Rough Guides now number more than 350 titles, covering: phrasebooks, waterproof maps, music guides from Opera to Heavy Metal, reference works as diverse as Conspiracy Theories and Shakespeare, and popular culture books from iPods to Poker. Rough Guides also produce a series of more than 120 World Music CDs in partnership with World Music Network.

Visit www.roughguides.com to see our latest publications.

Many Rough Guide travel images are available for commercial licensing at www.roughguidespictures.com

Rough Guide credits

Text editor: April Isaacs
Layout: Sachin Tanwar
Cartography: Katie Lloyd-Jones, Ed Wright
Picture editor: Sarah Smithies
Production: Aimee Hampson
Proofreader: Andrew McCulloch
Cover design: Chloë Roberts
Editorial: **London** Kate Berens, Claire Saunders, Ruth Blackmore, Polly Thomas, Richard Lim, Alison Murchie, Karoline Densley, Andy Turner, Keith Drew, Edward Aves, Nikki Birrell, Alice Park, Sarah Eno, Lucy White, Jo Kirby, Samantha Cook, James Smart, Natasha Foges, Roisin Cameron, Joe Staines, Duncan Clark, Peter Buckley, Matthew Milton, Tracy Hopkins, Ruth Tidball; **New York** Andrew Rosenberg, Steven Horak, AnneLise Sorensen, Amy Hegarty, Ella Steim, Anna Owens, Joseph Petta, Sean Mahoney
Design & Pictures: **London** Scott Stickland, Dan May, Diana Jarvis, Mark Thomas, Jj Luck, Harriet Mills, Nicole Newman; **Delhi** Umesh Aggarwal, Ajay Verma, Jessica Subramanian, Ankur Guha, Pradeep Thapliyal, Anita Singh, Madhavi Singh, Karen D'Souza
Production: Katherine Owers
Cartography: **London** Maxine Repath; **Delhi** Jai Prakash Mishra, Rajesh Chhibber, Ashutosh Bharti, Rajesh Mishra, Animesh Pathak, Jasbir Sandhu, Karobi Gogoi, Amod Singh, Alakananda Bhattacharya, Athokpam Jotinkumar
Online: **New York** Jennifer Gold, Kristin Mingrone; **Delhi** Manik Chauhan, Narender Kumar, Rakesh Kumar, Amit Kumar, Amit Verma, Rahul Kumar, Ganesh Sharma, Debojit Borah
Marketing & Publicity: **London** Liz Statham, Niki Hanmer, Louise Maher, Jess Carter, Vanessa Godden, Vivienne Watton, Anna Paynton, Rachel Sprackett; **New York** Geoff Colquitt, Megan Kennedy, Katy Ball; **Delhi** Reem Khokhar
Special Projects Editor: Philippa Hopkins
Manager India: Punita Singh
Series Editor: Mark Ellingham
Reference Director: Andrew Lockett
Publishing Coordinator: Megan McIntyre
Publishing Director: Martin Dunford
Commercial Manager: Gino Magnotta
Managing Director: John Duhigg

Publishing information

This first edition published April 2007 by **Rough Guides Ltd**,
80 Strand, London WC2R 0RL
345 Hudson St, 4th Floor,
New York, NY 10014, USA
14 Local Shopping Centre, Panchsheel Park,
New Delhi 110017, India
Distributed by the Penguin Group
Penguin Books Ltd,
80 Strand, London WC2R 0RL
Penguin Group (USA)
375 Hudson Street, NY 10014, USA
Penguin Group (Australia)
250 Camberwell Road, Camberwell,
Victoria 3124, Australia
Penguin Books Canada Ltd,
10 Alcorn Avenue, Toronto, Ontario,
Canada M4V 1E4
Penguin Group (NZ)
67 Apollo Drive, Mairangi Bay, Auckland 1310,
New Zealand
Cover concept by Peter Dyer.

Typeset in Bembo and Helvetica to an original design by Henry Iles.

Printed and bound in Singapore by Toppan Security Printing Pte. Ltd.

304pp includes index

A catalogue record for this book is available from the British Library

ISBN: 978-1-84353-662-8

3 5 7 9 8 6 4

Help us update

We've gone to a lot of effort to ensure that the first edition of **The Rough Guide to Yellowstone and Grand Teton** is accurate and up to date. However, things change – places get "discovered", opening hours are notoriously fickle, restaurants and rooms raise prices or lower standards. If you feel we've got it wrong or left something out, we'd like to know, and if you can remember the address, the price, the time, the phone number, so much the better.

We'll credit all contributions, and send a copy of the next edition (or any other Rough Guide if you prefer) for the best letters. Everyone who writes to us and isn't already a subscriber will receive a copy of our full-color thrice-yearly newsletter. Please mark letters: "**Rough Guide Yellowstone and Grand Teton Update**" and send to: Rough Guides, 80 Strand, London WC2R 0RL, or Rough Guides, 345 Hudson St, 4th Floor, New York, NY 10014. Or send an email to **mail@roughguides.com**

Have your questions answered and tell others about your trip at **www.roughguides.atinfopop.com**

Acknowledgments

The author would like to thank all of the invaluable people who helped out during both the researching and writing stages of this guide, including but certainly not limited to: all of the exceedingly helpful tourism and travel folks, including Anna Olson, Carol Shively, Chris Waters, Cinda Culton, David Troyanek, Dax Schieffer, Donnie Sexton, Karen Ballard, Marysue Costello, Mike Harrelson, Mona Mesereau, Pam Gosink, Robin Hoover, Samantha Denny, and Susan Albrecht; George Bumann, one of the Yellowstone Institute's finest instructors; Alf, Christian, and Cam for the Rockies piggyback ride; Jill Anderson Pyatt for a place to crash along with helping out with some of the hikes; the GDP – Jon, John, Randy, Ted, and Justin – for the epic days of riding in Jackson Hole, Grand Targhee, and Big Sky; my incredible parents, for continued support and friendship; and, finally, to Sandra, quite simply for everything. At Rough Guides, hearty handshakes to all involved, including: Andrew Rosenberg for the opportunity, April Isaacs for her fine and steady editing, Sarah Smithies for the wonderful photo research, and the entire cartography and production staff for all of their hard work.

The editor would like to thank Stephen Timblin for his wonderful writing, research, and dedication to the project. Also, a huge thanks to Amy Hegarty, Steve Horak, Katie Lloyd-Jones, Andrew McCulloch, Anna Owens, Maxine Repath, Sarah Smithies, Ella Steim, Sachin Tanwar, and Ed Wright for all of their help.

Photo credits

All photos © Rough Guides except the following:

Title page
Aspen trees in fall, Grand Teton © David Stubbs/Getty Images

Full page
Grand Canyon of the Yellowstone © Jean Hall/FLPA

Introduction
Mother bison and calf crossing river © Ingo Arndt/Minden Pictures/FLPA
Bald eagle © David Hosking/FLPA
Fly-fisherman hiking in Yellowstone © Tom Montgomery/Getty Images
Elk herd at Mammoth Hot Springs © David Hosking/FLPA
Tourists viewing the Morning Glory Pool © Geoff Renner/Alamy
Lupine flowers, Grand Teton © Lorenz Britt/Alamy
Yellowstone Lake with hot spring vent formation © Altrendo Nature/Getty Images

Things not to miss
01 Lamar Valley © Stephen Timblin
02 Grand Prismatic Spring © Holger Leue
03 Hayden Valley © Dennis Frates/Alamy
04 Sunset at Lunch Tree Hill © Stephen Timblin
05 Wolf-watchers © Stephen Timblin
06 Menor's Ferry Historic District © Stephen Timblin
07 Old Faithful Geyser © Holger Leue
08 West Thumb Geyser © Holger Leue
09 Snake River Brewery © Snake River Brewing
10 Bechler Meadows © Stephen Timblin
11 Fly-fisherman in Yellowstone River © Raymond Gehman/Getty Images
12 Artist Point © Chuck Pefley/Alamy
13 Osprey Falls © Stephen Timblin
14 Climbing Grand Teton © Brad Mitchell/Alamy
15 Bison foraging in snow beside Old Faithful Geyser © Pete Cairns/Nature Picture Library
16 Old Faithful Inn © National Park Services
17 Rafting on Gallatin River © Kevin R. Morris/Corbis
18 Buffalo Bill Historical Center © Stephen Timblin
19 Cheeseburger at Helen's Corral Drive-In © Stephen Timblin
20 Jackson Hole Mountain Resort © Jackson Hole Mountain Resort
21 Heart Lake and Mount Sheridan © Stephen Timblin
22 Tetons and Jenny Lake © G.R. Richardson/Robert Harding Picture Library

Color section: The wolves of Yellowstone
Gray wolf chasing its prey © Jeff Vanuga/Corbis
Wolf biologist with the Yellowstone wolf reintroduction project © William Campbell/Corbis
Wolf playing with pups © Norbert Rosing/Getty Images
Gray wolf guarding its elk kill © Tom Murphy/Getty Images
Wolf pack, Yellowstone © Jess Lee
Wolf-watching © National Park Services

Color section: Hydrothermal Yellowstone
Aerial shot of Grand Prismatic Spring © Holger Leue/Alamy
Thermal plumes © David Hosking/FLPA
Morning Glory Pool © America/Alamy
Lone Star Geyser © National Park Services
Sapphire Pool, Biscuit Basin © Gary Black/Masterfile

Fountain Paint Pots © Jamie and Judy Wild/ Alamy

Black and whites

p.48 Mammoth Hot Springs © David Hosking/ FLPA
p.54 Bison in Lamar Valley © Gordon McGregor/ Alamy
p.60 Grand Canyon Falls © Stephen Timblin
p.63 The Golden Gate © Stephen Timblin
p.70 Great Fountain Geyser © Norbert Rosing/ Alamy
p.73 Fishing cone © National Park Service Historic Photograph Collection
p.81 Yellowstone Lake © Age Fotostock/ SuperStock
p.86 Hayden Valley © Stephen Timblin
p.94 Moose crossing Gros Ventre River © David Hosking/FLPA
p.97 Moulton Barns and Grand Teton © Philippe Clement/Nature Picture Library
p.111 Colter Bay Marina © Stephen Timblin
p.126 Mount Washburn © Stephen Timblin
p.128 Seven-Mile Hole © Stephen Timblin
p.135 Grizzly bear © Philippe Clement/Nature Picture Library
p.158 Hiker on the Teton Crest Trail © John Brecher/Corbis
p.164 Fly-fishing on Snake River
p.179 Skier at Lone Star Geyser © Greg Vaughn/ Alamy
p.187 Lake Yellowstone Hotel © Yellowstone National Park Lodges
p.188 Roosevelt Lodge Cabins © Yellowstone National Park Lodges
p.192 Jackson Lake Lodge © Grand Teton Lodge Company
p.197 Old West Cookout © Yellowstone National Park Lodges
p.199 Jackson Lake Lodge Pioneer Grill © Grand Teton Lodge Company
p.202 Ranger-lead tour at Upper Geyser Basin © Betty Johnson/Dbimages
p.213 Downtown Jackson © Zach Holmes/Alamy
p.214 Arc of Elk Antlers © David Ball/Corbis
p.232 Lone Mountain © Big Sky Resort
p.243 Emigrant Peak in the Absaroka Ranges, Paradise Valley © Carol Polich/Getty Images
p.246 Cooke City © Stephen Timblin
p.253 The Irma Hotel © Stephen Timblin
p.256 Historic Trail Town © Stephen Timblin
p.274 Poached bison heads © National Park Services
p.281 Elk with interlocked horns © Konrad Wothe/Minden Pictures/FLPA

Index

Map entries are in color.

E

F

G

geysers

geysers...(cont.)

H

hot springs

I

J

K

L

M

N

O

P

Q

Y

INDEX

Map symbols

maps are listed in the full index using colored text

- State boundary
- National Park boundary
- Other park boundary
- Caldera boundary
- Continental divide
- 50 US highway
- 41 State highway
- Limited-access road
- Other road
- H22 Recommended hiking trail
- Other trail
- River
- Peak
- Point of interest
- Park entrance
- Ranger station
- Regional airport
- Viewpoint
- Waterfall
- Hydrothermal feature
- Accommodation
- Campground
- Information office
- Post office
- Gas station
- Golf course
- Hospital
- Picnic area
- Building
- Glacier
- Park
- Geyser Basin fill